GREEK TRAGEDY
IN NEW TRANSLATIONS

GENERAL EDITORS
Peter Burian and Alan Shapiro

FOUNDING GENERAL EDITOR
William Arrowsmith

FORMER GENERAL EDITOR
Herbert Golder

THE COMPLETE SOPHOCLES, VOLUME II

The Complete Sophocles, Volume II

Electra and Other Plays

Edited by
PETER BURIAN
and
ALAN SHAPIRO

OXFORD
UNIVERSITY PRESS

2010

OXFORD
UNIVERSITY PRESS

Oxford University Press, Inc., publishes works that further
Oxford University's objective of excellence
in research, scholarship, and education.

Oxford New York
Auckland   Cape Town   Dar es Salaam   Hong Kong   Karachi
Kuala Lumpur   Madrid   Melbourne   Mexico City   Nairobi
New Delhi   Shanghai   Taipei   Toronto

With offices in
Argentina   Austria   Brazil   Chile   Czech Republic   France   Greece
Guatemala   Hungary   Italy   Japan   Poland   Portugal   Singapore
South Korea   Switzerland   Thailand   Turkey   Ukraine   Vietnam

Electra Copyright © 2001 by Anne Carson and Michael Shaw

Aias Copyright © 1999 by Herbert Golder and Richard Pevear

Philoctetes Copyright © 2003 by Carl Phillips and Diskin Clay

Women of Trachis Copyright © 1978 by C. K. Williams and Gregory W. Dickerson

Compilation Copyright © 2010 by Oxford University Press, Inc.

Published by Oxford University Press, Inc.
198 Madison Avenue, New York, NY 10016

www.oup.com

Oxford is a registered trademark of Oxford University Press.

Library of Congress Cataloging-in-Publication Data
Sophocles.
[Works. English. 2009]
The complete Sophocles / edited by Peter Burian and Alan Shapiro
     v. cm. —(Greek tragedy in new translations)
Contents: —v. 2. Women of Trachis / translated by C. K. Williams and Gregory W. Dickerson.
Electra / translated by Anne Carson ; with introduction and notes by Michael Shaw.
Philoctetes / translated by Carl Phillips ; with introduction
and notes by Diskin Clay.
ISBN 978-0-19-538782-7; 978-0-19-537330-1 (pbk.)
1. Sophocles—Translations into English.   2. Mythology, Greek—Drama.
I. Burian, Peter.   II. Shapiro, Alan, 1952–   III. Title.
PA4414. A1B87   2009
882'.01—dc22   2009023762

Printed in the United States of America

EDITORS' FOREWORD

"*The Greek Tragedy in New Translations* is based on the conviction that poets like Aeschylus, Sophocles, and Euripides can only be properly rendered by translators who are themselves poets. Scholars may, it is true, produce useful and perceptive versions. But our most urgent present need is for a *re-creation* of these plays—as though they had been written, freshly and greatly, by masters fully at home in the English of our own times."

With these words, the late William Arrowsmith announced the purpose of this series, and we intend to honor that purpose. As was true of most of the volumes that began to appear in the 1970s—first under Arrowsmith's editorship, later in association with Herbert Golder—those for which we bear editorial responsibility are products of close collaborations between poets and scholars. We believe (as Arrowsmith did) that the skills of both are required for the difficult and delicate task of transplanting these magnificent specimens of another culture into the soil of our own place and time, to do justice both to their deep differences from our patterns of thought and expression and to their palpable closeness to our most intimate concerns. Above all, we are eager to offer contemporary readers dramatic poems that convey as vividly and directly as possible the splendor of language, the complexity of image and idea, and the intensity of emotion as the originals. This entails, among much else, the recognition that the tragedies were meant for performance—as scripts for actors—to be sung and danced as well as spoken. It demands writing of inventiveness, clarity, musicality, and dramatic power. By such standards, we ask that these translations be judged.

This series is also distinguished by its recognition of the need of nonspecialist readers for a critical introduction informed by the best recent scholarship, but written clearly and without condescension. Each play is followed by notes designed not only to elucidate obscure references but also to mediate the conventions of the Athenian stage as well as those features of the Greek text that might otherwise go unnoticed. The notes are supplemented by a glossary of mythical and geographical terms that should make it possible to read the play without turning elsewhere for basic information. Stage directions are sufficiently ample to aid readers in imagining the action as they read. Our fondest hope, of course, is that these versions will be staged not only in the minds of their readers but also in the theaters to which, after so many centuries, they still belong.

A NOTE ON THE SERIES FORMAT

A series such as this requires a consistent format. Different translators, with individual voices and approaches to the material at hand, cannot be expected to develop a single coherent style for each of the three tragedians, much less make clear to modern readers that, despite the differences among the tragedians themselves, the plays share many conventions and a generic, or period, style. But they can at least share a common format and provide similar forms of guidance.

1. *Spelling of Greek Names*

Orthography is one area of difference among the translations that requires a brief explanation. Historically, it has been common practice to use Latinized forms of Greek names when bringing them into English. Thus, for example, Oedipus (not Oidipous) and Clytemnestra (not Klutaimestra) are customary in English. Recently, however, many translators have moved toward more precise transliteration, which has the advantage of presenting the names as both Greek and new, instead of Roman and neoclassical importations into English. In the case of so familiar a name as Oedipus, however, transliteration risks the appearance of pedantry or affectation. And in any case, perfect consistency cannot be expected in such matters. Readers will feel the same discomfort with "Athenai" as the chief city of Greece as they would with "Platon" as the author of *The Republic*.

The earlier volumes in this series adopted as a rule a "mixed" orthography in accordance with the considerations outlined above. The most familiar names retain their Latinate forms, while the rest are transliterated; -*os* rather than Latin -*us* is adopted for the termination of masculine names, and Greek diphthongs (as in Iphige*neia* for Latin Iphigenia) are retained. Some of the later volumes continue this practice, but where translators have preferred to use a more consistent practice of transliteration of Latinization, we have honored their wishes.

2. *Stage directions*

The ancient manuscripts of the Greek plays do not supply stage directions (though the ancient commentators often provide information relevant to staging, delivery, "blocking," etc.). Hence stage directions must be inferred from words and situations and our knowledge of Greek theatrical conventions. At best this is a ticklish and uncertain procedure. But it is surely preferable that good stage directions should be provided by the translator than that readers should be left to their own devices in visualizing action, gesture, and spectacle. Ancient tragedy was austere and "distanced" by means of masks, which means that the reader must not expect the detailed intimacy ("He shrugs and turns wearily away," "She speaks with deliberate slowness, as though to emphasize the point," etc.) that characterizes stage directions in modern naturalistic drama.

3. *Numbering of lines*

For the convenience of the reader who may wish to check the translation against the original, or vice versa, the lines have been numbered according to both the Greek and English texts. The lines of the translation have been numbered in multiples of ten, and these numbers have been set in the right-hand margin. The (inclusive) Greek numeration will be found bracketed at the top of the page. The Notes that follow the text have been keyed to both numerations, the line numbers of the translation in **bold**, followed by the Greek lines in regular type, and the same convention is used for all references to specific passages (of the translated plays only) in both the Notes and the Introduction.

Readers will doubtless note that in many plays the English lines outnumber the Greek, but they should not therefore conclude that the translator has been unduly prolix. In most cases the reason is simply that the translator has adopted the free-flowing norms of modern Anglo-American prosody, with its brief-breath-and-emphasis-determined lines, and its habit of indicating cadence and caesuras by line length and setting rather than by conventional punctuation. Even where translators have preferred to cast dialogue in more regular five-beat or six-beat lines, the greater compactness of Greek diction is likely to result in a substantial disparity in Greek and English numerations.

ABOUT THE TRANSLATIONS

The translations in this series were written over a period of roughly forty years. No attempt has been made to update references to the scholarly literature in the Introductions and Notes, but each volume offers a brief For Further Reading list that will provide some initial orientation to contemporary critical thinking about the tragedies it contains.

THIS VOLUME

Only seven plays of Sophocles have come down to us complete, a small fraction of the hundred and twenty-three whose titles we have. These seven are, nevertheless, sufficient to establish Sophocles among the greatest of poets and playwrights. Those who know only *Oedipus* or *Antigone* may be surprised to discover how varied our small sample of Sophocles' art really is—and how unsettling and provocative still. This volume contains the surviving tragedies that are not connected to the history of the troubled family of Oedipus. *Aias* [*Ajax*], *Electra*, and *Philoctetes* are based on episodes from the Trojan saga; *Women of Trachis* dramatizes the death of the greatest of Greek heroes, Herakles.

Sophocles' life spanned almost the entire fifth century. He was most likely born in 495 BC, the same year as Pericles, and he is said to have led the boys' chorus in the celebrations of the Athenian triumph at Salamis in 480. He won his first victory at the City Dionysia competing against Aeschylus in 468, and went on to win eighteen more first prizes there (each prize for a tetralogy, for a total of seventy-two plays), and an unknown number at the smaller Lenaean festival. In addition, Sophocles had a significant public career, serving as elected general, as Hellenotamias (treasurer of the Athenian Empire), and in other important posts. He also introduced the cult of the healing god Asclepius to Athens. Sophocles died in 406, having become one of the most admired men of his day and having played a central role in a time and place of singular ferment and achievement, political, intellectual, and artistic.

Chance has left us with plays from something like the last forty years of Sophocles' very long life. Of the four in this volume, *Philoctetes* can be firmly dated to 409; *Electra* only very tentatively to around 415; *Ajax* may go back as far as the 450s BC, though (as our translators suggest) 445–40 may be closer to the mark; and *Women of Trachis* seems altogether undatable, with some claiming to find in it early traits, some late. Our translators suggest a date in mid-career, close to that of *Ajax*.

Ajax is often described as a "diptych" tragedy, since it appears to fall into two parts: one action that culminates in the hero's suicide, and a second in which his burial is contested by his enemies but finally assured. This division used to be taken by scholars as a defect (or at least a sign of dramatic immaturity), but it can be easily shown that the two parts, contrasting in tone as well as perspective, are part of a single, carefully planned dramatic progression. The action begins after Ajax has been humiliated by his comrades, who awarded the arms of the fallen Achilles to Odysseus, rather than to him. In terms of the "heroic code" portrayed in Homer's *Iliad*, in which the stalwart warrior's sense of self is entirely invested, Ajax has had his honor stolen from him and must act to reclaim it. This he chooses to do by killing those he holds responsible for his humiliation, Odysseus and his allies Agamemnon and Menelaus. Athena saves them by turning Ajax's wrath against the army's sheep and cattle instead. We first see Ajax in the depths of his delusion, then awakened from his madness to the realization that his attempt to salvage his honor has led only to further humiliation. The hero sees suicide as the only means of preserving his honor, and despite the pleas of his loved ones and his own attempt to find some accommodation with the new reality in which he now moves, he falls on his sword, still cursing his enemies.

The play opens with the goddess Athena, implicated as fully as her human victim in the harsh code of honor and revenge, inviting Ajax's great enemy Odysseus to exult with her over his ruin. Significantly, Odysseus declines to do so, saying that he pities "the poor wretch, though he's my enemy. / He's yoked to an evil delusion, / but the same fate could be mine" (148–50 / 122–24). This broader human sympathy provides an alternative to the Homeric code and provides a key to the action that follows Ajax's death. Ajax has rejected the notion that one's friends can become one's enemies and that one must yield to the inevitability of such change. It must be said that the poetry of this play is largely invested in his magnificent defiance. In a sense, however, his world dies with him, to be superseded by one that is less uncompromising and more magnanimous. The great monologues of Ajax now yield to the fractious and unattractive posturing of the debates that pit Ajax's brother Teukros (or Teucer), who fights for his brother's honor, against Agamemnon and Menelaus, who exult in their enemy's defeat and want to seal their triumph by forbidding his burial. It is Ajax's other enemy, Odysseus, using his art of persuasion (a fundamental attribute of the new democratic consciousness) to wrest consent from his comrades for the hero's last rites.

Ajax, whose home island of Salamis was Athenian territory in historical times, was a major sacred hero, nowhere more than in Attica; he gave his name to one of the ten Athenian tribes and his cult was especially celebrated at Salamis, where it was said that he rallied the Greeks in their victory over the Persians. Sophocles' *Ajax* suggests ways in which such a figure could be adapted to the needs of a different age and a new political culture. Teucer's positioning of Ajax's concubine, Tekmessa, and her child, Eurysakes, as suppliants at the fallen warrior's corpse (1312–26 / 1171–82), both to protect it and to offer them protection, suggests the hero who will emerge from the wreckage of this great, ill-fated man to be revered as a tutelary spirit of the polis.

Women of Trachis shares with *Ajax* a "diptych" structure and the theme of a great hero's death. Herakles may be said to dominate the play even in his absence but for most of its length, the action is centered on, and largely focalized through, Herakles' wife, Deianeira, whose love for him leads her to make the tragic mistake that will kill him—and when she recognizes what she has done, to kill herself. The final fourth of the play brings Herakles on stage at last to enact both an astonishing representation of his death agonies and a recognition of his own: that all this was foretold and that he must now take charge of his death to fulfill the oracles he received long ago.

Deianeira is portrayed with great sympathy in her anxiety for her missing husband, her pity for the captives he has sent before him as booty from the city he has destroyed, and then her desperation when she understands that one of them, the princess Iole, has supplanted her in Herakles' heart. We watch as, overcome by passion, she tries to recapture her husband's love by smearing a cloak with a "love potion" given to her by the centaur Nessos. Nessos had tried to rape her and had been fatally wounded by Herakles' arrows. Deianeira only recognizes that Nessos' "charm" was in reality poison from those arrows when she hears that Herakles' body is being horribly ravaged by its contact with his skin. In effect, it destroys her, too.

As so often with Sophocles, the ending is unsettling. Herakles, hearing from his son Hyllos about Nessos' revenge, realizes that death is upon him and takes charge of his own dying. He makes Hyllos swear a solemn oath to do his bidding no matter what, then commands his son to burn him alive on a funeral pyre and to marry Iole, the source of so much grief. Hyllos recoils in horror at Herakles' apparent cruelty to him and at the gods' apparent cruelty in inflicting such pain on Herakles, son of Zeus though he be. The meaning of the ending, however, is far more open and equivocal than Hyllos' bleak vision suggests. Sophocles withholds any overt suggestion of the traditional conclusion to the story of Herakles' immolation on Mt. Oita, his ascent to Olympus and immortal life among the gods. The original audience would have known and been primed for that ending, but Sophocles denies them the satisfaction of having their knowledge confirmed. Nevertheless, Herakles' sense that out of this suffering something good will yet come ("I want the finish of this welcome, unwelcome work / to be joy," 1212–13 / 1262–63), and the play's final words ("nothing is here // ... that is not Zeus," 1225–27 / 1278) hold out that possibility at the very least.

This play is one of several Greek tragedies that deserve to be called "neglected masterpieces." Such was William Arrowsmith's claim in his foreword to the original publication of this translation, calling *Women of*

Trachis "a staggering achievement, one of the very greatest of Greek plays. For sheer tragic power and horror, it is the equal of anything Sophocles wrote—superior in every way, I think, to *Electra* and even *Antigone*. A great play, and an incredibly neglected one." Some may find this judgment hyperbolic, but readers who open themselves to this drama will find its emotional and physical extremes both uncomfortable and amply rewarding.

Electra returns us to the aftermath of the Trojan War and one of tragedy's most familiar subjects. Indeed, this is the only story for which we have surviving versions by all three surviving tragedians. In Aeschylus' *Libation Bearers* (or *Choephori*), the second play of the monumental *Oresteia* trilogy of 458, Orestes' killing of his mother, Clytemnestra, is sanctioned by Apollo but comes as the culmination of a long series of crimes and retributions that are themselves new crimes that call out for revenge. Vengeance leads in the third play to Orestes' pursuit by his mother's Furies, until at last finally, in the city of Athens, a resolution is reached that brings Orestes' acquittal in a court of law and the transformation of the Furies into *Eumenides*, the "kindly ones" of the play's title. Some decades later, Sophocles and Euripides each wrote an *Electra*—most likely between 420 and 410, although we do not have a precise date for either, or know which came first. These plays have in common, in contrast to the multigenerational scope of the Aeschylean trilogy, a more limited focus on the revenge killings of Clytemnestra and her new consort, Aegisthus. They also give the central role to Orestes' sister Electra, whose role in Aeschylus was more limited and more passive.

Beyond that, the two dramas are very different in character and tone. Euripides, at his revisionist best, gives us an Orestes reluctant to kill his mother and pushed to act by a sister dominated by self-pity and anger at her own circumstances rather than a sense of righteous vengeance. Aegisthus and Clytemnestra are drawn with unexpected sympathy and murdered in entirely unheroic ways. Both Orestes and Clytemnestra feel shame and remorse when the deed is done, and question the validity of Apollo's command. Sophocles' version is both subtler and morally more ambiguous. On the one hand, his Electra is the most sympathetic and emotionally engaging character in the play. Her suffering becomes almost unbearable when, in the play's central deception, Orestes presents her with the bronze urn said to contain his own ashes; her joy at the discovery that he is still alive is unbounded. Yet she becomes almost a kind of fury as she exults in her mother's execution and stages the play's final deception, catching Aegisthus in her trap by pretending that Clytemnestra's shrouded corpse is that of her dead brother.

In the versions of Aeschylus and Euripides, Clytemnestra's death comes only after the usurper Aegisthus has been disposed of, as the climax of the action. The fact that Orestes kills his mother first in Sophocles, with the final scene dedicated to the punishment of Aegisthus, suggests a certain muting of the issue of matricide. There is no hint of pursuit by the Furies, as in Aeschylus, and no apparent need for contrition or remorse, as in Euripides. It is sometimes said therefore that Sophocles has reverted to the version of the story we find in the *Odyssey*, where Orestes' retribution is treated as praiseworthy and unproblematic. The nineteenth-century German critic A. W. Schlegel famously described the play as "a mixture of matricide and high spirits."

A more generous conclusion would be that Sophocles has left the door open for the spectator to connect his telling to the traditional tale of the Furies' pursuit and its final resolution—but he doesn't take us through that door himself. What he does do is show the internalization of the Furies, so to speak, in Electra herself. She knows that her sufferings have grievously distorted her nature: "By dread things I am compelled. I know that. / I see the trap closing" (295–96 / 221). When the moment of revenge arrives, a harshly triumphant Electra emerges to greet it: "Hit her a second time, if you have the strength" (1883 / 1415), she yells to Orestes as he stabs their mother; and, as Aegisthus is led to the slaughter, "Throw his corpse out / for scavengers to get" (1974–75 / 1487–89), the ultimate act of degradation. Sophocles' heroine confronts us with the effects on the human soul of vengeance deferred and vengeance achieved.

The plot of *Philoctetes* involves a hero cast out by his comrades because of the festering (and seemingly ill-omened) wounds from a snake bite, then sought again by those same comrades when they discover that they must bring him (and the unerring bow and arrows he inherited from Herakles) to Troy if they are to win the war. Like *Electra*, this is a play of deception, but the moral debate that deceit engenders is made far more central. Sophocles' tragedy is the only one of that name to survive, but we do have indirect evidence for earlier Philoctetes dramas by Aeschylus and Euripides, largely thanks to orations by Dio Chrysostomos, a rhetorician of the later first-century CE. From his comparison of the three dramas, we learn that Sophocles made two decisive innovations. First, Lemnos becomes a desert island, so that Philoctetes' banishment has cut him off from any human community, completely alone in his agony. Second, he adds Neoptolemos, Achilles' young and inexperienced son, as a partner in the mission to fetch Philoctetes (in the epic tradition, it was the seasoned warrior Diomedes; in Aeschylus, Odysseus; in Euripides, both). In this version, it is not only

Philoctetes who must choose what course to take but also Neoptolemos. For Philoctetes, there can be no thought of helping the comrades who have betrayed him to such extreme misery. Neoptolemos, on the other hand, is torn between the glory he hopes to win in the conquest of Troy and the pity for the suffering Philoctetes that increasingly weighs on his conscience.

Odysseus appears in one of his accustomed roles on the tragic stage, as a sort of ur-Sophist, able to make any means seem acceptable if it achieves the desired end. Since he cannot possibly appear in person before Philoctetes, who sees him as the most villainous of his enemies, he makes Neoptolemos his agent. Neoptolemos plays his role effectively, but with ever greater discomfort. Part of the fascination of the drama is the uncertainty we feel from moment to moment: Is what Neoptolemos says about himself and Odysseus representing his true feelings or is it part of the ruse, or perhaps both? Does the sailor (disguised as a trader) whom Odysseus sends to pass along the prophecy that Philoctetes must be brought to Troy by persuasion—adding that Odysseus will nevertheless use force if he has to—provide, despite the ruse, a true report, or is his whole speech just another ruse? In the end, revulsion for deceit and pity for the suffering hero win out in Neoptolemos. After facing down Odysseus, and then Philoctetes when he aims an arrow at Odysseus, Neoptolemos makes his best honest effort at persuading Philoctetes to overcome his bitterness and sail to Troy, conveying the prophecy that only at Troy can he be healed. When Philoctetes still refuses, Neoptolemos agrees to take him home after all.

Of course, this cannot be. Philoctetes and his bow must go to Troy and Troy must be taken. A special irony of this play is that Odysseus, however flawed the means he employs, has the right end in view, for his community and for Philoctetes. Sophocles has brought the play to a Euripidean *aporia* (many critics have pointed out that Philoctetes shows the influence of Euripides on his older colleague), and he uses a Euripidean device to get the myth back on track. Philoctetes' old patron and friend, the now deified Herakles, appears *ex machina* to persuade Philoctetes to do what he must do. The result is, however, another form of the very Sophoclean open ending we have noted in the other plays in this volume. Herakles offers nothing more than what Neoptolemos has already promised—healing and glory in Troy—but he does it in the voice of a beloved and trusted comrade. And, speaking to Neoptolemos, he emphasizes the need for human solidarity: "you aren't strong enough to take Troy / without him, nor he without you, but each of you must guard the other / even as two lions that feed together" (1626–29 / 1434–36). We are left to decide for ourselves what to make of the promise of healing and human solidarity in a world so rife with deceit. When we think about the questions raised in this drama about how to balance ends and means, the needs of the community and decent treatment for the individual, it is well to remember that for the audience that witnessed *Philoctetes* in 409, this was a moment of particular discomfort and anxiety. Two years earlier, Athens had suffered an oligarchic coup, and it still stood in danger of losing a war that might mean the end of the polis itself. Of course, moments of discomfort and anxiety are hardly rare, and there is much in *Philoctetes* that should give us cause for reflection today.

The plays in this volume were originally published between 1978 and 2003. ANNE CARSON is a Canadian classicist, essayist, translator, and a widely read and honored poet. Among her many books are *Eros the Bittersweet* (1986), *Glass, Irony, and God* (1992), *Autobiography of Red: A Novel in Verse* (1998), *Men in the Off Hours* (2001), and *If Not, Winter: Fragments of Sappho* (2002). In addition to Sophocles' *Electra*, Carson has translated tragedies of Aeschylus and Euripides. RICHARD PEVEAR, best known for his many acclaimed translations of Russian novels in collaboration with Larissa Volokhonsky, has also translated from French and Italian and published two volumes of his own poetry. CARL PHIL-LIPS, a poet who has garnered many awards, is the author of ten books of poems, including *Cortège* (1995), *The Tether* (2001), *The Rest of Love* (2004), *Quiver of Arrows: Selected Poems, 1986–2006* (2007), and *Speak Low* (2009); and a book of prose, *Coin of the Realm: Essays on the Art and Life of Poetry* (2004). The award-winning books of C. K. WILLIAMS, one of America's best-known poets, include *Lies* (1969), *Flesh and Blood* (1987), *Repair* (1999), *The Singing* (2003), and *Collected Poems* (2007). He has also published a translation of Euripides' *Bacchae* and volumes of poetry from French, Polish, and Japanese. He is the author of a memoir, *Misgivings* (2001). DISKIN CLAY is RJR Nabisco Professor of Classical Studies, Emeritus, at Duke University and the author of a number of distinguished books and monographs on classical literature and ancient philosophy, including *Lucretius and Epicurus* (1983), *Paradosis and Survival: Three Chapters in the History of Epicurean Philosophy* (1998), *Platonic Questions: Dialogues with the Silent Philosopher* (2000), and *Archilochos Heros: The Hero Cult of Poets in the Greek Polis* (2004). Among his published translations is Euripides' *Trojan Women* (2005). GREGORY W. DICKERSON is Professor Emeritus of Greek at Bryn Mawr College. HERBERT GOLDER, a former editor of this series, currently edits *Arion: A Journal of Humanities and the Classics* at Boston University, where he is Professor of Classical Civilization. He has published a translation of Euripides' *Bacchae* (2001). MICHAEL SHAW is Associate Professor of Classics at the University of Kansas.

CONTENTS

CONTENTS

AIAS [AJAX]

Translated by

HERBERT GOLDER

and

RICHARD PEVEAR

INTRODUCTION

"The ancient simplicity into which honor so largely entered was laughed down and disappeared," wrote Thucydides (3.83), describing the moral decline of the late fifth century B.C. That same judgment might equally well be applied to the story of the Homeric warrior Aias, whose betrayal and tragic suicide embodies the final eclipse of ancient honor itself. In the arts of war and in sheer magnificence, Aias, Homer's "bulwark of the Achaians," was second only to Achilles. By rights, after Achilles died, his armor, the highest prize of honor, was owed to Aias. But the Greeks denied Aias his due, awarding the arms instead to the wily Odysseus. To Aias, the man of action, that *his* prize should be given to Odysseus, the man of words, was intolerable. Outraged and humiliated, noble Aias did as his honor demanded, dying on his own sword.

Sophocles inherited an Aias tradition from Homer's *Iliad* and other epic poems. Aeschylus and Pindar, Sophocles' older contemporaries, had also presented versions of Aias' story. Together, these versions create the convention against which Sophocles shaped his own radically different Aias. But Sophocles' concept of heroism is also deeply rooted in the tragic heroism of Homer's *Iliad*. "Always to be best" (*aien aristeuein*) was the charge given to Achilles, Homer's greatest hero—the epitome of epic heroism. To the modern ear this may perhaps sound like mere competitive egoism. But being "best" (*aristos*) in Homer meant rather a *striving* for excellence or *arete*, a suprapersonal ideal pursued without compromise, even at the cost of life itself. In his first speech, Sophocles' Aias sounds the Homeric note: "Honor in life / or in death: if a man is born noble, / he must have one or the other" (**530–32** / 479–80). Thus the hero dies as he lives—absolutely. The stress is on the manner, not merely the matter, of living and dying. The word *aristos* ("best") in Greek is clearly related to the word *arete*, usually translated as "excellence." But *arete* is not merely an ethical term. It is above all a quality of character, to be realized only in action, by active fulfillment of one's *daimon*, or "indwelling destiny." "Character," said Heraclitus, "*is* destiny." Sophoclean tragedy explores and dramatizes this dynamic; character emerges through the act, or agony, of becoming. And, at a certain point, action becomes fatal, revealing, finally, the hero's destiny. The hero is therefore involved in a great struggle with his *daimon* "to become the thing he is," to adapt Pindar's noble phrase. Sophocles inherited this concept of heroic *arete*, in which character and destiny are one. But, in the case of Aias, the identity of character and destiny seems conspicuously absent: Aias, the man of honor, dies in shame. This paradox is at the heart of Sophocles' play. But only in the context of the received traditions can the full import of the Sophoclean Aias' "fatal" act be revealed.

Homer's Aias exemplifies ancient honor almost as much as Achilles himself. A giant of a man, famous for tenacity and valor rather than eloquence, Aias seems at first sight an Achilles manqué—the inarticulate man of action. But Achilles and Aias represent two complementary, tragic types; together they provide a fuller sense of the tragic hero than either hero alone. Achilles was passionately volatile and famous for swiftness, which made him deadly, especially on the attack. Aias, in contrast, was the steady, immovable defender; his colossal size and obdurate relentlessness made him quite literally the "bulwark of the Achaians." Each had his unique *daimon*, which disclosed his essential character through his acts. By inactivity, Achilles resisted his *daimon*; he is less than himself when he sits idly on the beach and talks of returning home to a long, inglorious life. By the same token, Aias, when forced by Zeus to retreat, ceases to be Aias:

> But Zeus on high drove fear upon Aias so that he stood
> amazed *and threw the seven layered, oxhide shield behind him,*
> terror in his eyes, he glared all around like a cornered beast
> and backed up slowly, turning this way and that like a fiery lion
> beaten back from the cattle-yard by dogs and farmers,
> . . . furious but afraid
> Aias retreated from the Trojans, *his heart sinking, much unwilling . . .*
> *hard to move as a mule* in a cornfield, who stays feeding
> though beaten with sticks . . ."
>
> (*Iliad* 11.544–61)

Though peerless in war, Aias loses three times in the games at Patroklos' funeral. He is, by nature, too inflexible to play "games." He is most himself when most serious—in mortal combat with Hektor, or when he single-handedly drives off the Trojans from Patroklos' body, or prevents the enemy from firing the ships. Standing firm against a worthy adversary or impossible odds is the real genius of Aias:

> ...holding back the Trojans, *as a timbered rock ridge*
> *holds back water,* one stretching the length of a plain,
> with flooding currents from strong rivers pounding against it,
> still holding and beating the waters right back across the plain,
> no wave having nearly strength enough to break it,
> so the two Aiases held off the attacking Trojans forever.
>
> (*Iliad* 17.747–53)

To move unmoving Aias is to change him: the mountain ceases to be a mountain if it moves. But for both unbending Aias and swift-footed Achilles, a defining strength is also a fatal weakness.

Each man suffers a different temporal tragedy. Achilles is "swift-footed," but the intensity with which he fights and lives ensures that he will be "swift-fated"; his life will be brief. Aias, the immovable man of honor, is instead bound to outlive his world, to see it change and time pass him by. He is not "a man for all seasons." Achilles is at least spared the pathos of living on in an unheroic age. But Aias lives to see his heroic labors come to nothing. His tragedy, however, is not simply that of individual obsolescence, but also that of a society that sacrifices its highest ideals of honor and nobility to expediency. The expedient Odysseus is the canny and flexible opportunist, Homer's "man of many turns"; his *arete* is an ability to adapt, to change with the times. No hero was more strikingly different from both Achilles and Aias. "As the gates of Hades," says Achilles to Odysseus (*Iliad* 9.312–13), "I hate the man who hides one thing in his heart and says another." But to Aias, who has spoken bluntly of honor and friendship, Achilles replies, "You have spoken, Aias, like a man after my own heart" (*Iliad* 9.645).

Homer does not tell us how Aias fell. Epic poems, lost to us but known to Sophocles' audience, narrated the grisly sequence of events. Like Aeschylus and Pindar before him, Sophocles was free to adapt this story as he chose, counting on his audience's familiarity with the mythical variants. By emphasizing, omitting, or innovating, the poet could use a myth to express his own vision. No spectator would fail to notice variations on stories known by heart; the poet knew what his audience knew and therefore what that audience might expect. The conventions, established by previous treatments of Aias' suicide, created the expectations with which, and against which, Sophocles wrote.

From fragments the episodes of the epic cycle can be pieced together. A quarrel arose between Aias and Odysseus over Achilles' arms; unable to choose between them, the Greeks asked Trojan prisoners to judge. Though accounts vary, the supple talker and thinker, Odysseus, prevailed. Shamed by defeat, Aias disappeared into his tent to die, "blameless" in Greek eyes; later, he was given a hero's funeral. In still another version, Aias' rage turns to madness, which leads in turn to suicide. In yet another—the one employed by Sophocles here—Aias went mad and slaughtered the Greek livestock before taking his own life; for this, he was denied a hero's burial. In presenting an Aias drama, Sophocles could choose from a number of potentially dramatic accounts and a variety of interpretations. All the variants raise questions about the three aspects of the myth that Sophocles chose to confront directly: madness, suicide, and burial. Precisely these elements determine whether Aias is to be considered heroic, and in what sense. The verdict is moot, and Sophocles is therefore free to explore what meaning he might find among the various Aias legends.

Aeschylus had already offered a comprehensive interpretation of the legend. His Aias trilogy presented a sequence of events that suggest a heroic, even divine, Aias, and a moral progression that characterizes Aeschylean theater. In Sophocles the suicide is the dead center of a single play, overshadowing everything else; in Aeschylus the suicide was only one of three equally significant theatrical events—the debate, the suicide, and the establishment of Aias' hero-cult on the Athenian island of Salamis. Like the *Oresteia*, the trilogy exhibited a redemptive pattern: Aias' anger was the "Fury" that, in the final play, was redeemed. Far from being the center of the trilogy, the suicide and events preceding it were not dramatized at all but reported by an eyewitness. A curious mythical variant regarding the hero's invulnerability was also introduced. When, bent on suicide, Aias failed to find the vulnerable point, a god appeared to aid him. He died, in other words, befriended by heaven and nearly godlike in his invulnerability. Finally, in the last play, Aias' death was revealed as part of a more universal scheme. And since both Salamis and Aias were "Athenian," Aeschylus' dramatic portrayal of Aias enshrined upon Salamis surely redounded to the glory of Athens herself.[1]

But to the Theban aristocrat Pindar, the death of Aias represented the end of the heroic age. Indifferent, even hostile, to Aeschylus' cosmic optimism, Pindar presented an Aias whose loss irreversibly diminished the world. Greece had betrayed its own greatness when it abandoned noble Aias in favor of crafty Odysseus. Pindar, moreover, injected an anachronistic

---

1. The three plays were *The Award of the Arms*, frg. 174–78aN; *The Women of Thrace*, frg. 83N; and *The Women of Salamis*, frg. 216N. My reconstruction of this trilogy is, of course, conjectural.

political meaning into his treatment of the myth, linking Aias not to Salamis (and Athens) but to his favorite city, Aigina, a bastion of conservative, aristocratic Greece (and perhaps no less important, the enemy of Athens). Having been betrayed by its ally Sparta, Aigina now "belonged" to Athens. So it is tempting to see in Pindar's ode, composed for an Aiginetan victor at the Nemean games, an equation between the defeat of this "unAthenian" Aias and that of Pindar's city of heroes—a victory of immoral intelligence, that famous "Attic cleverness," over honor:

> Envy's fang bit into the flesh of Aias and twisting inside
> ran him through with a sword.
> Strong—even in silence—he is eclipsed by that hateful fight,
> the greatest prize given for the flashy lie,
> the Greeks flattering Odysseus, their secret ballot leaving
> Aias stripped of the golden arms, alone
> to wrestle with death.
>
> But the winner was no match for Aias at ripping
> wounds in warm flesh, when his long spear
> was their only shield in the fight that raged
> over Achilles' body, or in a thousand other struggles
> in those days of too much dying.
> Despicable, even then, the art of guile
> —weaving webs of words, twisting thoughts, casting blame,
> working to no good end—drives splendor into darkness
> and honors the obscure, holding up a glory
> rotten to the root.
>
> (*Nemean* 8.23–34)

To this vividly implicit condemnation of Athens, Sophocles responds by immediately, in the first scene, rehabilitating Pindar's villain, Odysseus. But by isolating Aias, by focusing solely on the suicide, and finally by suppressing the confident Aeschylean coda, Sophocles also refuses Aeschylus' optimistic marriage of the divine hero with Athens. Everything essential to Sophocles' interpretation, moreover, has been condensed into a single play, and the suicide is the midpoint climax to which it builds. Thereafter Aias' huge corpse dominates the stage.

But dramatizing Aias' suicide creates genuine problems for an Athenian playwright passionately concerned, like Sophocles, with human greatness. There was simply no precedent for heroic suicide. For Greek males, suicide was, unlike the *seppuku* of the Japanese samurai, not an honorable death. Under extreme circumstances, heroes might long for death; and while they often chose courses of action that led to death, they never took their own lives. Suicide was a desperate act, restricted in tragedy solely to women. Far from confirming heroism,

Aias' suicide in fact marks the end of the heroic tradition, just as the victory of Odysseus signals the beginning of a new and less heroic age.

In Athens, where Aias was the eponymous hero of one of the ten tribes, suicide may have raised moral questions. His statue, paid divine honors, stood prominently in the marketplace, and clans claiming descent from Aias were among the city's most illustrious citizens. "Divine" Aias was honored by all of Greece, along with Poseidon and Athene, for his tutelary role in the Greek victory over Persia at Salamis in 480 B.C. Athens was justly proud of its link to the deified hero and its role as savior of Greece. Hence, the ignominy of Aias' suicide was hardly the most propitious subject for artistic representation; and in Attic art generally, it is Aias' military prowess, not his suicide, that is emphasized. So we can be reasonably certain that Sophocles' insistent, dramatic focus on the "forbidden" subject must have surprised his audience, violating, as it did, their expectations.

Still more surprising is the characterization of Aias as eloquent and reflective. The Homeric ideal as embodied by Achilles was excellence in both word and deed. But the Homeric Aias is clearly lacking in eloquence and mental agility. A staunch defender, he is never depicted as a strategist, nor does he participate, like the other heroes, in the councils of the chieftains. At one point, his tenacity in battle is compared to that of an ox (*Iliad* 13.703–7), a comparison invidiously "re-called" by Agamemnon in this play ("An ox, for all / its great girth, is driven down the road / with a little whip," 1403–5 / 1253–54); elsewhere, his steadfastness invites comparison with a stubborn ass (cited above). His great size and simplicity helped to create the traditional image of the hulking brute. Even in death, in his sublime Homeric moment, Aias is famous for what Longinus called his "eloquent silence": the refusal of his shade to speak to Odysseus in Hades. By contrast, the Sophoclean Aias dominates the stage, not only with his imposing presence, but with four of the most remarkable speeches in drama. One must go to Shakespeare—to Richard II's prison monologue or Macbeth's "brief candle" speech or even Hamlet's "to be or not to be"—to find anything like Aias' prodigious speech on time (712–69 / 646–92). These are lines, Bernard Knox writes, "so majestic, remote and mysterious, and at the same time so passionate, dramatic, and complex, that if this were all that had survived of Sophocles he would still have to be reckoned as one of the world's greatest poets."[2] The profound novelty of this eloquent and deadly lucid Aias is absolutely crucial to the reader's understanding of the play.

<hr/>

2. Bernard Knox, "The *Ajax* of Sophocles," *Word and Action: Essays on the Ancient Greek Theater* (The Johns Hopkins University Press, 1979), p. 125. Reprinted from *Harvard Studies in Classical Philology* 65 (1961).

II

The great Sophoclean Aias emerges in his confrontation with death. Through the speeches that arise from that confrontation he comes into being. It is his reflections and the transforming urgency of his rhetoric that make his suicide wholly unconventional in its metaphysical resonance. The hero's deftly paced and penetrating words detach him completely from the ignominy traditionally associated with his death; at the same time, they give his suicide a meaning radically different from that of the Aeschylean apotheosis. This Aias is neither the deified hero of Athenian cult nor the archaic warrior who dies in shame—not the hero whom time has passed by, but rather the *man* who steps beyond time.

Sophocles begins his play, however, with the familiar figure of Aias disgraced. Exploiting the most sensational version of Aias' fall, the dramatist presents an Aias at the extreme epic end. His audacious words and savagery seem brutish simplicity beside the humane Odysseus, whose vision of human transience ("we who live / are all phantoms, fleeting shadows," 151–52 / 125–26) makes him sound more like Pindar himself ("Creatures of a day. What is man? What is he not? Man / shadow of a dream," *Pythian* 8.95–96) than the immoral schemer of *Nemean* 8 ("twisting thoughts, casting blame, working to no good end"). Timeless Greek wisdom stands behind Odysseus' compassionate humility, whereas Aias is tainted by horror and a blood-lust fueled by violent hatred, Homeric self-assertion taken to a murderous extreme. Smeared from head to toe with the gore of his animal victims, mad Aias visibly confirms the death throes of Homeric heroism. Worse still, if Athene had not deterred him and driven him mad, he would have been soaked with human blood. This dark and savage project of murdering the Greeks in the night is Sophocles' own invention. The Aias of the *Iliad* had moved in the light, preferring death in light to life in darkness: "Father Zeus," he once cried in battle, "remove us from darkness, let our eyes see bright aether, / and then destroy us in shining daylight, / since this is now your pleasure" (*Iliad* 17.645).

Sophocles' Aias himself has become a vision of darkness. The sight of him conjures up "phantoms" and "fleeting shadows" before Odysseus' eyes; and "Darkness, my light! / brightest gloom" (430–31 / 394–95) is Aias' own vision when he wakes from madness. The archaic warrior seems now an avatar from some dark and brutish past, more like a pre- than a post-Homeric memory. He could not be more degraded, more ludicrously absurd.

Tekmessa's description of the night's events only darkens the initial image; she reports Aias' insane joy in inflicting torture, breaking necks, and flaying victims alive. The worst, she warns, is yet to come. The following scene does little to mitigate her forebodings and our revulsion: "sprawled / in the wreck of his fate" (**351–52** / 323), a saner Aias is wheeled out into view on the trundle stage, the *ekkyklema*—but nothing has changed except that his delusions are gone, replaced by his fatal shame. Aias still hates the Greeks; his only regret is that his hand missed its true target. Even when he is allowed to recall something of his former Homeric greatness—

> Skamander, river
> hostile to the Greeks,
> there is one man your water
> will not mirror
> again—I will have
> my full say—a man
> like none Troy ever set eyes on.   (**455–61** / 418–25)

—the spectacle of the hero-butcher overwhelms us, intensifying his dreadful fall.

But here, at Aias' lowest point, his transformation begins. No tragic characters sink lower, or rise higher, than those of Sophocles. Their savage degradation is vividly depicted—Philoctetes' oozing wound, Oedipus' bleeding eyes, Herakles' pain-racked body—in order to intensify their godlike struggle against that degradation. Disgraced, drenched in animal blood, victim of his own brutality, Aias discovers his agony as a mortal. He now knows his true fate: his name, *Aias* (from *aiadzein*, "to cry in pain," cf. **468–72** / 430–33), *is* his destiny. Aias stands before us polluted with gore; but this brute blood is tragic confirmation that he, too, is a creature of blood—mortal, born to die and therefore to cry *aiai*.

The anguished cry *aiai*, which begins Aias' speech (**468** / 430), and the heroic finale "Honor in life / or in death" (**530–31** / 479) express the range of his character; beyond this, as Aias concludes, "You've heard all there is to say" (**533** / 480). The outcry and the avowal of silence frame Aias' lament for a greatness the world has lost. We get a hint of what he might have become, if the world had not changed: a man like his father, Telamon, shipmate of Herakles and sacker of Troy, who sailed home with the highest prize of honor. But dishonored now, Aias can never return to face such a father. A shadow of his Homeric self, surviving in a world that has outlived his kind of *arete*, Aias sees that the only heroism left him is the essential human achievement—dignity in dying, "some act that will prove / [his] nature" (**520–21** / 470–72). This is the man the world has lost:

> To stretch your life out when you see
> that nothing can break its misery

is shameful — day after day
moving forward or back from the end line
of death. (523–27 / 473–27)

Though diminished by the changing world he abhors, enough of Aias is left for him to speak like the hero who led the fight against Troy: Better all at once to take our chances at living or dying, / than be worn away slowly by the dreadful slaughter... (*Iliad* 15.511–12).

Even his farewell to Tekmessa and Eurysakes pointedly recalls the famous Homeric scene of Hektor's farewell to Andromache and their son (*Iliad* 6.390–496). Hektor hears words from Andromache remarkably like those of Tekmessa here; he also instructs his young son on the warrior code. In a scene at once harsh and tender, epic and human, Aias appears not only as a shadow of his former self but also as the shadow of Hektor, the archenemy to whose fate his own is ironically linked. Now, more visibly than ever, through this shadow play of his enemy's fate, Aias appears little more than a memory, a "fleeting shadow" of that lost heroic world.

But Sophocles undercuts even this humanly revealing moment. The outmoded epic hero is finally too implacable to assume his new human role with grace. Displaced from his epic context, as in the opening scene, Aias appears absurdly ruthless; but, even in this Homeric farewell scene, he seems relatively grim. He has no such consoling words for Tekmessa as Hektor had for Andromache, whose day of slavery grieves him more than the deaths of all his family. Hektor's are strong words, but there is nothing like them in Sophocles' play: "She will win my praise / if she does what I command" (589–90 / 527–28) is all that Aias says. Tekmessa's appeal does not persuade Aias to accept her tragic view — "My lord, there is no greater evil / among us than inescapable / chance (538–40 / 485–86) — although his own fate confirms her words. She who was once Aias' captive now loves him; the Greeks who were his friends now hate him. Odysseus whom he most hates pities him; and, "by chance," Aias the man "like none other" reenacts the fate of the enemy he fought so hard to destroy. In madness Aias was degraded. But even in his farewell to Tekmessa and his son he is hard and stubborn: "It is foolish," he says to Tekmessa in parting, "to think you can school me now!" (673 / 594–95).

III

Aias has now made his exit, and the Chorus sings: "Let Hades hide him, his affliction has gone / beyond all measure" (702–3 / 635), and "Oh, luckless father, you've yet / to learn what unbearable end / your son has come to" (707–9 / 641–42). The Chorus confirms what has been antici-pated: Aias has gone to die. At this point, the audience doubtless expects the great messenger speech of the play, like that perhaps of Aeschylus' vivid account of the hero's last moments: "like a man stretching a bow, he bent back the sword on his impenetrable skin" (frg. 83N).

Instead, expectations are disappointed. What follows is indeed the play's great speech. Not a messenger's speech *about* Aias, but a meditation on mutability delivered *by* Aias. The audience believes that Aias is in his tent, either dead already or dying. But Sophocles has surprisingly reshaped the myth so as to reveal now the emergence of the new Aias, whose speech and suicide will transform the mean-ing of his myth:

> Great, unfathomable time
> brings dark things into the light
> and buries the bright in darkness.
> Nothing is too strange, time seizes
> the most dread oath, the most hardened
> mind. Even I... (712–17 / 646–50)

The play has indeed brought a "dark thing to light": that mad, bloodstained Aias, who inspired Odysseus' reflections on our tragically shadowy existence. Pindar had attributed the eclipse of Aias to human treachery: "Guile...drives splendor into darkness and honors the ob-scure." But Sophocles' Aias sees *beyond* his own tragedy into a universal darkness; there is a brutal mutability at the heart of things—betrayal, god-inflicted madness, and degradation are merely its symptoms. No Sophoclean play is so concerned with time and so saturated with tem-poral expressions ("always," first word of the play in Greek, "sometimes," "in time," "whenever," "never"). But Aias is the first to see clearly what the Chorus will realize only later—much too late—when it sings, "Time, since the best men / contended for the arms of Achilles, / has been a potent begetter of sorrows" (1032–34 / 933–36). The world of Aias is a universe in flux, modeled perhaps on Heraclitus' river of change but without the philosopher's comforting hint of continuity. In this world only one thing is certain: uncertainty. From this law nothing is exempt, not "the most dread oath, the most hardened / mind." Not even Aias.

This speech is the heart of the play, the moment of fatal choice. Aias sees the world for what it is but, by deciding to move *against* the flow, *becomes* himself. Because Tekmessa and the Chorus misunderstand Aias' resolve, the speech has been dubbed the "deception speech." Nothing could be further from the truth. Sophocles has not composed this speech, surely one of the greatest in Greek drama, so that the man of absolute honor may tell lies. In fact, Aias does not even speak to Tekmessa and the Chorus. He enters, deep in thought, and delivers an unprecedented monologue-in-the-presence-of-others. This tragic isolation of the hero, even while surrounded by his friends, is profoundly Sophoclean. Aias no longer belongs to the world of others. He is involved in a final struggle with his own *daimon*, which, like its emblem the sword, now appears hostile and alien.

Here and only here Aias speaks with two voices. But these are not voices of uncertainty. Rather, we see two Aiases: one Aias who recognizes the law of change by which all else lives and dies; another Aias who will act in accord with the absolute law of his own nature. The speech is pure drama, in the sense that its meaning is inseparable from its dramatic context. As T. S. Eliot remarked of some of Shakespeare's great speeches:

> The lines are surprising, and yet they fit in with the character; or else we are compelled *to adjust our conception of the character in such a way that the lines will be appropriate to it* . . . dramatic . . . poetry . . . does not interrupt but intensifies the dramatic situation . . . you can hardly say whether the lines give grandeur to the drama, or whether it is the drama which turns the words into poetry.[3]

The Aias who *seems* to soften, who *seems* capable of living in a world of double meanings, is the *fondo* from which the new Aias, the fatal Aias, emerges. The drama lies in the agony with which the warrior-hero speaks, first words of pity, then words of reconciliation ("we will know / how to yield to the gods," **739–40** / 666–67), and finally in the scorn with which he describes submission ("bow down before the Atreidai," **741** / 667). Aias uses the same word (*loutra*) of cleansing and purification ("I will go to a bathing place," **724** / 654) that is later used to describe the ritual of his death (**1597** / 1405). His fate speaks *through* and *in* his *daimon*, even as his words appear to deny it.

At the outset Aias describes himself as "unbending / in action" (**718–19** / 650). He now asserts his presence among "the most unbending" elemental powers, though they are, ironically, his models of submission:

> . . . snow-tracked
> winter yields to the rich growth
> of summer, dark-vaulted night
> gives way to the shining, white-horsed

3. T.S. Eliot, "Poetry and Drama," *On Poetry and Poets* (Farrar, Straus & Giroux, 1975), p. 89 (originally published 1951); "Yeats," *idem.*, p. 305 (originally published 1940).

> brightness of day, a blast
> of appalling wind stills the sea's rage,
> even all-overwhelming sleep
> binds only to let go... (744–51 / 670–76)

The succession in each case—winter to summer, night to day, storm to calm—is characterized by movement from "dark" to "light." The final term is sleep, but the antithesis—waking—is missing. The ellipsis will be answered by an action. "All-overwhelming sleep" epitomizes the world's condition, tossed to and fro in the oblivion of change. Yet, even as he speaks, Aias is on the threshold of "awaking" into another order, "a world elsewhere."

Moving purposively from the god-sent "storm" of darkness, Aias at last arrives at fatal clarity. He speaks with sarcasm ("Then how / shall we not learn wise restraint?" 751–52 / 677), which betrays absolute certainty. In his closing reflection on the frailty of friendship and enmity alike, Aias tells what cosmic mutability means in human terms:

> I know now to hate an enemy
> just so far, so that another time
> we may befriend him. And the friend
> I help, I will not help too greatly,
> knowing that one day will find him
> my enemy. (753–58 / 678–82)

In a world where nothing lasts, where even the inexorable forces of nature change, little can be expected of fragile human feeling. The Aias who ends his speech with a *topos* on treachery ("For most mortals / friendship is a treacherous harbor," 758–59 / 682–83) has already decided that he will no longer live in *this* world—and still be Aias. He now *knows*: the absolute moment of his life is his death. To *go on* being Aias he must end his life—beyond choice, chance, change. At the close of the speech there is no further ambiguity. Aias *becomes* himself—by ceasing to be.

Something innately human has pushed Aias beyond contingency: love, the other side of his equally absolute hatred. His first intelligible word was a call for his son (370 / 339), followed by a cry for his brother (373 / 342), then an address to his "friends, / my only true-minded friends" (381–82 / 349). Moreover, he has left specific instructions for the care of his old parents, that his son be brought to "ease the weight of their years" (642 / 570). And just before he dies, between his farewell to the light and invocation of death, Aias will think of his poor parents' grief. But what of his brusque way with Tekmessa? Surely he rebuffs her because he is vulnerable to her above all. Between them is a kindness (*charis*) greater than kinship. As the Chorus said, Aias won her by the spear, but she won his heart (229–31 / 210–12). His harshness with her is a resistance to what she alone can do, what even time cannot do: change Aias. "Even I, whose will / was tempered like iron, unbending / in action, for a woman's sake / am become a woman in my speech" (717–20 / 650–52). His seeming callousness conceals his real human vulnerability. Aias loves absolutely; and so to achieve permanence—the principle that preserves love itself—he must paradoxically leave those he loves. He will not accept a world in which the absolute values of love, friendship, oaths, honor, even hatred do not last. The words spoken by another unconditional lover, Shakespeare's Cleopatra, in the scene leading to her triumphant suicide, might have been those of Aias: "...and it is great / To do that thing that ends all other deeds; / Which shackles accidents and bolts up change" (*Antony and Cleopatra*, act 5, scene 2).

An overpowering human force drives Aias beyond the human, allowing him to transform death into destiny, without relinquishing his absolutes. Only an immutable act can defeat the enemy that undermines all "human things"—"great, unfathomable time." That Tekmessa and the Chorus fail to understand his words only heightens the power of the speech and dramatizes the solitude in which the hero's fatal struggle with his *daimon* has taken place. "I will go," says Aias, "where I have to go" (767 / 690).

IV

The certainty of his final words, however, dissolves in the Chorus' sudden ecstatic reaction to them. There was matter in the speech itself to induce hope and prepare the audience for a denial of the suicide convention. Song and dance, moreover, are strong medicine ("Desire thrills in me, joy gives me wings!" 770 / 693), and an audience cannot remain wholly unaffected. Sophocles was famous for these odes of joyous delusion, but perhaps nowhere else are they used to such dramatic effect. We now *feel hope* as we felt *despair* in the preceding choral dirge. Suspense and song draw us into the choral world of change, possibility, and therefore hope. "*Time truly is great... / nothing's too strange / if Aias can turn / his heart from hatred*" (791–94 / 714–17 [emphasis added]), the enrapt Chorus sings, echoing Aias' words but reversing his meaning. The poet *dramatizes* the gulf separating us from Aias and his fatal certainty.

Even the messenger who at last arrives is, contrary to expectation, a harbinger of uncertainty. In place of the long-awaited account of the hero's death, we are told that Aias' life is contingent upon "this [one] day's light" (832 / 753)—the point is stressed four times—the length of Athene's anger. Aias has scorned those men whose lives are measured by days, "day after day / moving forward or back from the end line / of death" (525–27 / 475–76), and it is just this which Tekmessa and the Chorus' to-ing and fro-ing, in the hope of saving Aias, now dramatizes. The messenger also presents still another distortion of the traditional image of Aias. Speaking the familiar language of Greek morality, the messenger describes Aias as a man of *hybris*—an "outsized body" (838 / 758) untamed by human thoughts. His account of Aias' blasphemous words to Athene ("Go . . . / stand by the rest of the Greeks. / The line won't break where I hold it," 857–59 / 774–75) has no epic precedent and consorts strangely with Aias' words of gratitude for what he earlier thought was Athene's divine alliance.

But Aias has "let [his mind] go beyond the human" (840 / 761) and truly "owe[s] nothing more to the gods" (668 / 590), though not in the sense that such presumptuousness is usually understood. Aias has indeed passed so far beyond both the "human" and the messenger's "divine" that Sophocles feels it necessary to empty the stage—an extremely rare occurrence in extant drama—in order to prepare for Aias' appearance. We are suddenly in another world, a liminal space where the opposed realities of land and sea, heaven and earth, converge. The grave tableau—Aias beside his upright sword—is now rolled out on the *ekkyklema*. At last, the true nature of his defiance, that of the *metaphysically* stiff-necked man, will be revealed.

The "killer" sword stands ready, firmly planted by Aias. In Homer the sword symbolized certainty and honor; here it is the visual emblem of change, an image of Aias' fate, a present from Hektor, "an enemy's gift" (737 / 665) to the man who won only enmity from friends. Sharpened on the "iron-eating stone" (915 / 820), the sword is destiny for the rocklike man, "whose will / was tempered like iron, unbending / in action" (717–19 / 650–51). But in the sword we also have an image of that force behind all flux, Aias' real enemy—Time. Imagine how this sword might have appeared to those sitting in the Theater of Dionysus: the blade straight up, in the early morning light, it must have cast a long shadow—like the needle of a giant sundial—across the *ekkyklema* on which Aias stands. It is "Time's sword," moving even as Aias speaks. The hero's character now requires that he enact the truth of his own words. As Time's sword moves "against" Aias, so he moves to make Time stop.

Zeus, Hermes, even Death are now, in Aias' words, made to wait on him. The gods he invokes are not, like Athene, powers of contingency who meddle with men. He invokes these gods solely as guardians of the dead, divinities of passage to man's "long home," beyond time, beyond change. Curses in the name of the primeval Furies assure his *eternal* hatred of the Greeks. But his most striking and significant address is to Helios, specifically as heavenly charioteer. Speaking in mythical terms, Aias commands Helios to rein in his chariot: to halt the Sun is to stop Time. Aias has transformed his death into an epiphany of permanence. His huge body covering the sword, he will eclipse Time and die, not in darkness, but, as his final invocation suggests, radiantly in the light. Now the unbending, immovable Aias has at last appeared. There is no trace of the lamenting Aias or the mad Aias of the opening scenes, or the shadowy "relenting" Aias of the Time speech; there is only the inflexible, commanding presence that here triumphs and destroys itself. We see his *ethos* become his *daimon*. He exceeds the world he is in, and passes beyond it. But in contrast to Homer's mute shade, this Aias promises speech in death: "I *will speak* to the dead in Hades" (965 / 865 [emphasis added]), or, as *mythēsomai*, his final word, declares, "live on as undying 'myth.' "

Aias has decided; and the "day" has been made to attend upon his decision. Even Odysseus' tragic wisdom about "fleeting shadows" has been refuted. Indeed, Aias' stature grows until he literally touches the divine. He demands and achieves something that is not of the temporal world. His final invocation of heavenly light and sustaining earth ("...O radiance! / O holy ground," 957–58 / 859) suggests something like the apotheosis of Oedipus at Colonus. The hero belongs to both heaven and earth. Elemental powers—divine *physis*, the eternality of Nature herself, not her changing seasons—are summoned from above and below to converge upon the hero. For Sophocles, men at the peak of their powers *reveal* the gods who are *there* but unrealized until men disclose them.

V

Does the suicide take place in view of the audience or not? The question is crucial, but unfortunately, our text provides no unequivocal answer. If, as Aias spoke his last words, he leapt on his sword, this would be the unique instance of dramatized violence in Greek tragedy. In any case, Sophocles is not concerned with a sensational suicide but rather with the *meaning* of the act. As with the Oedipus' self-blinding, it is the vision—it is the outward seeing transformed into inward sight—that matters, not the violence of the plunging blade. Aias finally had to move beyond words, to the enactment of his truth; at this point, verbal meaning becomes visual. And it is this that takes place in the coming scene with Teukros.

Teukros' arrival has been long awaited. Aias has three times referred to his coming (373–74 / 342–43, 631–34 / 562–64, 764–66 / 688–89), and now Tekmessa anticipates it (884–94 /797–804, 1018–20 / 921–22). The significance of his arrival is linked to the preceding events. As Aias finishes his speech, he and the sword are trundled inside the stage building. The Chorus enters the orchestra in confusion, followed by Tekmessa beside the body of Aias on the *ekkyklema*. But the Chorus does not in fact see Aias (1008–9 / 912–14). More important, its request to see him is emphatically refused by Tekmessa: "He must not be seen! I will cover / his body, I will wrap him completely / in my mantle" (1010–12 / 915–16).

If the Chorus cannot see the body, neither can the audience. The concealment suggests that later the body will be uncovered. But Tekmessa, who had urged Aias to accept contingency and who, like the Chorus, is resigned to the tyranny of time, is not the proper person to uncover the body and reveal the heroic truth Aias has enacted.

The following scene is all revelation. The question "Where is Teukros?" is at last answered. The plot requires his coming in order to protect Aias' dependents, but his arrival is carefully linked to the concealing of the body (1010–20 / 915–22). His long speech begins with three sight words: "... of all my eyes have seen / this is the most painful sight" (1099–1100 / 992–93). The point could hardly be more emphatic. Teukros now asks for visible confirmation of what he has heard. "Uncover him," he finally says to Tekmessa, "let me look at the whole evil" (1109–10 / 1003).

The *face* of Aias is what he sees: "that hard face, / that grim self-command!" (1111–12 / 1004–5)—literally, "that face hard to see, full of bitter daring" (*o dystheaton omma kai tolmēs pikras*). The line makes it clear that Aias has fallen sideways on his sword, and that he now lies impaled *face-up*. His fierce face is a constant feature from Homer on; bright eyes and an eagle glare characterize him in the play (100–101 / 84–85, 187–91 / 167–72). This same grim face—staring up at radiant light—must be what Teukros is describing. Aias has faced death as he faced his enemies: head on, without fear. He is now revealed as a man who has dared to look at the world's truth and face its consequences rather than suffer its uncertainties. Anything but a "fleeting shadow," Aias dies at the height of his powers, a hero "in the light."

VI

The dead Aias dominates the stage more than ever, but the heated dispute over his burial now jeopardizes his *meaning*. A hero's burial had an aura of mystery quite alien to us. Like a canonized saint, the hero had the power to bless the land in which he was buried and the people who revered him. To deny Aias burial is not only to dishonor a great man and deny the "otherness" he embodies, but to violate the sacred laws that bind the living to the dead. When the hero refused burial is also an Athenian hero, the morality of the "sacred city" itself is at stake.

But the tangible dramatic difference of the second half of the play has led critics to complain that the play is clumsily composed. The hero is "gone" by midpoint, and the remainder of the play seems merely an extended debate. Plays such as *Antigone*, *Oedipus Rex*, or *Women of Trachis* close with a crescendo. The diminuendo here is undeniable. But the purpose is certainly to dramatize how the world would be without an Aias. The unheroic tone of the speeches with their threats, boasts, and insults reveal the meanness of this new world. Heroism seems to have died with Aias on his sword. The great speeches earlier, rich with noble epic language, are all spoken by Aias. The lyric mode itself, tragedy's "higher voice," fades away; the first half of the play contains four choral odes, the last half has only one. Grandeur of every kind diminished or vanished, the loss of Aias becomes achingly real. Absent, he is powerfully present in a world of smaller men. Even as a corpse, he dwarfs the survivors (good and bad alike). As the Chorus sang in its entrance song, "... small men / crumble without the great" (181–89 / 158–59).

When presented, the *Aias* reportedly aroused a violent reaction. We will never know what nerve the final five hundred lines of this play touched. But something in Athenian experience must surely be related to the passing of the heroic age that these last scenes dramatize. Tentatively dated to c. 445–40 B.C., the play would seem to have been produced at a time when Athens was examining the policies and perhaps the morality of her empire. Political arrogance resonates in the rhetoric and power politics of the very un-Homeric Agamemnon and Menelaos. But nothing is served by identifying the particular contemporary types represented by the Atreidai. They may be Spartan oligarchs or the amoral expansionists of imperial Athens. In any case, they are despots who possess political, not moral, authority and whose power rests upon fear and exploitation of others. Such men are found almost anywhere, at almost any time. Aias' greatness was based upon the *arete* implicit in Odysseus' description of him. But true greatness is rare, and the Atreidai's "principled" outrage is merely a perversion of Aias' heroic *hybris*. Aias' supreme self-assertion was of an altogether different order, anything but the basely selfish "morality" of the Atreidai.

Which leaves Odysseus as Aias' improbable moral heir. The compassionate and conciliatory Odysseus of the last scene (the only favorable portrayal of him in extant tragedy) represents the new ethos of democratic Athens at its best. In his speech on Time, Aias predicted that harshness would yield to gentleness. *Aristos*—the term earlier applied to Aias—is now applied to Odysseus by Teukros. Like Aias, Odysseus also honors friendship, recognizing that the *arete* of the dead Aias trivializes their former enmity: "I am moved more by his greatness / than by my enmity" (1537–38 / 1357).

Odysseus' final exchange with Agamemnon paradoxically engages the terms *friend* and *enemy*. For Odysseus, they are relative terms: a confirmation of the contingent morality resolutely rejected by Aias. But, though canny and adaptive, Odysseus is no moral opportunist. He speaks as a man who understands that since all men suffer the same fate, compassion and compromise are the appropriate virtues. And he is therefore able to adapt even the self-willed exceptional man, Aias, to his democratic vision. As in the earlier scene, the sight of Aias inspires Odysseus' tragic view of humanity. His earlier reflection of human transience is a tragic *topos*, poetically expressed ("phantoms, fleeting shadows"); his advice to Agamemnon arises from this same vision but is put very differently. Now Odysseus' words suggest a practical strategy with political implications—a basis, in other words, for human (and Athenian) democracy:

> AGAMEMNON I must let them bury the body,
> is that what you say?
> ODYSSEUS It is.
> I will face the same need some day.
> AGAMEMNON It is all one, then, and each man works
> for himself.
> ODYSSEUS There is reason in that.
> Who else should I work for?
>
> (1547–52 / 1364–67)

This is not Homeric individualism in the grand manner; but neither is it the opportunistic selfishness of the final years of the Athenian fifth century. It is both political and tragic wisdom: the foundation for a society in which compassion is perceived as the basis of preservation. Thucydides wrote:

> ...men too often take upon themselves in the prosecution of their revenge to set the example of doing away with those general laws to

which all alike can look for salvation in adversity, instead of allowing them to subsist against the day of danger when their aid may be required.

(3.84, Crawley transl.)

Odysseus, contrary to expectation, shows how society might preserve not only "that ancient simplicity into which honor so largely entered" (3.83) but also those endangered "general laws."

But Sophocles refuses full closure. The audience instead is challenged by a paradox. Despite his mediating role, Odysseus is not allowed to touch the hero's body; Aias, even dead, is resolute in his hatred. If that huge body commanding the stage is seen as inimical to Odysseus, then how can the spirit that animated it ever be domiciled in Athens? In the single choral ode after Aias' death, an ode beginning in despair but ending in hope (1331–66 / 1185–1222), the Chorus strives for a resolution. How long, it asks, will the Trojan War last, and it recalls happier times, days of wine, song, sleep, and love-making. These sentiments of ordinary life, seemingly anomalous in high tragedy, compel us to ask what impulse lies behind them? Surely, what the Chorus *sees*—the tableau of Aias protected by his loved ones that dominates the play at its close.

Tekmessa and Eurysakes kneel over the body. The boy holds three locks of hair, with which he supplicates his dead father. Mother, son, and father form a tableau of *philia*, the "human bond" by which the dead and the living are joined in sacrament. Moved by the spectacle, the Chorus remembers *its* "world elsewhere," that of its loved ones, the joy and peace it has left behind. It then laments the loss of the man on whom its return depended, its "great wall / against weapons and terrors / under the pall of night . . . relentless Aias" (1355–57 / 1211–13). What joy is left, the Chorus asks, now that its Aias is dead (1361–62 / 1215–16)? It concludes, however, by expressing its yearning to sail toward the "wooded rampart of Sounion" and "holy Athens" (1363 / 1220, 1366 / 1222). What it might have hoped for while Aias lived—the pleasures of peace and home—now lies in Athens, the city so renowned for its compassion toward exiles and suppliants.

The point is made and confirmed by the poet's fusion of hero and city in the double image of a "bulwark": "relentless" Aias, "the great wall" (*probola*, 1355 / 1212) and the "rampart" (*problēma*, 1363 / 1217) of Sounion, the promontory where Attica most vividly meets the sea. Epic bulwark and Attic headland merge into what even the Theban Pindar had hailed as the "bulwark of Greece, holy Athens" (frg. 76). In the final scene, by applying to Odysseus the epithet *aristos*, elsewhere reserved for Aias, Teukros signals the emergence of a new *arete*, different from that of Aias, but originating nonetheless in his myth. By reconciling others to Aias, Odysseus demonstrates that the hero—daimonic even in hatred—is an enduring "presence," a power indispensable to that city that claimed to be "the education of Hellas." Just as the city needs the hero, so the hero, at least in death, needs others, needs the city and the human solidarity it represents. But now the burden of heroism must belong to all; aristocratic *arete* must be democratized. But ultimately the Chorus' new "bulwark" preserves the image of unyielding Aias—Homer's "wave-beaten ridge," that Sophoclean "rock in the sea" which, like old Oedipus, "abides the coming of the waves." For the "divine" in "human things," for the values of endurance, tragic solitude, and heroic hybris—the basis of the permanent values that energize the democratic city—Aias is the paradigm.

And so the play rightly closes with Aias. The final image is an image of blood—not animal blood as in the first scene, but the human blood of Aias. Body, burial, a hero's blood—these are now the final revealing images. Teukros, Eurysakes, and the chorus lift Aias whose "black life force...still flowing out / of his warm veins" (1601–2 / 1411–13) now covers those who hold him. Blood-violence has become blood-bond, the link that binds living and dead, city and hero, "radiance" and "holy ground."

HERBERT GOLDER

ON THE TRANSLATION

The dialogues in this version of the *Aias* are composed in sprung rhythm, with three stresses to a line. There is no set pattern in which the stresses fall and no rule governing the number of unstressed syllables in the line. The stresses may be single or doubled. This system allows for lines as brief as

I will bury Aias

or as long as

There were swords drawn. It would have gone badly

to be read as prosodically equivalent. Sprung rhythm is the natural rhythm of speech heightened by the formal constraint of a fixed number of stresses and the ear's perception of regularity behind the irregularity. Keeping the number of stresses in mind will also help the reader (or actor) to hear how the lines should be spoken.

The choral odes and other more formal passages in the play (162–279 / 134–262, for instance) are also in sprung rhythm, with lines of one to five stresses. They mirror the structures of the original. The entrance of the Chorus (*parados*, 162–91 / 134–72) is composed in a rocking four-stress line, as is the final *exodus* (1594–1608 / 1402–20), with its brief anticipation in lines 1304–8 / 1164–67.

I hope that these poetic principles have enabled us to avoid the effect of the double iambic trimeter, the meter of dialogue in Greek drama ("I see you've come on foot, not riding on a horse"), which can be rather ludicrous in English, and at the same time to make an actable version of the play that keeps some sense of the high formality of Greek tragedy, so often lost in free-verse translations.

Mention should be made of our use of certain Greek outcries and lamenting words: *Io! Io moi moi! Omoi! Aiai!* English has almost no such words, yet to eliminate them from the *Aias* seemed a grave loss. Instead, we have followed the example of Paul Claudel, whose great French translation of the *Agamemnon* allows for such cries as: *Otototoï! Iô popoï! Iou iou!* and *oïmoï!* The reader will understand that these are not so much words as noises. King Lear makes his last entrance with the line: "Howl, howl, howl, howl! O, you are men of stones!" And so I always read it. Only when I saw the play performed did I realize that the old man enters *howling*.

RICHARD PEVEAR

AIAS [AJAX]

Translated by

HERBERT GOLDER

and

RICHARD PEVEAR

CHARACTERS

ATHENE

ODYSSEUS

AIAS

CHORUS of sailors from Salamis

TEKMESSA wife of Aias

EURYSAKES son of Aias

MESSENGER

ATTENDANTS of Aias

TEUKROS half-brother of Aias

MENELAOS

ARMED ATTENDANTS of the Atreidai

AGAMEMNON

Line numbers in the right-hand margin of the text refer to the English translation only, and the Notes beginning at p. 81 are keyed to these lines. The bracketed line numbers in the running heads refer to the Greek text.

The scene is the Greek camp on the coast at Troy. The stage building represents the
quarters of ATHENE *surrounded by a stockade with double gates in the center.*

ATHENE *appears aloft.*

ODYSSEUS *enters from the side.*

ATHENE I always see you like this,
Odysseus, hunting out some advantage
against your enemies. Now
you're sniffing around where Aias
and his sailors pitched their tents
at the end of the battle line,
pacing over his fresh tracks, wondering
if he has gone in or is still
out roaming. The scent has led you
like a sharp-nosed Spartan bitch   10
to the right place. No need
to peer through the gates: he's there,
his head and sword-slaying hands
still dripping sweat. But tell me,
why are you pursuing him?
You may learn from what I know.

ODYSSEUS Athene! No god is closer
to my heart! I cannot see you
but your words ring like a bronze-mouthed
trumpet in my mind. You're right,   20
I'm hunting an enemy, circling
his footprints: Aias, the great shield
Last night he did something inconceivable—or he may have done it,
nothing's sure, we're still bewildered.
I took the burden of proof
on myself. Just now we found
all our spoil of cattle,
herds and herdsmen, butchered,
torn to pieces by some monstrous   30

27

hand—his hand, we think.
A witness claims he saw him
leaping across the field
alone, swinging a wet sword.
When I heard that, I sought out
the trail, and it led me here.
But these tracks baffle me; some
I know are his, but the others
are hard to make out. You've come
when I most needed you, goddess!   40
Your hand has <u>always</u> steered me
and <u>always</u> will.

ATHENE   I knew that.
I've been following you <u>for some time,
caught up in the hunt myself.</u>

ODYSSEUS Then my tracking has not gone wrong?

ATHENE I assure you, the man did everything
you have said.

ODYSSEUS   A reckless hand!
What drove him to it?

ATHENE   Rage
over the award of Achilles' armor.

*rage
of wrath of Achilles*

ODYSSEUS But why slaughter the cattle?   50

ATHENE He thought he was smearing his hands
with your blood.

ODYSSEUS   With ours?
<u>Then he meant to kill Greeks?</u>

ATHENE   And would have
if I had not been watching.

ODYSSEUS What nerved him, what made him dare?

ATHENE He came stalking you in the darkness.   *no answer*

ODYSSEUS Was he close? Could he have struck?

ATHENE He was at the two generals' gates.

ODYSSEUS And so eager to kill—what stopped him?

ATHENE I stopped him. Spinning illusions   60
        of his own most deadly joy,
        I drew him to your captured herds   *Spinning illusions*
        milling in the field. He fell on them,
        hacking at sheep and cattle,
        crushing their spines, carving out
        a bloody circle around him.
        Sometimes he thought the Atreidai
        were in his huge grip, then he struck
        at another chief and another,
        roving up and down in a sick frenzy.   70
        And I urged him on, I drove him
        deeper into the net.   *net*
        At last he grew tired of killing,
        bound up what cattle and sheep
        were left alive and dragged them
        to his camp—all horns and hoofs,
        but he thinks they're men. He has them
        inside there now. He's torturing them.
        But I want you to see this sickness
        with your own eyes and proclaim it   80
        aloud to all the Greeks.

                ODYSSEUS *averts his eyes and turns to leave.*

        Stay! Face him! What he has become
        is no threat to you. I'll bend
        the light of his eyes away.
        He won't see you standing there.
                                        Aias!

Leave off chaining your captives
and come out here!

ODYSSEUS   Athene!
            Do not call him out!

ATHENE   Quiet!
            Or shall men say you're a coward?

ODYSSEUS By the gods, no! But leave him inside.   90

ATHENE Why? Isn't he the same man he was?

ODYSSEUS The same, yes, and still my enemy.

ATHENE And is any laughter sweeter
            than laughter at an enemy?

ODYSSEUS Even so, let him stay inside.

ATHENE Are you afraid to look in the eyes
            of a madman?

ODYSSEUS   If he were not mad
            I would face him.

ATHENE   Face him now, then.
            Even this close, he won't see you.

ODYSSEUS How not, if he has the same eyes?   100

ATHENE Bright as they are, I'll darken them.

ODYSSEUS Gods can contrive what they please.

ATHENE Stand there and say nothing.

ODYSSEUS If I must, I will, but I would sooner
            be far from this place.

at stake

allies

alliances

connections

ATHENE   Aias!
          I call you again. Does your ally
          count for so little now?

          A blood-smeared AIAS *enters through central gates. His*
               speeches are interspersed with savage laughter.

AIAS Hail to you, Athene, hail to you,
          daughter of Zeus! Ah, how well
          you stood by me in this night's work!   110
          I'll crown you with gold for it!

          recognition
          but he'd act on them

ATHENE Beautiful words. But tell me,
          did your sword drink deeply of Greek blood?

AIAS I boast it did. Why deny it?

ATHENE Did your spear find the Atreidai?

          honor

AIAS Aias will not be dishonored
          by those two again.

ATHENE   They're dead,
          if I understand you?

AIAS   Dead!
          Let them rob me of the armor now!

          prize

ATHENE And what of the son of Laertes?   120
          Where does he stand between you
          and his ill fate? Has he escaped you?

AIAS That slinking weasel—you ask me
          where he is now?

ATHENE   Yes,
          that great obstacle of yours—Odysseus.

AIAS My sweetest triumph, goddess.

He's cowering inside there, in chains.
I don't want him to die yet.

ATHENE What more would you have first?

AIAS First tie him to a post in the yard.   130

ATHENE The poor wretch. What will you do then?

AIAS Then flay his back with this whip
before I kill him.

ATHENE   Ah!
Poor wretch, must he suffer so?

AIAS Be content to have your way
in all else, Athene. The man
will pay that price and no other.

ATHENE As you please, then. Let your hand
know the joys your mind is bent on.

AIAS I go back to my work. And you, goddess,   140
I charge you, always stand by me
as you did in this past night.

ho .

AIAS *exits through the gates, which close behind him.*

ATHENE You see how strong the gods are,
Odysseus. Was there ever a man
of greater foresight than Aias
or prompter in the shifts of action?

*foresight
prompter in the
shifts of action
!*

ODYSSEUS None that I know. Yet I pity
the poor wretch, though he's my enemy.
He's yoked to an evil delusion,
but the same fate could be mine.   150
I see clearly: we who live
are all phantoms, fleeting shadows.

ATHENE Consider him well, then, and never
allow yourself to speak arrogant
words against the gods,
or feel proud if your hand strikes harder
than another's or wealth heaps higher
around you. One day can lift up
and bring down all human things.
The gods favor wise restraint   160
in men and hate transgressors.

of chorus Ag,

> ATHENE *disappears,* ODYSSEUS *exits. The* CHORUS *enters*
> *marching in rhythm with their words.*

CHORUS   *parodos*
Son of Telamon, holder of power
on deep anchored, sea-ringed Salamis,
    when you do well I rejoice.
But to see you struck by Zeus, to hear
the Greeks cry slander against you, I tremble,
    dove-eyed terror comes over me.
Now from the fading night a loud murmur
has risen, disgracing us, saying you broke
across the horse-maddening meadows, killing   170
sheep and cattle, the plunder of allied
    spears in a blaze of iron.
Odysseus, persuasive Odysseus, shaped
these whispering words and finds ears eager
to hear them among your rivals, and each one
takes more pleasure in the tale, cursing
    your pain with outrageous laughter.
A great soul makes an easy target.
The same things said against me would miss.
Envy dogs the man of power.   180
Yet as a wall of defense small men
crumble without the great; when a great man
leads them, they rise and hold him higher.
    Fools will learn that the hard way.
Now they are shouting you down, and we have
no strength to turn away their attacks

33

without you, lord. Safe from your eye,
they chatter like a restless flock of starlings.
But show yourself, let a great eagle suddenly
tower above them, you'll see them huddle   190
    terror-struck, spechless with fear.

(The entrance chant turns to lyric invocation.)

Artemis of the bull cult, daughter   *strophe*
of Zeus—O terrible rumor, O
    mother of my disgrace—was it
she who drove you against the Greek herds
because of some victory left unpaid-for?
    Was it shining battle spoil
she was cheated of, or gifts of the deer hunt?
Did bronze-chested Ares or Enyalios
curse the work of your spear, spinning   200
a night plot to avenge the outrage?

Your own mind, son of Telamon,   *antistrophe*
would not have led you so far wrong
    to war against sheep and cattle.
It must be some sickness sent by the gods.
Zeus, Apollo, save us from slander!
    If they are spreading lies,
if the great kings or that son of the vile
race of Sisyphos whisper evil,
O lord, do not sit in your tent by the sea   210
and let their malice go unopposed.

Up from your seat!   *epode*
    You've been stuck fast
too long in this embattled silence.
    Ruin fires heaven!
Enemy arrogance is fanned to flame
by a high wind in the wooded valleys.
    While they all flee
    with cutting tongues,
        my grief cannot move.   220

TEKMESSA *enters through the gates.*

TEKMESSA Friends who serve on the ship of Aias,
    sons of the earth-born race of Erechtheus,   *Athenian*
    we who care for the distant house
    of Telamon must cry out, cry out now!
    Our awesome, great, relentless hero   *fallen*
    Aias has fallen
       afflicted by a darkening storm.

CHORUS What burden has the night exchanged for the day's?
    Daughter of Phrygian Teleutas,
    hard-driving Aias won you for his bed   230
    in war, but you have won his affection.
       Tell us if you know what happened.

TEKMESSA How can I say the unspeakable? You
    will hear about a suffering bitter
    as death: madness struck him in the night,
    his fame is defiled. There are such horrible
    things in his tent, sacrificial victims
    soaked in their own blood, oracles all
       too revealing of the hand that killed them.

CHORUS   *strophe*
          What you say   240
        of that fiery man is the same
        unbearable, inescapable
    rumor the Greek commanders have spread,
        and their telling makes it greater.
          Oh, I'm afraid
          of what will come now—
          his death shines in it.
          His frenzied hand
          and dark sword cut down
          the herds and herdsmen.   250

TEKMESSA Oh, that's it, that is where he came from!
    The beasts were tied up, he dragged them inside,

self-inflicted suffering

threw them to the ground and cut their throats
  or tore them apart barehanded.
Then he seized on two quick-footed rams,
slashed out the tongue of one, cuts its head off
and threw the carcass aside; the other
  he bound to a stake and lashed
with a heavy leather harness, a hissing
two-thonged whip, reviling it in words   260
so inhuman, so full of evil, a daimon
  must have spoken through him.

rage
disorientation

CHORUS   *antistrophe*
      Time to cover
    our heads and slip away
     on foot somehow,
or board ship, bend our backs to the oars,
   and go wherever she wills.
     The double-ruling
    Atreidai churn up
    such threats, I fear   270
    stones raining death
    on him and us, held
    by one awesome doom.

TEKMESSA But it's over now. The way flashing lightning
    dies with a gust of the south wind, he's come
    back to his senses. And found fresh pain.
    When a man looks at his own grief and knows
    that no one else was the cause of it, how much
     deeper the suffering cuts!

suffering greatest
when self-inflicted

CHORUS But fortunately it is over.   280
    Evil means less once it's passed.

TEKMESSA Which would you choose if you could:
    pleasure for yourself despite
    your friends, or a share in their grief?

CHORUS Two griefs are worse, woman.

TEKMESSA Then his recovery is our ruin.

CHORUS I don't see what you mean.

TEKMESSA Those evils trapped him, but he
            took great pleasure in them
            because of his madness. For us   290
            they were agony. Then the madness
            passed, he caught his breath,
            and now he's hounded, driven
            to the limits of pain as we are.
            Is that not twice the evil?

CHORUS You're right. I'm afraid some god
            has struck him. It must be so
            if his pain grows worse as the sickness
            passes.

TEKMESSA   Strange, yet it's true.

CHORUS But tell us, how did this evil   300
            come swooping down on him?
            We, too, suffer the harm of it.

TEKMESSA Since you are sharers, I'll tell you
            all I know. Long past midnight,
            when the torches were dead, he took
            his two-edged sword and groped
            his way to the door and the empty
            paths outside. I objected:
            "Aias, no one has called you,
            no messengers have come, no trumpets   310
            have sounded, the army's asleep.
            What are you doing?" His answer
            was brief, the much-sung refrain:
            "Silence becomes a woman,
            woman." So I let him teach me.
            He rushed out alone.
                            What happened

then I can't say, but he came back
dragging bulls, sheep dogs, sheep,
all tied together. He took some
and broke their necks, threw others   320
on their backs and slaughtered them, cutting
to the bone. A few he bound
and tortured as if they were human.
At one point he ran outside
and spoke with some shadow, dredging up
words against the Atreidai
and Odysseus, mixed with laughter
as violent as the revenge
he claimed he had taken. Then he rushed
back in where I was, and there   330
slowly, painfully, in time,
came to his senses. He looked
at the place and all the carnage
around him, beat his head
and howled, and fell blood-smeared
among the broken bodies, clawing
at his face and hair.
                                        He lay
for a long time without speaking.
Then he turned to me and threatened me
with terrible words if I wouldn't   340
explain what had happened, asking me
where he stood now. Oh, my friends,
I was frightened, I told him everything
just as I'd seen it. And he wailed,
he wailed in anguish. Never
have I heard such sounds from him.
He used to say wailing was fit
for cowards and the heavy-hearted.
When he groaned it was no shrill
lament but deep like the bellow   350
of a bull.
                        Now the man lies sprawled
in the wreck of his fate, surrounded

in time

AIAS [AJAX]   [324–45]

by the herds his iron brought down,
strangely calm, refusing to eat
or drink. It's clear he intends   *what will it be ?!*
to do some dreadful thing.
It sounds in his words and laments.
My friends, that's why I came out to you.
Go in, see if you can stop him.
Friends may win their friends back.   360

CHORUS Tekmessa, daughter of Teleutas,
by your words, the man's misfortunes
have brought him to a dread extreme
of possession.

                                              lament

AIAS   Io moi moi!

TEKMESSA There is worse to come, it seems.
Did you hear that distorted howl?
That was Aias!

AIAS   Io moi moi!

CHORUS He's still mad, or sick from seeing
what he did in his madness.

AIAS Io! Boy! My boy!   370

TEKMESSA Boy? Eurysakes! He wants you!
Oh, god, what for? Where are you?

AIAS Teukros! Where is Teukros! Forever   *Son of Telamon*
out raiding while I die here?   *half-brother of Aias*

CHORUS The man seems to be in his senses.
Open the gates. If he sees us,
shame may bring him back.   *to what?*

39

TEKMESSA They are open. Now you can see
        how he is and what he has done.

> TEKMESSA *opens the gates and* AIAS *is wheeled forward on*
> *a raised platform. He is sprawled among the carnage, and*
> *remains so as he addresses the* CHORUS *in song.*

AIAS   *strophe*

        Io!   380
    Shipmates, friends,
    my only true-minded friends,
      look at me, look
      at the storm-driven wave
      of blood that has swamped me!

CHORUS You were right, too right! See
       how far the madness drove him!

AIAS   *antistrophe*

       Io!
    My men, skilled oarsmen,
    who ply the sea with your blades,   390
      you, you alone
      can end this suffering.
      Join now to kill me!

cf. Herakles

CHORUS No! Never say it, Aias!
       If you try to cure evil with evil
       you will add more pain to your fate.

AIAS   *strophe*

    These hands that broke men,
    that drove back armies, brought down
    their terror on cattle! Oh,
    the laughter! the outrage I've suffered!   400

TEKMESSA My lord, do not say these things!

AIAS Are you still here, woman?

Can you find no other pasture?
            aiai! aiai!

TEKMESSA Give way, by the gods, relent!

AIAS   My hard fate to let   *regret*
                those devils slip through
                my hands, to fall
                on horned bulls and bright flocks
                spilling their dark blood!   410

CHORUS What's done is done, reliving   *they don't see Aias'*
            the harm will not undo it.   *regret, position*

AIAS   *antistrophe*
                Spying everywhere, tool
                of all evils, filthiest scum
                of the army, Odysseus, you must be
                somewhere laughing and gloating now!

CHORUS The gods say who laughs or cries.

AIAS Only let me set eyes on him . . . !
                Io moi moi!

CHORUS Your words are too big, you forget   420
            how deep in trouble you are.

AIAS   O Zeus, father   *Still wants*
                of my fathers, let me   *revenge*
                kill that skulking
                schemer and the two
                high kings, and die!

TEKMESSA Pray for my death, too, then.
            What good is my life with you dead?

AIAS   *strophe*
                    Io!
                Darkness, my light!   430

41

              brightest gloom, take me, take me
              to you, take me down into
              your house, I am not worthy
                  anymore to look
          for good from eternal gods or men of a day.
                  Zeus' daughter,
                  the armored goddess,
              tortures me to death!
              Where can I escape?
              What place will keep me?   440
              My honor is dead,
              my friends, as dead as these creatures.
              I've been caught by my own fool's prey,
              and the whole army would gladly
                  kill me twice over!

TEKMESSA It is hard to hear a great man
              say words he would once have despised.

AIAS   *antistrophe*
                      Io!
              Sea-roaring straits,
          sea caves, groves, salt meadows   450
              by the shore, you've held me
              a long time at Troy, but
                  no longer, no longer,
          not with breath in me, I promise you that!
              Skamander, river
              hostile to the Greeks,
              there is one man your water
                  will not mirror
                  again—I will have
                  my full say—a man   460
              like none Troy ever set eyes on
              in all the armed host coming over
              from Greece. But now I lie here
                  in filth and dishonor!

CHORUS I do not know how to stop you

42

or how I can let you go on,
seeing the evils you're caught in.

AIAS *rises slowly to his feet as the*
CHORUS *finishes speaking.*

AIAS Aiai! My name is a lament!
Who would have thought it would fit
so well with my misfortunes!   470
Now truly I can cry out—aiai!—
two and three times in my agony.
For I am a man whose father,
when he made war on this land,   *past glory*
came home with the greatest fame
and with the most beautiful spoils,
while I, that same man's son,
who brought as much strength to Troy,
whose acts were no less than his,
have won disgrace from the Greeks   480
and utter extinction!
                        Yet I know
one thing: if Achilles himself   *Achilles*
had declared which man among us
was worthiest to bear his arms,
no one else would have touched them.
But the Atreidai seized the prize
instead, and gave it away
to a schemer, a man of all minds.
They scorned my mastery! I tell you,
if my eyes and mind had not   490
been wrenched wide of their mark,
those two with their ballots and voting   *miscarriage*
would turn no matter of justice   *of*
against anyone again! But the grim-eyed,   *justice*
unbending daughter of Zeus
caught me as I brought my right hand
down on them, and drove me to madness.
I bloodied my hands on cattle.
They escaped, through no fault of mine,

43

actions not words

and now they exult in their triumph,   500
laughing at me. With the help
of a god's tricks, any coward
can escape his betters.
                 What now?
The gods hate me, that much is clear.
The Greek army detests me.
All Troy and the wide Trojan plain
are hostile to me. Shall I quit
this harbor, sail home across
the Aegean, and leave the Atreidai
to themselves? But what face can I show   510
my father Telamon? Could he bear
to see me come back stripped
of the high marks of honor that he
won here himself? Never.
Shall I go up to the walls of Troy
alone, take the army on, one
against all, show what I can do,
and die there? But that would only
please the Atreidai.
                No,

Achilles

I must find some act that will prove   520
my nature and show my father

act = nature

that his son was not born gutless.
To stretch your life out when you see
that nothing can break its misery
is shameful—day after day
moving forward or back from the end line
of death. There's no joy in that.
Any mortal who warms his heart
over empty hopes is worthless
in my eyes. Honor in life   530
or in death: if a man is born noble,
he must have one or the other.
You've heard all there is to say.

CHORUS No one will claim those words
         are false to your birth or your heart,

Aias. But let them go now,
give your friends some part in your purpose.

TEKMESSA My lord, there is no greater evil
among us than inescapable
chance. My father was a free man,   540
as rich and powerful as any
in Phrygia. Now I am a slave.
I owe that to the gods, it seems,
and to your strength most of all.
Since the day I came to your bed
I have always done you honor.
Now I beg you by Zeus of the hearth
and by that bed which binds me to you,
do not think so little of me   *Andromache*
as to leave me exposed to the scorn   550
of your enemies or the will of their hands.
If you die and abandon me,
know I'll be taken that same day
and dragged off with your son
to eat slave's food. And the Greeks,
my masters, will throw bitter words
in my face: "Do you see that woman?
Once she was concubine to Aias,
the strongest man in the army—
an enviable life. Now servitude   560
is all her reward!" They'll say more
and worse. The pain of that fate
will strike me, but the shame
of their words will strike you and all
your race.
                    Revere your father,
left alone in the misery of old age,
and your mother, with her portion of years,
who so often prays to the gods
that you will come home alive.
Pity your son, my lord,   570
facing his youth robbed of you,
in the keeping of indifferent strangers.

If you die, these are the evils
you will leave us to. There is nowhere
I can turn but to you. My homeland
vanished under your spear.
Fate took my mother and father down
to the dead in Hades. What other
home or wealth do I have?
You are my life. But remember,   580
my lord, what I've been for you.
If a man has known some pleasure,
he ought to be mindful of it.
Kindness begets kindness.
A man who takes his pleasure
and forgets it, cannot be noble.

CHORUS If your mind can be moved to pity
as mine is, Aias, you will praise
her words.

AIAS   She will win my praise
if she does what I command.   590

TEKMESSA I will always obey you, Aias.

AIAS Bring my son here, let me see him

TEKMESSA Of course. It was only from fear
that I sent him away.

AIAS   Fear of this?

He points to himself and the gory spectacle.

Or of what else?

TEKMESSA   Fear that he might
cross paths with you and die.

AIAS Yes, that would suit my fate.

TEKMESSA I was guarding against that.

AIAS You did well. I praise your foresight.

TEKMESSA Then how may I serve you now?   600

AIAS Let me see my son's face. I would speak with him.

TEKMESSA Very well. He is close by.
The attendants are watching over him.

AIAS Then why is he not here yet?

TEKMESSA Eurysakes, your father wants you.
Take his hand and bring him here.

AIAS Are they crawling? Do they refuse
to obey you?

TEKMESSA   They're coming now.

They approach AIAS.

AIAS Lift him up to me. The sight
of fresh blood will not frighten him   610
if he's truly my son. The colt
must be broken early to his father's   *cf Astynax*
rough ways, and so be made like him   *6.494 ff*
in nature.

The boy is lifted into AIAS' *hands.*

My son, I pray
that chance will prove kinder to you
than she was to me. If you match me
in all else, you will not do badly.
Oh, I could envy you even now,
because you cannot see the evil
in these things. Life is sweetest   620
when we know nothing. But a day will come

47   *echoes* Women of Trachis

when you learn about joy and grief.
Then show your father's enemies
what sort of man you are
and what sort he was who bred you.
For now, feed on soft breezes,
let your young soul play, and be
a joy for your mother.
                              The Greeks

why the confidence?

will not dare to harm or insult you
even without me, I know that.   630
Teukros will guard your gates
and raise you—a man unstinting
in his care, though now the hunt
for his enemies keeps him away.

when will he return?

You who manned my ships
and shared my battles, must share
that kindly service with him.
And give this command to Teukros:
he must take the boy home and present him
to Telamon and to my mother   640
Eriboia. His youth will forever
ease the weight of their years,
until they go down to the deep god.
And my arms must not be set up
by arbiters as a prize
in any warlike contest.
They must not fall to the Greeks,
not to the man who disgraced me!
You were named for this shield, Eurysakes—

Eurysakes
shield
son

sevenfold unpierceable oxhide.   650
Hold it by the thick braided grip
like this. The rest of the arms
will be buried with me.

> *In a slow, almost ceremonial fashion,* AIAS *places*
> *his small son's hand on the huge grip.*

                              Quick now,
take him in and lock the gates.

48

This is no place for tears, woman.
How you all love to weep! Go inside.
A skillful doctor does not
moan prayers when a sore needs cutting.

CHORUS I don't like this sudden hurry.
Your words have too sharp an edge.   660

TEKMESSA Aias, my lord!
Say what your heart intends!

AIAS Stop questioning and prying!
Wise restraint is best.

TEKMESSA I beg you in the name of your son
and the gods, do not betray us!

AIAS You vex me! Can you not see
I owe nothing more to the gods?

TEKMESSA That is impious!

AIAS   Save your words.

TEKMESSA Can't I move you?

AIAS   No more of that!   670

TEKMESSA I'm frightened, my lord!

AIAS   Shut the gates!

TEKMESSA For god's sake, soften!

AIAS   It is foolish
to think you can school me now!

TEKMESSA, EURYSAKES, *and* ATTENDANTS *exit through
the gates, followed by* AIAS *as the platform is rolled back.*

49

CHORUS   *first stasimon*
    Famous Salamis, you   *strophe*
must still be there, wave-beaten, fortunate,
    bright in the sea forever.
My misery is being gone from you
these long years under Ida, wasting
    away month after month,
    camped in the grassy fields,   680
    knowing I may win only
to an end in unseen, unfaceable Hades.
    Now Aias, too, is my care   *antistrophe*
taken over, omoi, beyond all cure
    by a god's madness, the man
you sent to win fame in the fury of Ares.
He brings grief to his friends, feeding
    his secret thoughts alone,
    and the honor due his great
    past deeds has fallen, fallen   690
friendless between the hate-filled Atreidai.

    I can see his mother, grown with time   *strophe*
to white old age, on the day she hears
    how madness ravaged his mind—
    ailinon! ailinon!
There will be no nightingale's soft lament
    from her, ill-fated woman,
    but a sharp, keening cry
    drawn from deep inside,
    hands beating her breast   700
again and again and tearing her gray hair.

    Let Hades hide him, his affliction has gone   *antistrophe*
beyond all measure, son of a great race,
    best of the battle-worn Greeks.
      His nature no longer
true-bred in anger, he wars with himself.
    Oh, luckless father, you've yet
    to learn what unbearable end
    your son has come to, the first

internal

time

of all the Aiakidai   710
to find fate set hard against him.

AIAS *enters through the gates, followed*
by TEKMESSA *and* EURYSAKES.

AIAS Great, unfathomable time
brings dark things into the light
and buries the bright in darkness.
Nothing is too strange, time seizes
the most dread oath, the most hardened
mind. Even I, whose will
was tempered like iron, unbending
in action, for a woman's sake   *cannot be*
am become a woman in my speech.   720
Yes, the thought of leaving her a widow,
surrounded by enemies, and my son
an orphan, moves me to pity.
    But I will go to a bathing place
and the salt meadows to be cleansed
of this filth, and I may still escape
the weight of the goddess's anger.
And finding some trackless place,
I will dig up the earth and bury
this sword of mine, the most hostile   730
of weapons, where no one will find it.
Let night and Hades keep it
safe from all eyes, for I swear   *Hektor's sword*
since the day I took it in gift   *an exchange after*
from Hektor, my greatest enemy,   *the truce*
I have had no love from the Greeks.
It is true, then: an enemy's gift
is no gift but a bringer of loss.
    And in time to come we will know
how to yield to the gods and learn   740
to bow down before the Atreidai.
They command and we must obey.
For even the most awesome powers
submit to authority: snow-tracked

winter yields to the rich growth
of summer, dark-vaulted night
gives way to the shining, white-horsed
brightness of day, a blast
of appalling wind stills the sea's rage,
even all-overwhelming sleep   750
binds only to let go. Then how
shall we not learn wise restraint?
    I know now to hate an enemy
just so far, for another time
we may befriend him. And the friend
I help, I will not help too greatly,
knowing that one day may find him
my enemy. For most mortals
friendship is a treacherous harbor.
    But these things will all turn out well.   760
You, woman, go and pray to the gods
that my heart may see its desires
carried through to the end. Pray with her,
my friends. And when Teukros comes,
tell him these are my orders:
to look after us and treat you kindly.
I will go where I have to go.
Do as I've said. Fate is hard now,
but you may soon hear I am safe.

AIAS *exits by the side.* TEKMESSA *and*
EURYSAKES *reenter* AIAS' *tent.*

CHORUS   *second stasimon*
Desire thrills in me, joy gives me wings!   *strophe*   770
    Io Io Pan! Pan!
    Sail from the snow-whipped
    crags of Kyllene,
O dance-maker of the gods!
    Join us, launch me
    in the impulsive
dance, the ecstatic Knosian,
the Mysian step—now, now I want dancing!

Come, Lord Apollo,
from Delos, cross over   780
the Icarian sea
in splendor, your favor stay with us now!

Rage has lifted its darkening terror.   *antistrophe*
  Io Io Zeus! Now
  white day dawns
  on our sea-sped ships!
For Aias has put pain away
  and gone in good mind
  to fulfill the saving
sacrifice to the gods.   790
Time truly is great, it quenches all things,
      nothing's too strange
      if Aias can turn
      his heart from hatred
and the huge struggle against the Atreidai.

                                   MESSENGER *enters.*

MESSENGER Friends, I have messages. First,
Teukros just came back
from the mountains of Mysia, but he ran
into trouble by the generals' tent.
When the Greeks saw he was here,   800
they closed in, circling around him,
beating him down with insults—
no one stayed out of it—calling him
half-brother of a madman
and traitor to the army, threatening
to stone him to a bloody death.
There were swords drawn. It would have gone badly
if the elders had not spoken up
and stopped it.
                    But where is Aias?
I must make my report to him.   810
Your commander should know what's happened.

CHORUS He has just now gone, a new man
yoked to a new purpose.

53

MESSENGER Then I'm afraid I was sent too late
                       or took too long in coming.

CHORUS What do you mean? Why too late?

MESSENGER He was not to leave the tent.
                       He was to stay in and wait for Teukros.

CHORUS But he left in good mind, resolved
                   to end his anger at last   820
                   and make peace with the gods.

MESSENGER You're talking nonsense, if Kalchas
                       has any skill as a prophet.

CHORUS What do you know about it?

MESSENGER What I heard with my own ears: Kalchas
                       stepped out of the circle of leaders
                       alone, apart from the Atreidai.
                       He went over to Teukros, gave him
                       his right hand in friendship, and enjoined him
                       to keep Aias inside by all means,   830
                       absolutely forbid him to go out
                       for as long as this day's light lasts,
                       if he hoped to see him survive it.
                       The anger of the goddess Athene
                       will drive him for this day only.
                       So Kalchas declared. He said
                       the gods strike down unwieldy
                       and outsized bodies, men grown
                       from the human branch who let
                       their minds go beyond the human.   840
                       The man's father warned him against
                       such recklessness when he saw him
                       rushing headlong to war
                       with these noble words: "My son,
                       may your spear prevail over all,
                       but always with a god's protection."

too confident? the perfect hero?

But Aias answered with a high
and thoughtless boast: "My father,
any nobody can win victories
with the help of a god. I trust   850
I can draw enough glory to me
without them." That was the size of it.
Then a second time, when Athene
was urging him on in his deadly
work against the Trojans,
he turned to her and uttered
unspeakable words: "Go, mistress,
and stand by the rest of the Greeks.
The line won't break where I hold it."
What he gained with such crude talk   860
no man wants: the goddess's anger.
But if he outlives this day,
with the god's help we may save him.
     That is what Kalchas said.
I was sent at once to bring you
orders from Teukros and see them
carried out. If we're too late,
if what Kalchas said is true,
Aias is no more.

CHORUS   Tekmessa, born for all suffering,   870
         come and hear this man's story!
         It shaves too painfully close.

                    TEKMESSA *and the boy enter from* AIAS' *tent.*

TEKMESSA Am I not wretched enough?
         Must you call me out here again
         when my troubles have just relented?

CHORUS   It was my own pain that called you.
         Hear what he says about Aias.

TEKMESSA What is it, man? Are we ruined?

55

MESSENGER You may or may not be. My fear
is for Aias, if he has gone out.   880

TEKMESSA He has gone out. Why do you frighten me?

MESSENGER Teukros sent orders to keep him
under cover of his tent and not let him
go out alone.

TEKMESSA   Where is Teukros?
Why did he say these things?

MESSENGER He has just returned. He thinks
that Aias may meet destruction
if he goes out there.

He points toward the fateful exit.

TEKMESSA   Ah, no!
What man told him that?

MESSENGER   The prophet
Kalchas. He says this day   890
means death or life for Aias.

TEKMESSA Ai! Help me, friends, protect me
against inescapable chance!
You, go and meet Teukros. Hurry!
The rest of you divide up and search
both the dawn and sunset arms
of the harbor. Find out where his dark will
has led him. He has deceived me,
I see it now, he has torn
all care for me from his heart.   900
Child, what shall I do? I can't
sit waiting, I must go with them
as far as my strength will let me.
Come all, let's be quick. The man
is in a hurry to die.

CHORUS No more words. We're ready.
Let the speed of our feet speak for us.

The CHORUS *splits into two groups and exits by both sides.*
ATTENDANTS *lead* EURYSAKES *back inside as* TEKMESSA
hurries after one part of the CHORUS.

The stage is emptied.

The scene changes to a deserted part of the coast.
The tent now represents a grove near the sea,
the gates a small clearing out of which AIAS *now*
appears on the wheeled platform. He stands over
his sword which is buried point up in the ground.

AIAS The killer, the sacrificial knife
is set now to be most cutting,
if there were time for such thoughts.   910
Hektor gave it to me, of all guest-friends
the man I most hated the sight of;
it stands in enemy earth,
Trojan earth, the edge newly ground
on the iron-eating stone,
planted firmly for one clean
and kindly stroke.
All is in order.
Zeus I call first, as is right,
not asking for some great prize,
but that you send the hard word   920
of this death to Teukros. Let him
be the first to find me and lift me
off of the streaming sword,
before my enemies come
and order my body cast out
to the dogs and crows. That is all
I ask of you, Zeus. And I call
on Hermes, guide of the underworld,
to take me down without struggle—

a quick leap, the sword's point breaking   930
up through my ribs.
                          And I call
on the everlasting virgins, the avengers
who see all mortal sufferings,
the dread, long-striding Furies,
to look at the wretched end
the Atreidai have brought me to.
Vile men! Come and take them!

still wants revenge

And as you see me self-slaughtered,
so make them die vile deaths,
cut down by the hands of their dearest   940
offspring. Feed on them, you swift
and punishing Furies, feed
on the whole body of the army!
Spare none of them!
                          And you, Helios,
driving across the steep sky,
when you come to my homeland pull back
on the gold-flashed reins and report
this ruin and doom to my father
and the unhappy woman who nursed me.
When she hears it, her weeping will sound   950
through the whole city. But why
think of weeping—I must act quickly.
   O death, come, death, attend me
or I will come to you there.
O Helios, bright light of day,
I greet you one last time
and never again, O radiance!
O holy ground of Salamis,
hearth of my fathers, famous

greatness of Athens

Athens, and our one people,   960
springs, rivers, and the wide plain
of Troy—you have all sustained me.
Farewell! Aias calls out
his last word to you. The rest
I will speak to the dead in Hades.

*The platform is wheeled back, disappearing into the
grove as* AIAS *speaks his last words. There is a pause.*

The two parts of the CHORUS
rush on stage from both sides.

CHORUS A   Pain brings pain more pain.
                I've searched, searched
                everywhere and everywhere the place
                     has kept its secret.
                Listen! A noise! Who is there?   970

CHORUS B Your shipmates.

CHORUS A   What news?

CHORUS B   We searched
                the whole west side of the harbor.

CHORUS A And found?

CHORUS B   Much work, nothing more.

CHORUS A Nor has he come to light
                anywhere on the eastern side.

CHORUS   *strophe*
                     If only some labor-loving
                     son of the sea at his sleepless
                          hunt, some nymph
                          of the hills or the quick-
                     flowing Bosphorus who can see   980
                     where the raw-hearted man
                          is wandering now
                     would call out and tell us! For me
                     this toiling aimlessness
                     is a hard thing, with no wind-
                blown speed, no sight of fleeting Aias.

TEKMESSA   Io moi moi!

CHORUS Who cried out by that grove?

TEKMESSA   No, no, no!

The gates open and the elevated platform is wheeled out
with TEKMESSA *kneeling over, and partially blocking,*
                                    AIAS' *body from view.*

CHORUS I see her, Tekmessa, the captive,   990
            the young wife, stricken with grief.

TEKMESSA All is ended, all destroyed for me, friends!

CHORUS   What is it?

TEKMESSA Aias is here, newly killed —
            his body draped over his sword.

CHORUS   Omoi, no homecoming!
            Oh, I am cut down, too,
        lord, your luckless shipmate!
            Such suffering, woman!

TEKMESSA He's dead! Weep for him! Ah, Aias!   1000

CHORUS But how, who, whose hand did it?

TEKMESSA His own. The sword he fell on,
            stuck here in the ground, convicts him.

CHORUS   Oh, my blindness! Alone, your life bleeding
                    away, no friend there
            to prevent you! And I, dull-witted, all
                    unheeding, to fail so!
            Where is he, where is intractable
            Aias, named to no good end?

recognizes
short-coming)

60

TEKMESSA He must not be seen! I will cover   1010
his body, I will wrap him completely
in my mantle. No one who loved him
could bear to see the dark blood
pouring from his nostrils and the raw
wound his own hand made.

                    TEKMESSA *enshrouds the body of* AIAS.

Oh, what must I do now?
Which friend should lift you up?
Where is Teukros? If only he'd come
in time at least to help me
prepare his brother for burial!   1020
Ah, to lie fallen here was no fate
for a man like you, Aias!
Even your enemies would weep to see it.

CHORUS   *antistrophe*

It had to have happened in time,
stiff heart, you had to have brought
        your boundless agony
        to this fulfillment.
I see it now. Night long and day long
your mind raged, your bright hatred cried out
        against the Atreidai.   1030
How else could such deadly passion
have ended? Time, since the best men
contended for the arms of Achilles,
has been a potent begetter of sorrows.

where is
their loyalty?

TEKMESSA   Io moi moi!

CHORUS True grief goes to the heart.   *echoes Aias*

TEKMESSA   Io moi moi!

CHORUS I don't wonder that you cry out twice
in pain for so dear a loss.

TEKMESSA You see how it seems, but I know it.   1040

CHORUS   You are right.

TEKMESSA Oh, child, what a yoke of slavery
          we're bound for, what cold-eyed masters!

CHORUS   No! What you say
          is unthinkable, that the ruthless
          Atreidai would add still more to your grief!
          May god prevent it!

TEKMESSA Is this not the gods' work?

CHORUS   Yes,
          they've laid an unbearable weight on you.

TEKMESSA It's the sort of bane the dreaded   1050
          daughter of Zeus will breed
          for the sake of her dear Odysseus.

CHORUS   What outrage that much-enduring
                          man commits
          in his black heart! He laughs a great laugh
                  at these frenzied calamities,
          and the double-ruling Atreidai
          listen and laugh with him!

TEKMESSA Let them laugh, then, let them rejoice
          at his destruction! They had   1060
          no use for him alive, but now
          in the press of battle they may well
          lament his death. Evil-minded
          men never see what good
          they have till they've thrown it away.
                  His death is more bitter for me
          than sweet for them, but for him
          it is joy. The end he so passionately
          yearned for, he brought about

by himself. What can they laugh at?   1070
He died by the gods, not by them. No!
    Let Odysseus hurl his useless
insults, Aias won't hear them.
He is as far from their laughter
as he is now from my grief.

emphasizes
drama ?
change later

TEUKROS   Io moi moi!

CHORUS Listen! I think that was Teukros.
The tune of his cry goes straight
to the mark of this ruin.

           TEUKROS *and* ATTENDANTS *enter in haste.*

TEUKROS   Aias!
Dear brother, bright eye of my blood!   1080
Have you done as rumor says?

CHORUS The man is dead, Teukros.

TEUKROS   Ai!
A heavy fate bears down on me!

CHORUS So it is.

TEUKROS   Ah, woe for me!

CHORUS You're right to lament.

TEUKROS   It breaks over me!

CHORUS Yes, it is terrible, and sudden.

TEUKROS The boy, his son, where is he
in all this Trojan country?

CHORUS Alone by the tents.

TEUKROS   Find him, then,
and bring him here, or some enemy   1090
may snatch him up like a lion cub
strayed from its mother. Go,
go quickly, help him! Believe me,
men love to mock the dead
when they have them at their feet.

                                        TEKMESSA *exits.*

CHORUS That is well done, Teukros. His final
order was for you to take care
of the boy, as you're doing now.

TEUKROS Oh, of all my eyes have seen
this is the most painful sight.   1100
No other road I've walked
has torn my guts the way this road
did, oh, Aias, when I learned
it was your death I was tracking.
        Word of it cut through the Greeks
with godly suddenness. Hearing it
before I could reach you, I groaned.
But now I see, and the sight
destroys me! Ai! Uncover him,
let me look at the whole evil.   1110

                    AIAS *is revealed, impaled face up on his sword.*

        Oh, bitter sight, that hard face,
that grim self-command! What griefs
you've sown for me with your death!
Where can I go, among what men,
when I was no help to you
in your struggle? Oh, yes, Telamon,
your father and mine, will meet me
with pleasant smiles when I come home
without you. Of course! The man
never smiled at the best of luck.   1120

[handwritten annotations: "thinks of himself" next to lines 1100–1103; "Life without Aias" next to line 1111]

What will he hold back, what vile names
will he not turn against me—bastard
gotten by a hostile spear, coward,
weakling who let you die
out of fear—oh, Aias, my brother!
Or he'll say I betrayed you to get
your place and power on Salamis.
Ill-tempered, quarrelsome, overbearing
old man! I'll be banished, driven out
with his word—*slave*—on my head.   1130
That waits for me at home, while here
at Troy I have enemies everywhere
and little help. So much
for the good your death has done me!
　　What now? How can I drag you
from that bright, biting sword-point,
the slayer that took your last breath?
Did you see that Hektor would finally
destroy you, even though he was dead?
　　By the gods, look at the fates   1140
of these two men! With the wide belt
that Aias gave him, Hektor
was lashed to the chariot and dragged,
mangled, till the spirit left him.
Aias took this sword in gift
from Hektor and died falling on it.
Was it the Furies who forged this sword?
Did that savage workman Hades
fashion the belt? Not just these things,
I say, but all fates always   1150
are worked against men by the gods.
Whoever has no stomach
for my words can look for comfort
in his own thoughts. Those are mine.

CHORUS Don't stretch this talk any further.
　　You had better think how to get him
　　buried, and what you will say next.
　　I see someone coming, an enemy,

        no straight-hearted man, I'm afraid,
        who may mean to laugh at our suffering.   1160

TEUKROS Which one of the army is it?

CHORUS Menelaos, whom we sailed here to help.

TEUKROS I see him now. From this distance
        it is not hard to tell who he is.

                  MENELAOS *enters with* ARMED ATTENDANTS.

MENELAOS You, keep your hands off that corpse,
        I order you! Do not try to lift it.

TEUKROS Those are big words—what stands behind them?

MENELAOS My judgment, and the chief commander's.

TEUKROS On what grounds, may I ask?

MENELAOS We brought him here thinking he was   1170
        a friend and ally. We've learned
        that he was a more dangerous enemy
        than any Trojan, a traitor
        who plotted to murder our army
        and came in the night against us
        to cut us down. One of the gods
        blocked his attack, otherwise
        the disgrace of this death, which is his lot,
        would have fallen to us, and he
        would be alive now. As it happened,   1180
        the god turned his outrage on shepherds
        and sheep.
                  I say throw him out!
        No man, not one of you here,
        has the power to put him in a grave.
        Let him lie on the yellow sand
        somewhere and feed sea birds. And you,

glory → obedience (handwritten)

don't work yourself up against us.
I grant you, we failed to control him
when he was alive, but he's dead now,
and like it or not we will have   1190
our way with him. At no time, so long
as the breath was in him, would he ever
obey me.
        Indeed, it's a mark
of baseness in a man from the ranks
to deny the need for obedience.
Can laws keep the city on a prosperous
course if no one fears them?
In the same way, an army cannot
be governed wisely without
a strong bulwark of fear and respect.   1200
For however large a man grows,
he must bear in mind that one small
defect can bring him down.
Where fear and shame come together
in a man, they act to preserve him.
But where there is wantonness
and license, the city, though she
be speeding before a fair wind,
will plunge to destruction. Fear
is the cornerstone of all order,   1210
I say. We should not take pleasure
and deny pain equal measure.
One comes on the other's heels.
Not long ago this man blazed
with insolence. Now it is I
who have big ideas, so I warn you:
if you dig a grave for him,
you yourselves may fall into it.

CHORUS Menelaos, you have spoken wisely
    of restraint. Do not outrage the dead.   1220

TEUKROS Why should it surprise me, friends,
    when a man of no birth does wrong,

(handwritten annotations in margins: *all twisted*; *all negative*; *lies distortions*; *= Aias*; *awful state of existence*; *reminder reasonable remarkable*)

67

if one presumed to be noble
can speak such twisted words?
     Let me hear it again. You say
you brought him here, you yourself,
as an ally of the Greeks? He came
under his own sails, you know that!
What right could you have to command him
or the men he led from home?   1230
Your power extends to the Spartans,
not to us. Nothing ever gave you
any claim to rule him, or him you.
In fact, you came here under orders,
not as general of us all.
You command Aias? Rule the men
you're entitled to rule, punish them
with your pompous talk. Your mouth
does not frighten me. Forbid it,
get the other general to forbid it—   1240
I will bury Aias
as justice demands. He did not join
this expedition for the sake
of your wife, like the drudges you brought here,
but because of oaths he had sworn,
And not because of you. He never
honored nonentities.
                Go on, then,
bring more heralds, bring the commander
himself. All your noise will not sway me
as long as you are what you are.   1250

CHORUS We have trouble enough without
these sharp words. Even if they're true,
they cut too deep.

MENELAOS   The archer
has a high opinion of himself.

TEUKROS I am not ashamed of my skill.

MENELAOS He'd boast more if he carried a shield.

TEUKROS I'll match all your bronze barehanded.

MENELAOS Can your heart be as fierce as your tongue?

TEUKROS As proud as my cause is just.

MENELAOS It is just to defend a killer?   1260

TEUKROS How strange, to be killed and yet living!

MENELAOS A god saved me, but in his mind
I was dead.

TEUKROS   So the gods saved you
and now you dishonor the gods?

MENELAOS What divine laws have I broken?

TEUKROS You hinder the burial of the dead.

MENELAOS I am right in that. We were enemies.

TEUKROS When did Aias oppose you in battle?

MENELAOS You know we hated each other.

TEUKROS He had good reason to hate you.   1270
He knew you fixed the vote.

MENELAOS It fell as the judges decided.

TEUKROS You could put a good face on your cheating.

MENELAOS Those words may cause someone pain.

TEUKROS No worse for me than for you.

MENELAOS I tell you Aias will not
be buried!

TEUKROS   I tell you he will!

MENELAOS I saw a man once whose bold talk
had pressed a ship's crew to set sail
in winter. A storm broke, the waves   1280
piled higher and higher, and he
grew quieter and quieter, huddled
in the stern under his cloak. The sailors
stepped on him in the confusion
and he said nothing at all.
So, if a great storm blows up
from a small cloud, it may silence
your big voice in the same way.

TEUKROS I, too, saw a man once, full
of his own stupidity, who insulted   1290
his neighbors in their grief.
Someone who looked like me,
and was like me in temper, warned him:
"Man, do not outrage the dead.
If you do, it will be your own ruin."
So the fool was told to his face.
I can still see him now: I think
he's none other than you, Menelaos!
Am I talking in riddles?

MENELAOS   Enough!
It's shameful for me to trade insults   1300
with you when I can use force.

                    MENELAOS *and* ATTENDANTS *exit.*

TEUKROS Creep away! It's shameful for me
to waste time on your empty words!

CHORUS A struggle is coming, a great strife.

Hurry, Teukros, find some hollow
trench to serve as his dank tomb —
rotting earth to receive his body,
his memorial among men everlasting.

> TEKMESSA *and* EURYSAKES *enter and*
> *approach* AIAS' *body.*

TEUKROS See, now, his near ones are coming,
his son and wife, when we   1310
most need them to perform the rites
for these poor remains.

> *Mother and son strike a pose of formal supplication.*

                    Come, child,
kneel here and touch the body
of the father who gave you life.
Come, hold on to him. Keep
a lock of my hair in your hand,
a lock of your mother's hair,
and a third lock of your own.
This is a suppliant's treasure.
And if anyone comes from the army   1320
to drag you away from this corpse,
may the wretch be cast out, unburied,
cut off with the whole of his race,
as I cut off this lock of hair!
Hold on to him, child. Guard him.
Let no one move you. And you,
remember you're men, not serving girls!
Defend him until I come back.
I'll go and prepare a grave for him
whether they permit it or not.   1330

> TEUKROS *exits.*

> TEKMESSA *and* EURYSAKES *remain as suppliants*
> *beside the body of* AIAS.

CHORUS   *third stasimon*
      What year? I wish I knew   *strophe*
what year will be the last of my wandering
years and waves of spear-driven, ruinous
     toil coming against me
     over the plains of Troy,
bringing bitter disgrace to the Greeks.

      The man who invented war,   *antistrophe*
if only he had vanished in the steep sky or sunk
to the common darkness of Hades before
     he taught men to use the tools   1340
     of hateful, heedless Ares—
oh, pain breeding pain—for the slaughter of men.

      He has robbed me of garlands   *strophe*
      and deep wine bowls,
kept me far from the joy of friendship, the sweet
     clamor of flutes,
     he has cut me off
       from the night-
       long joys
     of sleep and love and lovemaking.   1350
Ai, I'm abandoned out here
with thick dew soaking my hair,
a constant, cold reminder
     of alien Troy.

      Once my great wall   *antistrophe*
      against weapons and terrors
under the pall of night was relentless Aias.
     He lies here now
     offered up to the baleful
      force of his fate.   1360
      What joy
have I left? Oh, I wish I were sailing
past the wooded rampart of Sounion
where the rock juts into the sea,

and shouting out my praises
to holy Athens.

TEUKROS *enters in haste.*

TEUKROS Look there, it's Agamemnon!
I turned back when I saw him coming.
He'll let his crude tongue loose now!

AGAMEMNON *enters with great pomp, accompanied
by* MENELAOS *and* ARMED ATTENDANTS.

AGAMEMNON Teukros! I've heard some amazing   1370
reports about you. Do you think
you can talk so boldly against us
and go unpunished? A slave's son?
No doubt if your mother was noble
you'd boast even higher, prancing
around on the tips of your toes!
What does all this defiance amount to?
A nobody defending nothing!
So you claim that we're not generals,
not captains of ships for the Greeks,   1380
not for you? And that Aias sailed here
under his own command?
Is it not monstrous to hear
such things from a slave?
                                    Who is
this man you're bellowing about?
Where has he stood in battle
that I was not standing with him?
Are there no other men in the army?
Oh, it was a bad day for us,
the day we declared the contest   1390
for Achilles' armor. Now Teukros
denounces us everywhere,
unable to yield to what
the majority of judges decided
and accept defeat. You were beaten,
and now, like others of your kind,

you turn to insults and treachery.
No laws can stand firm if we drive out
the rightful victors and bring
men up from behind to replace them.   1400
    Such tendencies must be checked!
It's a wise mind, not a broad back,
that prevails. An ox, for all
its great girth, is driven down the road
with a little whip. You may feel
the sting of that treatment yourself
if you cannot listen to reason.
Behind all this outrage and loud talk
what is there? A man who's no more
than a shadow!
                        Know your place, Teukros.   1410
And since you lack the qualities
of a free man, bring someone else
to plead your case for you.
I can learn nothing from your way
of talking. Such barbarous speech
is foreign to my ears.

CHORUS You both should listen to reason,
        that is the best I can say.

TEUKROS Hah! a man dies, and how quickly
         all gratitude fades and is lost   1420
         in betrayal! Oh, Aias, you count
         for nothing in this man's memory,
         though you laid your life out so often
         toiling with your spear for him.
         It's all gone, all thrown away now.
             You who just spoke so many
         and such thoughtless words, can it be
         you've forgotten the time you were driven
         behind your own walls in a rout
         of spears? Your war was lost,   1430
         but he came alone and saved you.
         And when fire was already licking

74

at the stern rails of our ships,
and Hektor leaped over the trenches
among the black hulls, who stopped him?
Was it not this man? Were you
standing with him, as you say?
He did what was right. And again,
he met Hektor in single combat—
not on your orders. They drew lots.   1440
Did Aias put in a wet lump
of earth that would sink to the bottom?
No, he put in the lightest
bit of clay, and when the plumed helmet
was shaken, it leaped to the top.
That's the sort of man he was.
And I was beside him, the slave,
the barbarian woman's son.

      Wretched man, where are you looking
when you taunt me with that? Wasn't Pelops,   1450
you father's father, a barbarian
Phrygian? And what about Atreus,
who sowed your seed? What unholy
meal did he serve his brother?
The man's own children! Your mother
was a Cretan woman, who was caught
by her father making love
with a stranger and sent to her death
among speechless fish. And you
insult me? I am Telamon's son.   1460
His consort, my mother, was royal—
Laomedon's daughter. He received her
as the highest prize for valor
from Alkmene's son, Herakles.
Having sprung from two such noble
parents, how could I bring
dishonor on a man of my blood
who has fallen, whose corpse you shamelessly
order to be left unburied!

      I warn you, if you cast him out,   1470
you must cast out the bodies of us three

this brave corpse

as well. It would be much nobler
for me to die here in the light
for his sake, than to die for that woman
of yours, or I should say your brother's.
Look to your own affairs
and leave mine to me. If you cross me,
you'll find it would have been better
to be a coward than to act so boldly.

ODYSSEUS *enters.*

CHORUS Lord Odysseus, you have come at need,   1480
if you mean to loosen this struggle
and not to bind it tighter.

ODYSSEUS Men, what is happening here?
From far off I heard the Atreidai
shouting over this brave corpse.

AGAMEMNON And we, Lord Odysseus, have just heard
outrageous talk from this man.

change

ODYSSEUS How, outrageous? I understand
a man who meets insults with anger.

AGAMEMNON Yes, he has listened to insults,   1490
because he has acted against me.

ODYSSEUS Indeed? What harm has he done you?

AGAMEMNON He says he will not leave this corpse
without its portion of earth.
He will bury him, in defiance of me!

ODYSSEUS Can a friend speak the truth and still
pull his oar beside you?

AGAMEMNON   Speak.
I would be foolish not to listen
to my chief friend of all the Greek host.

76

restrain violence

ODYSSEUS Hear me, then. Before the gods,   1500
do not dare to cast this man out
unburied, so callously! Never
let violence drive you so far
in your hate that you tread on justice.
I, too, found him hateful once,
more than any other man,
after I won the armor of Achilles.
But though he held to his enmity,
I would not repay him now
with dishonor, or deny that in my eyes   1510
he was the greatest of all
who came to Troy, second only   *why admit it now?*
to Achilles. If you dishonor him,
there can be no justice in it.
You will not harm him, you will harm
the laws of the gods. To strike
at a brave man when he is dead
can never be just, no matter
how much you hate him.

AGAMEMNON   Odysseus,
you are fighting for him against me!   1520

ODYSSEUS Yes, though when honor demanded,
I hated him.

AGAMEMNON   Does honor not tell you
to trample him now that he's dead?

ODYSSEUS Do not glory, son of Atreus,
in such an ill-gotten advantage.

AGAMEMNON A ruler does not always find it
easy to be pious.

ODYSSEUS   But it's not hard
to honor a friend's good advice.

AGAMEMNON A good man should yield to authority.

77

ODYSSEUS Enough of that! You can prevail   1530
          by giving way to your friends.

AGAMEMNON Remember who you are asking
           this favor for!

ODYSSEUS   My enemy,
          it's true, yet once he was noble.

AGAMEMNON And you mean to show such respect
           to an enemy's corpse?

ODYSSEUS   Yes.
          I am moved more by his greatness
          than by my enmity.

AGAMEMNON I distrust such unstable natures.

ODYSSEUS I assure you, most men are that way,   1540
          now friendly, now hostile.

AGAMEMNON   And are these
           the sort of friends you would praise?

ODYSSEUS I would not praise an obstinate mind!

AGAMEMNON You will make us look like cowards.

ODYSSEUS Not cowards but men of justice—
          so all the Greeks will call you.

AGAMEMNON I must let them bury the body,
           is that what you say?

ODYSSEUS   It is.
          I will face the same need some day.

AGAMEMNON It's all one, then, and each man works   1550
           for himself.

ODYSSEUS   There is reason in that.
            Who else should I work for?

AGAMEMNON   Well, then,
            let it be your decision, not mine.

ODYSSEUS Either way you will do what is right.

AGAMEMNON If you asked for a much greater favor,
            I would grant it, be sure of that.
            As for him, he is hateful to me
            whether he lies on the earth or under it.
            Do what's necessary with the body.

        AGAMEMNON, MENELAOS, *and* ARMED ATTENDANTS *exit.*

CHORUS There is wisdom in you, Odysseus.   1560
            Whoever denies it is a fool.

ODYSSEUS Now let me say to Teukros
            that as much as I was his enemy
            before, I will be his friend
            from this day on. If he will,
            I would like to share with you
            in the work and the rites of burial,
            leaving out nothing that a mortal
            can do for the best of men.

TEUKROS You're a noble man, Odysseus.   1570
            I praise you for all that you've said.
            How greatly I misjudged you!
            The man he most hated was the one man
            of all the Greeks who stood by him,
            and would not endure while he lived
            to see outrage done to the dead —
            to leave him unburied, defiled,
            as those two, the thundering general
            and his blood brother, wanted. For that
            may the father who rules Olympos,   1580
            the remembering Furies, and all-

fulfilling Justice bring them
to as vile an end as they wished
for him!
                    But, son of Laertes,
I cannot let you touch his body,
for fear of offending the dead.
You may take part in the rest.
If you bring others from the army
to honor him, that will be well.
I must work now. What you have done   1590
is noble. We will not forget it.

ODYSSEUS I wished to help, but with all
respect for your thoughts, I will leave.

Exit ODYSSEUS.

TEUKROS   *exodos*
Come, too much time has passed already.
We must dig the grave, set the tall tripod
up and the cauldron ringed with fire
for the sacred bath. Bring his arms from the tent
in trophy, covered by the great shield.
I need your love and your small strength, child.
Help me to lift your father—gently,   1600
the black life force is still flowing out
of his warm veins. Come, you who called him friend,
and work for this man's sake, who was noble
in all that he did. For while Aias lived,
I say there was no better man in the world.

TEUKROS, EURYSAKES *and the* CHORUS, *who now*
approach the elevated platform, lift the body of
AIAS *off the sword.*

CHORUS Mortals know what their eyes can see,
but of what will come out of time there is
no seeing, no knowing what the end will be.

All exit in procession bearing the body of AIAS.

NOTES

TIME AND PLACE

The wooden stage building (*skene*) represents Aias' camp; the central, double doors, or gates, lead to his quarters. Two side entrances, one of which was probably used to represent the "Greek" side, that is, the side leading to and from the Greek camp, and the other the side by which Aias and those close to him come and go, visually reenforce the play's thematic polarities. As the tracking scene suggests, the time is very likely dawn, the traditional starting time of the day's first play. Since the Theater of Dionysos was open, the dramatist made "the world" his stage. The reader should try to visualize the effect: day dawns as the strange tracks leading to Aias become clear. By involving the natural world in his drama, Sophocles creates an immediate sense of the cosmic scope of Aias' tragedy. (Cf. Aeschylus' use of dawning light to dramatize the world-dimension of his *Agamemnon*.)

STRUCTURE OF THE PLAY

The play is, like all Greek plays, made up of spoken dialogue, monologues, choral lyrics, and lyric exchanges. "Acts," encounters, and speeches involving the principal characters are divided by lyrical interludes sung and danced by the chorus. Scholars regularly refer to the speeches and / or dialogue preceding the entrance of the chorus as the "prologue," the choral entrance song as the "*parodos*" (162–220 / 134–200), the exchanges between the principals as "episodes," and the choral songs as "*stasima*" (stasimon in the singular). The lyric parts of the play are evenly distributed between choral songs, of which there are four, and lyric dialogues, of which there are three. We should note several things about the structure of this play. First, all but one of the choral *stasima* occur in the first half of the play (the significance of which is discussed in the Introduction). Second, there is also a relatively high concentration of (dramatically heightening) lyric dialogue in the first half of the play, that is, sung exchanges (in lyric meter) between a principal character, such as Tekmessa or Aias, and the Chorus, who becomes a virtual second actor in the first part of the drama. In other words, the lyric structure of this play is quite intricate, and so the balance of spoken and sung parts should be taken into consideration when thinking about the dramatic effects, mood, tone, and feeling of the play.

1–161 / 1–133 *Prologue*

1 / 1 *I always* Always (*aei*) is the first word of the play, and the first of many temporal expressions. Always (sometimes rendered forever in our text) is Aias' word, the voice of his *daimon* (e.g., **141 / 117, 373 / 342, 641 / 570**). The play is concerned with "time," divine permanence vs. human transience, even in the subtlest details of its language.

1–16 / 1–13 *I always see . . . what I know* Is Athene actually visible? Odysseus states that he can hear but not see her. If the goddess is present (presumably, she would appear above on the *theologeion*, literally the place for "god-speech," on the roof of the *skene*), Sophocles visually confronts his audience with a contrast between Aias' and Odysseus' perspectives. Aias, blinded by Athene, nonetheless sees her. Odysseus, her favorite and the character in Homer who most often sees Athene when others do not, here cannot see her. Physically and metaphysically, Sophocles suggests the two men are very different. Like so much else in this play, the scene is unparalleled. The scene perhaps glances at *Iliad* 1.194–222, where Athene appears to Achilles to stay him from shedding Greek blood. But Athene's intervention there produces honor, not humiliation. This daimonic Athene is finally unlike anything in Sophocles, closer in fact to a Euripidean goddess, a divine *alastōr*, like Aphrodite in the *Hippolytos*.

4 / 4 *around where Aias* Aias is his Greek name. Despite the familiar Latinized form, Ajax, we have used the Greek form throughout, chiefly for reasons of sound. The Greek name suggests a cry of pain, which is dramatically exploited by Sophocles (see l. **468 / 430**).

10 / 8 *sharp-nosed Spartan bitch* The keenness of Spartan hounds was proverbial.

19–20 / 16–17 *your words ring like a bronze-mouthed / trumpet* Athene was said to have invented the first trumpet; the instrument was also blown in the Theater of Dionysos at the beginning of a play. Perhaps these words confirm that the trumpet blows as Athene begins speaking her prologue.

22 / 19 *the great shield* A warrior's arms were an intrinsic part of his identity. Hektor had his helmet, with its "frightfully nodding horse-hair crest"; Achilles, his "divine" armor and the Pelian ash spear that only he could lift. Aias was famous for his huge, seven-layered, ox-hide shield. His colossal size together with his shield made him Homer's "bulwark of the Greeks."

48–49 / 41 *Rage / over the award of Achilles' armor* Achilles' armor, described in Book 18 of the *Iliad*, was made for him by the god Hephaistos. "Immortal": the armor shone so brilliantly that Achilles' enemies were nearly blinded by it. It was in this armor that Achilles avenged the death of Patroklos and won his *aristeia* (heroic glory).

56 / 47 *He came stalking you in the darkness* Crafty Odysseus is the hero chosen by the Greeks for "night-raiding." In *Iliad* 10, he and Diomedes kill many sleeping Phrygians. But such an act is totally out of character for Aias, whose single combat with Hektor stops promptly at nightfall (*Iliad* 7.282–312).

93 / 79 *And is any laughter sweeter* To laugh at your enemy's misfortune is part of ancient Greek morality: love your friends and hate your enemies. The precept was still acceptable in Sophoclean Athens; not seriously challenged before Plato, it might be argued that Odysseus here anticipates Plato's challenge to it. Derisive laughter or fear of laughter haunt the play. Aias, Tekmessa, and the Chorus all fear that Aias has become a laughing-stock.

145–46 / 119–20 *greater foresight...shifts of action?* This is unexpected. Aias, the "great bulwark of the Achaians," is known for relentlessness in battle, not especially for his "foresight" or "timeliness in action" (literally what the Greek says). He is once called "wise" by Hektor (*Iliad* 7.288–89), but this is at an unusually gracious moment. This is perhaps the first hint, along with the allusions to the brightness of Aias' eyes (84 / 69–70, 101 / 85), that Sophocles' Aias is not merely the lumbering hulk of tradition.

158–59 / 131–32 *One day can...all human things* Another image of man's ephemerality. The metaphor in Greek is one of balance scales and comes from Homer's image of Zeus weighing men's fates. The novelty here is that the "day" metaphorically becomes the scale (cf. Aias' description of time as a succession of days moving back and forth, **523–27** / 473–76). Using the same metaphor, Athene identifies divine pleasure and displeasure with the vagaries of Time (also cf. lines **834–44** / 756–57).

162–220 / 134–200 *Parodos* (choral entrance song) The choral range of expression runs from spoken dialogue to chant to full song. Distinctions between song and chant should be obvious from shifts in tone, and are noted in stage directions, when, as in this *parodos*, the difference between them seems an important part of Sophocles' dramatic texture. Note, for example, the shifts in emotional level as the Chorus enters in a discursive mode, chanting (**162–91** / 134–72); then invokes the gods and Aias in lyric (**192–220** / 173–200); then addresses Tekmessa, whom it first questions in chant (**228–32** / 208–13), and then afterwards in song, when she has told it about Aias (**240–50** / 221–32, **263–73** / 245–56); finally, also note the Chorus' first "spoken" words after the lyric intensity has abated: "But fortunately it is over" (280 / 263), referring to the assault of Aias' madness, with which its lyric excitement has kept pace. The choral leader "spoke" for the Chorus in ancient practice.

189 / 169 *let a great eagle* Aias, according to Pindar (*Isthmian* 6.49–54), was named after the eagle—Aias from *aietos*. Sophocles conjures up the eagle glare but carefully avoids using Pindar's etymology. Instead, he uses the more unusual *aigupion* (normally meaning "vulture") for "eagle," which sounds nothing like Aias.

209 / 189 *race of Sisyphos* An alternative (and pejorative) genealogy of Odysseus, normally son of Laertes (as in the *Odyssey* and in *Aias*, 120 / 101). Sisyphos was king of Corinth and infamous for cunning and deceit.

221–673 / 201–595 *First episode*

222 / 202 *earth-born race of Erechtheus* Allusion to the autochthony of the Athenians, who regarded themselves descendants of "earth-born" Erechtheus. Sophocles is here assuming the identity of the Salaminian sailors as Athenians, which Aias (**958–60** / 859–61) and the Chorus (**1362–66** / 1217–22) will again reenforce.

227 / 206–7 *afflicted by a darkening storm* Literally, turbid or "muddy" storm. Traditionally, the madness is described as an "insane flashing" (words of the physician and skilled diagnostician, Podaleirius, from the *Aithiopis*) in his eyes. Sophocles describes Aias' madness with images of darkness, his recovery with images of light.

240–79 / 221–62 The chanting rhythm with which the episode began becomes a full lyric exchange (or *kommos*) between Tekmessa and the Chorus.

261–62 / 243–44 *a daimon / must have spoken through him* Though our word "demon" comes from *daimon*, the two are not to be confused. The Greek word can mean several things: a man's "destiny" (as in Latin, *genius*) or a "divine being" (the two are not always mutually exclusive in Greek experience). It is quite often used, as here, indefinitely—that is, when the speaker senses the presence of the divine but not of a particular divinity.

274 / 257–58 *The way flashing lightning* The Greek literally says, "as swift south wind having darted ceases without flashing lightning." Numerous attempts have been made to explain this strange phrase.

320–22 / 298–99 *broke their necks... to the bone* Almost unutterably alliterative and onomatopoeic in Greek: *euchenidze... esphadze karrachidze*. All the rhetorical stops are pulled in these speeches relating an offstage horror. The effect is sensory preparation for the greater horror to come. In this case, the appearance of Aias sprawled in the carnage: the vision of a Homeric hero turned mad butcher.

360 / 330 *Friends may win their friends back* The Homeric Aias also honored friendship. Cf. *Iliad* 9.641–42 where it forms the basis of his appeal to Achilles.

362–64 / 332 *man's misfortunes... possession* Literally, "possessed by Apollo." Aias is, in a sense, about to become Apollo's creature: insight and then revelation follow his madness. For the confluence of Apollo's visionary gifts and madness consider the case of Cassandra in Aeschylus' *Agamemnon*.

380–464 / 348–427 *Kommos* (dirge) In the usual *kommos* a principal character and the chorus engage in lyric dialogue; here only Aias sings in lyric meter, whereas the Chorus and Tekmessa respond with spoken dialogue. See ll. 240–79 / 221–62 for such a lyric exchange.

422 / 387 *O Zeus, father* Zeus was Aias' great-grandfather. The genealogy is: Zeus, Aiakos, Telamon, Aias.

441–42 / 405–6 *My honor is dead... as these creatures* These lines are obscure in Greek. Aias seems to be referring to "something" that has perished, which is contrasted with his "present state." We prefer the reading in the manuscripts (now accepted by Lloyd-Jones and Wilson, the editors of the most recent OCT edition of the play [Oxford, 1990]), which can mean "these creatures."

468 / 430 *Aiai! My name is a lament!* In Sophocles, name is sometimes destiny: Oedipus, "swollen-foot" and "knowing one"; Philoctetes, "possessor of friends." This "tragic" etymology is Sophocles' innovation.

473–76 / 434–36 *For I am a man . . . most beautiful spoils* Telamon stormed Troy with his friend Herakles after King Laomedon refused to reward them for rescuing his daughter, Hesione, from a sea serpent. Herakles gave Hesione, the highest prize of honor, to Telamon. She became the mother of Aias' half-brother Teukros. Before their expedition to Troy, according to some accounts, Heracles prayed that Telamon should have an invincible son. Zeus' eagle, for which Aias was named (see note on 189 / 169), appeared as an omen and Aias was born to Eriboia. Both the contrast with his father and the new etymology of his name remind the audience how far Aias has fallen. Aias actually speaks of the prize as most "beautiful," which is a fifth-century anachronism, where *kalos*, "beauty," connotes moral as well as physical sublimity. He uses a similar expression at lines 530–31 / 479 when he speaks of "Honor in life / or in death."

482–84 / 442–43 *if Achilles himself / had declared which man . . . / was worthiest* After losing the armor that was stripped from Patroklos by the Trojans, Achilles says that he could wear no man's armor except Aias' (*Iliad* 18.192).

494 / 450 *grim-eyed Gorgopis* Literally means "Gorgon-eyed," a contemptuous substitute for Athene's regular epithet, *glaukopis*, "gray-eyed." Athene wore the Gorgon head in the center of her shield, which she doubtless carried with her in the prologue.

522 / 472 *not born gutless* The word in Greek is *asplagchnos*. The *splangchnon*, "innards," was regarded as the seat of deep emotion and heroic spirit. When he learns of Aias' death, Teukros will use the same term (1102 / 995).

523–33 / 473–80 *To stretch your . . . all there is to say* The lines are striking and contain an unusual image from a board game, that of pieces moved forward and backward.

530–32 / 479–80 *Honor in life . . . or the other* The literal sense is "to live nobly (*kalos*), to die nobly is necessary for the well-born (*eugene*) man." *Kalos* and *eugenes* were the fifth-century moral equivalents of the Homeric *arista / aristos* (best).

538 / 486 *there is no greater evil* In Sophocles, the hero's moderate-minded foil, the *sōphrōn*, always argues for accepting "inevitable chance," whatever form it may take. Jocasta (*Oedipus the King*) urges Oedipus to live "at random." Deianeira (*Women of Trachis*) argues that men must submit to the vagaries of ineluctable eros. This is tragic wisdom, the kind of "human thoughts" that the messenger says that Aias rejects (838–40 / 760–61). The hero is by nature a metaphysical malcontent who cannot, like other men, accept limits. Both hero and *sōphrōn* are essential to Sophocles' vision, and his drama draws much of its power from the tension between these two opposed—and yet interdependent—types.

540–86 / 487–524 Tekmessa's speech closely resembles that of Andromache to Hektor at *Iliad* 6.406–39, the epic prototype of the departure scene here. As in Andromache's case ("Hektor . . . you are father to me . . . mother . . . brother, and husband") the appeal is particularly strong because of the totality of her dependence upon Aias—he is mother, father, wealth, and homeland. One interesting difference is Tekmessa's assertion that it will be to Aias' "shame" if he dies. Cf. Tekmessa's words at 557–61 / 501–3 with the following words, not of Andromache but of *Hektor*: "This is the wife of Hektor, greatest warrior / of the horse-breaking men of Troy . . . so someone will say of you; and for you it will hurt again to be widowed of such a man . . ." (6.460–63). Aias' gruffness is markedly different from the tenderness of Hektor, whose words to Andromache are perhaps the gentlest in the *Iliad* (esp. 6.450–65).

575–76 / 515 *My homeland / vanished* No pre-Sophoclean version of Aias' destruction of Tekmessa's homeland, Phrygia, is known. Andromache (see note on 540–86 / 487–524) makes the same point to Hektor, but it was Achilles, not her husband, who destroyed her homeland. Although she evokes Aias' violent pillaging of her country, Tekmessa also implies, at the end of her speech, a real intimacy between her and Aias.

609 / 545 *Lift him up to me* Parallel to the Homeric scene of Hektor with his young son, Astyanax (6.466–81). The implicit contrast between Aias and Hektor is strong, for example, in their respective addresses to their sons. When Hektor raised his son in his arms, the boy cried out in terror at the sight of his father's famous bronze helmet with its dreadfully nodding crest.

Laughing, Hektor removed his helmet and kissed the boy, then prayed to
Zeus that the boy might be "a better man than his father."

649–50 / 574–76 *You were named . . . unpierceable oxhide* The name Eurysakes literally means "broad shield."

674–711 / 596–645 *First stasimon* ("act-dividing" choral song)

712–69 / 646–92 *Second episode*

712–59 / 646–83 Aias' sudden, unannounced appearance is unusual in extant tragedy.
Customarily, characters entering after a choral ode are put into some
clear verbal rapport with other characters on stage, either through direct
address or choral introduction. The enormous size of the Greek theater,
as well as its use of masks requires that stage relations between characters
be firmly established, often with lengthy verbal introductions. The
absence of either introduction or addressee signals the unusual character
of the speech.

716 / 649 *most dread oath* Oaths were sacred and inviolable, and no less a god than
Zeus himself punished those who broke them. Aias swore a "dread oath"
when he sailed for Troy: together with the other Greek princes, he swore
to protect the honor of the man who married the beautiful Helen. As
Teukros states later, Aias only fought for the Atreidai because a great
oath bound him (1245 / 1113).

726 / 654–55 *this filth* "Pollution" was taken very seriously by the Greeks,
and represented something far more complicated than our "guilt."
It was sometimes as much a god-sent disease (cf. the threats made
by the Furies at the end of Aeschylus' *Eumenides*, 778–92 / 808–22) as
the consequence of immoral action. A man could be polluted by a
bad dream, contact with death or certain repellent diseases, and by
the stain of murder—or that of some other terrible crime—like Aias'
here. A polluted man must be ritually purified of the "bad blood" or
even, in certain cases of indelible pollution, like that of Oedipus,
driven into exile because his pollution might blight land and popu-
lace, innocent and guilty alike. Aias' words, however, are ambiguous.
The "bathing place" (724 / 654), by which Aias implies he seeks
purification, is the same expression used later by Teukros to
describe the place (the "sacred bath") for washing the dead body
(1597 / 1405).

734 / 661–62 *took it in gift* In the *Iliad*, the two champions exchanged tokens of honor after their single combat, which ended in a draw as night fell. Hektor proposed the exchange, offering his silver-studded sword in order that, in his words, "any Achaian or Trojan may say that / we who fought in heart-devouring hate parted joined together as friends" (*Iliad* 7.300–302). Aias, in turn, gave Hektor his purple loin guard (7.305).

753–59 / 678–83 *I know now . . . treacherous harbor* Words like those of the Cynic, Bias (cf. Aristotle, *Rhetoric* 1389b 24–25). This is the unheroic morality, the ethos of contingency, based on the universal uncertainty Aias describes. Similar words spoken by Hektor to Aias in the *Iliad* (see note on **734 / 661–662**) come to opposite moral conclusions and even sound, in the heroic context, a note of moral triumph. Cf., however, the moral conclusion drawn by Odysseus, based on Aias' same principle of uncertainty, at the end of the play (**1500–1519 / 1332–45**).

770–95 / 693–718 *Second stasimon*

783 / 706 *Rage* The Greek word is Ares, god of war, to whom Aias is often compared by Homer, and here the personification of Aias' anger.

796–1330 / 719–1184 *Third episode*

796–824 / 719–47 A messenger bringing news of the hero's death is doubtless what the audience expects, that is a "speech" but not the suicide itself, since acts of violence were never performed on the Greek stage. The spectator often bore witness to the aftermath of violent acts, the spectacle of mortality—a dead body or dying man—but not the monstrous act that caused it. For example, we see the bodies of Agamemnon and Cassandra but not their murder, the fragmentary remains of Pentheus but not his dismemberment, and blood-soaked Aias but not the slaughter of the livestock—awful revelation, not brutal realism. Contrary to expectations, however, this messenger introduces another postponement of the hero's death. Instead of delivering a conventional eyewitness account of the hero's death, the messenger reports what has been "said" about Aias and introduces the possibility that he may survive. Note the stress on what was merely "said" rather than actually "seen," an important distinction in Greek—**825–31 / 748–54, 836 / 757, 841 / 763, 856–57 / 773, 864 / 780, 868 / 783**.

825–69 / 748–83 This messenger speech is unusual in several ways. That the messenger's stories are without traditional precedent and that the messenger has them secondhand possibly suggests that his account belongs merely to the realm of "words" and "possibilities"—a realm that Aias has moved beyond.

838–39 / 758–60 *outsized bodies... grown / from the human branch* Aias is *perissos*, "huge," "prodigious," "exceptional," a man who exceeds the limits set by nature. The adjective regularly used to describe him in Homer, *pelorios*, "gigantic," is generally used to describe monstrous prodigies, such as the Cyclops, Skylla, or the Gorgon, etc.

841–52 / 762–69 *The man's father warned him... glory to me / without them* These two stories appear to be Sophocles' invention, and they set Aias apart from the gods on whom others pin their hopes. Aias prefers his own certain courage to the uncertain gods. In the *Iliad* Aias is not represented as hostile to the gods, though he never figures in their plans or considerations. Unlike other heroes, such as Achilles or Odysseus, Aias had no divine patron.

939–41 / 841–42 *so make them die... hands of their dearest / offspring* Agamemnon did indeed die at the hands of his own wife, but Aias' was not the only curse on his house. The root of his family's afflictions goes back to Tantalos, a mythical son of Zeus, who served the gods a feast of his son Pelops' flesh. However, Menelaos returned home to a charmed life with Helen.

953–57 / 854–58 *O death... and never again* These lines are bracketed by many editors, including Lloyd-Jones and Wilson. In general, they object to the strangeness of Aias' addressing the Sun above (945 / 846), then invoking Death ("come, death, attend me," 953 / 854) and then, as if he were stalling ("or I will come to you there," 954 / 855), then the Sun a second time, (955 / 857). But the sudden shift away from Death and back to the Sun, as well as the pointed invocation of its heavenly light (955 / 857), make the surprisingly unconventional association of the suicide with radiance and vision that much more emphatic.

964–65 / 865 *The rest / I will... in Hades* Aias' last word in Greek is *mythēsomai*, "I will speak," suggesting perhaps that dead, Aias will enter what Stanford has called a "Communion of Heroes." There is an irony here—and a hint that Sophocles' Aias is being differentiated from the conventional Aias; in Hades Aias was famous above all for his "silence," when his shade refused to speak to Odysseus (*Odyssey* 11.563–64).

965 / 865 *the dead in Hades* A thicket of scholarly controversy has grown around the question of how the suicide itself is managed. But most commentators deal only with technical aspects of stagecraft: whether Aias jumps behind a bush or through the stage door, when and how a dummy is substituted for the body, so that the actor playing Aias can, in keeping with the "three actor rule," reenter to play another part (for a summary of the main arguments, see Gardiner, "The Staging of the Death of Ajax," *The Classical Journal* 1979, 75, 10–14).

966–1058 / 866–960 *kommos*

994 / 898 *Aias is here* Suicide was not morally tainted in Greek, as opposed to Christian, culture because the Greeks did not regard fate and divine providence as coterminous. Suicide then did not interfere with "God's plan." Aristotle would later describe suicide as an antisocial act, since it deprived the community of a potential productive member. His categories, however, do not really apply to the hero who is always beyond the city in his tragic isolation. But that suicide was not held in heroic honor can be glimpsed in scenes from archaic art, where Aias, the sole "heroic" suicide, is mostly hunched over his sword, hideously gored, prone, or on all fours like a huge beast.

1011–15 / 915–19 *I will wrap him... raw / wound* Cf. the words spoken by Aeschylus' Tekmessa (from the lost *Women of Salamis*, frg. 216N) upon discovering Aias' body: "If only there were a shroud like heaven." The words of Sophocles' Tekmessa are as visceral as those of Aeschylus' are tinged with transcendence. The image of the impaled Aias that Sophocles conjures here and whose traditional associations he later confounds is one avoided even by Attic vase painters. Once a popular subject in archaic art, the suicide virtually disappears in Attic art from the early sixth century, when Salamis becomes an Athenian possession and Aias an Athenian hero.

1111–12 / 1004 *that hard face, / that grim self-command!* Aias' fierce face was proverbial. Describing a Hellenistic portrait gallery, the ancient writer Philostratus wrote, "You can recognize Aias by his grim look" (*Imagines* 350). The adjective *blosuros*, "fierce," "grim," used in Homer to describe Aias' face (*Iliad.* 7.212) is also used of lions, the Gorgon, and of Fear on Herakles' shield in Hesiod.

1122–23 / 1013 *bastard / gotten by a hostile spear* On Teukros' genealogy see ll. 473–76 / 434–36.

1129 / 1019 *I'll be banished* After returning home to Salamis, Teukros went into exile at Cyprus. Aeschylus dealt with this subject in the third play of his Aias trilogy, *The Women of Salamis*. Sophocles also wrote a play about Teukros, dealing with the aftermath of this play. In it, according to Aristotle (*Rhetoric* 3.15, 1416 b1), Odysseus prosecutes Teukros for having abandoned Aias!

1136 / 1024 *bright, biting sword-point* Literally, "a thing that bites." The sword is also personified (908 / 815), as if it were a living force. Cf. Pindar's description of Envy "biting" Aias "with a sword," *Nemean* 8.23. The comparison is worth noting because Sophocles also recalls several other curious details from Pindar's Aias ode in his description of the sword.

1138–46 / 1026–33 *Did you see... falling on it* Homer says only that Achilles tied and then dragged Hektor, already dead, behind his chariot, and no mention is made of Aias' loin-guard (see note on **734**). Sophocles, however, conceives of Hektor dragged alive and describes the paradoxical link between the two men's fates as though well known (from a lost epic?) to his audience.

1165–1301 / 1047–1162 With Menelaos' entrance, a heated debate over Aias' burial now ensues. The conventional sequence of debate and death has in fact been dramatically reversed. The loss of a great debate / quarrel with Odysseus over Achilles' arms preceded and partially caused Aias' death. Aeschylus presented this debate in his *The Award of the Arms* (frg. 174–78aN), and it appears to have been a popular subject in fourth-century drama and rhetoric. But in Sophocles' play, "debate" is relegated to the aftermath, and turned into a mean-spirited volley of abusive insults.

1165 / 1047–48 *hands off that corpse* Just before at **1156 / 1043**, the Chorus refers to Aias ("him") specifically as a "man," *anēr*, normally used of the living. Now, to Menelaos, he is a merely a corpse, *nekros*.

1200 / 1076 *bulwark of fear* Sparta honored Fear itself with a statue. Menelaos is King of Sparta. In the fifth century, Menelaos' emphasis on discipline and fear here make him sound like a fifth-century Spartan.

1245 / 1113 *oaths he had sworn* Aias, like the other Greeks who had been Helen's suitors, swore the oath to protect the man who finally married her. Teukros alleges that it was only the sacred oath which brought Aias to Troy. Nothing perhaps better illustrates the fundamental difference between Aias the true aristocrat and Menelaos the autocrat: Aias came under his own sails, bound by his word of honor, not a superior's commands.

1253–54 / 1120 *The archer / has a high opinion of himself* The prejudice in favor of spearmen over archers goes back to Homer and continues in fifth-century B.C. literature (e.g., Euripides' *Herakles* 157–64). The (democratic) bow was, at least until the battle of Delium (424 B.C.), held in contempt by aristocratic Athenians: it was used by the city police, always barbarian slaves and was the weapon of the Persians. But Teukros was the greatest of the bowmen in the *Iliad,* and other great archaic heroes, such as Philoctetes and even Herakles himself, were famous bowmen.

1271 / 1135 *fixed the vote* The *Odyssey* and epic fragments suggest that, because the Greeks were unable to choose between Odysseus and Aias, Trojan captives were asked to decide the award. The Greek "vote" was possibly introduced by Pindar in his Aias ode, *Nemean* 8 (elsewhere, he also disparages the Greek choice of Odysseus: see *Nemean* 7.23–27 and *Isthmian* 4.36–40); he almost certainly introduced the notion that the voting was "fixed," which he refers to as "something new." Sophocles pointedly recalls the Pindaric variant, partly because his play is a response to the condemnation of Athens implicit in Pindar's ode. The play cannot be dated with certainty (see Introduction, section VI), although public reaction to it was compared (by Libanius, *Declamatio* 14.20) to that accorded Phrynichus' disturbingly topical *Siege of Miletus,* for which the playwright was allegedly fined.

1278 / 1142–50 *I saw a man once... I, too, saw a man once...* Oblique insults and threats in allegorical form were old, popular types of abuse.

1313 / 1171 *kneel here* The return of Tekmessa and the child sets the stage for the *tableau vivant* that visually dominates the end of the play. The mourning group has the power of the dead and the inviolability of suppliancy (protected by Zeus) on their side, thereby suggesting that the actions of the Atreidai border on sacrilege.

1331–66 / 1185–1222 *Third stasimon*

1367–1593 / 1223–1401 *Fourth episode*

1410 / 1257 *than a shadow!* Precisely Odysseus' word in response to the spectacle of Aias fallen ("we who live / are all phantoms, fleeting shadows," **151–52 / 125–26**), but spoken now with contempt, not compassion.

1412 / 1260 *bring someone else*. . . In fifth-century Athens persons not born of free parents
were denied the rights of full citizenship and were therefore not entitled to
plead their own case. The anachronism is worth noting, and, in general,
the pointedness, for contemporary Athenians, of Sophocles' writing.

1419–48 / 1266–89 *a man dies*. . . *barbarian woman's son* Teukros responds by recalling
Aias' greatest Homeric moments in the *Iliad*: his lonely effort to prevent
Hektor from firing the Greek ships (15.415–564); his single combat with
Hektor (7.181–312). Menelaos had volunteered to fight Hektor, but Agamemnon, fearing the outcome, persuaded the Greek champions to draw
lots. The lot freely thrown into the helmet by Aias, "the lightest / bit of
clay" (1443–45 / 1286–87), contrasts sharply with the Greeks' "fixed"
voting for the arms (1271 / 1135).

1455–56 / 1295–97 *Your mother / was a Cretan woman* Cretans had a bad reputation in
fifth-century Athens for, among other things, dishonesty. Aëropē, Agamemnon's mother, was from Crete and had been caught in adultery by
her father, Katreus, and sentenced to death by drowning. However, she
was spared by Katreus' friend, Nauplios, and married Atreus, whom she
betrayed with his own brother. (See also ATREUS in Glossary.)

1511–13 / 1340–41 *greatest of all*. . . *to Achilles* Odysseus confirms the esteem in which
Aias is held throughout Homer (*Iliad* 2.768–69, 17.279–80; *Odyssey*
11.550–51, 24.17–18).

1594–1608 / 1402–20 *Exodos*

1604–5 / 1415–17 *while Aias lived*. . . *no better man in the world* Although the meaning
is reasonably clear, the text of these lines appears corrupt and no editor
has satisfactorily explained them. Teukros' strange, temporal emphasis
(even stronger in Greek) on the nobility of Aias "while he lived," though
the play has dramatized his greatness in facing death, may be Sophocles'
way of separating at the coda the timeless hero from the rest. George
Eliot remarked that those who survive the Sophoclean hero go on living
"life at the lower end."

1606–8 / 1418–20 *Mortals know*. . . *end will be* Sophocles ends five of his seven extant
plays with choral comment. Modern readers are cautioned against the
tendency to look too deeply into these stylized codas. (Euripides uses
one particular coda, similar to this, in six of his plays.) Nonetheless,
these words contrasting mere sight with vision are appropriate.

WOMEN OF TRACHIS

Translated by

C. K. WILLIAMS

and

GREGORY W. DICKERSON

INTRODUCTION

I

Mutability; uncertainty; a universe of precipitous change: these are at the heart of three of the seven surviving tragedies of Sophocles. In *Ajax* the hero confronts abrupt changes in human values and relationships, recognizes them as part of the pattern of universal flux, and escapes submission by self-destruction. In *Oedipus* sight is annulled by blindness, illusion by truth, intellect by irrationality. But nowhere have these themes been elaborated with more urgency or austerity than in *Women of Trachis.* There are no gradual alterations in this tragedy, no subtle shifts of fortune, but stunning and total reversals, moving forward with the relentlessness of a turning wheel: thesis, crushing antithesis, and—at the moment of transformation—violence and destruction. This pattern of opposition and cyclicity prevails throughout the play. Things occur, occur again, in another form, to another person, until, by the end, characters, images, past and present, all seem to have fused under a single mask of human helplessness, of subjugation to time and change, of bitterness and defiance.

The *parodos*[1] serves as a programmatic statement of this design, prefiguring many of the tragedy's themes and movements. Cyclicity and opposition are embodied in its very architecture—in its return at the end to its initial image of "shimmering night" (132 / 132–33, 94 / 94) and in its confinement of Herakles and Deianeira, the play's two principal opposing figures, within isolated stanzas, just as they are isolated from each other in their lives and in the drama itself. Everything in the

---

1. We have used this technical term for the entrance song of the Chorus as a matter of convenience. For the same reason we have used the traditional designations first stasimon, second stasimon, and so on, for the strophic choral odes at 481–516 / 497–536, 616–45 / 633–62, 806–44 / 821–62, and 922–29 / 947–70. The choral interlude at 201–20 / 205–24 belongs to a separate category of brief, metrically asymmetrical songs.

ode, in fact, is divided and at odds: night and day, darkness and light, sleep and consciousness, despair and hope, pain and exaltation. The young women of the Chorus sing of life's mutability as a succession of alterations, of sudden comings and goings: "The shimmering night won't stay, wealth / won't, calamity won't, not / for humans won't at least, but suddenly, suddenly / it's disappeared, gone [*aphar bebake*], and someone else, some poor else, / is under them; the joy, the deprivation" (132–36 / 132–35). And the drama's past and present are punctuated by just such movements. Herakles arrives to confront Achelöos, and Deianeira is saved, only then herself to be "suddenly, gone [*aphar bebakh'*]," torn from her mother like a calf (515–16 / 529–30), and condemned to endless anxiety over the further comings and goings of her husband: "All I know is that he's disappeared [*bebēken*] again" (44 / 41). And later, when the truth—that the hero is now gone forever—comes home to Trachis, it comes with the same abruptness: "...look how suddenly, suddenly [*aphar*], it's come breaking / on us, the word, the god-word..." (806–7 / 821–22).

Like the constellations in their "spinning paths" (131 / 131) the themes of the parodos circle through the tragedy, as the shadow and light of pain and joy, loss and recovery, despair and hope play over the participants. The Messenger arrives to set the Chorus "spinning" (216 / 220) with the news that Herakles is finally coming home, but Deianeira's melancholy immediately returns, prompted by a characteristically Greek anxiety over the dangers implicit in her husband's success and then reinforced by her compassion for the victims of his triumph (286–95 / 293–302). Iole she pities most of all, for she sees mirrored in the young girl's fate her own subjection to peripety. Youth and beauty, which once, like some disembodied force, uprooted her from her virginal security, have whirled onward to strike at another (26 / 25; 41 / 38; 451 / 465). And this perception suddenly darkens the bright joy of Deianeira's initial response to the news of Herakles' return (cf. 196–200 / 200–204). With the even more painful recognition of Herakles' faithlessness and destructive lust, Deianeira's gloom intensifies. She is driven to find hope in the darkness—the darkness of passion, in the love-charm which fuses the blood of Nessos, "the black-haired beast" (823 / 837–38), with the "black poison" of the Hydra (557 / 573–74). But this hope, too, is taken from her, first fading into doubt over the propriety of her action and then obliterated by the dread inspired by the portent of the self-consuming wool. When Hyllos arrives to confirm her fear, she can only return to the despair in which she began the play. Joy, illusory, has come—and gone. Confronting the fulfillment of her premonition that her "deprivation" would be widowhood (172–73 / 177–78), she chooses to die, leaving the

Nurse to announce the violent irony that the wife, whose reunion with her husband was the focus of all her hope and energy, has, at the moment of his homecoming, "disappeared [*bebēke*] ... her last journey" (855 / 874).

As the Chorus has predicted, it is now the turn of "someone else" to be stunned by peripety. The report which annihilates Deianeira's last hope begins by describing the new joy of Herakles and Hyllos—the son's happiness at seeing his father (738 / 755), and the hero's proud delight in the robe his wife has sent him. Then an ominous light begins to play over the account of the scene of sacrifice. The "bloody fires" start "blazing" (748 / 765–66); and within that image, flame against dark gore, shines the same lethal mutability possessed by the sun-slaughtered "shimmering night" of the parodos [*aiola nuks*: 94 / 94, 132 / 132–33], the "shimmering" serpentine metamorphosis of Achelöos [*aiolos drakon*: 14 / 11–12] and the "shimmering" Hydra [*aiolos drakon*: 818 / 834] whose venom strikes at Herakles from within Deianeira's gift of love. The pain which Herakles' own arrow struck long before into the "side" of the centaur Nessos (664 / 681) comes back to him, clinging to his "sides" (751 / 768) and ruthlessly devouring him. And onward the agony drives, to strike Deianeira, too, in "the side, where life lives" (904 / 931) and then Hyllos, lying "side by side" with her corpse, crying over his double loss (913 / 938–39).

Death brings Deianeira back to her marriage bed. In the final scene her husband's circle closes. Hyllos has rescued his father from the "shrouds of smoke" (779–80 / 794) but not from the darkness from which it swirled. Herakles appears in a death-like sleep; he awakens to vindictive desperation (991–92 / 1036–39, cf. 1057–62 / 1107–10). Then the moment of his enlightenment arrives, the realization that the radiance of his mortal heroism has been smothered in the robe's embrace: "Finished! FINISHED! My light—it's over now" (1094 / 1144). But there is one more light to be. The oracles which Herakles has received from his father, Zeus, become "clear" now, "brilliant" (1124 / 1174), leading him to surrender to the light itself, to fire lit with a "flaming torch" (1148 / 1198). To consummate this last heroic act he returns to the shelterless expanses from which he came, confident that there he will rediscover "joy" (1213 / 1262–63).

II

It is this thematic flux which gives the tragedy its surface tension. But there is an even deeper theme, a particular aspect of mutability which Sophocles has selected from the myth and emphasized throughout the play. This is the constant resurgence of irrational bestiality in the world, the tragic, primeval struggle of civilized humanity to stifle or exclude the savagery and violence which threaten it both from without and from within.

Sophocles' obsession with this theme is vividly evident in his treatment of Deianeira. He has given her a rich psychological complexity which makes her one of the more memorable figures in Greek tragedy. But, more important, he has also shaped her to embody humanity's fundamental desire to achieve that secure stability which serves as the basis of civilized life; and in so doing, he has both drastically altered and refined the Deianeira tradition current at the time of the play's composition.

In that tradition, Deianeira entered the Herakles myth only after the end of his labors for Eurystheus; that is, she was merely the last of that restless hero's many women. Sophocles, by contrast, has raised her to the status of legitimate wife in a marriage which has lasted throughout Herakles' adult career. By so doing he has created a counterpoise to Herakles' world of challenge, change, and movement—a potential for the permanence of a securely rooted family. At the same time, he has carefully excluded all elements of Deianeira's traditional background which might clash with her function as a single-minded domesticating—and domesticated—force. No hint is given of the original Amazonian persona to which her name—"Fighter-with-men" or "Hostile-to-men," or even "Man-killer"—attests, a role in which she was long remembered, even after Sophocles' very different Deianeira had come to dominate the literary tradition, as a woman who "drove a chariot and practiced the arts of war."[2] In fact, with the exception of a few references to her father Oineus, the poet has obliterated all traces of her fierce Aetolian family. Her mother Althaia, notorious in myth for the murder by magic of her son Meleager, is never mentioned, nor is Meleager himself, the famous hunter of the Kalydonian boar and the killer of his uncles in battle. Even Deianeira's birthplace is arbitrarily changed from Kalydon to Pleuron,[3] as if to dispel the aura of violence that comes with her traditional Kalydonian context.

For savagery is something before which this Deianeira characteristically retreats, as long as retreat is possible, to the safety of distance—as in her terrified withdrawal from the scene of Herakles' combat with

2. "Apollodoros," *Library* I. viii. 1.

3. Deianeira situates her family in Pleuron at line 7 of Sophocles' text. We have omitted the reference from the translation as an obscure geographical detail of no consequence for a modern audience.

Achelöos (509–11 / 523–25)—or to the shelter of the marriage bed, the symbol of her hopes for security and the site of her nocturnal fears (106–11 / 106–10). She is, finally, the most timid of all Sophoclean protagonists, static and passive; her mode of survival is to wait danger out, to do nothing—or to try to do nothing.

In the prologue it is the Nurse who must provide her with the almost absurdly obvious remedy for her anxieties—to send out one of her children to find Herakles (52–62 / 49–60). Ultimately, however, the play illuminates the logic of this: throughout, Deianeira's thoughts thrust obsessively toward her own hearth, toward the security of family and home. Even the similes and metaphors she uses reflect her world of domestic values and concerns—a farmer visiting his fields (34–36 / 32–33), delicate plants protected from nature's violence (144–46 / 144–47), the dust falling from a saw (683 / 699), the ritual wine (686–87 / 703–4). Similarly, the metamorphoses explicitly worked upon her by the poetry of the play give no hint of violence; she is a helpless bird (105 / 105), a frightened calf (516 / 530).

In the end, of course, Sophocles brings her to discover the tragic truth, the same lesson which the poet's contemporary Thucydides read in human history: that the forces of savagery, though temporarily dormant or concealed, never entirely disappear from the civilized world. At the very moment when she believes that Herakles' final victory has shut these forces out, they march in upon her in the person of Iole, the silent token of her husband's brutality and lust, penetrating the palace itself and striking at Deianeira's citadel—her marriage bed. Passive withdrawal is no longer possible; her deliverer is now himself the source of danger. This is the moment of crisis which sparks the recollection that for years she has had with her, safely confined in a dark corner of her house, the essence of that same fearful power which permeates her husband's world: the poisoned blood of Nessos.

Deianeira's moment of equivocation (565–71 / 582–87) reflects the desperate deflection of simple caution and civilized conscience required by her decision to use this force as a love-charm. But she is soon disabused of her delusion. The omen of the wool drives her to acknowledge the danger implicit in her action, and Hyllos arrives to confirm her fear: she has unloosed something more savage than the lust she wanted to "tame" (643–44 / 661–62). The "charm" by which she hoped to attach her husband's affections has struck—and stuck—"like venom from a snake" (754 / 771). She can only wilt and, in another cruel irony, "crawl away" (798 / 813) into the palace to find, in suicidal violence, her final escape from brutality. There she reaffirms her lifelong dream of domestic peace, carefully making up the marriage bed and slaughtering herself upon it: dead wife dutifully awaiting the return of the dying husband (891–904 / 912–28).

III

Herakles was rarely portrayed as a sympathetic hero by the Greek tragedians.[4] In his nature there was, in addition to an occasional element of buffoonery, a brutishness which made him singularly unsuited for heroic treatment. In this play, however, this very trait is an asset and is incorporated, with all its raw vitality, as an integral part of Sophocles' design. Herakles here is the embodiment of all that is antithetical—and ultimately inimical—to the world of civilized constraint which Deianeira tries to shape. He belongs to a world of limitless space, the vast landscape against which the Chorus pictures him in the parodos, a lonely figure "spinning" on the troubled seas of his life (116–19 / 116–19). It is a world of "woods / and seas" (970–71 / 1012), inhabited by forces of inhuman savagery: man-eating lion; Hydra; monstrosities, half-men, half-horse; wild boar; three-headed whelp of the Viper; and watchful dragon (1040–52 / 1091–1102).

His heroic mission—the endeavor which earns him the epithet of "the greatest man who ever lived" (173 / 177; 797 / 811)—has been to overpower these forces by sheer strength. It is a particularly primitive form of heroism, not self-chosen but imposed, a kind of licensed exercise of savagery which is distinguishable from the bestial elements it destroys only because it claims to serve civilization's purpose. From the beginning humanity has required such champions—and found them, to its ruin as well as to its salvation, in those men of obsessive violence represented by the Herakles of this play.

Here the hero is revealed as a figure of crushing strength, uninhibited by the constraints of conscience and family loyalty which bind Deianeira to the civilized world. Serenely he offers up to Zeus the spoils of a city pillaged by his lust (733–37 / 750–54). He makes no effort to conceal from his wife his intention to replace her with the young captive he sends to be welcomed in her house (459–67 / 474–83). He is without compassion, maintaining stony indifference to Hyllos' anguish throughout the finale, just as he has earlier, in a chilling perversion of the conventional tragic gesture of self-sacrifice, compelled his son to risk death to rescue him (782–87 / 797–802). He murders Lichas despite the herald's denial of complicity in his ruin. The proof of Deianeira's

---

4. Of the three major tragedians, only Euripides is known to have attempted such a treatment. The successful result has fortunately been preserved in his *Herakles*.

innocent intentions evokes from him no word of pity or regret. Action means everything; motive, nothing. He remains, until his mysterious moment of enlightenment in the final scene, wholly preoccupied with the instrument rather than the aim of his heroic mission: with the once invincible body invoked in his hymn to his own epic achievement: "O hands, my hands... Shoulders... Chest... My arms.../ Is it still you?" (1039–40 / 1089–91). All these he sees as incomprehensibly torn to shreds: "Pieces. Waste" (1053 / 1103). Stripped of his muscle by a "weak, / meaningless woman" (1011–12 / 1062), he feels himself stripped of his manhood: "Look at me, / moaning, bellowing like a wispy girl.../ Look! The hero! / All that time I was a woman!" (1021–26/ 1070–75). The ravaging of his body has left him with nothing but a desire for an impossible revenge: "I might be nothing, / paralyzed in nothingness, but the one who did this / will know these hands..." (1057–59 / 1107–9).

IV

What finally penetrates Herakles' blind obsession with his flesh, what restores his heroic spirit and frees him from despair, is the sudden discovery that his father Zeus has not betrayed him, that the oracular promises have, in fact, been fulfilled. Of these two oracles—one predicting that his release from toil would follow upon the sack of Oichalia (77–83 / 76–81; 163–70 / 166–72; 1119–22 / 1169–73), the other that no living creature would be able to kill him (1107–10 / 1159–61)—there are no traces in what survives of the mythical tradition from which Sophocles drew. It may well be that he has invented them; it is certain that he has included them to serve the tragic meaning of the action: to explain to the hero, and to the audience, why his career must at this time and in this way end.

It must end now, at the moment when Herakles has destroyed Eurytos' city, because that act in itself confirms a catastrophic shift in the focus of his energies. The violence of his spirit, which has been harnessed by civilization to attack its monstrous enemies, has broken rein; there is nothing left alive brutal enough to confront him with the threat of death, with genuine heroic challenge. And yet his thirst for savagery remains, seeking further victims—and finding them, as violent heroes too often have, in the very humans he once defended. The rampage of the beast can only be ended now by a kind of miracle, the resurrection from the dead of a former bestial adversary, by the resurrection, in other words, of his own heroic past. For the source of the poison which Nessos sends back to kill this murderer-rapist is in fact Herakles' own arrow, shot long ago at the same target: animal lust.

Sophocles does not have Herakles articulate this meaning after he senses the coherence of his destiny. This would be not only out of character but also dramatically superfluous; for by this point the special logic underlying the oracular ambiguities of the play has already revealed its meaning.

The development of this logic is initiated at the very beginning of the play by emphasis on certain disturbing changes in the pattern of Herakles' behavior. Deianeira's deliverer, slaving away as civilization's heroic laborer (35 / 38), has turned murderer and found service of a shockingly different sort. He has "killed poor Iphitos" (41 / 38); the poet needed to have Deianeira say nothing more, for the atrocity of this crime had already been told in Homer's *Odyssey* (21.11–44). And when Hyllos reports the sequel to this murder, "slavery" to a barbarian woman, his mother is astonished: "If he stood for that, then anything is possible" (72 / 71).

But this subservience to barbarism is only the ominous prelude to Herakles' complete rejection of the constraint upon which his claim to heroism is founded. The servitude to Omphale is over. The hero's savagery has become its own master—and we are confronted with the results: with the miserable victims of his latest triumph, with Lichas' brain-splattered death (762–68 / 779–85), and, finally, with the spectacle of Herakles himself consumed by violence. The Chorus in the third stasimon has foreseen the truth: for a man like Herakles, escape from the limitations of servitude is inevitably linked to the death of the heroic spirit: "Because how, how would the empty-eyed, the see-nothing, / still have work, toil to do, / bondage, if he's dead?" (813–15 / 828–30).

Herakles has succumbed to the monstrous world in which he has lived; he has become, in fact, another Nessos. This transformation is underscored throughout the play by images of animal violence. In Deianeira's account of the combat with Achelöos the outlines of man and monster remain distinct (9–22 / 9–21). But later, when the Chorus takes up the theme in the first stasimon, the distinction begins to blur: the conflict ends in a confusion of identities, a battle of bulls over a calf (502–8 / 517–22). Immediately thereafter, Deianeira sends the gift which her husband is to open "when he makes the bull-kill" (593 / 609) and which reduces him to the thrashing, eye-rolling, bellowing beast described by Hyllos in the following scene (769–81 / 785–96). Horrified, the Chorus articulates the ghastly image of Herakles "fused to the spirit / of the Hydra" (821–22 / 836–37). First bull, then snake: the hero has become indistinguishable from Achelöos. In the finale these images find their culmination. The hero is at last brought before the audience, tortured by an invisible and inescapable monster: "driving its teeth in me," "pouncing, lunging…leaping, destroying," Herakles' bestialized nature has, in the end, recoiled upon itself (945 / 987; 984–85 / 1027–30).

V

Of all the many changes enacted in the world of *Women of Trachis*, this is the most devastating: the greatest man who ever lived is reduced to a shrieking woman. The play's climactic transformation, however, is still to come—in the reversal of Herakles' mood after he has perceived the accuracy of Zeus' oracles.

In an instant, all the rage and bitterness of his first cry to Zeus are gone (cf. 942–75 / 983–1017). Until this moment, Herakles has impotently struggled to escape his pain, lamenting the loss of his manhood. Now he proclaims Hyllos the physician he has despaired of finding: "healer… doctor… / Only you can cure this evil" (1158–59 / 1208–9). But it is the patient himself who specifies, with an icy assurance and an indomitable strength of will, his paradoxical treatment: death, fiery destruction on a pyre to be constructed with ritualistic precision (1146–50/ 1195–99).

Sophocles refuses any explicit clarification of this change. On the contrary, he stresses the uncanniness of the hero's recovered confidence through Hyllos' unanswered pleas for explanation. Instead the answer has been left beneath the surface of the dialogue, in the shape of the action itself. Herakles, after the vindication of his father's oracular word, seems to find liberation in a meticulously prescribed pattern of behavior. The inference is irresistible that the source of this prescription is in these same oracles, or, more precisely, in certain unspecified aspects of these privileged communications between Herakles and Zeus.

Sophocles has clearly hinted that these oracles are more than the usual Olympian edicts issued by a detached divinity. Early in the play he refers to them as "convenants" (*xunthēmata*, 156 / 158), a word suggesting a kind of contract, struck by mutual consent and defining mutual obligations carefully inscribed, in good Greek legal fashion, on a tablet. And it is precisely this peculiar contractual aspect of the oracles which is reinforced by the superficially strange behavior of the hero at the end. The fulfillment of Zeus' word has made binding the pact which the son thought broken by his father's betrayal; at once Herakles initiates the execution of his own obligations: self-immolation upon Mt. Oita. As he does so, moreover, the nature of this unstated confrontation between Zeus and hero is revealed by the parallel confrontation between Herakles and Hyllos. Herakles demands from his son no less than Zeus has demanded of him, blind obedience to the paradoxical commands of an implacable father: "You ought to know at your age that obedience / to the father is the most important law" (1127–28 / 1177–78).

?

Such mystification, extraordinary for a Greek tragedian, can only be explained by Sophocles' determination to mark the change in Herakles for what it is: a miracle, a transformation possessed of no logic communicable to common mortals, its origins obscured in secrets between demigod and divine father. Zeus' son confronts the revelation that his ultimate adversary is his own ferocity, that his body, which has been the instrument of his triumphs, has in the end been the instrument of his defeat; and he finds in unprotesting acceptance of this paradox a new source of strength. As he leaves the stage it is no longer his ruined body which he invokes, but rather his spirit, directed now to reaffirm the forgotten heroic task by curbing the beast which has broken rein: "Soul, be hard now! . . . / Put the steel bit in your teeth" (1208–9 / 1260–61). With this metaphor Herakles departs to complete the sacrificial ritual which has been interrupted by Deianeira's gift—the triumphant bull-kill in which the celebrant has himself become the consummating victim.

The hero is convinced that the outcome of this "welcome, unwelcome work" must be "joy" (1212–13 / 1262–63). To find cause for jubilation in self-destruction is to transcend the limits of mortal vision. Herakles has been transformed from something less than human into something more than hero, an austere god-figure, enforcing his inexplicable will with pitiless compulsion and confronting the future with omniscient assurance. Here, surely, lies the reason why so many critics have failed to find in him the sympathetic hero conventional to Sophoclean tragedy. Men, not savages or gods, move audiences to pity.

god more than man

It is far more for Hyllos, the surviving son, than for Herakles that the close of *Women of Trachis* evokes compassion. Here the untroubled youth of the opening scene becomes a man. His father, with the indifference of life itself, compels him to accept the justice (1194–97 / 1245–48) of a world where killing is cure and marriage to the instrument of a mother's ruin a filial obligation. For those who live there can be no escape from violence. Hyllos must live with the knowledge that he has been an accomplice in his father's death; and he will be bound to Iole, a permanent reminder of the savagery which has destroyed his parents. In this enforced submission to inexplicable realities he, unlike his father, can find no joy but only bitterness. He is, after all, not a son of Zeus.

The austerity of the tragedy's climactic vision contrasts strikingly with the optimism of Sophocles' last play, *Oedipus at Kolonos*. There, too, mystery and paradox play critical roles. Oedipus, like Herakles, possesses a "covenant" (*xunthēma*, 46) with a god, Apollo. He has been assured that upon reaching the Grove of the Furies at Athens he will be released from his life as a blind pariah and transformed into a sacred hero with eternal powers to help his friends and harm his enemies. At the end of the play this divine promise is realized in the spectacle reported by the Messenger: thunder rolls, the voice of "heaven" is heard, and Oedipus is miraculously spirited out of sight.

Sophocles could easily have used a similar means to refute Hyllos' closing cry of protest and to confirm the Chorus' stubborn faith in the benevolence of Zeus toward his children (138–39 / 139–40). He needed only to appropriate the happy ending already present in the myth. There, in the deification with which Herakles' self-destruction was rewarded, lay proof of the heroic spirit's capacity to survive its conflict with bestial impulse; to win eternal victory over death and change. Sophocles has encouraged his audience to expect such an ending, both by making Mt. Oita, the traditional site of Herakles' ascent to Olympos, a conspicuous feature of the play's landscape and by giving to the hero's instructions for his pyre suggestive overtones of religious ritual. But in the end Sophocles produces no stage divinity to confirm the crowning glory which awaits the hero. Instead, after opposing Hyllos' bleak vista of senseless human misery to Herakles' mysterious prospect of joy, he abruptly ends the play with no suggestion of a final resolution; without so much as the conventional closing word from the Chorus.

It is from this suspension of final judgment that *Women of Trachis* derives its stunning tragic impact. Through it the poet compels us to share the pain of Hyllos' confrontation with a divine justice which transcends the logic of human experience. Such justice is, by definition, unknowable; and Sophocles, by his pointed refusal to realize the apotheosis, proclaims his unwillingness to provide the comfort of any illusion to the contrary. Hyllos assumes the burden of unquestioning faith in his father as the price for his escape from despair. Herakles departs to die, stifling all impulse to mourn his end—confident that the unwelcome will become welcome, that defeat will become victory. But Sophocles has made the *finality* of his triumph a matter of agonizing doubt. *Ajax* and both Oedipus plays clearly affirm mankind's capacity to transcend impermanence by heroic moral courage. For the problem he has addressed in *Women of Trachis* Sophocles offers no such certain answer. The possibility of humanity's *ultimate* victory over inherent savagery is no more than a bright, unrealized hope. There is but one certainty in the unpredictable universe of this play. It is affirmed at the end by Hyllos: "... nothing is here, / nothing, / none of all of it, that is not Zeus" (1225–27 / 1278).

VI

In view of the lack of firm evidence it is impossible to feel much conviction in assigning *Women of Trachis* even an approximate date.

The attempt to establish its dependence on Euripides' *Alcestis* of 438 B.C. seems at best inconclusive. About all that can safely be said is that the play can be shown to possess, in its vocabulary and technique, certain affinities with *Ajax* and *Antigone*, both generally thought to be the earliest of the seven surviving Sophoclean tragedies. This would suggest a production around 440 B.C., in the middle years of the poet's career.

As the basis of our translation we have used the text of R. C. Jebb, *Sophocles: The Plays and Fragments: Part V: The Trachiniae* (Cambridge, 1892). Occasionally (at ll. 643–45 /660–63, 825–29 / 841–50, 885 /905, and 890 / 911) we have preferred the manuscript tradition to the emendations accepted in his edition, and in one instance (201–4 / 205–8) we have adopted the reading of A. C. Pearson's *Sophoclis Fabulae* (Oxford, 1955).

We are grateful to the many who have encouraged and assisted us throughout our collaboration. Our specific debts have been separately acknowledged below.

GREGORY W. DICKERSON

C. K. WILLIAMS

ACKNOWLEDGMENTS

This work was completed with the help of the Guggenheim Foundation.

I wish to thank Erving Goffman, Guy Davenport, Stephen Berg, Paul Zweig, and Lorand Gaspar, who all, at one time or another, offered ideas, criticism, tactics, and encouragement; William Arrowsmith, for whom the term "editor" does not begin to capture the degree of his labor and the quality of his involvement, and Catherine Mauger, for everything. C. K. W.

I am grateful to the President, Directors, and Trustees of Bryn Mawr College for their generous award of the year's leave of absence during which this collaboration has been completed. To Richmond Lattimore and Richard Hamilton, colleagues past and present, and to William Arrowsmith, I give special thanks for their scrutiny of the Introduction and Notes. My debt to their perceptive criticisms and suggestions is enormous. The responsibility for whatever errors, idiocies, or imperfections that still remain is solely mine. G. W. D.

ON THE TRANSLATION

THE CHORUSES

The major difficulty in rendering the choruses is of course that they were originally set to music, sung, and danced, and that we have too little notion of what the music was to attempt to re-create it or "make it new." There are, then, two problems: how can the choruses achieve an integral, energetic role in the drama, given the fact that they must be simply spoken poetry and not music; and what is a valid approach to their performance?

I have tried to meet these problems first by trying to determine what the critical difference is between poetry and music. What is the irreducible element of each, irrespective of its elaboration in any particular work?

The basic unit of poetry is clearly the word. The basic unit of music might at first seem to be a sound, but this does not distinguish it from poetry since a word is itself a sound. So I would go further and say that music's basic element is repetition: the *repeated* sound. The repetition must occur in a pattern and this pattern can have a harmonic context, a rhythmic one—one of volume, duration, intensity, decay, etc.—or any or all of them. The human animal, given two sticks, will sooner or later produce at least a simple music. On the other hand, the most aesthetically complex culture will create a scale or scales, of however many modes, and a scale is at base a system of repetition. Once familiar with an individual mode, we need no more than a few notes of any phrase to predict without any intellection whatsoever what the resolution of the tonic—the unit of repetition—will be.

It would be beyond the scope of these remarks to inquire what exactly in the organism responds so precisely and dramatically to music. The pulse, the brain-patterns, the rhythms of life on the planet itself; every possibility has been suggested. We can say with certainty though that the consciousness assumes an entirely unique kind of functioning while experiencing music: it seems to dissolve itself strangely into the body—we "hear" a drum or a cello, for instance, in our rib-cage—and music is simply not experienced at all unless there is this organic connection.

This is not true of poetry. It would be impossible to confuse the most lyrically complex poetry with the most resolutely simple song because this physical reaction is of an entirely different, more cerebrally determined order, and when we speak of the "music" of poetry, we do so only because there is no other word for what so profoundly happens to us as we experience it. The repetitive possibilities—sound, syllable, foot, phrase, line—for one thing cannot begin to approach those of music, but aside from this, poetry, and in particular tragedy as poetry, is in some sense the antithesis of music, the other limit of our range of responsiveness. We might go back and say that the basic unit of poetry is meaning: meaning experienced, struggled with, surrendered to; and tragedy is a continual spinning out of meaning and configurations of experience in a relentless, unresolving fugue of revelation; of the unknown and unknowable.

Perhaps we can further postulate that the function of the musical chorus in Greek tragedy, like that of comedy in Elizabethan, is to offer a chance for us to come to ourselves, as it were, to the other end, the source, the body, in order to gather the entire organism's resources to go on with this.

There is another factor, basic to any consideration of chorus. That it is, at least to a great extent, unison. It is, in its very substance, the audience, the community, experiencing itself, and this presents another problem in the presentation of chorus without music. Choral speaking, even at its very best, always has something about it of school children reciting. There is always an imperceptible pause while the group awaits one voice to lead it out of the silence, and any given sentence can actually have—from an orchestral point of view—an entirely different harmony, according to which voice had the courage to begin that particular sentence. What generally happens is that a kind of sing-song rhythm is generated—the same rhythm that children give to nursery rhymes, and adults to Bible-reading. I think this is because the human voice simply does not function in unison—in community—without music; perhaps for the fundamental reason that music is a simplification of time, an organization of the movement of our voices through time, and, without music, we founder.

In rendering the choruses of *Women of Trachis*, I have tried to take into account as many of these difficulties as possible. In trying to make at least a facsimile of the basic musical experience of the chorus, I have had to violate some of the precision of grammar and image that would normally be expected, and I have taken what might at first seem to be extraordinary liberties with the literal text by using many repetitions, generally of single words, but, occasionally, of phrases and whole line units. All these repetitions, however, I have taken from the variance of complex meanings which are carried by a word from one language to another. The texture I have tried to evoke obviously does not have as its "mode" any known musical structure. The resolution, to use musical terms, can happen within a few lines or a few words, in an obvious repetition, or it can extend over almost the length of the play, following the sub-pattern of repetition that Sophocles himself used (the word "shimmering" for instance).

The unison-speaking problem I have tried to resolve by substituting the control of sound through time with that of sound through space. There is, strictly speaking, no unison at all. Each single, descending line, as I have rendered it, represents an *individual* voice, coming from a spatially distinct point on the stage. By doing this, I have hoped the audience would experience the flow of lyric meaning both visually and aurally, and thus, by involving another sense as well as by breaking down the normal expectation of meaning-unit, a more organic — i.e., musical — reaction would be evoked.

The director obviously has a critical task in organizing the choruses spatially, and the speeches themselves will require greater skill from actors than ordinary choral "chant." Many of my notions here are, in fact, based on the exercise developed by Peter Brook to create a greater sense of dramatic community among his actors. A group of actors stands in a circle, one word of a Shakespearean line is given to each and then the group attempts to reproduce the line as it would be spoken by an individual. The results, Brook says, at first chaotic, are ultimately liberating for the actors and exhilarating for listeners. Some such exercise, possibly not quite as rigorous, would be needed here if the poetry is to cohere.

THE TRANSLATION

Statements of translating practices seem a particularly futile procedure. The translator may qualify, formulate or excuse, but the *fact* of the text speaks for itself; it is insolubly, or inconsolably, concrete. To readers who know the original language, a translation is an exercise in literary craftsmanship, and the attempt is defined from the beginning as one degree or another of failure. To those unfamiliar with the original, however, the search into the translation becomes a quest for the seed, the kernel, of sublimity and passion which presumably reside in the original, and a failure in this is of an entirely different order. It does not imply a mere rejection of the translator's effort, but a loss of the whole potential experience embodied in the work.

At the same time, a non-failure, a blossoming, however partial, of that kernel; a glimmer of the strength and relevance of the original, is a bringing forth of what previously was not. It is at this hopeful point that translation becomes in itself an art-form, and here a whole new area of difficulties is encountered: those of the given linguistic, poetic possibilities of the translator's own historical moment.

Lyrical range, philosophical urgency, intensity of expression, complexity of rhetoric, and metaphoric ingenuity: there is always, in any work, a balancing, one might almost say a bargaining, among all these, and their availability in a vital combination is determined more by the translator's cultural, literary milieu than by his own resources. The literatures we find compelling and significant always seem to us to delicately and judiciously fuse these elements. Other works, the ones to which we feel no affinity, never seem to. And of course our values, our needs, change relatively quickly and in a few years what was loved can seem stilted or opaque or simply exhausted, and what was previously brushed aside can suddenly illuminate.

In confronting such a cultural monument as one of Sophocles' tragedies, the translator becomes all too quickly aware of his own literary economics and its limitations; but at the same time there has to be a clearing away of some of the accumulations of reverence that confuse the work and the genius who made it. The translator begins to realize the compromises the poet Sophocles was constrained to make with *his* tradition and, perhaps more importantly, the compromises, often non-literary in origin, which were made for him.

Antonio Machado said: "Before writing a poem, one must imagine a poet capable of writing it." It is much the same with a translation. A Sophocles must be re-created who not only speaks in the language we do, but who in a sense lives in our own time with us, with our thoughts, culture, and tradition layered over his own. And this Sophocles must begin to make his choices over again. I suppose a sense of somewhat guilty presumption is inevitable.

WOMEN OF TRACHIS

Translated by

C. K. WILLIAMS

and

GREGORY W. DICKERSON

CHARACTERS

HERAKLES hero of the famous labors, the son of Zeus

DEIANEIRA his wife

HYLLOS their son, approaching manhood

NURSE

LICHAS Herakles' herald

MESSENGER

OLD MAN

CHORUS of young women of Trachis

LEADER of the Chorus

CAPTIVES young women of Oichalia

IOLE one of them, the daughter of Eurytos

SERVANTS

Line numbers in the right-hand margin of the text refer to the English translation only, and the Notes beginning at p. 169 are keyed to these lines. The bracketed line numbers in the running heads refer to the Greek text.

Dawn.

The palace of Keyx, king of Trachis. Massive doors. To one side, a statue of Zeus,
with an altar.

Enter from the palace, DEIANEIRA. *Behind her and unseen by her, the* NURSE.

DEIANEIRA Men have been telling each other since time
started: if you're going to say happy or unhappy
about a human life, wait for it to be over.
Me, though, my life—I don't need Hell to teach me
the turns in my life or how much it weighs.
Even when I still lived at home with my father
Oineus... Girls are afraid of marriage,
you're supposed to be. I was a girl, but nobody
ever felt the ice I felt. There was a river.
His name was Acheloös, and it was that,   10
a river, *that*, who wanted me. My father
would see shapes. I was being wooed by shapes!
There'd be a torrent of a bull, it would be him,
then a snake, coiled and shimmering—him—
then something with the face of an ox, a man's body
and a thick beard gushing jets of water.
Again, him. I'd look at him—my admirer—
and I used to pray to die if they brought me
anywhere near a bed with a thing like that in it.

Then finally Herakles arrived. I soared!   20
The famous Herakles. Alkmene's child, the son of Zeus.
He faced the other, fought him, I was saved.
If you want to know about the battle itself,
ask someone who wasn't paralyzed, who wasn't ice,
who didn't sit there overwhelmed with the dread
that my own beauty was going to spin curses for me.
However it did happen, though, the part of god
who watches these war things made it come out right...

115

If right really is right, because ever since I've been
with Herakles, sharing his bed, standing with him,   30
all I seem to have done is nurse terror for him.
One night is fear, the next drives that fear out
with new fear.
                        We had children, of course.
He sees them the way a farmer sees his back fields:
he drops a seed and comes around once in awhile
to check the harvest.
                        All right, that was his life,
home, gone, home and then slogging away again
to labor for some master or another. But now
he's supposed to have risen above all that
and now my anxieties are worse than ever.   40
He killed poor Iphitos and we've been uprooted since,
exiled in Trachis, the guests of people
we hardly know and where is he? Tell me.
All I know is that he's disappeared again
and that I'm being torn to bits for him again.
And it's been so long this time . . . ten months . . .
no, five more even than that and not a word.
What kind of trouble will it be this time?
He gave me something to keep for him
when he left, a tablet. I only hope   50
it doesn't mean more suffering for me.

The NURSE *comes forward and addresses* DEIANEIRA.

NURSE Queen . . . Deianeira . . . I've watched you for such a
              long time
        groaning and carrying on about Herakles being away.
        I've never said a word: you are the Queen
        and I the slave. Would you forgive me now
        if I suggested something? You have so many children—
        why haven't you ever sent one of them to search
        for your husband? Hyllos is old enough. Why not?
        Look, he's running home right now.
        If it doesn't bother you that it's my idea,   60
        why don't you use it and him along with it?

116

(handwritten) How does her comment characterize Herakles?

Enter HYLLOS, *returning from a game or hunt, running.*

DEIANEIRA Son, sweetheart, good advice
can come from anyone, apparently. This woman's
my slave, but you'd never know from what she says.

HYLLOS What advice, Mother? Am I allowed to hear?

DEIANEIRA Shouldn't you be ashamed, she says, all this time,
never trying to find where your father is?

HYLLOS But I know where he is, or I hear rumors, anyway.

DEIANEIRA What rumors? What are you talking about? Where?

HYLLOS All last year, they say, he was a slave in Lydia,   70
to a woman; some barbarian. The whole year, he ploughed.
(handwritten) effeminized

DEIANEIRA If he stood for that, then anything is possible.

HYLLOS Well, he's supposed to be out of it now.

DEIANEIRA Out of it where? Is he alive?

HYLLOS He's making war, they say, or getting ready to,
against Euboia, Eurytos' kingdom.

DEIANEIRA Son, listen to me. Don't you know about that place?
That he gave me prophecies about that place?

HYLLOS What kind of prophecies, Mother?

DEIANEIRA Important ones. They say: he dies, there, now.   *(handwritten)* uncertainty   80
They say: if he survives the there and now,   *(handwritten)* or
his labors will be over. What's left will be happiness,
peace and quiet for his life.
Hyllos, his future
is in the balance. Go help him. If he's safe,
so are we. If he's not, we're finished, too.

shimmering

HYLLOS   Mother, if I'd known about all this,
         prophecies like this, I'd be there now.
         With all the luck he's had, though,
         I didn't think we had to worry. About him,
         or anything. All right, I do know now.   90
         I'll find the truth, no matter what.

truth

DEIANEIRA   Go ahead, then. If news is good,
            it does good, late or not.

why would it be good?
not always!

            Exit NURSE *into the palace. Exit* HYLLOS. *Enter* CHORUS.*

CHORUS   The night, the
                          shimmering night, is
                             slaughtered, her armor
                       torn from her for you
                          to be unwombed and then she
                             beds you back in her, burning,
                       on fire! SUN!
                          Listen!
                             You should know,
                       Sun—listen!
                          The child,
                             the child of Alkmene,
                       listen, where
                          is he, we're
                             asking, where, the child,
                       is he?
                          O brilliance! O
                             fire-thing,   100
                       in the sea-pit is
                          he?
                             On
                       the doubled continents,
                          asleep—
                             is he there?

violence   *moon*   *virgin*
sex

Sun

Sun
Sea   *vagina*

         breasts

---

* The Chorus does not speak in unison. Each descending line is meant to be
spoken by a different voice. See pp. 109–12.

Listen! Listen! You
   could see it! Eye-Lord!
     Seeing-Lord!
Because Deianeira, her,
   the heart-torn, o
    and she
was fought for, she,
   I've heard that she,
    her eyes,
like the blinded
   bird, the eyelids
    torn
with longing,
   never, never
    puts her
eyes
   away
    to sleep, not
dry, not dry, but nurses
   fear after
    fear for her husband,
his wanderings, and
   the obsessive bed,
    the widowed
bed,   110
   and doom,
    the
consuming,
   terrible, the
    expectation.

The sea! The
   sea! The way, look
    the way
the inexhaustible
   wind, look, sucks
    north
waves, south

waves, coming, look,
　　coming
farther,
　　endless,
　　　endless, so
Herakles, seed
　　of Kadmos,
　　　so his life, that way,
one wave
　　spinning it,
　　　another,
like the deep
　　sea at Crete,
　　　swelling it
into labor.
　　But listen, a god,
　　　one of them, the gods,
one of the knowers,   120
　　always holds
　　　him
away, always, away
　　from Hell, at least away
　　　from that house, always.

　　　　　　　　They turn to DEIANEIRA.

And that's the reason
　　I offer two mouths to
　　　you now,
for how you're acting.
　　Respect, yes,
　　　but reproach, too, and
blame. Because you can't,
　　no, shouldn't,
　　　no, never, mustn't,
ever, let
　　hope, not all of
　　　hope, not

Spinning

Dei.

respect
reproach

keep hope alive

hope, erode.
  It wasn't
    painlessness
the all-King,
  all-Doer,
    Kronos-heir,
worked
  out for
    humanity. But
it circles,
  pain, it
  circles,
exaltation, to
  all, all
  of us,
like the Great
  Bear, the spinning,
    the spinning paths.

The shimmering
  night
    won't stay, wealth
won't,
  calamity
    won't, not
for humans won't
  at least, but
    suddenly, suddenly
it's disappeared,
  gone, and someone else,
    some poor else,
is under them; the
  joy, the
    deprivation.
I tell you,
  Queen,
    keep
that always, ever,

[handwritten margin notes: suffering; circle; spinning; shimmering; all change; always expect Change]

130

121

virgin → wife = fear, anxiety (handwritten)

in your expectation.
Who, who
of anyone, has ever known
Zeus, not to think, the
god, of his children?

hope (handwritten)

DEIANEIRA You must have heard about my suffering.   140
That's why you're here. But without being me,
you'll never understand it,
and may you never have to.
All the sweet things growing in their good places,
the sun's burning never touching them, or the rain or wind;
living their happy little joyfulness, until the virgin's name
is wife and then she knows anxiety and the night
and how to tremble for a husband and children.
Someone who's been through that could begin
to know me, what I'm living.   150
She'd look at her own troubles.
Well, I've done my share of crying until now, but now
I'm going to offer you a grief that's more
than all of them. Just before Herakles
was leaving on his latest journey, he gave me
an old tablet with strange covenants carved on it.
As many times as he'd gone out on trials before
he'd never bothered to explain anything—
he always left to conquer, not to die—
but this time it was as though he knew some doom   160
about himself. He told me how much of our property
was mine and what his sons should have
and he told me when: that if a year
and three months passed and he wasn't back,
then he'd be dead. Live that long, though,
and he could rest, from that day on.
He said it was ordained by the gods: the end
of the labors of Herakles. It's what the sacred oak
told him through the twin dove-priestesses
at Dodona...And the time is now, now,   170
so that every blessed night I come awake,

suffering — singular experience? (handwritten)

universal (handwritten)

old tablet covenants (handwritten)

122

messenger

afraid that I'm a widow, that I'm deprived now
of the greatest man who ever lived.

LEADER Wait,   *what if not a widow, yet*
        quiet,   *deprived ?*
            doomed
        or not doomed, no more
        words: someone
            with a wreath: that's joy.

Enter MESSENGER.

MESSENGER Queen Deianeira. Your humble servant, madam,
        but with the news to liberate you from your unhappiness.
        Not only is Herakles alive, he's won his war
        and is bringing back spoils to give the gods.

DEIANEIRA What are you saying, old man?   180

MESSENGER That your hero husband will be home soon,
        by your side, more powerful than ever.

DEIANEIRA Who told you that?

MESSENGER In the pasture, you know, where they take the oxen
        in the summer? Lichas, the herald, is telling everyone.
        As soon as I heard, I ran ahead to be the first   *desire for*
        to tell you. I thought you might give me
        a reward or at least your gratitude.   *Compensation*

DEIANEIRA If it's such good news, why isn't Lichas here himself?
                                                      challenge
MESSENGER Why? Madam, it wouldn't be easy.   190
        All the people have got him cornered, asking questions
        and he can't move. They want to know
        what's happened and they won't pass him on
        until they do. He wants to come. They just won't let him.
        But you'll see yourself. He'll be here soon.

123

DEIANEIRA O Zeus...your sacred meadows...the grass...Oita...
It had to be so long, but now, finally...finally...
All right, you, women, inside; you, out here, now,
everyone, cry out...Sing!...We are so glad. This
is beyond...the light of it...beyond...hope...joy!   200

*ignores the
person of the
messenger*

> The CHORUS, *arms raised, dances.*

CHORUS   SOAR!
                    LET THIS
                        HOUSE SOAR!
                HEARTH-
                    CRIES! HOUSE-
                        CRIES! ALTAR!
                The house!
                    The husband—
                        hungry house,
                let it
                    SOAR!
                        Men!
                To Apollo
                    soar!
                        His brilliant
                arrow! Women! The healing,
                    the healing-hymn, Apollo!
                        Healing!
                The hymn!
                    Soar!
                        Virgins!
                And for the
                    Sown-with-
                        him!
                The Sister!
                    Artemis!
                        Buck-
                Striker!   210
                    Double-
                        struck!

And the neighbor
     bride-
          nymphs!   *both*

Their dance grows more and more abandoned. Enter
LICHAS, IOLE, *and the* CAPTIVES. *All but* LICHAS *are*
dishevelled, downcast.

CHORUS   Now watch
                   this! Watch
                        this have me!
                I'm letting it
                   have me!
                     It has
                me! Look!
                   Soaring! ME!
                      Can't think!
                JOY! ME!
                   Garlands!
                        Now! The intoxicated
                now!
                   It's spinning!   *spinning*
                      Whirling!
                RIGHT!
                   RIGHT
                      HEALER!
                LOOK!
                   WOMAN!
                      ANGEL!
                WHAT'S
                   CONFRONTING
                      YOU! RIGHT NOW!
                LOOK! IT'S   220
                   APPEARING!
                      APPEARING!

DEIANEIRA Here they are. Women, look:
          could my eyes' look-out ever miss this march?

Wonderful, Lichas! Welcome! You took so long for someone
bringing joy... That is the right word, joy?

LICHAS It's good to be back and good to hear you welcome us,
Queen Deianeira. Your words suit your husband's triumph —
they are the right ones.

DEIANEIRA Wonderful man, tell me:
do I get Herakles back, alive?

LICHAS You do. I left him alive,   230
in good health, flourishing.

DEIANEIRA Where? Here or somewhere else?

LICHAS At Cape Kenaion, by the cliff. Consecrating
altars to his father Zeus and sacrificing.

DEIANEIRA Why? Is it only a vow he's fulfilling
or is there a prophecy?

LICHAS   A vow he made.

Before he took his spear against the country of these women.

DEIANEIRA And whose daughters are they... sad things?
Lord, unless I'm wrong, they should be pitied.

LICHAS They're Herakles' captives. He picked them out, for himself   240
and the gods, when he sacked Eurytos' city.

DEIANEIRA Is that the same war that kept him gone
until I couldn't count the days?

LICHAS It wasn't only that. Most of the time he was a captive
in Lydia, and not just a captive, and he admits
this himself, but a bought slave. Don't be upset
about the word "slave," though: it was god's work.
As I said, he admits he spent that year
in slavery to Omphale, the barbarian woman.

126

vengeance
trickery

But he was so furious about being disgraced that way   250
that he swore when his turn came he'd make a slave
himself out of the man who'd made it happen,
and out of the man's wife and child, too.
And he meant it. When he was finally freed,
he hired an army and went to Eurytos' city
because he said Eurytos was the only human being
who'd had any part in his misfortune. He'd been
Herakles' friend and when Herakles came to his house
and beat his sons at archery, he mocked him.
"My sons still could whip you … It was those damned,   260
magical arrows of yours, not you."
And then he called him a slave. "You're a slave,"
he said, "a free-man's lick-foot, and broken-down besides."
Then had him kicked out of the house
after dinner when he was drunk. That hurt.
Which must be why when Iphitos, one of the sons,
came to Tiryns one day looking for horses
and was thinking about something else, Herakles
took him and threw him from the tower. But Zeus,
Father of us all, King, wouldn't stand for him   270
killing by deceit that way,
even if it was the only time he did it. So he had him sold.
Bondage. Slavery. It wasn't the killing,
but the guile. If he'd done it openly, Zeus
would have pardoned the vengeance and called it justice,
victory. Anyway, the big-mouths, they're all in Hell
and their city's the slave now. These are their women,
pitiful, yes. They've lost the life they had
and here they are, with you. That's what your husband
wanted and, dependable, it's what I've done.   280
He'll be here soon himself, I'm sure. When he finishes
the sacrifices to his father. Of all my good news,
that must be the part that makes you happiest.

LEADER Queen …

     your joy …

     part

himself!

lie?

insult

justification

affect on Deianeira
not addressed
exile

127

here, the rest
   promised...
     on the way...

         DEIANEIRA *approaches the* CAPTIVES.

DEIANEIRA Of course. Isn't it just and right to rejoice
    in my husband's successes? God knows, I have reason to.
    The response should match the outcome, shouldn't it?
    Still, someone who thinks carefully about it
    might be afraid that someone's luck could turn   290
    and bring him to his knees. Friends, I feel
    so strangely sorry for these miserable orphans, homeless
    and fatherless in a foreign place. Women like this,
    they might have been rich men's daughters
    and now...slaves, Zeus, Tide-Turner,
    I hope you never touch a child of mine
    and if you do, let it be when I'm dead.
    That's what I'm afraid of, looking at these women.

    (*to* IOLE)

    You: who are you, poor woman? A virgin? A mother?
    You look so innocent...are you a princess?   300
    Lichas, whose daughter is this one?
    Who are her mother and father? Tell me...
    there's something about her...I feel sorrier
    for her than the rest. She seems to know
    what's in store for her.

LICHAS Why ask me? How should I know? Maybe
    she's not the lowest of them, I don't know.

DEIANEIRA Could she be royal? Did Eurytos have a daughter?

LICHAS I don't know. I didn't ask.

DEIANEIRA And you didn't hear her name from the others?   310

read out loud

LICHAS No, nothing. I didn't go into it.

DEIANEIRA Poor thing.

(*to* IOLE)

                    If not Lichas, won't you tell me?
                    It's ridiculous not to know who you are.

LICHAS It would be something if she talked now.
       Let me tell you. Since we left, she hasn't said
       a word, she just goes on and on moaning like an animal
       about her disaster. The wind that raked us
       on our way says more than she does.
       It's hard for her, her silence is forgivable.

DEIANEIRA Let her alone, then. She has enough pain.   320
          I won't give her more. If it's what she wants,
          she doesn't have to talk. Come, we'll go inside,
          then you can start back when you want to.

          LICHAS *and the* CAPTIVES *enter the palace.* DEIANEIRA *is
          about to follow them but the* MESSENGER *touches her arm.*

MESSENGER Wait! I have to tell you something.
          You ... not them ...

          (*Indicating* LICHAS *and the women*)

          D.'s thoughts elsewhere?

                    Let them go ahead.
          I know things. You don't. You don't know anything
          because nobody's told you anything and you should.

DEIANEIRA What are you doing? Get out of my way.   *refusal*

MESSENGER Wait, listen. You liked my first story,
          maybe you'll like the next one better.   330

129

DEIANEIRA Should I call the others back? Or is what
he already told her you have to say only for my friends and me?

(*She indicates the* CHORUS)

MESSENGER You and them. Forget the rest.

DEIANEIRA They're gone now. Explain yourself.

MESSENGER That man, Lichas. He wasn't telling the truth
just now. Either that or he was lying before.

DEIANEIRA What are you saying? Don't give me riddles.
Tell me what you know.

MESSENGER I heard that same Lichas saying before—
and there were witnesses—that it was because of the girl   340
that Herakles destroyed Eurytos and his city.
If there was a god involved, it was Love
Love who fired him into making that war, Love,
not whatever happened in Lydia or being Omphale's slave
or killing Iphitos, however he did do it.
There's no Love in the story now, though,
is there? Supposedly, when Herakles
couldn't talk the father into giving him the girl
as his whore, he invented a pretext,
treachery some petty complaint, and went to war against her country—   350
Eurytos ruled there, that much is true—
and murdered him and looted the city.
Look yourself. He doesn't casually send the girl
ahead with just anyone . . . and not to be a slave, don't
think that for a moment. He wouldn't dream of it,
not when he's on fire for her.
I thought I'd better tell you what I heard back there,
Queen Deianeira. There were a lot of others
who could convict him along with me;
he said it right in the main square of Trachis.   360
If what I say isn't welcome, I'm sorry.
cf. 329–30 But it's the truth, the whole truth, nothing but.

lying is greatest treachery

DEIANEIRA O my god. What's happening to me?
Have I been stabbed? What kind of thing
have I brought under my roof? My god.
He swore she doesn't have a name. Does she?

MESSENGER Yes, she's royal. In birth and name.
She's Eurytos' daughter and her name was Iole.
Lichas didn't know... remember? He never asked?

LEADER All the treachery   370
there is,
forget,
compared to the monster
who degrades himself
lying!

doesn't know
DEIANEIRA Women... Friends... What should I do?   *what to do*
I'm paralyzed... Tell me what to do!

LEADER Lichas:
force him: make
him answer.
Maybe
he'll give you what   *which means what?!*
you want.   *hope?*
                                      pain?
DEIANEIRA I will. You're right. I will.

MESSENGER What about me? Do I wait, or what?

Enter LICHAS *from palace.*

DEIANEIRA You stay. He's coming out of the house
on his own. I don't have to send for him.

LICHAS Deianeira, is there any message you want   380
to give to Herakles? I'm leaving now.

131

DEIANEIRA It took you so long to arrive and here you are
rushing off and we've hardly spoken.

LICHAS Is there more? Ask anything.

DEIANEIRA If I do, you'll give me the truth?

LICHAS I swear, by Zeus. Everything I know.

DEIANEIRA Then who's that woman you brought here?

LICHAS She's from Euboia. I don't know her family.

MESSENGER Hey, you, Lichas! Look at me. Who are you talking to?

LICHAS Who's this? How dare you speak like that to me?   390

MESSENGER Never mind. You understood. Just answer.

LICHAS To the royal Deianeira. Unless I'm seeing things.
Oineus' daughter, Herakles' wife: my Queen.

MESSENGER That's what I wanted you to say. Your Queen, right?

LICHAS Of course, my Queen. Just as it should be.

MESSENGER Aha! What kind of *just*-ice should you suffer then
if I can prove you're being unjust to her?

LICHAS Injustice? What is this nonsense?

MESSENGER Nothing. You're the one who's talking nonsense.

LICHAS I'm leaving. I was a fool   400
to listen to you in the first place.

MESSENGER No, you don't. Not till you answer one short question.

LICHAS All right, what is it? You'll tell me anyway.

MESSENGER That girl you brought, the slave. You know
who I mean?

(LICHAS *glances toward the palace*)

LICHAS   Of course, well?

MESSENGER Yes, right, that one back in there, the one you didn't know.
Didn't you say before... didn't you say
that she was Iole, Eurytos' daughter?

LICHAS Said where? Show me a witness who'll testify   *deny*
to that, that he heard such a thing.   410

MESSENGER A lot of people heard you. In the square
at Trachis. The whole crowd.

*redefine
truth*

LICHAS   Now, wait.
That's what I *said* I *heard*. But that was an opinion.
It's not the same as accuracy. Not strictly.

MESSENGER Strictly! Didn't you swear you brought her here
to marry Herakles?

LICHAS   Me? Marry?
For god's sake, Queen, who is this man?

*divert attention
who is this
man?!*

MESSENGER Somebody who heard you say with your own lips
that Eurytos' city was destroyed out of love
for that girl. It wasn't the woman in Lydia   420
but Herakles' passion for the girl.

LICHAS Madam, get rid of this person. How can a sane man
argue with a lunatic?

DEIANEIRA Now, I'm going to beg you. In the name of Zeus,
of his bolts blasting the grass on his mountain Oita,
don't cheat me of my answer. Listen to me.

The woman you're talking to doesn't hold grudges.
I know what goes on with men, how things change,
how hearts change. The man's insane who tries to face
Love down, to go to blows with Love. Even the gods—   430
Love does what it wants to, even to them.
Do you think I'd expect a weak woman, me or anyone else,
to resist Love? I'd have to be mad to blame my husband
if he's sick for this girl. Or her. She can't hurt me.
Can I blame her? Never, impossible.
But if Herakles taught you to lie to me,
then you were low. And if you thought of it yourself
to keep from hurting me, you're lower still,
you're hurting me more. Just tell me the truth.
The brand of liar isn't worthy of you.   440
If you're thinking I won't find out what's happened,
don't. Too many heard who'll tell me anyway.
Are you afraid? That's absurd. *Not* to know,
that would cause me pain!
What's so terrible in knowing? Herakles
has loved more women than I can count—
did one of them ever have harsh words from me?
And neither will this one, no matter how
he's burning up for her. As soon as I saw her,
I felt compassion. As helpless and innocent   450
as she is and her beauty has still ruined her life
and enslaved her father's country. But all that's
waves in the wind, now. You, though: you lie
to someone else if you're going to lie, but not to me!

LEADER She speaks
        well,
             you'd do
        well
           to listen. You won't be
           sorry. We'll thank you, too.

LICHAS Deianeira … all right. I see you think
        the way we humans have to. We're weak.

134

I'll give you the truth, all of it.   *not a rumor?*
It's just the way that one said it was.   460
Herakles' soul was driven through with desire
for the girl and he did do it because of her—   *cf. Helen*
take his spear and go up against her father's city
and level it.
              But I have to be fair and tell you
that he never hid a thing and never asked
me to, either. I didn't want to hurt you,
so if there's a fault that way, it's mine.

Now you know what's been going on
but for your sake as much as for his,
let the girl be. Don't ever take back   470
what you said about her. His strength
has won so much for him but his passion   *out of control*
for this girl is more than he can master.

DEIANEIRA I realize. Don't trouble yourself.
I'm not going to make myself sick
fighting futile battles with gods.
Come, we'll go in. I'll tell you what message
to take to Herakles and give you gifts for him.
It wouldn't do to go back empty-handed
when you brought so much marching in.   480

Exit LICHAS *and* DEIANEIRA *into the palace. Exit* MESSENGER.

CHORUS   Some gigantic power,
                            huge, is what
                              Love, Love's goddess,   *Love*
                          Love, always seems
                            to wrench, always,
                              from carnage.   *carnage*
                          I won't tell
                            about the
                              gods, not

135

them, how even they,
  with love, the gods, how
    even Zeus, Father
of Fathers, was taken
  in
    by her,
and Death,
  even
    he, Death
who owns night, even
  he was taken
    in by her
and even the whole
  earth, the
    Breaker...
But who was it,
  who,
    when they wanted this
woman, who was it   490
  who both
    went into combat, both,
heroes,
  into blows,
    heroes, the
grime, to
  the end, the final
    finish?

One was a river,
  Acheloös
    gigantic,
horns high!
  Power! Appearing!
    Power!
Disappearing!
  The bull, power, the
    brute! And the other,
Theban, from the

Acheloös
Herakles

wine-country,
    bow-cocked,
spear, club-
    cocked, the
       breaker,
the son of
    Zeus, all
       his power.
They go in
    to find it, marriage
      in the heart
of it, the battle, and   500
    in it, heart of it, the
      battle, Love,
the goddess Love, the
    decider, her, her choosing
      wand, her wand.
Fist-
    crack! Bow-
      crack!
Then
    bull, then
      beast,
horn-
    crack, the
      swarming, the
confusion and then
    both,
      they were both,
both twisted, both
    strangling,
      groaning, both,
both
    groaning and
      groaning,
their faces
    broken, both,
      broken.

And she, all
   that while, she
     on her hill, in
the far distance, she   510
    gleaming, white,
     all in herself, frail,
she
   waited, waited
     there, husband-
waiting. And I
   can see it, I, and I,
    what I could tell
about that look of
   hers,
    that look, pitiful, they
both wanted, both
   needed, both,
    from her,
waiting, waiting, and
   then, suddenly,
    gone, she, suddenly she,
the calf, the calf torn,
   torn from its mother, bawling, gone,
    alone, lost, alone.

DEIANEIRA *enters from the palace, carrying a black casket*
with a seal.

DEIANEIRA Friends, our guest is still in there
saying goodbye but I had to slip out.
I want to tell you what my hands have done
and I want sympathy, too,   520
    for what I'm suffering.
             A virgin . . . no,
what virgin? A slut, cheap, outrageous trade,
has come into my house to weigh me down and now
we'll all spin under the same blanket.
That's the reward I have from Herakles,
my true, good love, for having taken care

138

of his home through all this miserable time.
Am I angry? I don't know how to be.
He's had the same infection often enough before...
But to have her here! To live with her,   530
to have to share him—can I stand for that?
And she's just blossoming. Men love plucking them
when they're like that. I'm on the path down,
drying up. Do you know what I'm afraid of?
That I'll be calling Herakles husband   *worse*
but that child will be calling him to bed.

                                                not going to be
                                                wife - denial?

But no, I told you, anger is wrong for a wife.
I accept that. And besides,
I have a way to get us out of this.
When I was still a girl, one of the monsters   540
from the old time gave me something that I've kept
sealed in a bronze jar ever since. It was Nessos,
the centaur. I took the life's blood from his wound:
it was his dying present, the hairy animal!
He used to ferry people in his arms across a river;
no boat, no oars, no anything, just him.
When I first left home after my father
married me to Herakles, he was carrying me like that
and when we got to mid-stream, he put his hands on me.
I screamed. Herakles shot an arrow in him,   550
deep, through his chest, to the lungs.
As he was dying, Nessos started to talk to me.
"You're Oineus' daughter, aren't you?" he said.
"Since you're the last person I'll carry across here,
I'm going to give you something. Pay attention.
If you take a handful of the clots from my wound,
from where Herakles stained the arrow
with black poison from the blood of the Hydra,   *true—*
you'll have a love-potion, a drug so strong   *he'll*
that Herakles would never look at another woman." 560 *be*
                                                       dead

Well, I thought of all that now because after he died,
I did it: kept it, locked up, hidden.
And now I've impregnated this robe with it,

exactly the way his last words told me to.

Knows it's evil?

It's done. I hate evil. I don't like
being obvious. I don't even like knowing about it

treachery

and I hate women who are that way...
But in this case, if charms or spells can defeat that girl,
can get Herakles back to me, then I'm ready...
Unless I'm being rash... Do you think so?   570
Say so if you do... I'll stop... I will...

LEADER No, it

what to do?

seems
          all right
to do
   if you think it can
      work.

DEIANEIRA I don't know for sure. He said
it would. I can't tell till I try.

LEADER Then you
      have
         to
try. No
   telling till
      you try.

Enter LICHAS *from palace.*

DEIANEIRA We'll know soon enough. There's the man
coming through the door. He'll be leaving soon.

*how is this
better than
lying?*

Only don't, ever, tell what I'm doing. No matter how shameful 580
what's done in the dark is, at least it stays there.

LICHAS Well, Oineus' daughter, tell me what
I should do. I'm late.

DEIANEIRA I was getting something ready, Lichas,
while you were in there with those strangers.

140

This robe. I want you to take it to my husband
as a gift from me. My own hands wove it.
When you give it to him, I want you to tell him
that he has to be the first to wear it, no one else.
And that it mustn't be seen by the sunlight or   590
the firelight or even the altar-fire until he comes out,
shining, in front of everyone to show it to the gods
when he makes the bull-kill.
I promised myself once that if he came home safe
and sound, I'd wrap him in it
and offer him reverently to the gods
like a newborn child, to be their sacrificer.

sacrifice

Here's my sign, set in the circle of my seal.
He'll recognize it. Now go.
But don't forget this time, you're a messenger,   600
keep out of it, don't meddle.
Do it right. We'll thank you, both of us,
he and I...

don't meddle

LICHAS Don't worry.
I'm not going to fall on my face.
I'll get it to him
and your exact words, too.

*not really
treachery*

DEIANEIRA Goodbye, then. You know how things are
with us here.

LICHAS   Everything's well, I know.
I'll tell him.   610

DEIANEIRA   And you'll tell him
how I greeted the girl, that I welcomed her?

LICHAS I was amazed by that, and moved...yes.

DEIANEIRA There's nothing more. I'm afraid
to say how much I miss him
until I'm sure it's the same there.

fearful

Exit LICHAS, *with the casket.*

CHORUS   O, anyone,
      anyone who lives
       by the harbor, anyone,
    by the rocks,
      the boiling
       streams, the crags;
    who lives
      by Oita, the mountain,
      lives
    by the sea
      that sits in land or by
      the shore
    the Huntress-Goddess   620
      owns,
       the golden-arrowed
    one: you know
      where,
       where the Greeks
    hold council, where
      the gates
      are . . .

    All of you, listen,
      you'll hear
       it soon, soon,
    the flute-voice, the
      life,
       the sweet life-music . . .
    O, gorgeous,
      not the hard, death-
      wail, the
    wailing but sweet,
      godly and soft, like
      strings, strings.
    Because the son
      of the woman
      Alkmene, the son

of Zeus, the god-son, is
   rushing, the hero,
      rushing, huge,
home, rushing
   home,
      with treasure.

He was gone   630
   so long, so
      long disappeared
from here, so
   long, twelve months,
      twelve, waiting.
He spun,
   the sea,
      we knew
nothing, nothing, and
   the darling
      wife, darling
sufferer,
   wretch, the
      heart-torn,
torn ... She ...
   she was perishing, she,
      every moment.
But now!
   Now and now! the stung-
      mad
war-god, now, has let
   it be unleashed, the day,
      the day!

O let him,
   let him get
      here! Here! Let
the oars not
   stop, never
      stop, not

until   640
    he gets
        here, not.
Let him leave
    that island, island-
        fires,
    leave the
        sacrifice he's
            doing
and get here, get
    here, get here,
        here, tamed, finally,
    tamed, soothed, with
        the robe, the ointment,
            soothed, soothed,
love   fused
        with it, the way the
            beast prescribed it.

                    DEIANEIRA *enters from palace.*

misgiving

DEIANEIRA Friends... Everything I did... my act...
        I'm afraid I've gone too far!

LEADER Deianeira,
        Daughter of Oineus,
            What?

DEIANEIRA I don't know, but I have a premonition
        that what I did in good faith is turning evil.   650

LEADER Is it Herakles'
        gift? Is it
            that?

DEIANEIRA Yes, that. Listen to me.
        If you have to act in the dark, don't act.

LEADER Tell us,
    you're afraid . . . of
    what?

DEIANEIRA Without my telling you, you wouldn't dream
    what happened. You couldn't conceive it.
    The thing I used to smear the ointment on the robe,
    a ball of sheep's wool: it vanished!
    And nothing in the house consumed it—it devoured itself,
    wasted and corroded itself on the pavement.   660
    Wait. Let me tell you everything, all of it.
    I didn't leave out anything that beast the centaur,
    as he was writhing and dying with Herakles' arrow
    burning in his side, told me:
    it was bitten into my memory ⎤ *like Herakles'*
    like a law on a bronze tablet. ⎦ *tablet*
    He ordered. I obeyed . . .
    To keep the drug in a dark, secret place
    away from fire, even away from the warmth of sunlight
    so I'd have it fresh when I was ready.   670
    And that's what I did. It was the time.
    Now. I was alone.
    I did the anointing with a tuft of wool
    I pulled from one of our sheep and then I folded
    the robe and put it in a casket
    to be out of the light . . . You saw that . . .
    But when I went back in, I saw—o god,
    how can I believe myself? . . .
    Somehow I happened to throw the used fleece
    into a patch of blazing light—sunlight—   680
    and when it was warm, it shriveled up and fell
    apart on the ground into a kind of powder
    that looked like the dirt a saw cutting wood makes.
    That's still there. But underneath, where it fell,
    clots of hot foam have boiled up
    the way the earth on a grave boils when you pour
    the dark wine of Dionysos on it.
    What can I think now?

I've done something hideous!
That monster: why, in thanks for *what*,   690
should he do kindnesses for me
when his dying was my fault?
O no! He was *lying* to me! *Using* me!
He wanted to get back at his killer.
I understand it now, now, when it's too late,
Unless I'm wrong, it's me, o god, me,
who's going to kill my husband.
Of course! The arrow
that wounded him even hurt Cheiron, and Cheiron
was a god! Whatever living thing it can touch, it kills!   700
And if it's the same poison that oozed black
out of the centaur's wounds,
how can it not kill Herakles? I'm afraid
it will, it will.
                    But I've decided. If he falls,
I go with him. I die, too. How could a woman
who believed in her goodness the way I did
go on living if her name meant infamy?

LEADER You're right
                    to be afraid but
                              don't
                    give
                              away too soon your
                                        hope.

DEIANEIRA If the trying was evil in the first place,   710
                    why keep courage with false hope?

LEADER But they'll
                    believe, you didn't
                              know.
                    Who could be angry when
                              you didn't
                                        know?

DEIANEIRA That's innocence. You did
no evil, what do you know?

Enter HYLLOS.

LEADER You'd better hush...
unless you want your son to know.
He's found his father; they're here.   *they don't know*

HYLLOS Mother, I wanted one of three things when I came here.
That I'd find you dead. That you wouldn't be my mother
anymore. Or that you'd be another person altogether,
with somebody else's heart inside you.   720

DEIANEIRA Hyllos! What have I done to make you hate me?

HYLLOS I'll give you what! The man, your husband, yes,
my father—him—you've slaughtered him!

DEIANEIRA Son, my god, what's coming out of you?

HYLLOS Truth. What has to be.
Who can undo the done?

DEIANEIRA What are you saying, Child? It's monstrous!
On whose authority can you accuse me?

HYLLOS *My* authority! *I* saw it! *My* eyes!
His agony...His fall...   730

DEIANEIRA Where did it happen? Were you by his side?

HYLLOS If you want to know, I'll tell you. All of it.
After he sacked Eurytos' city, he left
with the spoils, the first-fruits of what he'd won.
There's a sea-cliff at Euboia called Cape Kenaion.
He set up altars there and dedicated a grove
of sacred trees to his father, Zeus, and that's

147

where I found him. I loved him then. O I loved him.
Just as he was starting the sacrifice,
Lichas, his own messenger, came   740
and brought your gift, that murderous robe.
And he put it on, the way you said he should,
and began the killing. Twelve giant bulls,
the best he'd won. And more, a hundred
altogether; everything that was brought to the altar,
big and small. And he was so serene at first,
unsuspecting; so proud of that robe, so happy in it.
But when the bloody fires started blazing
with the pine tar and the dripping fat, sweat
suddenly bubbled up on his flesh and the robe embraced him,   750
clung to his sides, at every joint
as though somebody'd soldered it on. And then
a gnawing seemed to start on his bones, convulsing him,
eating at him like venom from a snake.
He shouted for poor Lichas, who'd had nothing to do
with it, and asked him why he'd brought that robe,
what kind of scheme did he have in mind?
But Lichas didn't know anything. He could only say
what you told him to say; that the robe was a gift
from you. When Herakles heard that,   760
a spasm of pain seemed to shoot into his lungs
and he grabbed Lichas by the foot, right
where the ankle pivots in the socket and just
threw him at a rock sticking out of the water.
His head shattered. The brains erupted
through his hair and blood and pieces of the skull.
Everyone in the crowd was shrieking with horror.
One was insane, the other dead,
but nobody dared come near him
because he kept throwing himself onto the ground   770
and leaping, howling and screaming, into the air
until the rocks were ringing from the mountains
at Lokris all the way back to the cliff at Euboia.
But when he couldn't move anymore, when he was too
exhausted with hurling himself

into the dirt and lay there on the ground,
groaning, cursing you, his marriage with you—you, vile!—
and cursing ever dealing with your father and ruining
himself, then he lifted up out of the shrouds
of smoke—his eyes were rolling in his head—   780
and picked me out where I was crying in the crowd.
And called to me. "Son, come here! Don't run away
from my pain. Even if you have to die   ⎤ *selfish*
my death with me, don't. Get me out of here!   ⎦
Put me someplace where I can't be seen,
or if you're too soft for that, at least
take me out of this country so I won't die here."
He didn't have to ask again. We put him
on our ship and brought him, or what was left of him,
the bellowing, the torment, and landed him here.   790
And you'll see him soon, just alive, or just dead.
These are the things, my Mother,
you've plotted, and executed, and been caught at.

I hope punishing justice finds you. I hope the Furies
pay you back. I pray for it and it's right.
I know it's right because you've crushed the right—
you've destroyed the greatest man who ever lived.

DEIANEIRA *starts toward the palace.*

LEADER Don't crawl
            away! Speak! Your
            silence...
        You're pleading
            for the
            prosecution.

HYLLOS Let her crawl! Let a gale blow up   800
        to crawl her out of my sight!
        Mother! The name mother in her—   *refuses her*
        it's a miscarriage.   *role of mother*

149

No, let her crawl off in her rejoicing
to find the same joy she's given my father.

Exit DEIANEIRA *into the palace. Then* HYLLOS.

CHORUS   O children, look, children,
                                       look how suddenly, suddenly,
                                          it's come breaking
                                       on us, the word,
                                          the god
                                          word
                                       out of the old-
                                          time, the prophecy
                                          from the old-time.
                                       It shrieked. It
                                          shrieked that when the twelve
                                          years, the twelve
                                       ploughing-times with   810
                                          them, the turning
                                          over of years, that then
                                       the labor of the son, the
                                          son of Zeus, would
                                          end, and it's
                                       accurate, exact,
                                          it's sailed, crashed,
                                          thundered, in on us.
                                       Because how, how
                                          would the empty-eyed, the see-
                                          nothing,
                                       still have
                                          work, toil
                                          to do,
                                       bondage,
                                          if he's
                                          dead?
                                       Because,
                                          because, if the murderous
                                          cloud, the venomous, clinging,

Comprehension

obscure cloud of
   the centaur-beast's eternal
     venom,
that came from death,
   nursed in the shimmering
    of the serpent,
if that's what
   stings
    him, his sides,
then how will he ever,   820
   ever, see another
    sun than this;
this man, only
   man, fused
    to the spirit
of the Hydra?
   The words
    themselves,
the words of the black-haired
   beast themselves,
    jumbled, obscure,
must seem themselves to
   be prodding, into
    him, boiling him themselves.

And none of this, none
   of it, the poor
    being, the woman, the
relentless, gigantic
   ruin, she saw none, impending
    for her family, none,
the new
   marriage bearing down...
    What would happen? Could
she know what would come
   from the beast-
    word,
the intercourse?

words - poison

O,
      O, she must
be bellowing   830
      with this, groaning
         hideously with
this,
   moaning,
      dissolving,
new tears, the
   dew, pervading,
      new tears...
And DOOM
   is coming
      and DOOM,
revealed, obscure again,
   gigantic,
      ruins... ruins...

An eruption...
   it must be an explosion!
      Hot tears!
An infection
   has poured down
      through the
other, the him, worse
   than any enemy, any, with
      hands, ever inflicted,
worse than anything Herakles
   suffered
      that we would give
pity for. The spear,
   the point,
      gored, victorious,
point, you brought   840
   this
      bride
so quickly
   didn't you? Quickly
      from the mountains

of Oichalia...
and Love...
and Love...
the servant
Love,
the silent, the
obedient, all that time
was the avenger! Maker!
Made these things!

Love ?

*A low, continual groaning is heard from
the palace:* HYLLOS.

LEADER Is that imagination
or
did somebody
groan inside
that house? Is
it pity? What
now? What
can I say now? It's no
illusion...
Another
wail of
misfortune
for that
house. More
Pain.
Look, the   850
old
woman,

The NURSE *enters from the palace.*

her face...
what is she
bringing? News?

NURSE Women...Daughters...the endless sorrow
that gift to Herakles has loosed.

LEADER Talk,
    woman, a new
      calamity?

NURSE Deianeira has disappeared...her last journey...
    without a single step.

LEADER You don't
    mean...not
      death?

NURSE You heard.

LEADER Death? Her?
    Pitiable
      her?

NURSE You heard. Again.   860

LEADER The lost
    soul lost.
      How?

NURSE Horribly. Horribly.

LEADER Woman, tell
    us, how
      did her doom come?

NURSE Her own hand. She finished it herself.

LEADER What rage
    she must have
      had! What frenzy!

NURSE A point. A weapon.

LEADER Alone?
    Death upon death and
      alone?

NURSE Steel. Freezing steel.

LEADER But you were
      there, fool;
         did you stand and watch?

NURSE I was there... I watched... I was there...   870

LEADER How did it happen? How
      did it happen? How
         did...

NURSE Her own hand... herself...

LEADER WHAT?
      WHAT?
      WHAT?

NURSE True.

LEADER The bride, the upstart,
      has given birth to giant
      Fury for this house.

NURSE You're right. If you were there
      to see it, you'd feel the pity even more.

LEADER Hands...
      A woman's hands...
        Could they?

NURSE They could, o yes, awful, yes they could.
      I'll tell. When she came into the house—she was alone—   880
      and saw her son making a litter up
      in the courtyard to bring his father in,
      she hid herself where no one could see her
      and then she fell on the altar, bellowing

that she was alone now, moaning...And when she'd touch
something she used to use, any old domestic thing,
the angel, before all this, she'd cry,
and if she met one of her servants, she'd cry again,
angel again, then cried that she was doomed,
no children anymore, nothing, for all time.   890
Then she suddenly stopped, all of it,
and I saw her rush into Herakles' room—she didn't know
I was watching, she couldn't see me—
and made the bed, her husband's bed,
and fell in it and dissolved in a burst
of brilliant tears. And talked to it.
"Dear bed...my dearest love-bed...Dear room,
      love...
You'll never welcome me again...Goodbye!"
And then was quiet. And with a violent spasm
tore her robe where it was pinned with a gold brooch   900
so that her left side and her arm were bare
and I ran as fast as I could to warn the son
but before we could get there she'd plunged a war-sword
into herself...into the side, where life lives.
The son shrieked when he saw it.
He'd learned from someone in the house, poor child,
but it was too late, that she'd acted
unintentionally,
that she'd only obeyed the word of the beast.
And he knew his rage had made her   910
do the thing. He kneeled, howling,
shattered, and kissed her
on the mouth and lay down side by side with her,
crying that he'd murdered her with slander,
crying again that he had to live his life
with no father and no mother now...an orphan.
And that's where it is inside this house.
Anyone who tries to see two days ahead
or more, is mad.
There's no tomorrow at all   920
until the day we're in is suffered through.

Handwritten margin notes:
- stripped of virginity, now maternity
- she could have saved her
- regret
- time has collapsed

156

Exit NURSE *into the palace. Enter* HYLLOS *from the palace with* SERVANTS *carrying the litter. It is of heavy, rough-hewn wood. The bed-planks, at waist-height, are strewn with skins and hides.* HYLLOS *and the* SERVANTS *exit.*

CHORUS

Who groan for
　　first? Which is the worse disaster?
　　　　Where begin? Misery.
Look, there's
　　one; we're waiting, there's
　　　　another. Pain, waiting, it's the same.
I wish a breeze would come
　　blasting out of the hearth
　　　　to carry me from here.
I'm afraid I'll die
　　of terror, of terror, to suddenly
　　　　look at the son of Zeus,
the giant, because he's coming
　　now, in incurable torment, a wonder
　　　　of unspeakable sorrowing.

Enter HYLLOS, *the* SERVANTS, HERAKLES *on the litter. He is unmoving, eyes closed. An* OLD MAN *is with them.*

It's right here,
　　now, then, what I was crying like
　　　　a nightbird for. Strangers. Coming.
How are they
　　bringing him? Sorrowfully.
　　　　Adoringly. Mournfully.
Silently.
　　Oh, it is he! And he's
　　　　silent. Is he dead? Sleeping?

HYLLOS　O my god.　　　　　　　　　　　　　　　930
　　Father ... my god ... what do I do?
　　Father, where ... my god ... what?

OLD MAN Shush, son. Don't wake up
his pain. It makes him savage.
He looks dead, but he's alive.

HYLLOS This...alive?

OLD MAN Let the sleeper sleep.
Don't wake up his frenzies,
His infection is still roaring.

HYLLOS O no...the weight...   940
I'm the one who'll be mad!

> HERAKLES *wakes, struggles to lift himself. He sees*
> *the statue of Zeus.*

HERAKLES Zeus! God! What place is this? Where am I?
Who are these people watching
this endless torment? I'm destroyed, destroyed!
O the thing again, it's driving teeth in me!

OLD MAN I told you. Didn't I tell you to be quiet,
to let the sleep stay in his eyes?

HYLLOS Am I supposed to stand
and watch...this?

HERAKLES Kenaion...The altar! All my sacrifices!   950
Mine! And you, Zeus! This...
Is this the thanks you give me back?
This agony you've made of me, this outrage?

I wish these damned eyes had never seen you
and never had to see myself this way,
this incurable madness blossoming in me.

Can't somebody sing spells to me?
Lay your hands on? Heal this horror?

[handwritten left margin: thinking more of Herakles or self?]

158

Do you need Zeus to say you can?
It would be a miracle to me.   960

The OLD MAN *tries to prop him up.*

Leave me alone! Let
me be! Let me die!
Alone!

Why are you touching me? Don't
touch me! You're killing me! Killing me!
You've woken up what was asleep!

It has me... Again. It's lunging through.
Where are the Greeks? Ungrateful!
I wore my useless life out
clearing monsters from your woods   970
and seas and where are you now? Somebody
put a sword in me! Set fire to me!

Tear the awful
head
from my abominable body!

OLD MAN You're his son, boy. Give me a hand. He's
too much for me. You're strong.
Your hands can help him more than mine.

HYLLOS I'm trying. My hands are trying.
But I can't make his life forget itself.   980
And neither can anyone. It's Zeus. He's doomed.

HERAKLES Son, where are you? Lift me.
Hold me... O god, what's happening to me?
The thing, again, again, it's pouncing,
lunging in me, leaping, destroying,
this unbelievable plague, this savage agony!

159

O goddess, Pallas, Sister, again, again!
Son, have pity on your father.
Take your knife. No one would blame you. Put it
in my chest. Heal the wild pain your damned mother   990
put there. O god, I'd give anything to see her suffer this,
the same destruction, this, she's given me.

Dear Death, you're God's brother. Do it!
End me! Let the pain sleep! Quick! Give me doom!

LEADER A great Lord
    to hear cry. What pain
    must have him! Huge!

HERAKLES It's torment even to speak of the sufferings
these hands have labored through; the hot, awful loads
on this back. But nothing Zeus' wife
or that contemptible slavedriver, Eurystheus,
ever made me do was anything to what the beautiful,   1000
two-faced daughter of Oineus has woven me in,
this net of Furies, this mutilation.
It's nailed in me... It's eaten to inside me...
It's moved in... Sucking my lungholes,
all my good blood is swallowed. Its coils
have wasted everything, my body, all my meat.
No one, no hero I ever fought, not even the horde
of giants born of the earth nor any monstrous,
savage animal could do it... and no Greeks either,
and not another place... Not anyone, from anywhere   1010
I ever purified, could do what she, a weak,
meaningless woman, without a sword, with nothing, by
        herself,
has done to me, defeated, conquered me, completely.
Son, if you are my son and not your mother's boy,
give me that woman, give me that dam of yours.
Take your hands. Put her in my hands.
I want to know which hurts you more... Me,
like this, my agony, or her, when I make her suffer
the punishment she deserves to suffer.

160

[Handwritten margin notes:]
Caught in net
Weaving — ? craft

Put down ♀ because she has thoroughly defeated him

wants to kill
Deianeira, wants Hyllos to help

hyper-male

Go on, boy. Don't be a coward. Pity me.   1020
Anyone else would. Look at me,
moaning, bellowing like a wispy girl. Nobody
ever saw me like this before . . . never,
no matter where my damned luck took me.

Look! The hero!
All that time I was a woman!

Come here . . . closer . . . I'll show you your father.
I'll show you what's been done to me.
Look, under the cover, here . . . LOOK! ME! LOOK!

body

EVERYONE! . . . My muscles . . . ruined, pitiful . . .   1030
      Look again . . .
O DESTROYED!

Pain! Fire! The torment! Another time! Again,
wait, again, it's coming, I have to fight it,
that cruel, that eating in my sides, eating, eating . . .
O Lord down in the dark of Hell, take me now!
Give me fire, Zeus! Blast your bolts down! KING! KING!
Here, Father, my head, here. The thing's
consuming me, it's blossoming, festering . . .

body

O hands, my hands . . . Shoulders . . . Chest . . .
            My arms . . .
Is it still you? Did I really kill the man-eating lion   1040
in Nemea with you? No one else could come close,
no less strangle it. And the Hydra
from Lerna, you tamed that. And that din
of double-creatures, monstrosities, half-men, half-horse,
who spoke to no one and had no law but violence
and power? And the wild boar of Erymanthos
and the three-headed whelp of the Viper, horrible,
who lived under the earth, in Hell, unconquerable,
and the dragon guarding the golden fruit
at the end of the world, him too.   1050
And all the innumerable others.
These hands: no one ever triumphed over them.

161

And now I'm broken. Pieces. Waste.
And by what? I can't see it! It's invisible!
ME! Whose mother everyone says was the noblest of all.
ME! They said my father was Zeus himself, King of
    Heaven...

But let me tell you this: I might be nothing,
paralyzed in nothingness, but the one who did this
will know these hands, what they can do: give me her!
I have a message she can take back to the world: 1060
I punished evil when I was alive
and I punished it when I was dead.

LEADER O Greece! What will you do
    without this man...
    Mourn... Mourn...

HYLLOS Father, while you're quiet, let me speak.
As sick as you are, I have to tell you something.
Try to control your rage for a moment.
Otherwise you'll never understand
that vengeance wouldn't bring you joy,
that your bitterness is useless.

HERAKLES If you have something to say, say it.   1070
I'm in too much pain to have you riddling.

HYLLOS I want to tell you about my mother. What happened.
The mistake she made. It was unintentional.

HERAKLES Damn you... You'd breathe her name to me?
Your mother, who killed your father?

HYLLOS The way she is, she needs more than silence.

HERAKLES Oh, you're right. She does. She does.

HYLLOS And what she did today, that needs it, too.

HERAKLES Go ahead. But don't betray me.

HYLLOS She's dead. Just now. Slaughtered.   1080

HERAKLES Who killed her? What an awful miracle!

HYLLOS Nobody killed her. She did it herself.

HERAKLES O god, I wish I'd done that. She needed me for that!

HYLLOS If you knew the rest, you wouldn't rage this way.

HERAKLES A good start. Now, what are you saying?

HYLLOS This: she made a mistake. But she meant well.

HERAKLES Meant? Damn. Meant well, to kill your father?

HYLLOS She thought it was a love-charm she was sending.
When she heard about your new marriage. That was the
    mistake.

HERAKLES Who could you get a drug that strong from here?   1090

HYLLOS It was Nessos, the centaur. In the old time.
He told her it would make you want her.

HERAKLES THAT!
        THAT!
            THAT!
            The agony. I'm lost!
Finished! FINISHED! My light—it's over now.
I understand it now, my end; I'm there.

Come here, Son. You have no father anymore.
Go call your family. Call my mother,
too: she slept with Zeus for nothing.

I want to give you all the oracles I know,
now, before I die.   1100

HYLLOS Alkmene isn't here, and neither are your children.
But there are enough of us
to do anything you could want. Just ask.

HERAKLES Then listen to what you have to do.
This is your chance to prove you're a man,
that you're the son of Herakles.
A long time ago, my father
prophesied that I wasn't going to die at the hands
of anything that breathed: something
would have to come from Hell to take me.   1110
And it's come true. I've been murdered by that brute
centaur: the dead kill the living, the holy promise.

Now listen again. In the mountains there are people
who still sleep on the ground, the Selloi.
They have an oak of my father's in their grove
and it speaks. No matter what your language is,
it speaks to you. It told me other things —
I even wrote them down — and they confirm the first.
This, now, the time we're living now,
is when I should have been released from labor.   1120
I thought it meant I'd prosper but it doesn't:
it means I die, that's all. The dead don't toil.

Son, look, it's
        revealed, look,
            everything, converging,
        clear, brilliant,
            look, all of it, LOOK!
                LOOK!

I need your help now. Don't make me be angry
to convince you. Just say yes, and do it.

164

I won't suffer, I'll keep my word.

You ought to know at your age that obedience
to the father is the most important law.

HYLLOS Yes, father. I'm afraid of where you're taking us,
but yes, I'll do what you say.   1130

HERAKLES Then give me your hand. Your right hand.

HYLLOS An oath? Why?

HERAKLES Give it! Now! Mind me!

HYLLOS There . . . Here . . . Anything you want.

HERAKLES Swear. On the head of Zeus. Swear. My father's head.

HYLLOS Swear what? Tell me that at least.

HERAKLES To do the thing I ask.

HYLLOS I swear. I will. In the name of Zeus.

HERAKLES And pray to suffer if you violate it.

not possible

HYLLOS I won't suffer. I'll keep my word.   1140

HERAKLES Do you know the summit of Oita, Zeus' mountain?

HYLLOS Yes, I've sacrificed at the great altar.

HERAKLES You have to take me there.
Get all the friends you need
but I want you, your own hands, to carry me.
Then cut logs from the hardest oaks you can find
and tough, gnarled branches from olive trees.
Then put me on them. Then take a flaming torch
and set it on fire.
                    And no mourning,

no crying or carrying on. You're my son.   1150
And if you don't do it, all of it, you'll have my fury
and my curse, even from the next world, for all time.

curse

HYLLOS What are you doing, Father? What are you asking me?

HERAKLES What has to be. And if you won't,
then get another father, I won't have you.

paternity denied

HYLLOS My god! Do you know what you're saying?
I'd be your murderer! Your blood would be on me!

HERAKLES Not murderer... healer... doctor...
Only you can cure this evil.

HYLLOS I heal your flesh by burning it?   1160

HERAKLES If you're afraid of that, at least the rest.

HYLLOS I'll take you to Oita. I can do that much.

(Philoctetes will light the fire)

HERAKLES And make the pyre the way I told you?

HYLLOS Not with my own hands, but I'll have it done.
Everything else, yes. I won't stop you.

HERAKLES That's enough. More than enough.
Now one other little favor.

HYLLOS Of course. Anything you ask.

HERAKLES Do you know the girl... Eurytos' daughter?

HYLLOS Iole.   1170

HERAKLES Yes. This is what I want, Son:
after I'm dead, if you want to honor me
and honor your promises and not disobey,
then marry her. I don't want anyone else

marry Iole

166

Hyllos struggles

being with her. She was mine, she slept with me.
I want you and her together, married. Say yes.
You've been obedient about so much that's important,
don't lose my good grace over something less.

asshole

HYLLOS   You don't get angry with someone who's sick,
but how can I stand listening to him, to this?   1180

HERAKLES   You won't do what I ask?

not 9's fault

HYLLOS   Who in the world... the woman whose fault it is
that my mother's dead and that you're *this*...
if someone wasn't swarming with avenging Furies,
would they choose her? Father, I'd be better off dead
with you than living with our bitterest enemy.

HERAKLES   He won't carry out my dying wish, it seems.
You'll see:
the gods will curse your disobedience.

HYLLOS   Tell me to do it now because you're sick.   1190

HERAKLES   I am! You're stirring up my pain again!

HYLLOS   What can I do? I'm trapped!

HERAKLES   Why shouldn't you be? You don't honor your father!

HYLLOS   Do I have to learn to do wrong, Father?

HERAKLES   It isn't wrong. Not if it gives me joy.

HYLLOS   Are you commanding it? Are you calling it right?

HERAKLES   I command it. Before the gods, I'm commanding it.

HYLLOS   Then I have to do it.

makes it ok?

As long as the gods know it's your doing.
Who could call it wrong, obeying my father?   1200

167

HERAKLES Finally. Good. No more words now.
Just the favor. Get me on that fire.
Don't let the pain bend me again.
Quick. Lift me up. It's true. My labors are over.
This is the end, the last and final end of Herakles.

HYLLOS Nothing's preventing it, Father.
You're commanding us. You're making us do it.

HERAKLES Soul, be hard now! Don't let the sickness start you
again. Put the steel bit in your teeth, weld it there,
clamp your lips on it, stone against stone.   1210
No tears.
I want the finish of this welcome, unwelcome work
to be joy.

> As HYLLOS *speaks, the* SERVANTS *lift the litter
> with* HERAKLES *and begin to exit.*

HYLLOS Lift him. Grant me forgiveness for what I'm doing.
But the gods, let their ruthlessness in this,
their cruelty, be remembered.
They have their children, us. We call them Father.
And they can bear to see such suffering.
No one knows the future, but there is a present
and the present is shame for them   1220
and mourning for us, and for the victim, pain;
solitude and pain.

(*to the* LEADER OF THE CHORUS)

Girl, leave that house.
You've seen dying, dreadful, and agony today
and hideous suffering and nothing is here,
nothing,
none of all of it, that is not Zeus.

> *Exit* HYLLOS, *following his father. Exit the* CHORUS.

> *Night.*

NOTES

1 / 1 *The palace of Keyx*... The manuscripts of Greek tragedy contain no stage
directions. We have been sparing in our reconstruction. In the original
production all performers were male and masked. Since the Greek
tragedians were allotted, in addition to a chorus, only three actors for
the performance of all speaking parts, it is probable that both Deianeira
and Herakles were played by the most accomplished of the three, the
protagonist appointed by the state. It is impossible to assess what effect, if
any, this conventional doubling of roles, so intriguing in terms of
twentieth-century psychology, exercised upon an ancient audience.

10 / 9 *Acheloös* Herakles' combat with this creature was a popular subject in ancient
literature and art. In order to magnify the importance of Deianeira in the
episode Sophocles omits reference to what seems to have been its
traditional center of interest—the Horn of Amalthaia, a magic cornuco-
pia, which Herakles carried away as his principal prize of victory.

14 / 11 *shimmering* The first occurrence of *aiolos*, one of the play's key words. The
adjective appears thrice hereafter (94 / 94; 132 / 132; 818 / 834) and is
found only twice elsewhere in all Sophocles' preserved work. The Greek
word evokes a complexity of associations, but primarily a sense of swift
mutability, sometimes from inertia to motion, sometimes from darkness
to light. When applied to human fortune and human behavior, however,
it has particularly unsettling implications of impermanence, unreliabil-
ity, and deception. Thus Aeschylus refers to the "mutable misfortunes
of men" (*ta aiol' anthrōpōn kaka, Suppliants* 328), Solon to the "shifty
speech of tyrants" (*epos aiolon,* Frg. 10.7), and Pindar to Odysseus'

capacity for the "shifty lie" (*aiolon pseudos, Nemean* 8.25). For additional comment, cf. the Introduction, I.

41 / 38 *He killed poor Iphitos* Cf. the Introduction, IV, and the note on **244–323**.

42–43 / 40 *people / we hardly know* By this vague reference to anonymous hosts Sophocles glancingly nods at the tradition which set the scene of this story at the palace of Keyx, king of Trachis. Elsewhere he ignores the dramatically inconvenient fact that Herakles and Deianeira are merely guests at the house where the action centers. All that follows creates and sustains the illusion that the palace and the loyalties of the local Chorus belong solely to the hero and his wife.

56 / 54 *so many children* Extant ancient tradition records four offspring of the Herakles-Deianeira marriage in addition to Hyllos. Here and in a passing reference at the end of the play (**1101 / 1153**) Sophocles acknowledges the existence of these siblings. The pre-eminence given throughout the play to Hyllos' filial role is crucial to some of the tragedy's most powerful effects, isolating the son in his suffering and preparing for the suggestive father-son parallelism noted in the Introduction, V.

61 / 61 *Enter* HYLLOS, *returning, . . . running* It is puzzling that Sophocles fails to provide Hyllos' running entrance with the explicit motivation commonly found in the other plays. The suggestion has been made that he rushes in to report fresh news about Herakles' Oichalian campaign. This seems unlikely; for neither does Hyllos behave like other Sophoclean "messengers," nor is he treated as one by the other characters on stage. More probably the vigorous mode of his entrance is intended to strike an effective contrast with the remarkably static pose struck by the passive Deianeira. Our stage direction is intended only to emphasize the necessity for a director to give some visible logic to an entrance which otherwise might strike an audience as somewhat absurd. Some such measure was surely taken by Sophocles in the original production.

71 / 70 *a woman . . . he ploughed* Lichas later (**248–49 / 252–53**) identifies this woman as Omphale. In the context of Deianeira's recent Herakles-farmer simile (**34–36 / 32–33**), the reference to "ploughing" (literally: "he has been toiling . . . throughout the past ploughing season") suggests a touch of Sophoclean irony. Deianeira will soon discover that her farmer-husband has indeed been laboring in another woman's "field." The Chorus later reveals (**810 / 825**) that Zeus' oracle also measured the hero's destiny by "ploughing-times." For the same metaphor, common in Greek, cf. *Oedipus Tyrannus* 1497.

94–139 / 94–140 Parodos

100 / 100 the sea-pit Probably the straits separating Greece from Asia Minor.

101 / 101 the doubled continents Precisely what vista the poet intends to evoke remains unclear. A reference to Europe and Asia is usually assumed. Others have seen an allusion to the Pillars of Herakles, which mark the Mediterranean's western outlet between Africa and Spain. This gives a more impressive sweep to the Chorus' vision.

105 / 105 like the blinded bird This may be intended to suggest no more than the picture of a bird lamenting the loss of nestlings, one of the commonplace sorrow-images of Greek tragedy. There may, however, also be a hint of the nightingale's eternal sorrow, a theme which, though no less shopworn, is particularly appropriate to Deianeira's case. Greek myth identified the nightingale with Prokne, who was driven by the discovery of her husband's infidelity to destroy her son, thereby condemning herself to ceaseless lamentation.

116 / 116–17 seed of Kadmos Geographically but not genetically accurate. Herakles was born at Thebes, of which Kadmos was the founder and first ruler, but he possessed no blood connection with the Kadmean line.

140–480 / 141–496 First episode

156 / 158 covenants A radical departure from the traditional interpretation of the word which Sophocles has written here. That word, *ksunthemata*, literally denotes objects of mutual agreement. The prevailing view is that the reference here is to the conventional symbols of writing, i.e., the letters of the alphabet. This specific usage, however, is unparalleled elsewhere in Greek literature, nor does the occasional application of the word to "codes" and "passwords" point in that direction; for such agreements imply elements of personal involvement and conscious consent, whereas the alphabet is merely a convention to which one is born, automatically accepted without any sense of voluntarily entering into an act of accord with all men of letters. We cannot, therefore, believe that Sophocles intended to write anything as otiose as "a tablet inscribed with the letters of the alphabet." A more reliable guide to his meaning is his own use of the word to denote compacts of a personal nature at the only two places where it appears elsewhere in his work. Both belong to *Oedipus at Kolonos*, where mention is made of a mysterious covenant between the hero and God (46) and of an agreement struck between Theseus and Perithöos in preparation for their descent to the Underworld (1594). For the implications of Sophocles' use of the word in Deianeira's speech, cf. the Introduction, V.

168–69 / 171–72 *sacred oak /. . . dove-priestesses* This venerable oracular shrine was originally consecrated to Zeus. By Sophocles' time Dione, an earth-mother figure, and Aphrodite, Zeus' daughter by Dione, were also worshipped there. Consultants of the oracle were brought before Zeus' sacred oak. Local priestesses divined the sense of the god's response from the movements of its leaves and branches and articulated the message for visitors. Why these priestesses were called "doves" is not clear, though it is probable that the term was to some extent connected with the prominence of doves in Aphrodite's cult.

174–75 / 178–79 *Wait. . . joy* Throughout the translation, lines belonging to the Leader of the Chorus have been subdivided into three descending units in order to maintain conformity with the typography of the passages spoken by the Chorus as a whole. In the case of the Leader's lines, however, this triadic arrangement is intended to imply neither the presence of lyrics in the original nor the necessity for each descending unit to be spoken by a different voice. In the Greek the Leader, except for one brief lapse into lyrics (see the note on 855–56), expresses herself in the regular iambic rhythms of spoken dialogue.

175 / 179 *a wreath* It seems to have been the custom for Greek messengers to wear garlands when bearing good news. Kreon, arriving from Delphi at the beginning of *Oedipus*, also wears a wreath.

196 / 200 *Oita* This is the first of four mentions of the mountain famous as the site of Herakles' self-immolation and apotheosis; cf. 425 / 436, 618 / 635, 1141 / 1191. For the importance of these references to the creation of false expectation in the audience, cf. the Introduction, V.

201–20 / 205–24 A brief choral song that responds directly to Deinaira's request for a joyful song to celebrate the good news she has just heard. This kind of lyric interlude within an episode is known as *hyporchema*, literally a dance song.

210 / 214 *double-struck* Literally: "double-fired"; she carries torches in both hands.

211 / 215 *neighbor bride-nymphs* In Greek the same word (*numphos*) serves to denote both "nymph" and "bride." Both senses have been asserted in the translation in order to preserve the ironic ambiguity of the original. The Chorus invokes the Nymphs of the Trachinian neighborhood; immediately a "bride" appears close at hand. It is Iole.

222 / 225–26 *look-out . . . march* Deianeira's use of military metaphor is another twist of Sophoclean irony. She will soon discover that Iole's arrival does in fact constitute a dangerous invasion. The metaphor of the "march" is repeated in the last line of this scene (480 / 496).

244–323 / 248–334 *It wasn't only that . . . / . . . when you want to* It is impossible to communicate to a modern audience the interplay of tensions with which Sophocles has charged this scene of deception. The Greek spectators, despite the poet's uncharacteristic failure to forewarn them of the herald's deceitful intent, were instantly alerted to his duplicity by their own familiarity with the traditional outlines of the story. They must have guessed at once the identity of the bedraggled princess whose absence from Lichas' narrative is no less conspicuous than her presence in the theater; and they must have clearly discerned the half-truths with which he tries to spare Deianeira's feelings and save his master's reputation. According to what seems to have been the orthodox version of the story, Iphitos was murdered not while searching for innocent strays (267 / 271) but while seeking to recover horses stolen from Oichalia—some said by Herakles himself in spite at Eurytos' refusal to surrender Iole. Similarly, the original audience must have sensed in Lichas' reference to the archery contest (259 / 266) the same oddity which compelled an ancient commentator on this passage to remark: "This is a peculiar version; for he (Eurytos) not only boasted about his children but also set Iole as a prize for archery and then failed to hand her over when Herakles was victorious." In the original, several passages of unusually stilted Greek in Lichas' long speech seem designed to reflect the embarrassment of an inexperienced and reluctant liar.

246–47 / 250–51 *a bought slave . . . / . . . god's work* Herakles' sale to Omphale was imposed by Apollo, at Zeus' request, to purify the pollution incurred by Iphitos' murder and to provide blood-money to the victim's relatives.

261 / 265 *magical arrows* Herakles possessed, as a gift from Apollo, a miraculous bow with infallible arrows. At his death the hero bequeathed these to Philoctetes, the kindler of his pyre, in whose hands they ultimately proved instrumental to the Greek victory at Troy.

262–65 / 267–69 *called him a slave . . . / . . . when he was drunk* There is no trace of these insults elsewhere in ancient tradition. They are meant by Sophocles to be recognized for what they are: something freely invented by Lichas to conceal the true motive behind Herakles' destruction of Oichalia.

273–74 / 277–78 *It wasn't the killing, / but the guile* A valiant attempt by Lichas to mitigate the seriousness of his master's crime. The original audience, familiar with Zeus' important role as guarantor of their venerable laws of hospitality, must have immediately sensed the special pleading. Far more outrageous than the stealthy execution of the murder was the hero's choice of victim: a helpless guest.

324–421 / 335–433 *Wait! . . . / . . . passion for the girl* There are clear hints of malicious pleasure in the bluntness with which the Messenger breaks the truth to Deianeira and cross-examines the embarrassed Lichas. The motivation for this spite—and for his refusal to quit the stage after performing his function as self-appointed messenger—has been left implicit in the action: he is frustrated by Deianeira's failure to respond to his pointed request for a reward (187–88 / 190–91) and chagrined at having his thunder stolen by the arrival of Herakles' herald. In his fondness for legal jargon and in his relish at assuming a prosecutorial role he has much in common with the victims of Athenian jury-mania satirized by Aristophanes in his Wasps. Of all Sophocles' anonymous minor characters, including the candid Watchman in *Antigone*, the Messenger is the most carefully and the most colorfully sketched.

395–98 / 409–12 *Just . . . just-ice . . . unjust . . . Injustice* The Messenger, in his forensic fervor, attempts to dazzle Lichas with malicious play upon *dikē*, the Greek word for punishment and justice.

416 / 428 *to marry* Literally: "as a wife (*damar*) for Herakles." Sophocles stresses that the hero intends Iole to play a permanent and prestigious role within his house. The Greek word *damar* always denotes legitimate wife, never concubine or mistress. It is unclear whether or not the audience is meant to assume that Herakles intends to divorce Deianeira. Deianeira obviously does not think so (cf. 520–31 / 535–46), but this may be intended to reflect a natural reluctance to face painful facts. The critical point established by the Messenger here is that Iole represents something far more dangerous than a philandering husband's passing fancy. It makes little difference whether Deianeira is confronted by divorce or by some intolerable form of bigamy. What matters is the unprecedented threat to the security of her cherished role as the only true "wife" of Herakles.

446 / 459 *more women than I can count* According to Greek tradition Herakles sired sons by some sixty different women, including Omphale. In equating his interest in Iole with these previous fleeting affairs Deianeira seems not yet to have grasped the key point stressed by the Messenger at 416 / 428; cf. the preceding note.

481–516 / 497–530 *First stasimon*

481 / 497 *Love's goddess* Aphrodite.

484–88 / 499–502 *Zeus...was taken in...and Death...and even the whole earth* Sophocles emphasizes two aspects of Love's dominion: its cosmic reach and its powers of deception. The first is implicit in its victories over Zeus (sky), Death (Underworld), and Poseidon (earth and sea); the second is explicitly affirmed as a hint of Deianeira's imminent resort to guile.

501 / 516 *her choosing wand* The effect of Sophocles' text is enriched by an untranslatable ambiguity between images of Love, wielder of the athletic umpire's staff, and Love, wielder of the sorceress' wand. Both are denoted by the word used here: *rhabdos*. The athletic image is charged with irony. Aphrodite stands serenely refereeing a contest in which no holds are barred.

512 / 526 *and I can see it...could tell* In the Greek the Chorus seems to say: "I am a mother in the sort of things I speak." All attempts to prove that some sense can be extracted from this inanity have failed. Faced by such incurable corruption in the text, we have found free invention the only recourse.

517–615 / 531–632 *Second episode*

522–24 / 537–40 *a slut.../...under the same blanket* Deianeira's sudden lapse into uncharacteristically coarse language is clearly intended to reveal the anger now rising to challenge her high principles of conjugal tolerance. This whole speech is remarkable for the subtlety with which it illuminates Deianeira's inner struggle to stifle unfamiliar and frightening forces of resentment.

548–49 / 564–65 *carrying me like that /... he put his hands on me* Sophocles pictures Nessos carrying Deianeira "on his shoulders." We have eliminated this detail, finding it an unlikely posture for the putting on of hands.

Sophocles makes Nessos' attack on Deianeira, like Herakles' on Iole, an unprovoked assault. There is some indication that in the traditional version of the story it was presented as revenge for a wound inflicted by the hero during the course of his battle with the centaurs. Cf. the note on 1044.

580 / 597 *No matter how shameful* Deianeira's sense of shame derives partly from the deceit to which she has been driven and partly from her resort to lover's magic, something the Greeks considered both dangerous and disreputable.

597 / 612 *like a newborn child* Again the Greek possesses untranslatable ambiguity. Deianeira has vowed that she will make Herakles a "new sacrificer in a new robe." For the Greeks "newness" had a double aspect. To the extent that it suggested freshness and ingenuity it was a quality to be desired; to the extent that it suggested the strange and unexpected it was considered distinctly ominous. Here Deianeira intends the first sense; but the original audience, already aware of the outcome, was intended to sense the ironic aptness of the second: Herakles will indeed soon become a "novel" sacrificer in a "novel" robe. Finding it impossible to reproduce this effect in English, the translator has substituted for sinister "newness" the vulnerability of the newborn.

605 / 621 *to fall on my face* Lichas uses a common Greek expression for failure: "I shall not be tripped up." By the choice of metaphor Sophocles ironically prefigures the moment when Herakles grasps the herald by the ankle and hurls him to his death; cf. 762–66 / 779–82. In the original, Lichas prefaces this assurance with the condition: "If I hold firm command of Hermes' escort-craft." There is an additional irony here deriving from Hermes' double function as both patron god of heralds and escort of souls to the Underworld. We have omitted the reference since its point would be lost on a modern audience.

616–45 / 633–62 *Second stasimon*

616–22 / 634–39 *the harbor . . . where the gates are* The features enumerated by the Chorus all belong to the local landscape: the hot springs from which Thermopylai (hot-gates) gained its name; the Malian Gulf; the eastern shore of central Greece; and Anthela, where the Amphictyonic Council met to administer the affairs of Apollo's shrine at Delphi.

620 / 638 *the Huntress-Goddess* Artemis, who seems to have been considered the protectress of this segment of the Greek coast.

631 / 647 *twelve months* There is an apparent discrepancy between this description of the duration of Herakles' absence and the critical period of fifteen months twice stressed previously by Deianeira (46–47 / 44–45; 163–65 / 164–66). Those who have attempted to explain away this inconsistency have argued either that the poet forgets what he has said in the earlier scenes, or that the reference is limited to the period of servitude in Lydia, or that it denotes the last of the twelve years which the Chorus first mentions nearly two hundred lines later (809–10 / 824–25). Few readers will find much consolation in such improbable answers to this perplexing question. Regrettably, a more satisfying alternative has yet to be suggested.

636–37 / 653 *the stung-mad / war-god* Ares. The Greek suggests a latent image of a bull, goaded to madness by the gadfly's sting. The passage thus provides a prophetic glimpse of Herakles bellowing under the sting of Nessos' poison; cf. 790 / 805, 1022 / 1072.

644 / 661 *soothed* Again Sophocles' language is charged with untranslatable ambiguity. The play is upon the Greek verb *khriō*, which, though usually used to denote the "smearing" of soothing ointments, is employed four times in Aeschylus' *Prometheus* to describe the maddening sting of the gadfly. It is the former sense which dominates here and in Deianeira's long speech at the beginning of the next scene, where this verb and its cognates are four times repeated. Its last recurrence is in the next stasimon, where Hyllos' disclosure prompts the Chorus to assert the secondary sense in their description of the "stinging" venom of the Hydra, cf. 819 / 834.

646–805 / 663–820 *Third episode*

658 / 675 *sheep's wool* Raw wool was prescribed by a variety of ancient rituals, including lovers' magic and sacrifice to the spirits of the dead. It is thus doubly appropriate for Deianeira's rite. She thinks she is binding Herakles' affections; in reality she is sacrificing him to the shade of his enemy, Nessos.

666 / 683 *like a law on a bronze tablet* By this simile Sophocles ironically recalls the tablet on which Herakles' oracles are inscribed; cf. 50 / 47, 156 / 154. The play's final scene reveals that Nessos' instructions do, in fact, reflect Zeus' ineradicable writing of the hero's destiny.

686 / 703–4 *the way the earth on a grave boils* Our own addition, designed to clarify the suggestions of chthonic ritual implicit in the Greek: "as when the

rich juice of the blue harvest from Bacchos' vine is poured out on the ground." The pouring of wine upon the ground is a conspicuous feature of Greek offerings to the dead. The suggestion of such ritual is particularly appropriate at the moment of Deianeira's discovery that she has sacrificed her husband to his dead enemy. Cf. the note on 658.

699–700 / 714–15 *even hurt Cheiron, and Cheiron / was a god* During the aftermath of their battle with Herakles (cf. the note on 1044) some of the centaurs fled to Cheiron for protection. One of the poisoned arrows launched by the hero in his pursuit passed through its intended target and struck his innocent friend. As the immortal victim of immortal venom, Cheiron would have been condemned to eternal agony had not the mortal Prometheus agreed to exchange lots with him, thereby enabling the centaur to suffer a merciful death.

780 / 794–95 *his eyes were rolling* For the Greeks rolling eyes were characteristic of both madmen and raging bulls. The latent animal image is consistent with Sophocles' emphasis on Herakles' bestialization throughout the play and is reinforced by the hero's "bellowing" a few lines below (790/804).

783 / 798 *Even if you have to die* Herakles' readiness to destroy his son stands in striking contrast with Deianeira's recently announced readiness to destroy herself as proof of her devotion.

798–804 / 813–20 *crawl . . . crawl . . . crawl . . . crawl* Hyllos, who has already—with unwitting accuracy—compared Deianeira's gift to the "venom from a snake" (754 / 770–71), finds an unexpected aptness in the verb innocently introduced by the Chorus and bitterly exploits its suggestion of reptilian movement by emphatic repetition. Though the verb in question (*herpō*) had already by Sophocles' time come into somewhat indiscriminate use for motion of all kinds, it is here intended to be felt in its original sense. One of the forms used by Hyllos (*herpetō*) strongly suggests the Greek word for reptile (*herpeton*—"crawling thing").

806–44 / 821–62 *Third stasimon*

809 / 825 *the twelve years* The play's first indication that Zeus' oracle specified twelve years as the period of Herakles' appointed toil. Few readers, we suspect, will share the distress felt by some critics at the Chorus' sudden revelation of a fact which, according to the strict logic of dramatic premise, they have no right to know. That the sudden clarification of the meaning

of the oracle is accompanied by a sudden clarification of its terms possesses a poetic logic of its own. For the ironic point of the reference to "ploughing-times" (810 / 825), see the note on 71.

843 / 860 *the servant, Love, the silent* In this climactic image Aphrodite, whose sovereignty over the action has remained unchallenged since its affirmation by the Chorus in the first stasimon, stands finally revealed as no more than the instrument of a higher power still—the will of Zeus. The impact of the passage is intensified by an ironic reminiscence of the two conspicuously "silent" women—first Iole and most recently Deianeira—whom Aphrodite herself has employed to serve Zeus' purpose.

845–922 / 863–946 *Fourth episode*

855–56 / 874–75 *Deianeira has disappeared...without a single step* The rather contrived formality of this remark suggests that the Nurse enters relatively composed and eager to deliver an impressive narrative of what has happened inside. During the exchange which follows (857–75 / 876–88) she becomes flustered by the Chorus Leader's increasingly impatient interruptions. In the original the aura of confusion is intensified by a break into irregular lyric metres (863–75 / 879–88) and by repeated shifts of speaker within the line.

884–85 / 904–5 *bellowing / that she was alone* A clear echo of the first stasimon's climactic image of Deianeira, the lost and lonely calf; cf. 516 / 530.

918–21 / 943–46 *Anyone who tries...is suffered through* These lines bear a striking resemblance to the commonplace expressions of resignation with which choruses frequently conclude Greek tragedies. By this suggestion of finality Sophocles brings into the highest possible relief the sharp line of demarcation between the play's two constituent tragedies and their isolated protagonists.

921–22 / 946–47 *Enter Hyllos...exit* Hyllos' movements at this point raise a difficult problem. There is no indication in the text that he appears at any time during the interval between his exit into the palace after 805 / 820 and the beginning of his exchange with the Old Man at 930 / 972. On the other hand, the text clearly suggests that in the finale he enters not from the palace but in the same party with Herakles and his attendants. If the action is to be intelligible, the route of Hyllos' return to Herakles with the litter which he has prepared inside "to bring his father in" (882 / 902) must somehow be clarified for the audience. Since the presumption of an invisible "backdoor" is alien to the conventions of Greek tragedy, we can only conclude that Sophocles caused Hyllos to enter and exit, in silence and without comment from those on stage, here at the end of the Nurse's speech and before the beginning of the final stasimon. Though this procedure is itself unparalleled elsewhere in Greek tragedy, it seems clearly preferable to the only alternative which has yet been suggested: Hyllos enters *from the palace* after 926 / 962 and finds his intention to return to Herakles anticipated by his father's arrival. If Sophocles intended the hero to arrive without any assistance from Hyllos he would hardly have created superfluous difficulties by stressing the son's preoccupation with the bed.

922–29 / 947–70 *Fourth stasimon*

927 / 963 *like a nightbird* Cf. the note on 105.

930–1227 / 971–1278 *Exodos*

930–94 / 972–1043 *O my god . . . / . . . Give me doom!* No translation can hope to do more than hint at the impact of this passage in its original production. Here Sophocles uses every available resource—spectacle, flute, and song—to raise his audience's emotions to an excruciatingly high pitch. During their approach to the palace the hero and his party chant in anapestic measures, a conventional marching rhythm (930–60 / 972–1003). At 961 / 1004 the attempt to move Herakles causes him to erupt in agonized song. Then the Old Man and Hyllos, succumbing to the lyric intensity of this outburst, themselves begin to sing (976–81 / 1017–1022). Not until the Chorus re-establishes the regular iambic rhythms of dialogue at 995 / 1044 does this frenzied music die. The unsettling effect of the whole lyric exchange (961–94 / 1004–43) is reinforced by a striking asymmetry of metrical structure and by an ironic exploitation of the dactylic hexameter, the rhythm of Greek epic, to underline the magnitude of Herakles' loss of heroic grandeur.

956 / 999 *blossoming* Many readers may be surprised to learn that Sophocles appropriated this striking metaphor from the technical terminology of Greek medicine, where "blossom" (*anthos*) denotes a pustulant efflorescence. He repeats the effect at 1038 / 1089. Since the metaphor is not likely to have died by Sophocles' time and since it may well be intended to echo ironically Deianeira's image of Herakles plucking Iole's youthful "blossom" (*anthos*, 532 / 549), the literal force of the word has been stressed throughout the translation.

987 / 1031 *Pallas, Sister* The goddess Athena, herself a child of Zeus. We have added "Sister" to stress the special intimacy of her relationship with the hero. In Greek myth she serves not only as his half-sister but also as his protectress, assisting him at various points in his career and ultimately aiding in his apotheosis by escorting him from Mt. Oita to Olympos.

993 / 1040 *Death...God's brother* Another relative. As Zeus' brother, Death (Hades) is also Herakles' uncle.

998 / 1048 *Zeus' wife* Hera, whose persecution of her husband's bastard son is notorious in Greek myth. It is she who sends serpents to destroy the infant Herakles in his cradle and who later drives the hero to murder, in a fit of madness, his children by the Theban princess Megara. Sophocles' allusion to Hera's malice is intentionally vague. His dramatic premise precludes any specific reference to the hero's previous marriage and its tragic outcome.

1008 / 1058–59 *giants born of the earth* These giants were spawned by Gē (Earth) and Ouranos (Sky) to attack Zeus and the other children of Kronos after they had usurped their father's throne and defeated his allies, the Titans, in battle. Warned by an oracle that the giants could only be destroyed by a mortal, Zeus enlisted the aid of Herakles, who subsequently destroyed them with his arrows.

1029 / 1078 *under the cover* Most probably the lion-skin which, though not anywhere mentioned in the text, serves everywhere in ancient art as one of the hero's indispensable identification marks. As such, it must have been made visible in the original staging of the scene.

1040–41 / 1092–93 *lion / in Nemea* The destruction of this beast was the first of the labors imposed upon Herakles by Eurystheus. After throttling it with his bare hands, the hero carried the carcass back to the king's palace. Eurystheus was supposed to have been so terrified by the sight of the creature that he ordered Herakles in the future to deposit his victims outside the city gates. The lion's hide became a conventional feature of the hero's costume; cf. the note on 1029.

1044 / 1095 *monstrosities, half-men, half-horse* The centaurs, who attacked Herakles in rage at his having sampled a special wine reserved solely for their own enjoyment. It was during the aftermath of this battle that the hero accidentally wounded Cheiron; cf. the note on 699–700.

1046 / 1097 *wild boar of Erymanthos* The destruction of this creature, another bane to the inhabitants of southern Greece, also belongs to the hero's labors for Eurystheus.

1047 / 1098 *three-headed whelp of the Viper* Kerberos, watchdog of Hades' gates. He was thought to possess, in addition to a forbidding multiplicity of heads, a mane of snakes and a dragon's tail. At Eurystheus' command Herakles descended to Hades, overpowered this creature without aid of weapons, and brought it back alive to the world above. Kerberos' mother, Echidna (Viper), was another monster, half-woman, half-snake. According to some ancient authors, the journey which brought Herakles to the palace of Oineus was prompted by an encounter with the shade of Meleager, Deianeira's brother, during this visit to the Underworld.

1049 / 1100 *the dragon guarding the golden fruit* Herakles was ordered by Eurystheus to bring back the golden apples presented by Earth to Hera as a wedding gift and entrusted to the Hesperides, daughters of Night, for safe-keeping. As a deterrent to thieves, Hera stationed a hundred-headed dragon to guard the miraculous fruit. Sophocles follows the tradition in which Herakles himself destroys this monster and makes away with the apples. According to an alternative version, the hero persuaded Atlas to steal the fruit.

1113–14 / 1166–67 *people / who... the Selloi* The local tribe which administered Zeus' sanctuary at Dodona. Homer, at *Iliad* 16.235, notes that in addition to dispensing with beds they failed to wash their feet. It is not clear whether these peculiar habits were noted as evidence of ascetic principle or as proof of barbarian origin.

1115–16 / 1168 *an oak... / and it speaks* Cf. the note on 168–69.

1121 / 1171 *I thought it meant I'd prosper* In view of Deianeira's vivid description of the gloomy mood in which Herakles left Trachis (**154–68 / 156–68**), the reference must be to recent confidence instilled by the release from Omphale and the victory at Oichalia.

1146–47 / 1195–97 *from the hardest oaks... /... from olive trees* Literally: "from the deep-rooted oak and the virile wild olive." The striking specificity of these instructions casts an aura of sacrificial ritual over the hero's sudden resolve to destroy himself by fire; cf. the Introduction, v. The two components of the pyre aptly represent the two partners in the compact which has produced it. Zeus' sacred oak has foretold the hero's destiny, and the wild olive was thought to have been brought to Greece by Herakles to provide shade and victors' wreaths for his father's festival at Olympia; cf. Pindar, *Olympian* 3. 13ff. and Pausanias V.7.7.

1161 / 1211 *at least the rest* Hyllos must be excused from the actual kindling of the pyre since Greek tradition reserves this service for Philoctetes (or his father). As the favor by which Philoctetes won the legacy of Herakles' miraculous bow, this detail of the myth was too important to ignore; cf. the note on 261.

1167 / 1214–15 *Now one other little favor* We remain unpersuaded by those critics who have attempted to deny the callousness of this casual addendum. The argument that Herakles' arrangement of a marriage for his captive is intended as proof of his capacity for compassion is patently inconsistent with Sophocles' emphasis on the hero's pitiless response to the pain which this "little favor" inflicts upon his son. Another view assumes that Sophocles felt compelled by audience expectation to account for the existence of this intrinsically improbable marriage in established Greek tradition. We find this inconceivable. At this overpowering moment no audience could be expected to be preoccupied with reflections upon mythical genealogies. The Hyllos-Iole marriage would never have come to mind had not the poet chosen to make an issue of it. For our view of the significance of this choice, cf. the Introduction, v.

1208 / 1260 *Soul, be hard now* Here the Greek text shifts from the iambic trimeters of spoken dialogue to chanted anapests. The change marks the beginning of the processional exit which closes the play.

1209–10 / 1260–61 *steel bit . . . / . . . stone against stone* An intentionally free rendering of Sophocles' perplexing phrase: "a stone-glued bit of steel." Herakles seems to picture himself as a marble horse to which, in accordance with a common practice of Greek sculptors, a metal harness has been welded with lead. The image is particularly suited to this context where the hardening and the taming of the hero's spirit are simultaneously affirmed. Others have assumed a reference to a particularly painful type of bit studded with sharp stones. This attractive suggestion is unfortunately unsupported by any evidence that stone-studded bits ever existed in Greece.

1223–27 / 1275–78 *Girl . . . Zeus* The manuscripts reflect great confusion as to whether these lines belong to Hyllos or the Leader of the Chorus. We unhesitatingly assign them to Hyllos. Their tone is consistent with the bitterness of his preceding remarks (**1215–22** / 1264–74), and they are readily intelligible as an instruction to the Leader to initiate the exit of the Chorus. Those who have supported the attribution to the Leader have been driven to a desperate search for a "girl" for her to address. Some have found her in Iole, assuming her presence in the scene despite Sophocles' failure to indicate this seemingly pointless reappearance at any point in the preceding dialogue. Others argue that the Leader uses the singular "girl" to address her fourteen fellow chorus members, an improbable procedure unparalleled elsewhere in Sophoclean tragedy. Such are the drastic measures required if the conclusion of the play is to be restored to orthodox form by providing a conventional closing remark from the Chorus. They reflect, in our view, a perverse reluctance to accept the obvious: that in omitting a choral tag Sophocles deliberately defies convention in order to sustain the agonizingly inconclusive effect which he has contrived for this finale.

ELECTRA

Translated by
ANNE CARSON

*With Introduction
and Notes by*
MICHAEL SHAW

INTRODUCTION

The long siege of Troy, a city on the coast of Asia Minor, is one of the major events in the world of Greek myth. The first surviving work of Greek literature, the *Iliad* of Homer, is largely concerned with it. The *Iliad* itself is about an event in the ninth year of that siege, a quarrel in the Greek camp between Agamemnon, the leader of the Greek rulers, and Achilles, their best warrior, that leads to Achilles' withdrawal. This in turn leads to a series of events that end with the death of the Trojans' best warrior, Hektor. But in the course of that story, Homer tells us much of the earlier history of the war and reveals that after Hektor's death Troy's fall will inevitably follow.

Homer's *Odyssey* is concerned with the ten years' wandering and eventual return home of Odysseus, another Greek leader at Troy. Here, too, other stories are brought in, among them the story of Agamemnon's return home and his murder by Aegisthus and his wife. While he had been in Troy, his cousin Aegisthus had seduced his wife, Clytemnestra, and upon his return home Aegisthus and Clytemnestra had arranged a feast for him at which he, his war-prize and concubine Cassandra, and his followers were murdered. Eight years later, Orestes, Agamemnon's son, returned to Mycenae and murdered Aegisthus and buried Aegisthus and Clytemnestra—Homer does not say who killed her. In the references to this event, Orestes' action is always viewed in a positive light—he is pointed out as an example for Odysseus' son Telemachus to follow as he comes of age and becomes dissatisfied with the suitors of his mother who have made themselves at home for several years and are consuming his estate.

The story of Agamemnon's return is much more elaborate in Aeschylus' dramatic trilogy, the *Oresteia*, which was produced some 250 years later (assuming Homer's date to be about 700 B.C.) in 458 B.C. In particular, the story has become much more problematic. In the first play, the *Agamemnon*, Clytemnestra has been given a new and powerful motive for killing her husband: his sacrifice of their daughter Iphigenia to Artemis so the Greeks could have fair winds for the voyage to Troy. When Orestes arrives in Argos in the second play, *Libation Bearers*, he is greeted by his sister Electra, who has long been praying for his return. She, like Iphigenia, is not mentioned by Homer. Electra bears witness to the scandal and welcomes Orestes, but she does not participate in the murder. In the final play, *Eumenides*, Orestes is pursued by his mother's avenging spirits, stands trial in Athens, and is acquitted, even though by a split decision. Although there are other episodes and variants found in other works, Aeschylus' trilogy is a fair representative of the model Euripides and Sophocles used when they created their two very different plays.

Euripides' *Electra* follows the conventional plot to a degree. Electra bears witness to her mother's crimes and she welcomes Orestes to Argos as avenger, but Euripides shows what the strain of her situation has done to her character. In his version, she has been removed from the palace by her mother and married to a poor but noble farmer in an outlying farm. Her witness-bearing occurs in a context where it is irrelevant, and this, too, has helped to bend her character. She has become obsessive, sexually confused (both repressed and prurient), and, most important, she is unaware of the consequences of murdering her mother. As Clytemnestra approaches, Orestes loses his nerve (or gains his sanity), but Electra forces him to persevere—a vivid dramatization of the force that works through her. However, once they have murdered Clytemnestra, Electra then becomes as extreme in her regret as she was in her vengefulness. She insists the fault is hers and not Orestes'. In the final scene, Euripides states, through a divine spokesman, that the murder was just, that it was wrong that Electra and Orestes should have done it, and also that Apollo is responsible. In other words, the cost of enacting justice is prohibitively high—in this case, it has destroyed Electra and Orestes.

Like Euripides, Sophocles focuses on the relationship between situation and character, but the character of Euripides' Electra is destroyed by her situation, while Sophocles' character resists. She admits that her actions are shameful in themselves, even though they are just, and thus she displays a self-consciousness that is completely lacking in Euripides' Electra. As she puts it, in order to do things that are right, she must do things that are wrong, and her only defense is that she has been forced.

This is a highly satisfactory vengeance drama. Sophocles emphasizes the pathetic aspects of Electra's situation: All the supports she has are gradually removed in the course of the play. Her sister chooses expedient silence; her mother threatens her with force; finally, her main support—the hope that her brother will return—is taken away when his death is falsely reported as part of his vengeance plot. Only then, when she is betrayed, alone, and completely lacking in hope, Orestes reveals himself to her. The play then wheels from noble suffering to vindication. Electra indulges herself in extreme joy at her brother's return, and her pleasure at the death of Clytemnestra and Aegisthus is grim but not excessive.

Those elements of the story that would destroy this effect have been dampened. Electra's antagonists display unprincipled expediency and violence. It is clear that Electra should prevail; since we the audience know that Orestes has arrived, we are certain that she will prevail. Once Orestes sets his plot in motion, he dispatches his mother quickly and after minimal verbal sparring he leads Aegisthus into the house to be killed in a manner we are not allowed to contemplate.

It is not hard to see why some have concluded that it is primarily a play of revenge. However, it is difficult to believe that our response should be so uncomplicated. Orestes' murder of his mother is monstrous behavior. This difficulty has to a great degree been suppressed in Sophocles' play. It is not repressed in Aeschylus' trilogy, and Orestes himself understands that what he is doing is monstrous: "I have been made into a snake in order to kill her." This monstrousness, externalized and personified as the Furies, threatens to destroy him. When Orestes and Apollo argue against the Furies in the law court setting of the third play of this trilogy, we see how closely balanced the arguments for and against the murder are, and how national interest, the highest of motives, only carries the day by the slimmest margin.

Although it is generally felt that Sophocles' Electra is an admirable person and that the revenge is necessary, it is possible to draw the conclusion that she and Orestes are driven by motives that they do not understand to perform an action of which no one—not even Apollo—approves, and that Electra becomes insane in the course of the play.[1] This dark reading is based on a relatively small number of passages. Electra undercuts her own position when she makes the point to Clytemnestra that vengeance leads to endless retaliation. Clytemnestra reveals that she has some maternal feelings for her son after hearing the account of his death. After Orestes reveals himself to her, Electra, who has devoted

1. See Sophocles, *Electra*, edited by J. H. Kells, Cambridge University Press, 1973, pp. 8–11, for the strongest version known to me of the dark reading, which he calls the ironic theory, basing his discussion on the two articles by J. T. Sheppard cited below. This discussion by Kells is the basis for this paragraph. C. P. Segal, *Tragedy and Civilization: An Interpretation of Sophocles* ("Martin Classical Lectures," vol. 26), Cambridge and London: Harvard University Press, 1981, discusses the "darker view," which he agrees with, in his chapter on *Electra*, pp. 249–91.

herself so absolutely to justice, makes several disturbingly opportunistic remarks. She agrees to deceive Clytemnestra so she can be true to "the good luck that now attends us,"[2] and later says (ironically) to Aegisthus that "I've learned to side with the winners" 1943 / 1465. Electra becomes increasingly out of touch with reality as the play progresses—first planning to kill Aegisthus herself, and later thinking that the Old Man is her father. Finally, she refuses to let Aegisthus speak in his own defense because she wants "satisfaction for her wounded feelings."[3]

In this reading, Sophocles' Electra is a near double of the Euripidean Electra. But it is possible to account for these passages and to come to less extreme conclusions about Electra's mental state. J. T. Sheppard suggests that Electra acts like a sane and moral person most of the time, but occasionally we see "hints of the chaos ruling in those tragic souls."[4] Thus, to respond to the dark reading it is necessary to consider not only the meaning of these passages but also the way they fit into the play's full context.[5]

The play begins in a manner that suggests it will follow the same course taken by Aeschylus in the *Libation Bearers*. Orestes enters with the Old Man, his former tutor, and says that he inquired of Apollo at Delphi how to exact justice from the murderers and that the god gave this answer:

> Take no weapons.
> No shield.
> No army.
> Go alone—a hand in the night.
> Snare them.
> Slaughter them.
> You have the right.   (46–52 / 36–37)

In this version, Apollo's oracle did not say why a trick was necessary. In the Aeschylean version, on the other hand, the oracle told Orestes to pursue his father's murderers "in the same fashion, death for death"

2. Kells' translation of line 1306, line 1740 in this translation. Our translation has "the god who stands beside us now," but a more literal translation says "the present *daimon*." A *daimon* is indeed a divinity, but in phrases like the one here the word only means "the spirit of the moment."

3. Kells, p. 11.

4. J. T. Sheppard, "*Electra* Again." *Classical Review* 41 (1927) 165. This and the two other articles by Sheppard concerning *Electra* remain among the most interesting treatments of this play: "The Tragedy of Electra, According to Sophocles." *Classical Quarterly* 12 (1918) 80–88; "Electra: A Defense of Sophocles." *Classical Review* 41 (1927) 2–9.

5. I have omitted one major claim of the dark reading, that Orestes asked the wrong question of the oracle, for reasons discussed in C. M. Bowra, *Sophoclean Tragedy*, Oxford: Clarendon Press, 1944, pp. 215–18. In brief, although Orestes failed to ask the oracle if he should murder his mother, the oracular response was not ambiguous, doubts are not raised elsewhere in the play, and the project seems here as in Aeschylus to have divine favor.

(*Libation Bearers* 273–74). When Aeschylus' Orestes refers to the trick, it is clear that he knows why a trick is necessary:

> You must hide what we have discussed here,
> so that those who killed a respected man with a trick
> might be taken with a trick, dying in the self-same noose,
> the way Loxias proclaimed,
> He who is Lord, Apollo, true prophet from of old.

(Libation Bearers 555–59)

Sophocles' Orestes does not have the benefit of this explanation, and he is uneasy about lying about his own death. His explanation is less than adequate: "Can a mere story be evil? No of course not— / so long as it pays in the end" (85–86 / 61). This is the cheap language of politics. The lie he has chosen, a chariot wreck at Delphi, reflects the limited perspective of a rich teenager of his times. In the midst of this pedestrian stuff he can suddenly inject language of a much higher level, "I come to cleanse you with justice" (97 / 69–70). But on the whole Sophocles' Orestes is a typical person of his age and class, who only partly understands what he has undertaken.

For the most part, this scene has been prosaic, and there is a sharp contrast with Electra's first word. A cry is heard from offstage—"O wretched me" is a close translation of *moi dystenos*—and Orestes immediately echoes that word, "Can it be *poor* [*dystenos*] Electra? / Should we stay here and listen?" (110–11 / 80). The Old Man seems to drag him away: "No. Nothing precedes the work of Apollo."

After the men leave, Electra enters. Perhaps she is in rags, but it is more likely that she is in the plain dress of a servant.[6] Her language continues to be highly emotional:

6. What is she wearing? The text does not give us much help on this point. In line 257 of this translation she says she is in "rags" but a closer translation is "unseemly dress" (line 193 in the Greek). Orestes asks, "It shocks me, the way you look: do they abuse you?" (1181). In a melodrama of this intensity, whether Electra is dressed as a commoner or is in rags is an important issue. My own feeling is that to dress her in rags would be too extreme. J. C. Kamerbeek implies that Electra has been doing harm to herself after hearing of Orestes' death, and if this is so it must occur on stage (*The Electra*, Leiden: Brill, 1974, note on 1177). This seems likely—in the rehearsals for the Kansas University student production that I attended in 1978, it was decided that she should roll on the ground during the messenger speech. It is also possible that she causes herself harm in a later scene. She announces that she is lying down at 819, and she may roll on the ground and lacerate herself in the *kommos*, 823–70, since such gestures are often referred to in similar passages in tragedy, although not here. The director, Bill Nesbitt, graciously allowed me to attend all aspects of this production, beginning with the auditions and ending with the faculty oral evaluation of the director. My reading of this play and my approach to Greek drama in general has been deeply influenced by this experience. I am especially indebted to Mr. Nesbitt, to Kathleen Warfel, who played Electra, and to Professors Ron Willis and Jack Wright.

O holy light!
And equal air shaped on the world—
you hear my songs,
you hear the blows fall.   (115–18 / 86–90)

It is as though the scene has suddenly shifted from black and white to
color. She is singing, for one thing. She does not speak about things so
much as she speaks to them, a mark of heightened emotion—she
addresses the light, the air, her father, Hades, Persephone. She turns
quickly to her father's murder:

No pity for these things,
there is no pity
but mine,
oh father,
for the pity of your butchering rawblood death.   (133–37 / 100–102)

We do not stop to think about it, but Orestes said nothing of how he
feels about his father. After Electra's speech ends, there is a lyric dialogue (*kommos*) between Electra and the Chorus. The tension between
them is visible from the beginning: "Your mother is evil / but oh my
child why / melt your life away in mourning?" (163–65 / 121–23). Choruses are typically suspicious of extreme behavior. Already the words
characteristic of the Sophoclean hero have begun to appear.[7] Electra
calls on Philomela (199 / 147) and Niobe (202 / 150), both of whom
lament "endlessly" (*aien*, a word associated with Sophoclean heroes).
The Chorus says "you go too far" (209 / 155) and urges her to find
a middle ground between hating and forgetting (237–38 / 177). It informs
her that she "must not / clash with the people in power" (293–94 /
219–20). It sounds as if Sophocles' earlier *Antigone* is being played out
again, and we will hear more echoes of that play, particularly in the
dialogues of Electra and her sister.

However, what happens next does not have a parallel in *Antigone*.
Electra does not answer the Chorus' remark in quite the way we expect
of Sophoclean heroes:

By dread things I am compelled. I know that.
I see the trap closing.
I know what I am.
But while life is in me
I will not stop this violence. No.   (295–99 / 221–25)

---

7. This aspect of the Sophoclean hero was brilliantly delineated by Bernard Knox in *The Heroic
Temper: Studies in Sophoclean Tragedy*, Berkeley: University of California Press, 1964.

Sophoclean heroes often say that they "must" do something. But the implication here is that Electra herself does not fully approve of what she is doing. A nuance in the Greek text, not found in this translation, adds to this impression. A close translation of line 296 / 222 ("I see the trap closing") would read, "my anger [*orga*] does not escape me." This self-awareness is unusual for a Sophoclean hero, and it also contrasts with the mood of the female avengers in the dramas by the other playwrights on this theme. Aeschylus' Clytemnestra only becomes aware that some sort of spirit has possessed her after the murder of Agamemnon. Euripides' Electra achieves a similar self-awareness, but only after she has participated in the murder of Clytemnestra.

Electra and the Chorus have been singing since she entered, the longest unbroken passage in lyric in Sophocles. She now shifts to iambics, that is, to something more like normal speech. And as often happens in tragedy, she reiterates the gist of what she has been saying in song. She begins with a word that is very important to her: "Women, I am ashamed before you: I know / you find me extreme / in my grief" (338–40 / 254–55). Shame is normally considered to be an enforcer of social conformity, but shame makes Electra a rebel. She imagines another person, like herself, doing just as she is doing:

> But how could I—
> how could a woman of any nobility
> stand
> and watch her father's house go bad?   (344–47 / 257–58)

These words suggest that she is not excessively self-absorbed. This "woman of any nobility" is partly a projection of herself, and partly another person; so she attempts to align herself with her society, although it is the aspect of society that reflects her own values.[8] This emphasis on gazing continues: "I see my father's throne / with Aegisthus on it" (358–59 / 267–68). This early in the play, we have already seen the most important aspects of Electra's character: her interest in shame, good conduct, proper religious practice.

Electra also raises another issue that will be important later. Is there any pragmatic justification for her behavior, or is she dangerously out of touch with reality? One answer to this question is that Electra functions as a Fury, and this speech contains the first of two hints that she does. Her mother, she says, "lives with that polluted object, / fearing no Fury"

---

8. This woman is not quite the same as the "imagined other," whom Bernard Williams discusses in *Shame and Necessity*, Berkeley: University of California Press, 1993, p. 82. However, she serves a similar mediating function.

(370–71 / 275–76). Yet when her mother hears that Orestes is coming, she is clearly not so unaffected as Electra has said: "then she goes wild, comes screaming at me: / 'Have I you to thank for this? / Isn't it your work?' " (399–401 / 294–96). Driving someone "wild" (*emmanes*) would seem to be an appropriate action for a Fury.[9] Although the threat comes from Orestes, Clytemnestra sees Electra's hand behind Orestes.

Furies are important characters throughout the *Oresteia* of Aeschylus, and in the final play in that trilogy, the *Eumenides*, they form the Chorus. They define themselves as the avengers of crimes of blood.[10] One of the ways that they answer the prayers of those unjustly murdered is to drive the guilty person out of his mind.[11] Clytemnestra herself will imply that Electra is a Fury, and at least one scholar sees this as the key to her character, a view that must be at least partially true.[12]

Chrysothemis, Electra's sister, enters when Electra ends her monologue. The contrast between her relatively fine dress and the plainer dress of Electra makes a dramatic point that will be raised in their conversation. She carries offerings in her hands, and clearly she is being diverted from some action to speak to Electra. In her opening words, she reveals that they have had this discussion before: "Here you are again at the doorway, sister, / telling your tale to the world! / When will you learn?" (444–46 / 328–31). What Electra has not learned is that she should not indulge her emotions when she can have no effect on the situation. This is essentially what Ismene said to Antigone, the first signal that the scenes between the two sisters will be an elaboration of the conflict of sisters in the *Antigone*.

The Chorus has emphasized at Chrysothemis' entrance that she is just like her sister, but there is something that distinguishes them, and Chrysothemis reveals it immediately: "Yes I know how bad things are. / I suffer too—if I had the strength / I would show what I think of them"(448–50 / 332–34). What differentiates the two sisters is found in that phrase, "if I had the strength [*sthenos*]." Electra is offended by this remark and throws the word back at her (*sthenos*, 471 / 348). The prudential Chrysothemis does not act when she knows she will not succeed: "Why pretend to be doing, / unless I can do some real harm?" (453–54 / 336). Sophoclean heroes, on the other hand, often say something like this: "I will be stopped if I don't have the strength" (*sthenei*,

---

9. See the Chorus' description of Clytemnestra in Aeschylus' *Agamemnon*, line 1428: "her mind is raging [*epimainetai*] because of the bloody action."
10. *Eumenides* 312–20.
11. Ibid., pp. 318–33.
12. See R. P. Winnington-Ingram, *Sophocles: An Interpretation*, Cambridge and New York: Cambridge University Press, 1980, pp. 217–47.

Antigone 91). That is, these characters are demonstrating in their quarrels the quality later to be known as *will*.

Chrysothemis continues with an even more revealing remark:

> And yet,
> it is true,
> justice is not on my side.
> Your choice is the right one. On the other hand,
> if I want to live a free woman,
> there are masters who must be obeyed. (456–61 / 338–40)

Chrysothemis uses a word for justice (*to dikaion*) that is frequently employed in contemporary discussion, as is the phrase she uses, "masters who must be obeyed."[13] In Athenian rhetoric of this period, matters would typically be considered in terms of justice and then in terms of the expedient.[14] The expedient can conveniently be defined as what works. In Sophoclean drama, this expediency language is usually found in the context of moral relativism, as in this remark made by Odysseus in Sophocles' *Philoctetes*:

> As the occasion
> demands, such a one am I.
> When there is a competition of men just and good,
> you will find none more scrupulous than myself.
> What I seek in everything is to win . . . [15]

The ironic usage of "free woman" in Chrysothemis' lines should not be passed by without notice. Normally those who obey masters are slaves. Chrysothemis is defining "free" in terms of expedience—that is, she means that she accepts her position as a de facto slave and thus

---

13. See Kells, note on line 1465, who refers to Thrasymachus' statement in Plato's *Republic* that justice is "going along with the stronger." The usual term for this concept is expedience (*to sympheron*). Although Chrysothemis does not use it here, Electra uses one form of this word in 1465 ("to *side with* [*sympherein*] the winners"). There is an extensive discussion of expediency argument in W. K. C. Guthrie, *The Sophists* (Vol. 3. Pt. 1. *A History of Greek Philosophy*), Cambridge, 1971, pp. 84–116.
14. The expedient is discussed with respect to Thucydides in Colin Macleod's article. "Form and Meaning in the Melian Dialogue," in *Collected Essays*, Oxford: Clarendon Press: New York: Oxford University Press, 1983, pp. 52–67. This remark is as true of tragedy as it is of Thucydides, "Now justice and expediency are what in rhetorical terms are called *telika kephalaia*, qualities human action should aim to have Rhetoricians often fuse them together. . . . to make the course the speaker advises or defends appear satisfactory from as many points of view as possible. . . . But, as is well known, it is particularly characteristic of Thucydides to contrapose the two" (p. 55). I am indebted to Macleod's essays in various ways in this essay.
15. Sophocles, *Philoctetes*, trans. by David Grene, in *Sophocles II*, Chicago: University of Chicago Press, 1957, ll. 1048–52.

assents to it. Electra will demolish this position, but not until much later. Chrysothemis' remark about Electra and justice is one of several times in this play when a character reveals what they are thinking but not saying openly; in all of those cases those internal thoughts are governed by Electra. This effect is more visible here than elsewhere, and so it may be well to consider its significance at this point. When William Arrowsmith used to discuss this play, he would refer to a passage from John Jay Chapman which still strikes me as particularly apt:

> The radicals are really always saying the same thing. They do not change: everybody else changes. They are accused of the most incompatible crimes, of egoism and a mania for power, indifference to the fate of their own cause, fanaticism, triviality, want of humor, buffoonery and irreverence. [!] But they sound a certain note. Hence the great practical power of consistent radicals. To all appearance nobody follows them, yet every one believes them. They hold a tuning fork and sound A, and everybody knows it really is A, though the time-honored pitch is G flat. The community cannot get that A out of its head. Nothing can prevent an upward tendency in the popular tone so long as the real A is kept sounding. Every now and then the whole town strikes it for a week, and all the bells ring, and then all sinks to suppressed discord and denial.[16]

When Electra replies to Chrysothemis, she tries to defend herself in terms of expediency:

> . . . what do I stand to gain if I cease my lament?
> Do I not live? Badly, I know, but I live.
> What is more,
> I am a violation to them.   (478–81 / 352–55)

"Gain" (*kerdos*) is a word often found in expediency arguments—it has the connotation of profit or the bottom line. Perhaps we should note that in the Greek text (l. 354) she says "but I live *sufficiently for me*." Chrysothemis will later point out that some forms of living are worse than death, and Electra here seems to admit that some level of physical comfort must be present before one can practice virtue. Electra is not simply an embodiment of the justice argument, just as Chrysothemis is not purely the expediency argument. Each is trying to accommodate the opposite view as well as her own.

There is no room for compromise between the justice argument and the expediency argument in this case, and it would be reasonable for this scene to end in mutual rejection, as happens in the parallel scene

16. "A sampling of letters and obiter dicta," edited by William Arrowsmith, *Arion*, third series, 2.2 and 3, 1992 / 3, p. 64. The passage is from *Practical Agitation*.

between Antigone and Ismene, but suddenly Chrysothemis remembers why she has left the palace and she tells about Clytemnestra's dream. That Clytemnestra had a dream is traditional, but Sophocles has changed its content. In Aeschylus she dreamed that she gave birth to a snake, put it to her breast, and it drew out blood mixed with milk. Here, Agamemnon returns to the light, sticks his scepter into the earth beside the hearth, and the scepter puts forth a branch that overshadows all of Mycenae. Aeschylus' version of the dream emphasized the violation of nature implicated in matricide; Sophocles' emphasizes the return of natural process when the heir returns. In Sophocles' play, it is Electra, not Orestes, who drinks Clytemnestra's blood. We are meant, of course, to recall that in the *Iliad* Achilles said that this very scepter would never bloom again. Here we see how it could bloom again, by the installation of the true heir in the palace.

When Electra asks Chrysothemis to tell of the dream, she makes a remark that hints very broadly at the fact that this is a play of intrigue: "Little words can mean / death or life sometimes" (566–67 / 415–16). Sophocles' *Electra* is, among other things, a thriller—we enjoy the helplessness of the good characters and their desperate hopes, not to mention the haughty speech of the bad people, because we are absolutely sure of the outcome.

The immediate effect of the dream is that Electra can now make another appeal to Chrysothemis. Her tone shifts from hostility to pleading. She asks Chrysothemis to throw away the offerings, which she will agree to do, precisely because Clytemnestra will never know. Instead, Electra says, she should take locks of her own hair and Electra's, and "this belt of mine / though it's nothing elaborate" (618–19 / 452). These are "meagre gifts (615 / 450)"—literally "little [*smikra*, 615 / 450] gifts"— just as Chrysothemis' words were "little" (*smikroi*) at 566 / 415. But they will be enough. There is a hint here of the justice versus expediency argument. Electra has nothing but the right, but that nothing is enough. After the wonderful student performance at the University of Kansas in 1978,[17] I was offered my choice of props. As I write these words, the belt of Electra hangs behind me from the ceiling of my office, entangled in the crown of Aegisthus.

The scene ends on a note of hope and of friendship, far different from the way it began. The next time Chrysothemis enters, the reverse will occur. In a play that is filled with emotion, nothing to me is more affecting than the shifting moods in these two sisters, who are "of one nature."

17. See note 6 above.

When Chrysothemis leaves, the Chorus sings its second song. First, it responds to the dream:

> Unless I am utterly wrong in my reading of omens
> unless I am out of my mind
> Justice is coming
> with clear signs before her
> and righteousness in her hands. (648–52 / 472–76)

It is not wrong, of course—we know that Orestes will momentarily appear. The dream is a clear sign of the approach of Justice. As often in the comments of this Chorus, there seems to be a hint of the traditional story. The theme of Justice is prominent in Aeschylus' version. These lines are also what we would expect in a play of action. They inform us that Apollo's plan is working out; Orestes will soon appear.

In their final stanza, the mood and subject suddenly shift: "O horse-race of Pelops,..." (678 / 504–5). Pelops, the person who founded the royal family at Argos, whose members include Orestes, Electra, and Aegisthus, bribed Myrtilus, the charioteer of the king Oinomaus, to rig the king's chariot so that Pelops might win the race and so take the daughter of Oinomaus as his bride. After the race, in which Oinomaus was killed, Pelops also killed Myrtilus. No wonder Orestes thought of the story that he had been killed in a chariot crash. But the Chorus refers to this old story because it thinks it has found a principle at work in this family:

> never
> since that time
> has this house
> got itself clear of
> rawblood
> butchery. (686–91 / 513–15)

It used the same word at the beginning of the song: the axe was used "to butcher the meat." It is a good word to end on. The butcher herself now enters.

Clytemnestra has a servant with her who carries offerings to be sacrificed. Thus we can see that she is of higher rank than Chrysothemis, who carried her offerings in her own hands. But in its general structure this scene resembles the preceding one: a woman enters with offerings, is diverted when she sees Electra and is drawn into an argument, after which she reveals the purpose of the offerings. Then the sacrifice is performed, offstage or on, but it has been altered by Electra. This parallel in the action suggests that Electra is dominating Clytemnestra's thoughts, just as she is those of Chrysothemis.

Clytemnestra does not make any pretense of politeness when she begins: "Prowling the streets again, are you? / Of course, with Aegisthus away" (692–93 / 516–17). Her first point, that Electra "embarrass[es] us" 695 / 518, has already been raised by Electra, who has admitted from the start that her behavior is shameful. But she quickly changes tack: "It was Justice who took him, not I alone" (705 / 528). When the Greek fleet was about to sail for Troy, it was becalmed at the Greek port of Aulis, and only the sacrifice of Agamemnon's daughter Iphigenia would gain favoring winds for the Greek fleet. She also claimed that she murdered Agamemnon to avenge Iphigenia in Aeschylus' *Agamemnon*. Clytemnestra has a strong case—indeed, its merits are still being discussed. Furthermore, Sophocles puts her case strongly, at one point even letting her sound like one of his heroines: "Did he have some share / in the pain of her birth? No—I did it myself!" (711–12 / 532–33). To an audience member who knows his Aeschylus and who routinely thinks in terms of justice versus expediency, it seems that Clytemnestra has challenged Electra on her own ground.

Electra attempts to refute Clytemnestra's justice argument by offering another version of the events at Aulis, in which Agamemnon had no choice but to sacrifice his daughter. This is not a particularly effective counter to Clytemnestra's argument, whose strongest point is that Agamemnon has violated Clytemnestra's rights as a mother. Even worse is the principle she cites at the end of her justice argument:

> By what law?
> Watch out: this particular law
> could recoil upon your own head.
> If we made it a rule
> to answer killing with killing,
> you would die first,
> in all justice. (777–83 / 579–83)

If this is true of Clytemnestra, it is also true of Orestes and Electra. But I do not think that we should follow the extreme version of the dark reading and assume that this shows that Electra is profoundly mistaken. For one thing, in the mythical time line, so to speak, the world of some higher form of justice than an eye for an eye is still to come. Indeed, Orestes is going to be the catalyst for its appearance.

More important, we must keep the context of this defective justice argument in mind. In the overall structure of this speech, it is not presented as the main argument. Electra began on quite a different note:

All right then. Yes.
You killed my father, you admit.
What admission could bring more shame?
Never mind if it was legal or not—did you care?   (749–52 / 558–60)

Anne Carson's translation catches the disdain of Electra for the legal issues involved here. She is mainly interested in reverence (*eusebeia*). Once she has ended her justice argument, Electra returns to this main theme of shame (emphasis added to line 791 / 589):

Tell me:
why do you live this way?
Your life is filth [*aischista* (most shameful)].
You share your bed with a bloodstained man:
once he obliged you by killing my father,
now you put him to use making children.
Once you had *decent* children from a *decent* father
[*eusebeis . . . eusebon* (reverent . . . reverent)],
now you've thrown them out.   (785–92 / 585–90)

She ends her speech with an explosive rejoinder to Clytemnestra's original charge that she was embarrassing her friends, "for if this is my nature / we know how I come by it, don't we?" (817–18 / 608–9). The Chorus draws attention to the passions of this speech: "Look, Anger is breathing out of her. / Yet she seems not to care / about right and wrong" (819–21 / 610–11). Although Carson's stage directions state here that these lines refer to Clytemnestra's apparently visible anger at Electra's speech, I assume that they refer to Electra herself. Scholars are divided, and the reader must decide. However, if the lines refer to Electra, as I believe, their remarks here support those who feel that Electra has simply lost control of her emotions. However, her points are valid and one does not talk about good and bad conduct in neutral terms. Clytemnestra's marriage to Aegisthus and her neglect of her children by Agamemnon are indefensible. Her subsequent behavior in this scene shows that she cannot answer these charges. One is left then with the impression that Electra has won this encounter where *reverence* is the issue, but that she has failed with respect to *justice*.

Clytemnestra herself breaks off the discussion which she had initiated: "By Artemis I swear, you will pay for this / when Aegisthus comes home" (845–46 / 626–27). Electra points out that she has turned from argument to threat. Clytemnestra makes no response, but instead asks Electra to be silent so she can make her sacrifice.

In the prayer which follows, Clytemnestra cannot speak freely because Electra is watching her. She tells Apollo that she must make a "guarded" (861 / 638) prayer. She cannot ask that Orestes not return, but instead she asks for "everything to go on as it is, / untroubled" (876–77 / 650). This remark's falsity is proved by the very conditions of this speech. Her behavior here also undercuts her earlier claim that "I feel no remorse" (737 / 549–50). She will admit to her true inner feelings once she thinks Orestes is dead.

She ends her speech in a conventional way, but what happens next gives it an unintended meaning:

> CLYTEMNESTRA It goes without saying,
> the children of Zeus see all things.
> Amen.
>
> OLD MAN Ladies, can you tell me for certain
> if this is the house of Aegisthus the king?
> (890–94 / 659–61)

Apollo has heard her prayer, and he responds. The Old Man will seem to bring her the answer to her prayers. We expect this kind of misdirection from Apollo, the great riddler, of whom the early philosopher Heraclitus said, "The god at Delphi does not say; he does not conceal; he gives a sign."

When the Old Man enters, a new stage in the sufferings of Electra begins. This process begins with a sudden jolt:

> OLD MAN Orestes is dead. That is the sum of it.
> ELECTRA OI 'GO TALAINA.
> My death begins now.
> CLYTEMNESTRA What are you saying, what are you saying?
> Don't bother with her. (907–11 / 673–75)

This short passage indicates to us the response that the two women will display through gesture during the Old Man's long and exciting speech.

Once the speech has ended, Clytemnestra responds: "To give birth is terrible, incomprehensible. / No matter how you suffer, / you cannot hate a child you've born" (1042–44 / 770–71). How do we take what she says here? There is no reason to doubt her sincerity. It is possible to conclude that some compromise between her and her children is possible and that the vengeance is wrong.[18] However, she will admit that

---

18. "And in this scene he subtly transfers our sympathy to her" (Kells, 8).

she thinks Orestes' death is a good thing just a few moments later. Seen in the full context of the scene, it would appear that Sophocles has simply given his Clytemnestra a human touch.[19]

The Old Man suggests that he should not have come, and she immediately admits that she feels relief. Because of Orestes' constant threats, "Time stood like a deathmaster over me.../ Now I am free" (1056–58 / 781–83). In her elation, she reveals thoughts she has denied until now:

> And to tell you the truth,
> she did more damage.
> She lived in my house
> and drank
> my lifeblood neat!   (1061–65 / 784–86)

Although she claimed that she felt no remorse when she first entered the stage (737 / 549–50), here she admits that she has been enervated and depressed. Her reference to Electra's drinking her blood shows that in her own mind Electra is something like a Fury.[20] Electra accuses Clytemnestra of *hybris* ("Orestes!.../.../ your own mother insults you," 1071–73 / 789–90), and gets her to express her pleasure at Orestes' death more openly: "Well you're no fine sight. / But he looks as fine as can be" (1075–76 / 791). Fine maternal feeling here!

At the end of this scene, Clytemnestra is still very much aware of Electra: "Stranger, you deserve a reward / if you really have put a stop on her traveling tongue" (1082–83 / 797–98). And her exit line is also concerned with her: "Just leave her out here / to go on with her evil litany" (1088–89 / 802–3). An audience steeped in this story might see here that Electra performs a function like that of a Fury, as a "distracter" (*parakopa, Eumenides* 339). In the similar scene in Aeschylus' *Libation Bearers*, Clytemnestra sends the messenger (in this version, Orestes himself) to the men's quarters and later sends a message for Aegisthus to come with his bodyguard. In this play, Clytemnestra sends no such message, and when Orestes arrives he is welcomed into the main hall where he stands beside Clytemnestra as she prepares the urn for burial. One reason that she does not show more caution is the distraction caused by Electra.

Electra is alone on stage with the Chorus, and she speaks of the effect on her of Orestes' death: "You have torn away the part of my mind /

---

19. This remark was made about her by Professor Jack Wright in his critique of the production I observed.
20. R. P. Winnington-Ingram (note 12 above), p. 233; "For all her bravado, she lived in fear."

where hope was— / my one hope in you" (1096–98 / 809–10). She had said at the beginning of the play that Orestes was her only hope. Now that support is gone, and "Life is no desire of mine anymore" (1117 / 822). She says that she will "lie / unloved" before the door to the palace (1111–12 / 819–20), and I assume she sings the following dialogue from a lying position, her physical position mirroring her mental depression.

The Chorus immediately turns to the gods, "Where are you lightnings of Zeus!" (1119 / 823). Electra resists; she does not want to turn to false hopes. The Chorus thinks of a parallel (it often does)— Amphiaraus, one of the Seven Against Thebes. Electra counters that he is a bad choice because his son avenged him by killing his mother. Electra remains focused on what she can do, on deeds with her own hands, like other Sophoclean heroes, and so she ends the *kommos*:

> Laid out
> somewhere
> not by my hands.
> Not with my tears.   (1162–65 / 869–70)

The mood abruptly shifts when Chrysothemis enters:

> I am so happy, I ran here to tell you—
> putting good manners aside!   (1166–67 / 871–72)

This should mark the beginning of the discovery and of the change of Electra's fortunes. Chrysothemis is absolutely certain that Orestes has returned: "I saw the evidence with my own eyes" (1181 / 886); yet she is easily persuaded by Electra that she is wrong ("What a fool I am...," 1236 / 934). Once again, Electra dominates the action.

Electra suddenly shifts to a new topic: "...But listen to me. / You could ease our sorrow" (1240–41 / 938–39). Chrysothemis responds to this with her characteristic common sense: "How? Raise the dead?" (1242 / 940). Chrysothemis agrees to display some "nerve," but with a significant condition: "If it *benefits* us, I will not refuse" (1246 / 944) (emphasis added). This is the language of expediency, and we know that this scene is headed into the same impasse with which their first scene began.

We expect talk here of loyalty, honor, and justice from Electra, and we will get it. But first she attacks Chrysothemis' expediency position with an unexpected vigor and clarity:

> Let's be blunt, girl, what hope is left?
> Your losses are mounting,
> the property gone and
> marriage
> seems a fading dream at your age —
> or do you still console yourself with thoughts of a
>   husband?
> Forget it. Aegisthus is not so naive
> as to see children born from you or from me—
> unambiguous grief for himself.   (1263–72 / 958–66)

Electra has destroyed Chrysothemis' position in her own terms. She has lost the property, and can never have children. In terms of benefit, little is left to her.

Chrysothemis' reply is equally strong. Her first argument, that they will fail if they try to kill Aegisthus, will only convince those so disposed. But failure is not the only prospect here, and Chrysothemis refers to two more:

> Death itself is not the worst thing.
> Worse is to live
> when you want to die.
> So I beg you,
> before you destroy us
> and wipe out the family altogether,
> control your temper.   (1323–29 / 1007–11)

Electra has already admitted the validity of this first point in their first scene when she said she lived "sufficiently for me" (my translation of line 354 in the Greek, line 479 in this translation). In Athens, slaves who were to give evidence in court were routinely broken on the rack. There are no illusions in such a place about the ability of human nature to endure anything. The second point is that one cannot pursue honor to the extent that it threatens the city or the family. This, too, an Athenian would recognize as valid. Chrysothemis and Electra are both advancing their arguments in very strong form, and so it is clear that there is no room here for compromise.

Electra suddenly shifts; instead of urging Chrysothemis to act, or castigating her, she turns to what she is suffering at Chrysothemis' hand:

> ELECTRA   At least realize you are driving me into dishonor.
> CHRYSOTHEMIS   Dishonor? No: foresight.   (1362–63 / 1035–36)

The word "dishonor" is important to Electra; Electra's life is devoted to honoring the dead (482 / 355–56). Chrysothemis' desertion of her is one in a series of dishonorings.

When Chrysothemis leaves, Electra appears to have lost all of her allies among the living. In this desperate situation, something unusual happens, so far as Sophoclean choruses are concerned. They depart from their usual caution and good sense, and they praise Electra precisely because she is powerless, "betrayed, / alone" (1422–23 / 1074). They praise her because she does *not* have forethought:

> Nor
> does she think
> to fear dying,
> no!   (1430–33 / 1078)

They end their song with an emphatic use of a word that means a great deal to Electra:

> you are the one who kept faith
> with the living laws,
> kept faith
> in the clear reverence
> of Zeus.   (1462–66 / 1095–97)

The word "reverence," which has been so important for Electra, is the entrance cue for Orestes. It is the moment of reversal, surely. But as soon as he enters, we realize that he will appear to be something quite different to Electra than the end of her troubles. Orestes says, of Orestes: "We have his remains in a small jar here— / for he's dead, as you see" (1484–85 / 1113–14). There could be no greater difference between what Electra sees and what she thinks she sees. Orestes, carrying out divine commands, will now push Electra even further into despair.

Orestes gives the urn to Electra, and she delivers a speech that was famous in antiquity and that remains emotionally powerful today. Although she occasionally refers to her specific situation, on the whole this is an extensive and accurate description of the feelings one has at the death of a loved person. The Chorus thinks her grief is excessive ("be reasonable," 1571 / 1171), but we do not share in that feeling because we know that everything will soon be all right.

Another reason for the power of this speech is the purity of spirit that Electra reveals. Reverence has been her theme word, and this speech is largely about reverence as it is acted out by a noble daughter and sister. She begins by addressing the urn itself, lamenting that her hopes have been dashed because Orestes now is "nothing" (1510 / 1129), and then recalls how she saved him with her own hands (1513 / 1132). She moves quickly to the next act with her hands that "reverence" would have required of her:

And I would have waited
and washed you ["with my loving hands," the Greek adds here]
and lifted you
up from the fire.... (1522–25 / 1138–40)

She addresses her wasted nurture of Orestes ("years of my love," 1532 /
1145; the Greek here refers to "a sweet labor").

Now she considers the loss of Orestes from another perspective. His
death meant also the disappearance of Agamemnon and the death of
Electra. From Orestes the person she nursed she turns to Orestes, who
had promised vengeance on her mother. This is her first overt reference
to Clytemnestra's death, but those who see this as sign of Electra's bloody-
mindedness take the comment out of context. For one thing, she says
Orestes has been saying that he would take vengeance on Clytemnestra,
and although Electra says here that Orestes' return would be "secret"
(1549 / 1155), Clytemnestra knew what he had been threatening to do
(1054 / 788–89). For another, Electra herself is stressing loss, not the
revenge that will never be. The thought begins "One day three people
vanished" (1542 / 1149), and so her reference to her enemies and to her
mother are illustrations of the nothingness that she now sees all around her.

She considers Orestes' remains again, his "ashes" (1554 / 1159), and
says he is a "shadow" (an image of human insignificance Sophocles has
used before).[21] By dying he has destroyed her, and she wishes to join him
in the urn:

Oh my love
take me there.
Let me dwell where you are.
I am already nothing.
I am already burning.
Oh my love, I was once part of you —
take me too!
Only void is between us.
And I see that the dead feel no pain. (1562–70 / 1163–70)

When Electra says "take me there," she means "take me into the urn
with you," as the Greek text makes clear. There is an echo here of the
greatest friendship in Greek literature; the ghost of Achilles' best friend,
Patroklus, asked Achilles to have his ashes placed in the same urn as his
own (*Iliad* 23.91–92).

The reference to herself as "nothing" (1565 / 1166) echoes what other
Sophoclean heroes say about themselves, or have others say about them, at

---

21. Odysseus says that all human beings are "shadows of smoke." *Aias* 126.

similar moments of ultimate evil fortune.[22] Although they are "nobodies," because of their extravagant failures, they are powerful in a fashion that is visible on the stage. For instance, in *Ajax*, Ajax's brother Teucer defends Ajax's right to burial, even though he had committed treason against the army. Agamemnon says that Teucer (a bastard) is "a nobody" who is standing up for a "nobody" (i.e., a dead man, 1231), just a few lines before Odysseus, Ajax's political enemy, arrives to defend him.

In this case, the person who will make Electra into the opposite of a "nothing" is standing beside her. Once again, a character in this play speaks lines that have a meaning in themselves, but they are given additional meaning because other characters are silently responding to those lines. It is not possible to say how much business Sophocles assigned to Orestes while this speech is going on. His mere presence on stage tells us that her suffering will soon end. But he also must be indicating the sympathy he will express soon after the speech ends.

The Chorus responds with traditional consolation for one who is grieving a death, but at this point there is a sudden shift. It is not Electra who responds to it, but the other character, Orestes: "What should I say? This is / impossible! I cannot hold my tongue much longer" (1576–77 / 1174–75). The moment we have been waiting for since the first lines of the play has arrived, and yet there is one more excruciating delay. Orestes has one request that to him seems trivial enough, but it leads to another emotional outburst:

> ORESTES Give back the urn, then, and you will hear
> everything.
> ELECTRA No! Don't take this from me, for Gods' sake,
> whoever you are.
> ORESTES Come now, do as I say. It is the right thing.
> ELECTRA No! In all reverence no please—don't take this
> away.
> It is all that I love. (1610–15 / 1205–8)

Again, Sophocles draws our attention to the stripping away from Electra of all that she cares for. And then he shows her losing yet one thing more:

---

22. The other passages are *Oedipus Tyrannus* 1188; *Oedipus at Colonus* 393; *Trachiniae* 1107; *Philoctetes* 1030. Only in the *Oedipus Tyrannus* is this paradoxical power not immediately visible. But even in that play the main character shows a strength that belies Creon's final line, in which he says that Oedipus power has not followed him to the end (1523).

ELECTRA Wrong to mourn my own dead brother?
ORESTES Wrong for you to say that word.
ELECTRA How did I lose the right to call him brother?
(1622–24 / 1212–14)

A more literal rendering of that last line would be "Am I so dishonored by the dead?" This word, "dishonored" (*atimos*), means a lot to Electra. When she defended herself to Chrysothemis the first time, she used the word "honor": "I am a violation to them. / And so, honor [*timas prosaptein*] the dead — / if any grace exists down there" (481–83 / 355–56). That the dead should not reciprocate the honor she has spent her life granting them is an annihilating thought.

This reference to being "dishonored" is the point of Electra's most complete degradation. In the very next line Orestes assures her that she has her honor: "Your rights you have" (1625 / 1215). In my experience, this is the most emotional passage in this drama. We have watched this stripping of Electra even longer than Orestes has. She sums that stripping up in one word, "dishonored." There has been no validation of her action, except by the Chorus. With Orestes' remark, her isolation has ended. We assent to his remark, and we feel relief that at last Electra knows the secret we have known since the beginning.

I would like to pause at this moment, just before Orestes announces that honor is hers by right, to ask why Sophocles should bring Electra to this point, stripped of everything she depends on. There is a discussion of this problem in Thomas Gould's last book, which has been of help to me.[23] Professor Gould observed that the passions aroused by literature were at the heart of the discussion of tragedy by Plato and Aristotle, although the passions are largely overlooked in modern criticism.[24] Plato would ban the sufferings (*pathe*) of Niobe, of the children of Pelops, and of Troy.[25] Aristotle admits in *Poetics* that suffering is necessary to the tragic, but he argues that our response to this suffering has a beneficial purpose, whatever "*katharsis*" may mean.

---

23. Thomas Gould, *The Ancient Quarrel Between Poetry and Philosophy*, Princeton University Press, 1991.
24. One classical scholar who did treat the passions in drama was Friedrich Nietzsche, whose book *The Birth of Tragedy* was first published in German in 1872. Another was Karl Reinhardt, whose *Sophokles*, first published in 1933, was translated by Hazel Harvey and David Harvey from the German in 1979, Oxford: Basil Blackwell. More recently, W. B. Stanford, *Greek Tragedy and the Emotions: An Introductory Study*, London: Routledge and Kegan Paul, 1983, notes there is "no comprehensive book on the subject" (p. 1). There are some remarks in Oliver Taplin, *Greek Tragedy in Action*, Berkeley: University of California Press, 1978; in particular, see chapter 10, "Emotion and Meaning in the Theatre."
25. *Republic* 2.380a 5–7.

Gould claims that Sophocles "brought the thrilling *pathe* of hero religion right into the theater and evidently felt that no explanation or apology was needed." That is, Sophoclean tragedy enables us to respond to the suffering and death that are part of human existence. In this play, those heroic sufferings occur in a special context: we know that Electra's sufferings are already over. And yet, this is one of the most tearful of all Greek dramas.[26] Perhaps we can only face hopelessness and death as fully as we do here when we are certain that everything will turn out all right.

But there is another explanation that I would like to suggest here. The stripping away of every support from Electra is reminiscent of a case posed by Glaukon in *The Republic of Plato*. Glaukon asks Socrates to compare two men, and to say who is the happier. The first man is completely unjust, but he has the reputation of being just and is successful in every way. Here is the second man, in Cornford's translation:

> Now set beside this paragon the just man in his simplicity and nobleness, one who, in Aeschylus' words, 'would be, not seem, the best.' There must, indeed, be no such seeming; for if his character were apparent, his reputation would bring him honours and rewards, and then we should not know whether it was for their sake that he was just or for justice's sake alone. He must be stripped of everything but justice, and denied every advantage the other enjoyed. Doing no wrong, he must have the worst reputation for wrong-doing, to test whether his virtue is proof against all that comes of having a bad name; and under this lifelong imputation of wickedness, let him hold on his course of justice unwavering to the point of death. And so, when the two men have carried their justice and injustice to the last extreme, we may judge which is the happier. (361b5–d3)[27]

Electra fits this situation from the beginning: she is a "just [woman] in (her) simplicity and nobleness," but she has "the worst reputation for wrong-doing." Like the man Glaukon imagines, Electra lacks both "rewards" and "honors" (*timai*).

This play poses the question of Glaukon, and it offers an answer. This answer is largely found in the play's action, in those many cases where it is implied that the other characters are under the authority of Electra, accepting that what she says is true and just. Thus, Orestes says something that we already know when he replies to Electra, "Your rights you have" (1625 / 1215). The exact phrasing of this line is significant; here is a closer version: "You are dishonored [*atimos*] by no one—that is not what is

---

26. There is a wonderful account by Fiona Shaw of the emotional impact of this play in Francis M. Dunn, editor, *Sophocles' "Electra" in Performance*, Stuttgart: M&P, 1996.

27. *The Republic of Plato*, translated with introduction and notes by Francis MacDonald Cornford, New York: Oxford University Press, 1945.

appropriate for you." This line thus refers to the phenomenon Arrowsmith had noted and that he thought John Jay Chapman had best expressed. That is, not only is it true that the dead honor Electra; everyone honors Electra. Chrysothemis' admission that Electra has justice on her side is honor. Clytemnestra's anguished mental state is honor as well. Everyone is taking their signal from Electra. Like Chapman's radical who sounds the note "A," Electra sounds "the just," and the just, in this play, is conversely what Electra sounds. This is why Clytemnestra's very-good-justice argument collapses and vanishes. Chrysothemis even assumes that whatever Electra says is true and doubts the evidence of her own eyes.

Electra has also been "happy" throughout this play. Electra herself explains how this could be so to Chrysothemis: she has an adequate life and she harms her enemies and honors her friends (479–82 / 354–56). On most realistic assessments this statement describes a happy life. But there is more to the answer than this: The play shows us Electra living on a different level of intensity from anyone else.

Orestes gives us a hint of this intensity early in this discovery scene, in which he uses the word "brilliant" ("famous" [*kleinon*], 1579 / 1177) to describe her: "Is this the brilliant Electra?" This word usually refers to a heroic reputation The usual explanation is that Electra is famous because of who her father was (as Orestes is "famous"),[28] but it seems to me that we have been aware that she is indeed "famous" since the beginning of the play, when Orestes wanted to wait and see her.

After Orestes has revealed himself and they have expressed their joy at being reunited, they shift to song and express the same emotions. Electra is lyric in mood and in meter; Orestes keeps urging her to control herself in prosaic iambic. Electra's opening lines are of considerable interest:

> IO GONAI.
> You exist!
> You came back,
> you found me—   (1650–53 / 1232–35)

One scholar translates the Greek text translated here as "You exist" literally as "Ah! birth—birth of a person to me most beloved ..."[29] This is not a normal form of address, but Orestes is the legitimate offspring (another meaning of *gone*), and it seems only apt that Electra, whose very name means the suppression of offspring,[30] should use it. When

28. *Sophocles ... Part VI. The Electra*, edited by Sir Richard C. Jebb, Cambridge: At the University Press, 1907, note on line 1177.

29. Kells, note on ll. 1232ff.

30. See the notes on ll. 663–69 and 1266–67.

Electra cries out that word she announces her release from that perverted marriage that she has been forced to witness and from the virginity forced on her by that polluted coupling. The manifest result of the deeds of Aegisthus and Clytemnestra has been the perversion of marriage and birth. Clytemnestra's legitimate children cannot inherit, and they cannot marry.

In the midst of this outpouring of love, Electra, for a chilling moment, remembers the horror of her past life

> ELECTRA Do not turn your face from me.
> Don't take yourself away.
> ORESTES Of course not. No one else will take me either.
> ELECTRA Do you mean that?
> ORESTES Yes, I do.   (1701–5 / 1276–80)

She reminds us, for a moment, of what she has had to see and what she has been forced not to see, all these years.

The singing ends, and Orestes immediately speaks as the cool planner: "We've no time for all that" (1722 / 1292). Electra agrees to help her brother and to deceive her mother in order to serve "the *daimon* who is now at hand," their momentary good luck—"the god who stands beside us now," as Carson puts it (1740 / 1306). This is a remarkable thing for a person to say who has been so closely identified with justice. Her own explanation is that she is so happy to see Orestes again that she can deny him in nothing. Perhaps we can forgive her this inconsistency because it is her heart that leads her to it. But one has come to expect so much of this woman. She ends this speech with a reminiscence of herself before her luck changed, Electra alone, desperate, and heroic: "Alone, / I would have done one of two things: / deliver myself or else die" (1760–62 / 1319–21).

The Old Man enters and urges them to hurry up. Orestes asks him how his mother has taken the news of his death. Another awkward moment; the Old Man does not tell all he knows

> ORESTES Are they happy at this?
> OLD MAN I'll tell you that later. For now,
> the whole plan is unfolding beautifully.
> Even the ugly parts.   (1786–89 / 1343–45)

What the Old Man means is not entirely clear. Some have suggested that he means that Clytemnestra's motherly feelings have distracted her and caused her to be taken in by the trick even more easily. Kells thinks that is what he means, and he concludes that Clytemnestra is not the evil woman Orestes and Electra take her to be.[31] However, there is plenty of evidence in this scene of her pleasure at Orestes' death and Electra's defeat. There is another possibility. In Aeschylus' trilogy, that evil gives rise to good is a pervasive theme; for instance, Athena says of the Furies in the *Eumenides*: "I see great profit to these citizens, coming out of those fearful faces" (990–91). The Old Man may well be referring to the broadest outlines of this traditional story.

Electra asks who the Old Man is, and upon learning that he is the very person into whose hands she committed the infant Orestes, she again breaks out in joy:

> Bless you, father!—Yes, father.
> That is who I see when I look at you now.
> There is no man on earth I have hated and loved like you
> on the one same day. (1814–17 / 1361–63)

It has been suggested that Electra's words here indicate mental instability.[32] That she is excited is undeniable. However, it is not irrational for her to see in the Old Man the reincarnation of her father. As the agent of Justice, the Old Man represents the dead man. For the same reason, it is reasonable for her to bless his hands and his feet. The Chorus has earlier described Vengeance as having many hands and many feet (663–64 / 489).

The ending of this scene suggests that Electra has not lost sight of her guiding principles, despite her excitement. After Orestes and Pylades bow to the gods before the house and go in, Electra prays, "show / how the gods reward / unholy action!" (*dys-sebeia*, "irreverence") (1843–45 / 1382–83). The word "reverence" introduced this scene (1465 / 1097). After the excitement caused by Orestes' appearance, she has regained her focus.

The Chorus now sings its third stasimon, which is very brief, as Sophocles' lyrics often are when the climactic action is about to occur. Once again its language recalls the traditional form of this story. Orestes and Pylades are identified with Furies, "the raw and deadly dogs" (1850 / 1388). The statement that "Hermes...guides him" (1857 / 1396) also has an archaic sound; in Aeschylus' *Eumenides*, Hermes was a silent character who guided Orestes from Delphi to Athens. The lyrics continue when Electra returns to the stage. Clytemnestra is heard

---

31. Kells, note on l. 1344.
32. Kells, p. 11.

off-stage, appealing to Orestes. Electra enjoys this awful event. These are grim lines:

> CLYTEMNESTRA Oh child my child, pity the mother who bore you!
> ELECTRA Yet you had little enough pity for him
> and none for his father! (1875–77 / 1410–12)

Harsh words but true. But Electra does not relent when Clytemnestra cries out:

> CLYTEMNESTRA OMOI.
> I am hit!
> ELECTRA Hit her a second time, if you have the strength!
> CLYTEMNESTRA OMOI MAL' AUTHIS.
> Again!
> ELECTRA If only Aegisthus could share this!
> (1882–87 / 1415–16)

There is no question that her words are harsh. But it is not clear what Electra means when she says "if you have the strength." Sophocles was famous for drawing a character in a single line and this time he has made only two words do the work of many: "does not *ei stheneis* ["if you have the strength"] imply something more than is to be expressed by loud and complicated lyrical lamentations about her feelings at that dreadful moment?"[33] This is true, of course, but there is also some significance in the fact that she spoke of those turbulent inner feelings. Even here, she is not so ignorant of the inner forces driving her as Aeschylus' Clytemnestra or Euripides' Electra. But she does not weaken; she looks forward to dealing with Aegisthus (1887 / 1416).

When Orestes enters, stained with blood, he and Electra have a short but significant exchange. This is a moment of great danger—one where one could commit a regrettable excess, or reveal mental instability. In their brief dialogue, both are markedly restrained:

> ELECTRA Orestes, how does it go?
> ORESTES Good, so far—at least so far as Apollo's oracle
> was good (1897–99 / 1424–25)

In the dark reading, this line can be taken to mean that Apollo's oracle was not valid, but Orestes himself means that it is for Apollo to say

33. J. T. Sheppard, "The Tragedy of Electra, According to Sophocles" (note 4 above), p. 88.

whether this was a good deed. In the Aeschylean version, he actually goes to Delphi after the murder and proceeds according to Apollo's instructions. There is also an echo here of the *Odyssey*. When the old nurse sees that the suitors are dead and is about to shout out in triumph, Odysseus restrains her by insisting that he was acting in accord with the gods:

> No cries of triumph now.
> It's unholy to glory over the bodies of the dead.
> These men the doom of the gods has brought low,
> and their own indecent acts.[34]

Electra is not satisfied with this answer. She must know exactly what happened:

> ELECTRA Is the creature dead?
> ORESTES Your good mother will not insult you anymore.
>   (1900–1901 / 1426–27)

The Greek word translated here as "creature" means nothing more than "wretch," the person who has suffered. If anything, it indicates some slight compassion.

In Orestes' response, the word here translated "insult" literally means "dishonor" (*atimesei*), and echoes his line that was discussed earlier, "You are dishonored [*atimos*] by no one—that is not what is appropriate for you." In both cases, Orestes reveals that relieving Electra of her dishonor is constantly on his mind and has almost the same status as the oracle of Apollo.

After this dialogue ends, the Chorus sees that Aegisthus is coming. It is in the spirit of things now: "You have won the first round. Now for the second" (1908 / 1434). It is no more troubled by deceit now than Electra seems to be: "Why not drop a few friendly words in his ear" (1913 / 1437–38).

Aegisthus speaks in the manner of a tyrant from the beginning. He makes no formal address but begins with a question, "Does anyone know..." (1916 / 1442). His address to Electra is even more insulting: "You! / yes you!—you've never been shy / to speak your mind" (1919–21 / 1445–46). He is completely lacking in sympathy—he asks her about the news because Orestes was a concern to her. He speaks as a tyrant when he orders the gates opened: "take my bit on your tongue / or learn the hard way" (1940–42 / 1462–63). Creon also spoke of his rule as a "bit" when he was at his harshest (*Antigone* 477). Electra plays along: "As for

34. Homer, *Odyssey*, translated by Robert Fagles, N.Y.: Penguin Books, 1996, Book 22, lines 436–39 (lines 411–13 in the Greek text).

me, I am playing my part to the end" (1942 / 1464). It appears that she is opening the gates herself—no matter what Aegisthus says, on this stage Electra is in control. She obeys him with a sarcastic acceptance of expedience: "I've learned to side with the winners" (1943 / 1465). Electra toys with Aegisthus. Some have found this baiting distasteful. There is a danger of excess, and she is close to the limit.

Aegisthus removes the cover from the body, expecting to find Orestes, and finds Clytemnestra instead. This is one of the most exciting moments in Greek tragedy. However, before Aegisthus raises the cover, Sophocles adds a subtle touch to his character. Up until this point, Aegisthus has been presented purely as a villain, but after he has said that the gods have caused Orestes' death, Sophocles has him restrain himself: "if that remark offends, / I unsay it" (1946–47 / 1467). By making this qualification, Aegisthus shows just enough human decency to make him a believable human being.

Aegisthus raises the sheet, realizes that he has been trapped, and asks (in the language of Aeschylus' version of the story) "whose is the net?" (a closer translation than "who set the trap?," 1960 / 1476–77). Orestes answers with another Aeschylean phrase: "Don't you realize yet / that you're talking to dead men alive?" (1961–62 / 1477–78). Just as when a messenger in the Aeschylean *Libation Bearers* says that "the dead are killing the living" (886), the words "the dead" refer to Orestes, but there is also the hint that Agamemnon himself is acting with Orestes.

To this point, the revenge has proceeded without major hindrance. Electra's savage remarks about hitting her mother a second time were unsettling, but Orestes' comments that Apollo sanctioned the murder and that Clytemnestra had maltreated Electra were restrained and persuasive. Indeed, we expect the actual butchering of the villains to be unproblematic since the play to this point has given us plenty of reasons to assent to it.

This is not the case. A number of troubling things occur between lines 1968 / 1483 and 2003 / 1507. Electra refuses to let Aegisthus speak, invoking a principle that calls her dedication to justice into question and displays a brutality that makes us doubt her human decency. With his final words, Orestes recommends the death penalty for every transgression of law (2001–3 / 1506–7), and this indicates a fundamental misunderstanding of justice and an insane trust in violence.

I have stated these difficulties in their strongest form because so much is at stake here. I personally believe in the noble Electra—I carry her with me as an "imagined other." She is part of my own moral dialogue. Further, after struggling with these problematic lines, I am convinced that Sophocles intended us to struggle with them.

Aegisthus, accepting that he has lost, asks permission to speak. At this
moment Electra breaks in:

> No!
> Don't let him speak—
> by the gods! Brother—no speechmaking now!
> When a human being is so steeped in evil as this one
> what is gained by delaying his death?   (1968–72 / 1483–86)

It is not clear exactly what the phrase translated "steeped in evils"
means,[35] but whatever that phrase means, the remark that there is no
benefit in letting the accused make speeches reveals an astounding
ignorance of the nature of justice. In Aeschylus' *Oresteia*, the next
phase of this story, when Orestes defends himself at the trial in Athens,
is largely concerned with the importance of persuasion. I do not think
we can defend this statement. Since her justice argument to Clytemnestra earlier was also flawed, I would suggest that she is consistently wrong
about larger abstract issues.

What Electra says next is more troubling: "Kill him at once. / Throw
his corpse out / for scavengers to get" (1973–75 / 1487–89). Electra
remains true to her own immediate experience when she says that she
wants the body "unseen by us" (not translated here). It was the sight of
Aegisthus that disgusted her. What she says about disposing of the body
is not so easily excused. Dishonoring a dead body was a sign of excess in
both *Antigone* and *Ajax*. If Electra means to feed Aegisthus to the dogs,
one might argue that she is no longer human. As so often in these critical
passages, we must examine what she says closely. The issue is not
whether Electra expects Aegisthus' body to be eaten by dogs and birds.
She does, and in one version of the story this was what happened.
Rather, it is whether this is something that she intends to enforce. In
the other cases, the ruler announced penalties against anyone who
buried the corpse. In the Greek text, Electra says it is "likely" (*eikos*,
1488) that he will get a certain kind of "grave-diggers" (a closer translation than "scavengers"). Nonetheless, it seems to me unworthy of her
even to consider what will happen to his body. That the dead are dead
and that it is insane to punish a body is a truism in Greek tragedy. On the
other hand, Electra's final lines seem to me to be carefully restrained:
"Nothing less than this / can cut the knot of evils / inside me" (1976–78 /
1489–90).

---

35. This phrase could mean either "considering all the evils in which all of us are tangled" (referring
to the whole messy history of the family) or "considering all the evils he has done" (referring to his
adultery and murder). Even if she refers to his adultery, he has the right to speak, even though the
death penalty is appropriate and treated as unproblematic in Aeschylus.

Electra says nothing of the future; rather, she speaks solely of release from the past. And this she will surely get. Whatever lies ahead for her, she will not be forced to witness the disgusting behavior of Clytemnestra and Aegisthus. This short passage forces us to consider the dark reading. The question is not whether Electra is stained by the events of this play. Rather, it is to what degree she has been stained. Karl Reinhardt takes a balanced position:

> she appears in a world of the wicked and the false as the extreme of great-heartedness which enables normal humanity to survive; she is the woman who loves and hates from the depths of her heart; because of her hate and her love, she suffers, is persecuted, and is even alienated from herself, disfigured, and consumed by her own fires.[36]

I would suggest that this view still gives too much weight to the negative aspects of Electra. Just as Clytemnestra had a touch of maternal feeling and Aegisthus a touch of decency, so Electra has a touch of the madness produced by bloodshed. She is not one of the raging mad-women of the stage, as Kells describes her. Rather, she is a person we admire and care for. We are pained to see her take on any taint. Thus we cannot completely dismiss the dark reading. Kells goes too far when he sees her becoming mad, but Sheppard's more subtle Electra is the one I have delineated here.

After Electra makes her intervention, Orestes and Aegisthus each seek to control the situation. Orestes, as has been noted, wants to introduce a symmetry into the revenge. Aegisthus must be killed in a specific place, "the spot / where you slaughtered my father" (1986–87 / 1495–96). Orestes pursues the issue of justice:

> AEGISTHUS You lead the way.
> ORESTES No, you go first.
> AEGISTHUS Afraid I'll escape?
> ORESTES You shall not die on your own terms.
> I will make it bitter for you.
> (1995–99 / 1502–6)

It has been suggested that in these lines Orestes is trying to make the punishment unpleasant in every way (so Jebb), or even that he is torturing Aegisthus.[37] However, the amount of pain involved here is so minute that Orestes must have some purpose other than making

---

36. Reinhardt (note 24 above), p. 138.
37. So Kells, note on l. 1503.

Aegisthus' death unpleasant. Since Orestes has just said that Aegisthus must die in the same place where he killed Agamemnon, it seems likely that here, too, he is trying to give this action the character of a just punishment.[38] If reciprocity is the principle involved, then it must be so that Aegisthus' death will resemble that of Agamemnon by being not what he wanted. However, it is also possible that Orestes is making certain that Aegisthus dies against his will, to preserve the quality of a punishment.

not really a challenge

Orestes' final lines, on the other hand, seem to be clearly flawed: "And let such judgment fall / on any who wish to break the law: / kill them!" (2000–2002 / 1505–7). Despite the crudity of Orestes' logic, it contains the concept of equity. It was a feature of the archaic laws of Drakon that every crime was punished by death, and it may be that what the first audience heard in Orestes' final lines is a primitive justice.

Electra and Orestes have played their parts well, but they do not fully understand what they have done, nor have they remained unmarked by violence. Electra has achieved near divine status in her martyrdom to right conduct, but she frequently errs when she speaks about the nature of justice and of just process. One of the main reasons Aegisthus should die is to relieve her of the sight of him, but he should be allowed to speak and should not be thrown to the dogs. Orestes is true to the letter of Apollo's oracle, by employing the trick, but also to the spirit of that oracle, by injecting proportionality into the punishment where he can. On the other hand, he has no inkling of the justice that will emerge when he goes to Athens to stand trial.

The Chorus ends the play with a careful statement, in its way as limited as those of Electra when she said that Aegisthus' murder is the release of pains for her: "O seed of Atreus: / you suffered and broke free . . ." (2004–5 / 1508–9). This seems to me to be true. No matter what Orestes suffers for killing his mother, he is a free man, in control, restored to his proper status; this also implies that the legitimate will inherit in the future. That is what I take it to mean when it says to the seed of Atreus, in its final line, "you have won your way through / to the finish" (2007–8 / 1510). Orestes is "the seed," but it is also true that "the seed" is the process of legitimate inheritance—only when legitimate inheritance exists is the seed really a seed. It does not say that the future will be without trouble, any more than Electra did. The substantial accomplishment here is that Argos and the house of Atreus are "free." Thus Electra's word, "release," is apt— the mood of the end of the play is the mood of release.

38. Orestes in Aeschylus' version also stresses proportionality when he says to Clytemnestra: "you killed one whom you should not have; now suffer that which you should not" (*Libation Bearers* 930).

We should not underestimate this mood of release. That this play is about a horrible act is indubitable, but it is also about the death of tyrants. Their rule rested on force and nothing else. And the Chorus' reference to freedom and order restored is of transcendent importance. On at least one occasion, a performance of this play turned into a celebration of democracy. The Greek of the Chorus' final lines contains the word "freedom." When I saw this play in Athens in the early 1970s, under the reign of the Colonels, after the play ended the crowd began to chant, "freedom, freedom." Men in military uniform scuttled out of the theater. Roses rained down on the actress who had portrayed Electra.

MICHAEL SHAW

ON THE TRANSLATION

SCREAMING IN TRANSLATION: THE ELECTRA OF SOPHOCLES

And how the red wild sparkles dimly burn
Through the ashen grayness

ELIZABETH BARRETT BROWNING

A translator is someone trying to get in between a body and its shadow. Translating is a task of imitation that faces in two directions at once, for it must line itself up with the solid body of the original text and at the same time with the shadow of that text where it falls across another language. Shadows fall and move. The following paper, based on my own attempts to render the Greek text of Sophocles' *Electra* into English, will indicate some of the moving shadows cast by this unusual and difficult play and describe how they have proven problematic for its translation into readable verse and performable drama.

First I will consider screaming. The presence in Greek drama of bursts of sound expressing strong emotion (like OIMOI or O TALAINA or PHEU PHEU) furnishes the translator with a very simple and intractable problem. It has been generally assumed that they represent a somewhat formulaic body of ejaculatory utterance best rendered into English by some dead phrase like "Alas!" or "Woe is

I am grateful to Francis Dunn (then) of Northwestern University in Chicago (now UC Santa Barbara), who gave me the opportunity to present this paper at the symposium *Sophocles' Electra: Greek Tragedy In Word And Action* cosponsored by the Departments of Classics and Theatre in May 1993. Greek texts are cited from the edition of Sir Richard Jebb, Cambridge, 1894. Works consulted include the translation of D. Grene in *Sophocles II*, Chicago, 1957, the commentary of J. C. Kamerbeek, Leiden, 1974, the edition of R. H. Mather 1889, and the translation of Ezra Pound and R. Flemming, New York, 1990.

me!" But I discovered when studying the language of Electra that her screams are far from formulaic. They contribute to her characterization as creatively as many other aspects of her diction.

Electra's diction, especially her verbs, is the second topic I will discuss. There is one particular verb, repeated seven times in the play, with which Sophocles takes linguistic risks that have no synonym in English. It is a verb that means "to cause pain" and Electra uses it in unique ways. The uniqueness of Electra's pain emerges not only from her diction but also musically. Thirdly and very briefly I will discuss the verbal and rhythmic music of Electra, especially in her interactions with the Chorus in the opening movement of the play.

Screaming is a fairly typical activity of characters in Greek drama. But it was Virginia Woolf who noticed, perhaps after a night of listening to the birds in her garden talking ancient Greek, that there is something original about the screaming of Sophocles' Electra. In her essay on this play in *The Common Reader* Virginia Woolf says:[1]

> ... his Electra stands before us like a figure so tightly bound that she can only move an inch this way, an inch that. But each movement must tell to the utmost, or ... she will be nothing but a dummy, tightly bound. Her words in crisis are, as a matter of fact, bare; mere cries of despair, joy, hate ... But it is not so easy to decide what it is that gives these cries of Electra in her anguish their power to cut and wound and excite.

Indeed it is not easy to decide what gives the screaming of Electra its power. Sophocles has invented for her a language of lament that is like listening to an X-ray: Electra's cries are just bones of sound. I itemize the cries of Electra as follows:

1. O
2. IO
3. PHEU
4. AIAI
5. TALAINA
6. OIMOI MOI
7. IO MOI MOI
8. E E IO
9. E E AIAI
10. IO GONAI
11. OIMOI TALAINA
12. OI 'GO TALAINA

---

1. London, 1925, p. 26.

13. ΟΤΟΤΟΤΟΤΟΙ ΤΟΤΟΙ
14. ΙΟ ΜΟΙ ΜΟΙ DYSTENOS

In range and diversity of aural construction Electra surpasses all other screamers in Sophocles, including Philoctetes who suffers from gangrene in the foot and Herakles who gets burned alive at the end of his play. Let us consider how Electra constructs her screams. It should be noted at the outset that none of them occur extra metrum: they scan, and are to be taken as integral to the rhythmic and musical economy of her utterance. As units of sound they employ the usual features of ritual lament (assonance, alliteration, internal rhyme, balance, symmetry, repetition)[2] in unusual ways. She creates, for example, certain unpronounceable concatenations of hiatus like E E AIAI or E E IO which hold the voice and the mouth open for the whole length of a measure of verse and are as painful to listen to as they are to say. The effect of such sounds is well described by Electra herself at 242–43, where she refers to her own language of lament in the phrase:

pterygas / oxytonôn goon
πτέρυγας / ὀξυτόνων γόων

literally, "wings of sharpstretched laments" or "wings of screamings that are strained to sharp points." The phrase in Greek undulates harshly, onomatopoeic of the cries themselves. But it has also an image of straining or stretching—the straining of sound and emotion against enclosing limits—which is important to the concept of the whole passage. Electra here is talking about the evil of the house of Atreus as if it were a trap that has closed around her life. She believes that nothing except her voice can penetrate the walls of this enclosure. "My cries are wings, they pierce the cage," is how I translated the verse, losing the sound effect of the Greek but retaining the aggressivity of the cries and also the terrible sense of stuckness that characterizes Electra's self-descriptions. For example at v. 132f. she summarizes her own stuck situation in the double negative construction:

oud' ethelô.../ mê ou...stenachein
οὐδ ἐθέλω.../ μή οὐ...στενάχειν
"I cannot not grieve..."

This same stuckness informs certain of the screams of Electra, for example the strangely compressed oi 'go talaina. This phrase is a

2. On characteristics of funeral lament, see M. Alexiou, *The Ritual Lament in Greek Tradition*. Cambridge, 1974.

three-part construction which combines the exclamation *oi* (conventionally translated "Alas!" or the like) with the first person singular pronoun *egô* ("I") and the standard adjective of tragic self-description *talaina* ("wretched, pitiable, miserable, sorry, sad, messed up"). These three components are forced together at high emotional pressure as if they formed a single entity of sound and self. It is an entity that elides Electra of part of her *egô*: the pronoun *egô* sacrifices its opening vowel to the encroachment of the exclamatory *oi* and then merges immediately with the epithet *talaina* so as to enclose Electra's *egô* in grief from both sides. As she says of herself at v. 147: "Grieving is a pattern that is cut and fitted around my mind" (*eme . . . araren phrenas*).

The mind of Electra is a remarkable machinery. It provides an unrelentingly lucid commentary on her stuck situation from the first moment she enters the stage. She begins the parodos, for example, by naming two other stuck people as paradigms for herself: Niobe, who is literally petrified by grief for her dead children; and Procne, who has been transformed into a nightingale by remorse for her dead son. But it is not their emotional paralysis that Electra venerates. For her, Niobe and Procne represent a victory of female sign language. They are women who have left behind human form and rational speech yet have not let go the making of meaning. The water that pours perpetually down Niobe's rock face, the twittering that pours perpetually from Procne's bird mouth, are analogues for Electra's private language of screams. Each of these three women manages to say what she means from within an idiolect that is alien or unknown to other people. Each of them manages, although stuck in a form of life that cuts her off from the world of normal converse, to transect and trouble and change that world by her utterance. Electra admires Niobe and Procne because each of them has a significatory power, as she does herself, to sabotage the world of other people and normal converse.

Now Electra has a special verb for this action of sabotage, which she has come to regard as identical with her own function. It is the verb *lupein* and it figures in one of the strangest sentences of the play. The Greek lexicon defines *lupein* in the active as "to grieve, vex, cause pain, do harm, harass, distress, damage, violate" and in the passive as "to be vexed, violated, harassed," etc. or "to grieve, feel pain." The cognate noun *lupê* means "pain of body" or "pain of mind" or "sad plight." Electra uses this verb to assert her philosophy of action at v. 355, where she says that public lament is her whole function in life because by this action she can *lupein*—grieve, harass, distress, damage, violate—her mother. In the following verses she summarizes her philosophy of self in a sentence formed around this same verb *lupein* (363–64):

emoi gar estô toume mê lupein monon / boskêma
ἐμοὶ γὰρ ἔστω τοὐμὲ μὴ λυπεῖν μόνον / βόσκημα
"For me yes let be not damaging me the only food."

"For me be it food enough that I do not wound mine own
conscience." (R. C. Jebb)

"For me let it be meat and drink not to put my self out." (R. H. Mather)

"All the food I need is the quiet of my conscience." (D. Grene)

"Keep my self-respect anyhow." (E. Pound)

During the days and weeks when I was working on this play I used to
dream about translating. One night I dreamed that the text of the play
was a big solid glass house. I floated above the house trying to zero in on
v. 363. I was carrying in my hands wrapped in a piece of black cloth the
perfect English equivalent for *lupein* and I kept trying to force myself
down through the glass atmosphere of the house to position this word in
its right place. But there was an upward pressure as heavy as water.
I couldn't move down, I swam helplessly back and forth on the surface of
the transparency, waving my black object and staring down at the text
through fathoms of glass. And I was just about to take the black cloth off
and look at the word so as to memorize it for later when I awoke, when
I awoke.

I never did discover, asleep or awake, what was under that black cloth.
I never did hit upon the right translation for *lupein*. But Electra's use of
this verb (particularly at v. 363) continues to disturb me because of the
way it sums her up. As Virginia Woolf says, "the stable, the permanent,
the original human being is to be found there."[3] When we look at the
syntax of v. 363 we see a sentence formed around a verb, the infinitive
lupein, but the verb is made into a negative by the addition of the adverb
mê ("to not vex, harm, damage, etc. . . . ") and then the negatived verb is
made into a noun by the addition of the article *to* ("the act of not vexing,
harming, damaging, etc. . . . "). So, too, in Electra's life we see all positive
action negatived by hatred and then this negative condition reified as
personal destiny. Actionless she feeds on her own negativity. "It is the
only Food that grows," as Emily Dickinson says of another equally
private religion of pain.[4] This strange black food is named again by
Electra, this time as a noun, at v. 822 in its full suicidal implication:

---

3. *The Common Reader* (note 1 above), 27.
4. T. H. Johnson, ed., *The Complete Poems of Emily Dickinson*, Boston, 1890. # 1555.

lupê d' ean zô· tou biou d' oudeis pothos.
λύπη δ', ἐὰν ζῶ· τοῦ βίου δ' οὐδεὶς πόθος.
"It is damage [pain, violation, etc.] if I continue to exist.
No desire for life [is in me]."

She expresses another death wish with the participle of the verb at v. 1170:

tous gar thanontas oukh horô lupoumenous.
τοὺς γὰρ θανόντας οὐχ ὁρῶ λυτουμένους.
"For the dead, I see, feel no pain."

Electra has a talent for brutal antithesis but these statements are not, I think, rhetorically formed. They touch a null point at the center of the woman's soul. And they have the same X-ray quality as some of her screams.

But for the translator the problem presented by Electra's screams and diction in general is contextual. She uses fairly common verbs and nouns, and Sophocles goes out of his way to show us her X-ray utterances projected on the ordinary language screen of other people. This creates an especially jarring effect when we hear them using her words. For example when Orestes, dismissing the notion that lying and deceit are bad things, tosses off the phrase (59–60):

ti gar me lupei touth'...
τὰ γάρ με λυπεῖ τοῦθ'...
"What harm does this do me [to die in words if I am saved in fact]?"

In Orestes' much more lightly maintained moral order, Electra's black verb *lupei* is little more than a synonym for "What's the problem?" A similar shock effect is felt when we hear Clytemnestra appropriate Electra's noun *lupê* to denote pain of childbirth. Clytemnestra is refer-ring to Agamemnon and Iphigeneia when she says (532–33):

...ouk ison kamôn emoi / lupês, hot' espeir', hôsper hê tiktous' egô.
...οὐκ ἰσον καμὼν ἐμοὶ / ὅτ' ἐσπειρ', ὥσπερ ἡ τκτουσ' ἐγώ.
"...Did he have some share in the pain [*lupês*] of her birth? No! I did it myself."

This is one category of pain that the resolutely asexual Electra will never know, and furthermore, as she tells us repeatedly throughout the play, the very idea of genetic connection or genital analogy between herself and her mother fills her with horror. "Mother she is called but mother she is not," Electra announces at one point to her sister. And although on one level Electra can be said to instantiate every girl's fear of turning into her mother, it is also true that in this case both the girl and the mother are prodigious—the mother for her shamelessness, the girl for her shame. It is not until we hear Clytemnestra decline Electra's word *lupê* to its most fleshly and female connotation that we understand Electra's shame in its full human and sexual aspect. There is something *unnatural*, something radical and alien, for Sophocles and his audience, about the way female shame has constructed around Electra a sort of life-size funeral urn which she inhabits as if it were a life.

Alienation is also indicated musically in the Sophoclean text. Electra's music is a standing discrepancy to tragic convention and other people's expectations. She takes over the stage musically from the first moment of her entrance—in fact from before her entrance, for the first sound Electra makes at v. 77 interrupts the iambic procedure of the prologue with an offstage scream in what seems an aborted lyric anapest. The monodic song of Electra that follows is intrusive in every way. It replaces the entrance song of the Chorus which should occur at this point and usurps the anapestic meter in which the Chorus conventionally sings the entrance song. Rhetorically, Electra's monody rivals anything in Greek drama for the sheer egotism of its address. She begins by saying (86–87):

ô phaos hagnon / kai gês isomoir' aêr...
ὠφάος ἁγνὸν / καὶ γῆς ἰσόμοιρ' ἀήρ...
"O holy light and equal air shaped on the world..."

and goes on to call the entire cosmos to collaborate in her private drama of mourning and revenge. But the odd thing about this cosmic song is that it both begins and ends with a metaphor of measure. In the first verse (87) she measures air against earth with the phrase *gês isomoir' aêr*, and in the last verse she measures herself against the whole history of evil in the house of Atreus saying (119–20):

mounê gar agein ouketi sôkô / lupês antirrhopon achthos.
Μούνη γὰρ ἄγειν οὐκέτι σωκῶ / λύπης αντίρροπον.
"Because alone the whole poised force of my life is nothing against this pain."

It is typical of Sophoclean heroes to set for themselves cosmic parameters of moral action. By framing Electra in images of measure Sophocles reminds us that she is someone off the scale. And he is able to make this heroic discrepancy clear, in the long lyric interchange between Electra and the Chorus that follows her monody, by a very simple musical effect.

The dramatic purpose of this interchange is to show Electra in interaction with a society sympathetic to her dilemma and realistic about her options. And moreover to show Electra, in the midst of such people, utterly alone. The antiphonal nature of the song emphasizes this. Antiphony organizes the song into alternating strophes and antistrophes. Each strophic pair follows a principle of responsion whereby the first verse of the strophe responds metrically with the first verse of the antistrophe, the second verse with the second verse, and so on. This arrangement is generally used to create a lyric dialogue between two voices. If Electra and the Chorus had sung strophe and antistrophe, respectively, the effect would have been one of shared thought or interwoven emotion. But Sophocles has chosen to further subdivide each strophe and antistrophe so that each six lines of Electra respond with another six lines of Electra, each six lines of the Chorus respond with another six lines of the Chorus. They are each talking to themselves. Musically, it is an anti-dialogue.

Conceptually also. Each time the Chorus talks it sends a drift of platitudes down over Electra, who knocks them away with one hand. Each choral utterance attempts to steer the discussion towards general truths and perspectives wider than the individual life. Electra keeps pulling the focus back to herself with a resolute first-person pronoun or verb. The Chorus talks strategies for going on with life, Electra declares life an irrelevancy. It is death that absorbs Electra's whole imagination and the darkness that is soaking out of this one fact seems to color the music and reasoning of everything she says in the song, especially when we see these continually measured against the bright banalities of the Chorus. And at the point where Electra's anger and despair finally boil over (236) she throws the metaphor of measure back at the chorus with a question as jagged as a scream:

kai ti metron kakotâtos ephu?
καὶ τί μέτρον κακότατος ἔφυ;
"And at what point does the evil level off in my life, tell me that!"

ANNE CARSON

ELECTRA

Translated by
ANNE CARSON

With Introduction
and Notes by
MICHAEL SHAW

CHARACTERS

PAEDAGOGUS, OR OLD MAN servant and former tutor of Orestes

ORESTES son of Clytemnestra and Agamemnon, king of Argos

CHRYSOTHEMIS daughter of Clytemnestra and Agamemnon

ELECTRA daughter of Clytemnestra and Agamemnon

CLYTEMNESTRA Queen of Argos

AEGISTHUS paramour of Clytemnestra

CHORUS of Mycenaean women

PYLADES Orestes' silent friend

Line numbers in the right-hand margin of the text refer to the English translation only, and the Notes beginning on p. 295 are keyed to these lines. The bracketed line numbers in the running heads refer to the Greek text.

The scene is at Mycenae before the palace of Agamemnon.

Enter the OLD MAN *and* ORESTES *with* PYLADES.

cf Philoctetes

Ag as point of reference

PAEDAGOGUS You are his son! Your father
marshaled the armies at Troy once—
child of Agamemnon: look around you now.
Here is the land you were longing to see all that time.
Ancient Argos. You dreamed of this place.
The grove of Io, where the gadfly drove her.
Look, Orestes. There is the marketplace
named for Apollo,
wolfkiller god.
And on the left, the famous temple of Hera.   10
But stop! There—do you know what that is?
Mycenae. Yes. Look at it. Walls of gold!
Walls of death. It is the house of Pelops.
I got you out of there
out of the midst of your father's murder,
one day long ago.
From the hands of your sister
I carried you off. Saved your life. Reared you up—
to this: to manhood. To avenge your father's death.
So, Orestes! And you, dear   20
Pylades—
Now is the time to decide what to do.
Already the sun is hot upon us.
Birds are shaking, the world is awake.
Black stars and night have died away.
So before anyone is up and about
let's talk.
Now is no time to delay.
This is the edge of action.

filial piety

ORESTES I love you, old man.   30
The signs of goodness shine from your face.
Like a thoroughbred horse—he gets old,

231

but he does not lose heart,
he pricks up his ears—so you
urge me forward
and stand in the front rank yourself.
Good. Now,
I will outline my plan. You
listen sharp.
If I'm off target anywhere,   40
set me straight.
You see, I went to Pytho
to ask the oracle how I could get justice
from the killers of my father,
Apollo answered:

Take no weapons.
No shield.
No army.
Go alone—a hand in the night.
Snare them.   50
Slaughter them.
You have the right.

That is the oracle.
Here is the plan:
you go into the house at the first chance.
Find out all that is happening there.
Find out and report to us. Be very clear.
You're so old, they won't know you.
And your garlands will fool them.
Now this is your story: 60
you're a stranger from Phocis,
from the house of Phanoteus
(he's the most powerful ally they have).
Tell them on oath that Orestes is dead.
An accident. Fatal:
rolled out of his chariot on the racetrack at Delphi.
Dragged to death under the wheels.
Let that be the story.
Meanwhile, we go to my father's grave,

political angle

chariot death

as Apollo commanded,   70
to pour libation and crown the tomb
with locks of hair cut from my head.
Then we'll be back
with that bronzeplated urn
(you know, the one I hid in the bushes).
Oh yes, we'll fool them
with this tale of me dead,
burnt,
nothing left but ash.
What good news for them!   80

As for me—
what harm can it do
to die in words?
I save my life and win glory besides!   *assessment of words*
Can a mere story be evil? No, of course not—
so long as it pays in the end.
I know of shrewd men
who die a false death
so as to come home   *why?*
all the more valued.   90
Yes, I am sure:
I will stand clear of this lie
and break on my enemies like a star.

O land of my fathers! O gods of this place!
Take me in. Give me luck on this road.
House of my father:
I come to cleanse you with justice.   *justice*
I come sent by gods.
Do not exile me from honor!   *honor*
Put me in full command   100
of the wealth and the house!
Enough talk.   *ready to act*
Old man, look to your task.
We are off.
This is the point on which everything hinges.
This is the moment of proof.

ELECTRA (*a cry from inside the house*) IO MOI MOI DYSTENOS.

OLD MAN What was that? I heard
a cry—some servant in the house?

ORESTES Can it be poor Electra?   110
Should we stay here and listen?

recognition
thinking of Electra

OLD MAN No. Nothing precedes the work of Apollo.
That is our first step: your father's libations.
That is the way to win: action.

god
action

> *Exit* OLD MAN *and* ORESTES *with* PYLADES. *Enter* ELECTRA
> *from the palace.*

ELECTRA O holy light!
And equal air shaped on the world—
you hear my songs,
you hear the blows fall.
You know the blood runs
when night sinks away.   120
All night I watch.
All night I mourn,
in this bed that I hate in this house I detest.
How many times can a heart break?
Oh father,
it was not killer Ares
who opened his arms
in some foreign land
to welcome you.
But my own mother and her lover Aegisthus: 130
those two good woodsmen
took an axe and split you down like an oak.
No pity for these things,
there is no pity
but mine,
oh father,
for the pity of your butchering rawblood death.

Never
will I leave off lamenting,
never. No.   140
As long as the stars sweep through heaven.
As long as I look on this daylight.
No.
Like the nightingale who lost her child
I will stand in his doorway
and call on his name.
Make them all hear.
Make this house echo.
O Hades!
Persephone!   150
Hermes of hell!
Furies, I call you!
Who watch
when lives are murdered.
Who watch when loves betray.
Come! Help me! Strike back!
Strike back for my father murdered!
And send my brother to me.
Because
alone,   160
the whole poised force of my life is nothing
against this.

                        Enter CHORUS.

CHORUS Your mother is evil   *strophe* 1
        but oh my child why
        melt your life away in mourning?   *comfort v. goad*
        Why let grief eat you alive?
        It was long ago
        she took your father:
        her hand came out of unholy dark
        and cut him down.
        I curse the one   170
        who did the deed
        (if this is right to say).   *why wouldn't it be?*

235

ELECTRA You are women of noble instinct
and you come to console me
in my pain.
I know.
I do understand.
But I will not let go this man or this mourning.

He is my father.   180
I cannot not grieve.

double negative

Oh my friends,
Friendship is a tension. It makes delicate demands.
I ask this one thing:
let me go mad in my own way.

antistrophe 1

CHORUS Not from Hades' black and universal lake can you lift
him.
Not by groaning, not by prayers.
Yet you run yourself out
in a grief with no cure,
no time-limit, no measure,   190
It is a knot no one can untie.
Why are you so in love with
things unbearable?

Myth – Procne – Tereus
Procne   Itys
killed Itys.
Tereus raped + ripped out tongue of Philomela, who wove story + sent it to Procne

ELECTRA None but a fool or an infant
could forget a father
gone so far and cold.
No.

no in glossary

child of Philomela + Tireus, Philomela killed Itys after Tireus raped her sister Procne.

Lament is a pattern cut and fitted around my mind—
like the bird who calls Itys! Itys! endlessly,
bird of grief,
angel of Zeus.   200
O heartdragging Niobe,
I count you a god:
buried in rock yet
always you weep.

brag   *Leto greater than ~~Apollo~~*
greater than Apollo & Artemis killed all her children she turned to rock in grief

Turned into a nightingale

CHORUS You are not the only one in the world   *strophe 2*
my child, who has stood in the glare of grief.

236

Leto – Titan generation w/ Zeus had Apollo & Artemis

Compare yourself:
you go too far.
Look at your sister, Chrysothemis: 210
she goes on living. So does Iphianassa.
And the boy—his secret years are sorrowful too,
but he will be brilliant
one day when Mycenae welcomes him home
to his father's place, to his own land
in the guidance of Zeus—
Orestes!

ELECTRA Him yes!
I am past exhaustion
in waiting for him—   220
no children,
no marriage,
no light in my heart.
I live in a place of tears.
And he
simply forgets.   *cf Orestes re Apollo*
Forgets what he suffered,
forgets what he knew.
Messages reach me, each one belied.
He is passionate—as any lover.   230
But his passion does not bring him here.

CHORUS Have courage,   *antistrophe 2*
my child.
Zeus is still great in heaven,
he watches and governs all things.
Leave this anger to Zeus: it burns too high in you.
Don't hate so much.
Nor let memory go.
For time is a god who can simplify all.
And as for Orestes   240
on the shore of Crisa
where oxen graze—
he does not forget you.

Nor is the king of death
on the banks of Acheron
unaware.

ELECTRA But meanwhile most of my life has slid by
without hope.
I sink.
I melt.   250
Father has gone and there is no man left
who cares enough to stand up for me.
Like some beggar
wandered in off the street,
I serve as a slave
in the halls of my father.
Dressed in these rags,
I stand at the table
and feast on air.

CHORUS One rawblood cry   *strophe 3*   260
on the day he returned,
one rawblood cry went through the halls
just as the axeblade
rose
and fell.
He was caught by guile,
cut down by lust:
together they bred a thing shaped like a monster—
god or mortal
no one knows.   270

*Offspring
monster*

ELECTRA That day tore out the nerves of my life.
That night:
far too silent the feasting,
much too sudden
the silence.
My father looked up and saw
death coming out of their hands.
Those hands took my life hostage.
Those hands murdered me.

I pray   280
the great god of Olympus
give them pain on pain to pay for this!
And smother the glow   (Aias)
of deeds like these.

CHORUS Think again, Electra.   *antistrophe 3*
Don't say any more.
Don't you see what you're doing?
You make your own pain.
Why keep wounding yourself?
With so much evil stored up   290
in that cold dark soul of yours
you breed enemies everywhere you touch.   enemies
But you must not
clash with the people in power.

ELECTRA By dread things I am compelled. I know that.
I see the trap closing.
I know what I am.   trap closing
But while life is in me
I will not stop this violence. No.
Oh my friends   300
who is there to comfort me?
Who understands?
Leave me be,
let me go,
do not soothe me.
This is a knot no one can untie.
There will be no rest,
there is no retrieval.
No number exists for
griefs like these.   310

CHORUS Yes but I speak from concern —   *epode*
as a mother would: trust me.
Do not breed violence out of violence.   violence

My cries are wings

ELECTRA Alright then, you tell me one thing—
at what point does the evil level off in my life?
You say ignore the deed—is that right?
Who could approve this?
It defies human instinct!
Such ethics make no sense to me.
And how could I nestle myself in a life of ease   320

while my father lies out in the cold,
outside honor?

bird

My cries are wings:
they pierce the cage.
For if a dead man is earth and nothing,
if a dead man is void and dead space lying,
if a dead man's murderers
do not give
blood for blood
to pay for this,   330
then shame does not exist.

*human
reverence*

Human reverence
is gone.

CHORUS I came here, child, because I care

like a mother

for your welfare as my own.
But perhaps I am wrong.   *give way to Electra*
Let it be as you say.

ELECTRA Women. I am ashamed before you: I know
you find me extreme
in my grief.   340
I bear it hard.
But I tell you I have no choice.
It compels. I act because it compels.
Oh forgive me. But how could I—
how could a woman of any nobility
stand
and watch her father's house go bad?
There is something bad here,

weep, melt

growing. Day and night   *bad growing*
I watch it. Growing.   350

My mother is where it begins.   *mother*
She and I are at war.
Our relation is hatred.
And I live in this house
with my father's own killers:
they rule me. They dole out my life.
What kind of days do you think I have here?
I see my father's throne
with Aegisthus on it.
I see my father's robes   360
with Aegisthus in them.
I see my father's hearth with Aegisthus presiding—
right where he stood when he struck
my father down!
And the final outrage: *sex*
the killer tucked in my father's bed.
Behold the man who pleasures my mother—
should I call that thing 'mother' that lies at his side?
God! Her nerve astounds me.
She lives with that polluted object,   370
fearing no fury. No,
she laughs!
Celebrates
that day—the day she took my father
with dances and song and slaughter of sheep!
A monthly bloodgift to the gods who keep her safe.

I watch
all going dark in the rooms of my house.
I weep.
I melt.   380

I grieve
for the strange cruel feast made in my father's name.
But I grieve to myself: *alone*
not allowed even to shed the tears I would.

No—that creature
who calls herself noble
will shriek at me:
"Godcursed! You piece of hatred!
So you've lost your father—is that unique?
No mortal mourns but you?   390
Damn you.
May the gods of hell damn you
to groan perpetually there
as you groan
perpetually
here!"
That's her style—
and when she hears someone mention Orestes,
then she goes wild, comes screaming at me:
"Have I you to thank for this?   400

Isn't it your work? Wasn't it you
who stole Orestes out of my hands
and smuggled him away?
You'll pay for it.
I tell you, you will pay."
Howling bitch. And by her side
the brave bridegroom—
this lump of bad meat.
With women only
he makes his war.   410

And I wait.
I wait.
I wait
for Orestes.
He will come! He will end this.
But my life is dying out.
He is always on the verge of doing something
then does nothing.
He has worn out all the hopes I had or could have.
Oh my friends,   420
in times like these,

Electra saved Orestes

self-control has no meaning.
Rules of reverence do not apply.
Evil is a pressure that shapes us to itself.

CHORUS Is Aegisthus at home?

ELECTRA No. Do you think I'd be
standing outdoors?
He is gone to the fields.

CHORUS That gives me courage
to say what I came to say.   430

ELECTRA What is it you want?

CHORUS I want to know—your brother—
do you say he is coming? Or has a plan?

ELECTRA Yes, he says so. But he says a lot. Does nothing.

CHORUS A man who does a great deed may hesitate.

ELECTRA Oh? I saved his life without hesitating.

CHORUS Courage. His nature is good, he will not fail his kin.

ELECTRA That belief is what keeps me alive.

CHORUS Quiet now. Here is your sister come from the house,
Chrysothemis, of the same father   440
and mother as you.
She has offerings in her hands,
as if for the dead.

    Enter CHRYSOTHEMIS *carrying garlands and a vessel.*

CHRYSOTHEMIS Here you are again at the doorway, sister,
telling your tale to the world!
When will you learn?

It's pointless. Pure self-indulgence.
Yes, I know how bad things are.
I suffer too—if I had the strength
I would show what I think of them.   450
But now is not the right time.
In rough waters, lower the sail, is my theory.
Why pretend to be doing,
unless I can do some real harm?
I wish you would see this.
And yet,
it is true,
justice is not on my side.
Your choice is the right one. On the other hand,
if I want to live a free woman,   460
there are masters who must be obeyed.

ELECTRA You appall me.
Think of the father who sired you! But you do not.
All your thought is for her.
These sermons you give me are all learnt
from mother, not a word is your own.
Well it's time for you to make a choice:
quit being "sensible"
or keep your good sense and betray your own kin.
Wasn't it you who just said,   470
"If I had the strength I would show how I hate them!"
Yet here I am doing everything possible
to avenge our father,
and do you help? No!
You try to turn me aside.
Isn't this simply cowardice added to evil?
Instruct me—no! Let me tell you:
what do I stand to gain if I cease my lament?
Do I not live? Badly, I know, but I live.
What is more,   480
I am a violation to them.
And so, honor the dead—
if any grace exists down there.
Now

244

you hate them, you say.
But this hate is all words.
In fact, you live with the killers.
And I tell you,
if someone were to give me
all the gifts that make your days delicious,   490
I would not bend. No.
You can have your rich table
and life flowing over the cup.
I need one food: ⎤ *true to self*
I must not violate Electra.   ⎦
As for your status, I couldn't care less.
Nor would you, if you had any self-respect.
You could have been called
child of the noblest men!
Instead they call you mother's girl,   500
they think you base.
Your own dead father,
your own loved ones,
you do betray.

CHORUS   No anger I pray.
There is profit for both
if you listen to one another.

CHRYSOTHEMIS   Her talk is no surprise to me, ladies.
I'm used to this.
And I wouldn't have bothered   510
to speak at all, except—
for the rumor I heard.
There is very great evil coming this way,
something to cut her long laments
short.

ELECTRA   Tell me what is the terrible thing?
If it is worse than my present life,   *near the edge*
I give up.

CHRYSOTHEMIS   I tell what I know:
they plan,   520

unless you cease from this mourning,
to send you where you will not see the sun again.
You'll be singing your songs
alive
in a room
in the ground.
Think about that.
And don't blame me when you suffer.
Too late then.
Now is the time to start being sensible.   530

Threat of punishment

sensible

ELECTRA Ah. That is their intention, is it.

CHRYSOTHEMIS It is. As soon as Aegisthus comes home.

ELECTRA May he come soon, then.

CHRYSOTHEMIS What are you saying?

ELECTRA Let him come, if he has his plan ready.

CHRYSOTHEMIS What do you mean? Are you losing your mind?

ready to die ELECTRA I want to escape from you all.

CHRYSOTHEMIS Not go on living?

ELECTRA Living? Oh yes   *Oiar*
quality of life   my life is a beautiful thing, is it not.   540

CHRYSOTHEMIS Well it could be, if you got some sense.

ELECTRA Don't bother telling me to betray those I love.

CHRYSOTHEMIS I tell you we have masters, we must bend.

ELECTRA You bend—you go ahead and lick their boots.
It's not my way.

CHRYSOTHEMIS Don't ruin your life in sheer stupidity.

ELECTRA I will ruin my life, if need be,
         avenging our father.

CHRYSOTHEMIS But our father, I know, forgives us for this.

ELECTRA Cowards' talk.   550

CHRYSOTHEMIS You won't listen to <u>reason</u> at all, will you?

ELECTRA <u>No. My mind is my own.</u>

CHRYSOTHEMIS Well then I'll be on my way.

ELECTRA Where are you going? Whose offerings are those?

Δ

CHRYSOTHEMIS Mother is sending me to father's tomb,
              to pour libation.

ELECTRA What? To her mortal enemy?

CHRYSOTHEMIS To her "murder victim," as you like to say.

ELECTRA Whose idea was this?

CHRYSOTHEMIS It came out of a dream in the night, I believe.   560

ELECTRA Gods of my father be with me now!

CHRYSOTHEMIS You take courage from a nightmare?

ELECTRA Tell the dream and I'll answer you.

CHRYSOTHEMIS There is little to tell.

ELECTRA Tell it anyway.
         Little words can mean
         death or life sometimes.

247

CHRYSOTHEMIS Well the story is
she dreamed of our father
and knew him again   570
for he came back into the light.
Then she saw him take hold of his scepter
and stick it in the hearth—
his own scepter from the old days,
that Aegisthus carries now.
And from the scepter sprang a branch
in full climbing leaf
which cast a shadow over the whole land of Mycenae.
That is as much as I got
from one who overheard her   580
telling the dream to the sun.
More I don't know, except
fear is her reason for sending me out today.
So I beg you, by the gods of our family,
listen to me.
Don't throw your life away on plain stupidity.
For if you spurn me now,
you'll come begging later
when the trouble starts.

ELECTRA Oh dear one, no.   590
You cannot touch this tomb
with any of those things you have in your hands.
It breaks the law. It would be unholy
to bring that woman's libations
to our father: she is the enemy.
No. Pitch them to the winds
or down a dark hole.
They shall come nowhere near his resting place.
But when she dies and goes below,
she will find them waiting.   600
Treasure keeps, down there.

God! Her nerve is astounding.
What woman alive would send gifts
to garnish her own murder victim?

Agamemnon
scepter
branch hearth
in leaf

indignant

248

And do you imagine
the dead man would welcome such
honors
from the hand of the woman who butchered him—
think! To clean her blade she wiped it off on his head!
You astonish me—do you really believe   ⌐   610
such gifts will cancel murder?   ⌐
Throw them away.
Here, instead
cut a lock from your hair
and a lock of mine—meager gifts
but it is all I have.
Take this to him, the hair
and this belt of mine,   E lectra's belt
though it's nothing elaborate.
Kneel down there and pray to him.   620
Pray he come up from the ground
to stand with us against our enemies.
Pray that his son Orestes lives
to trample his enemies underfoot.
And someday you and I will go in better style than this
to crown his tomb.
But I wonder. You know
I wonder—
suppose he had some part
in sending her these cold unlucky dreams.   630

Well, never mind that.
Sister,
do this deed.   ⌐
Stand up for yourself |
and for me and for this man we love |
more than anyone else in the world, |
this dead man. Your father. My father.   ⌐

CHORUS The girl speaks for human reverence.
        And you,
        if you have any sense, will do what she says.   640

CHRYSOTHEMIS I will do it. It is the right thing,
why dispute?
But please, my friends,
I need silence from you.
If my mother finds out,
the attempt will turn bitter for me,
I fear.

willing to yield to
Electra

fearful of Clytemnestra

Exit CHRYSOTHEMIS.

CHORUS Unless I am utterly wrong in my reading of omens *strophe*
unless I am out of my mind
Justice is coming   650
with clear signs before her
and righteousness in her hands.
She is coming down on us, child, coming now!
There is courage
whispering into me
when I hear tell of these sweetbreathing dreams.
He does not forget—
the one who begot you
the king of the Greeks.
She does not forget—   660
the jaw that bit him in two:
ancient and sharpened on both sides to butcher the meat!

Justice
righteousness

Courage

Snake

Vengeance is coming—her hands like an army,   *antistrophe*
her feet as a host.
She will come out of hiding
come scorching down
on love that is filth
and beds that are blood
where marriage should never have happened!
Conviction   670
is strong in me:
visions like these are no innocent sign for killers.
I say no omens exist
for mortals to read
from the cold faces of dreams

Vengeance

Conviction

or from oracles
unless this fragment of death steps into the daylight.

O horserace of Pelops,   *epode*
once long ago
you came in the shape of a wide calamity   680

to this land.
And from the time when
Myrtilus pitched and sank in the sea
his solid gold life
sliced off at the roots—
never
since that time
has this house
got itself clear of
rawblood   690
butchery.

                                        Enter CLYTEMNESTRA.

CLYTEMNESTRA Prowling the streets again, are you?
              Of course, with Aegisthus away.
              He was always the one
shame her   who kept you indoors where you couldn't embarrass us.
              Now that he's gone you pay no heed to me.
              Yet you love to make me the text of your lectures:
              What an arrogant bitchminded tyrant I am,
              a living insult to you and your whole way of being!
              But do I in fact insult you? No. I merely return   700
              the muck you throw at me.
              Father, father, father! your perpetual excuse—
              your father got his death from me. From me! That's right!
              I make no denial.
Justice   It was Justice who took him, not I alone.
              And you should have helped if you had any conscience.
              For this father of yours,
                                              real challenge
              this one you bewail,
              this unique Greek,
              had the heart to sacrifice your own sister to the gods.   710

my child∞

And how was that? Did he have some share
in the pain of her birth? No—I did it myself!
Tell me:
why did he cut her throat? What was the reason?
You say for the Argives?
But they had no business to kill what was mine.
To save Menelaus?
Then I deserved recompense, wouldn't you say?
Did not Menelaus have children himself—
in fact two of them,   720
who ought to have died before mine
in all fairness?
Their mother, let's not forget,
was the cause of the whole expedition!
Or was it that Hades conceived some peculiar desire
to feast on my children instead?
Or perhaps
that murdering thug your father,
simply overlooked my children
in his tender care for Menelaus'.   730
Was that not brutal? Was that not perverse?

I say it was.
No doubt you disagree.
But I tell you one thing, that murdered girl
would speak for me if she had a voice.
Anyway, the deed is done.
I feel no remorse.
You think me degenerate?
Here's my advice:
perfect yourself   740
before you blame others.

ELECTRA   At least you can't say I started it this time;
these ugly remarks are unprovoked.
But I want to get a few things clear
about the dead man and my sister as well.
If you allow me.

CLYTEMNESTRA Go ahead, by all means. Begin this way more often
and we won't need ugly remarks at all, will we?

reconcile ?

ELECTRA All right then. Yes.
You killed my father, you admit.   750
What admission could bring more shame?
Never mind if it was legal or not—did you care?
Let's talk facts: there was only one reason you killed him.
You were seduced by that creature you live with.   *lust*
Ask Artemis,
goddess of hunters,
why she stopped the winds at Aulis.
No, I'll tell you:
my father one day, so I hear,
was out in the grove of the goddess.   760
The sound of his footfall startled a stag out from cover
and, when he killed it, he let fall a boast.   *stag*
This angered the daughter of Leto.
She held the Achaeans in check until,
as payment for the animal,
my father should offer his own daughter.
Hence, the sacrifice. There was no other way.
He had to free the army,
to sail home or towards Troy.   *either way*
These were the pressures that closed upon him.   770

He resisted, he hated it—
and then he killed her.
Not for Menelaus' sake, no, not at all.
But even if—let's say we grant your claim—
he did these things to help his brother,
was it right he should die for it at your hands?
By what law?
Watch out: this particular law
could recoil upon your own head.   *and on Electra's or*
If we made it a rule   *Orestes'* 780
to answer killing with killing,
you would die first,
in all justice.

Open your eyes! The claim is a fake.
Tell me:
why do you live this way?
Your life is filth.
You share your bed with a bloodstained man:
once he obliged you by killing my father,
now you put him to use making children.   790
Once you had *decent* children from a *decent* father,
now you've thrown them out.
Am I supposed to praise that?
Or will you say
you do all this to avenge your child?
The thought is obscene —
to bed your enemies
and use a daughter as an alibi!
Oh why do you go on? I can't argue with you.
You have your one same answer ready: 800
"That's no way to talk to your mother!"

Strange.
I don't think of you as mother at all.
You are some sort of punishment cage
locked around my life.
Evils from you, evils from him
are the air I breathe.
And what of Orestes? — he barely escaped you.
Poor boy.
The minutes are grinding him away somewhere.   810
You always accuse me
of training him up to be an avenger —

Oh I would if I could, you're so right!
Proclaim it to all!

Call me
baseminded, blackmouthing bitch! if you like —
for if this is my nature
we know how I come by it, don't we?

Sex (margin note)

abandoned children (margin note)

CHORUS *(looking at* CLYTEMNESTRA)
Look, Anger is breathing out of her.
Yet she seems not to care   820
about right and wrong.   *response as mother*

CLYTEMNESTRA Right and wrong!
What use is that in dealing with her?
Do you hear her insults?
And this girl is old enough to know better.
The fact is, she would do *anything,*
don't you see that?
No shame at all.

ELECTRA Ah now there you mistake me.
Shame I do feel.   830
And I know there is something all wrong about me —
believe me. Sometimes I shock myself.
But there is a reason: you.
You never let up
this one same pressure of hatred on my life:
I am the shape you made me.   *teacher*
Filth teaches filth.

CLYTEMNESTRA You little animal.
I and my deeds and my words draw
far too much comment from you.   840

ELECTRA You said it, not I.
For the deeds are your own.
But deeds find words for themselves,
don't they?

CLYTEMNESTRA By Artemis I swear, you will pay for this
when Aegisthus comes home!

ELECTRA See? You're out of control.
Though you gave me permission to say what I want,
you don't know how to listen.

CLYTEMNESTRA Silence! If you allow me   850
              I will proceed with my sacrifice.
              You spoke your piece.

     ELECTRA Please! By all means! Go to it.
              Not another word from me.

CLYTEMNESTRA (*to her attendant*) You there! Yes you—lift up
              these offerings for me.
              I will offer prayers to this our king
              and loosen the fears that hold me now.
              Do you hear me, Apollo?
              I call you my champion!   860
              But my words are guarded, for I am not among friends,
              It wouldn't do to unfold the whole tale
              with her standing here.
              She has a destroying tongue in her
              and she does love
              to sow wild stories all over town.
              So listen, I'll put it this way:
              last night was a night of bad dreams
              and ambiguous visions.
              If they bode well for me, Lycian king, bring them to pass. 870
              Otherwise, roll them back on my enemies!
              And if there are certain people around
              plotting to pull me down
              from the wealth I enjoy,
              do not allow it.
              I want everything to go on as it is,
              untroubled.
              It suits me—this grand palace life
              in the midst of my loved ones
              and children—at least the ones   880
              who do not bring me hatred and pain.

              These are my prayers, Apollo.
              Hear them.
              Apollo,
              grant them.

controlled/ limited
by Electra

256

Gracious to all of us as we petition you.
And for the rest, though I keep silent,
I credit you with knowing it fully.
You are a god.
It goes without saying,   890
the children of Zeus see all things.
Amen.

Enter OLD MAN.

OLD MAN   Ladies, can you tell me for certain
if this is the house of Aegisthus the king?

CHORUS   Yes, stranger, it is.

OLD MAN   And am I correct that this is his wife?
She has a certain royal look.

CHORUS   Yes. That's who she is.

OLD MAN   Greetings, queen. I have come with glad tidings
for you and Aegisthus, from a friend of yours.   900

CLYTEMNESTRA   That's welcome news. But tell me
who sent you.

OLD MAN   Phanoteus the Phocian. On a mission of some
importance.

CLYTEMNESTRA   What mission? Tell me.
Insofar as I like Phanoteus, | political |
I am likely to like your news.

OLD MAN   Orestes is dead. That is the sum of it.

ELECTRA   OI 'GO TALAINA.
My death begins now.

CLYTEMNESTRA   What are you saying, what are you saying?   910
Don't bother with her.

257

OLD MAN Orestes—dead. I say it again.

ELECTRA I am at the end. I exist no more.

CLYTEMNESTRA (*to* ELECTRA) Mind your own affairs, girl.
But you, stranger—tell me the true story:
how did he die?

OLD MAN Yes I was sent for this purpose. I'll tell the whole thing.
Well:
he had gone to the spectacle at Delphi,
where all Greece turns up for the games.   920
Things were just beginning to get under way
and the herald's voice rang out
announcing the footrace—first contest.
When he came onto the track
he was radiant. Every eye turned.
Well, he leveled the competition,
took first prize and came away famous.
Oh there's so much to tell—
I never saw anything like his performance!—but
let me come straight to the point.   930
He won every contest the judges announced—
single lap, double lap, pentathlon, you name it.

First prize every time.
He was beginning to take on an aura.
His name rang out over the track again and again:
"Argive Orestes,
whose father commanded the armies of Greece!"
So far so good.
But when a god sends harm,
no man can sidestep it,   940
no matter how strong he may be.
Came another day.
Sunrise: the chariot race.
He entered the lists.
What a pack:
there was one from Achaea,

victorious

258

a Spartan,
two Libyan drivers,
and he in the midst on Thessalian horses
stood fifth.   950
Sixth an Aetolian man, driving bays.
Seventh someone from Magnesia.
An Aenian man, riding white horses, had eighth place
and ninth a driver from godbuilt Athens.
Then a Boeotian.
Ten cars in all.
As they took their positions,
the judges cast lots to line up the cars.
A trumpet blast sounded.
They shot down the track.   960
All shouting together, reins tossing—

a hard clatter filled the whole course
and a vast float of dust,
as they all streamed together,
each one lashing and straining ahead
to the next axle box, the next snorting lip,
and the horse-foam flying
back over shoulders and wheels as they pounded past.
Meanwhile Orestes
just grazing the post each time with his wheel,   970
was letting his right horse go wide,
reining back on the other.
The cars were all upright at this point—

then all of a sudden
the Aenian's colts go out of control
and swerve off
just as they round the seventh turn.
They crash head-on into the Barcaean team.
Then one car after another comes ramming into the pile
and the whole plain of Crisa   980
fills with the smoke of wrecks.
Now
the Athenian driver was smart, he saw

of course he was

259

what was happening.
Drew offside and waited as
the tide of cars went thundering by.
Orestes
was driving in last place,
lying back on his mares.
He had put his faith in the finish.   990
But as soon as he sees
the Athenian driver alone on the track

he lets out a cry that shivers his horses' ears
and goes after him.
Neck and neck
they are racing,
first one, then
the other
nosing ahead,
easing ahead.   1000

Now our unlucky boy had stood every course so far,
sailing right on in his upright car,
but at this point he lets the left rein go slack
with the horses turning,
he doesn't notice,
hits the pillar and
smashes the axle box in two.
Out he flips
over the chariot rail,
reins snarled around him   1010
and as he falls
the horses scatter midcourse.
They see him down. A gasp goes through the crowd:
"Not the boy!"
To go for glory and end like this—
recalls
Agamemnon
pounded against the ground,
legs beating the sky—
the other drivers could hardly manage
to stop his team and cut him loose.
Blood everywhere.   1020

He was unrecognizable. Sickening.
They burned him at once on a pyre
and certain Phocians are bringing
the mighty body back—
just ashes,
a little bronze urn—
so you can bury him in his father's ground.
That is my story.
So far as words go,
gruesome enough.   1030
But for those who watched it,
and we did watch it,
the ugliest evil I ever saw.

CHORUS PHEU PHEU.
The whole ancient race
torn off at the roots. Gone.

CLYTEMNESTRA Zeus! What now? Should I call this good news?
Or a nightmare cut to my own advantage?   *mother*
There is something grotesque
in having my own evils save my life.   1040

OLD MAN Why are you so disheartened at this news, my lady?

CLYTEMNESTRA To give birth is terrible, incomprehensible.
No matter how you suffer,
you cannot hate a child you've born.

OLD MAN My coming was futile then, it seems.

CLYTEMNESTRA Futile? Oh no. How—
if you've come with convincing proof of his death?
He was alive because I gave him life.
But he chose to desert my breasts and my care,
to live as an exile, aloof and strange.   1050
After he left here he never saw me.
But he laid against me
the death of his father,

261

he made terrible threats.
And I had no shelter in sleep by night or sleep by day:
Time stood like a deathmaster over me,
letting the minutes drop.
Now I am free!
Today I shake loose from my fear
of her, my fear of him.   1060
And to tell you the truth,
she did more damage.
She lived in my house
and drank
my lifeblood neat!
Now things are different.
She may go on making threats—but so what?
From now on, I pass my days in peace.

ELECTRA   OIMOI TALAINA.
Now I have grief enough to cry out OIMOI—   1070
Orestes! Poor cold thing.
As you lie in death
your own mother insults you.
What a fine sight!

CLYTEMNESTRA   Well you're no fine sight.
But he looks as fine as can be.

ELECTRA   Nemesis! Hear her!

CLYTEMNESTRA   Nemesis *has* heard me. And she has answered.

ELECTRA   Batter away. This is your hour of luck.

CLYTEMNESTRA   And you think you will stop me, you and Orestes?   1080

ELECTRA   It is we who are stopped. There's no stopping you.

CLYTEMNESTRA   Stranger, you deserve reward
if you really have put a stop on her traveling tongue.

262

OLD MAN Then I'll be on my way, if all is well.

CLYTEMNESTRA Certainly not! You've earned better
of me and the man who dispatched you.
No, you go inside.
Just leave her out here
to go on with her evil litany.

Exit CLYTEMNESTRA *and* OLD MAN *into house.*

ELECTRA Well how did she look to you—shattered by grief?   1090
Heartbroken mother bewailing her only son?
No—you saw her—she went off laughing!
O TALAIN'ECO.
Orestes beloved,
as you die you destroy me.
You have torn away the part of my mind
where hope was—
my one hope in you
to live,
to come back,   1100
to avenge us.
Now where can I go?
Alone I am.
Bereft of you. Bereft of father.
Should I go back into slavery?
Back to those creatures who cut down my father?
What a fine picture.
No.
I will not go back inside that house.
No. At this door   1110
I will let myself lie
unloved.   *Odysseus' dog*
I will wither my life.
If it aggravates them,
they can kill me.
Yes it will be a grace if I die.
To exist is pain.
Life is no desire of mine anymore.

CHORUS Where are you lightnings of Zeus!   *strophe 1*
         Where are you scorching Sun!   1120
         In these dark pits you leave us dark!

ELECTRA E E AIAI.

CHORUS Child, why do you cry?

ELECTRA PHEU.

CHORUS Don't make that sound.

ELECTRA You will break me.

CHORUS How?

ELECTRA If you bring me hope and I know he is dead,
         you will harm my heart.

CHORUS But think of Amphiaraus: *antistrophe 1*   1130
         he was a king once.
         snared by a woman in nets of gold.
         Now under the earth

ELECTRA E E IO.

CHORUS He is a king in the shadows of souls.

ELECTRA PHEU.

CHORUS Cry PHEU, yes! For his murderess—

ELECTRA was destroyed!

CHORUS Destroyed.

ELECTRA I know—because an avenger arose.   1140
         I have no such person. That person is gone.

CHORUS You are a woman marked for sorrow.   *strophe 2*

ELECTRA Yes I know sorrow. Know it far too well.
My life is a tunnel
choked
by the sweepings of dread.

CHORUS We have watched you grieving.

ELECTRA Then do not try—

CHORUS What?

ELECTRA To console me.   1150
The fact is,
there are no more hopes.
No fine brothers.
No comfort.

CHORUS Death exists inside every mortal.   *antistrophe 2*

ELECTRA Oh yes, but think of the hooves drumming down on him!
See that thing
dragging behind in the reins—   *imagines death*

CHORUS Too cruel.

ELECTRA Yes. Death made him a stranger—   1160

CHORUS PAPAI.

ELECTRA Laid out
somewhere
not by my hands.   *thinks of self*
Not with my tears.

Enter CHRYSOTHEMIS.

CHRYSOTHEMIS I am so happy, I ran here to tell you—
putting good manners aside!

tomb

> I have good news for you that spells release
> from all your grieving.

ELECTRA Where could you find anything to touch my grief? 1170
It has no cure.

CHRYSOTHEMIS Orestes is with us—yes! Know it from me—

plain as you see me standing here!

ELECTRA You are mad.
You are joking.

reversal

CHRYSOTHEMIS By the hearth of our father, this is no joke.
He is with us. He is.

ELECTRA You poor girl.
Who gave you this story?

CHRYSOTHEMIS No one gave me the story! 1180
I saw the evidence with my own eyes.

ELECTRA What evidence?
My poor girl, what has set you on fire?

CHRYSOTHEMIS Well listen, for gods' sake.
Find out if I'm crazy or not.

ELECTRA All right, tell the tale, if it makes you happy.

CHRYSOTHEMIS Yes, I will tell all I saw.
Well
when I arrived at father's grave
I saw milk dripping down from the top of the mound 1190
and the tomb wreathed in flowers—
flowers of every kind—what a shock!
I peered all around—
in case someone was sneaking up on me

but no, the whole place was perfectly still.
I crept near the tomb.
And there it was.
Right there on the edge.
A lock of hair, fresh cut.
As soon as I saw it, a bolt went through me—   1200
almost as if I saw his face,
I suddenly knew! Orestes.
Beloved Orestes.
I lifted it up. I said not a word.
I was weeping for joy.
And I know it now as I knew it then,
this offering had to come from him.
Who else would bother, except you or me?
And I didn't do it. I'm sure of that.
You couldn't do it—god knows you don't   1210
take a step from this house without getting in trouble.
And certainly mother has no such inclinations.

If she did, we would hear of it.
No, I tell you these offerings came from Orestes.
Oh Electra, lift your heart!
Bad luck can't last forever.
Long have we lived in shadows and shuddering:
today I think our future is opening out.

ELECTRA PHEU!
Poor lunatic. I feel sorry for you.   1220

CHRYSOTHEMIS What do you mean? Why aren't you happy?

ELECTRA You're dreaming, girl, lost in a moving dream.

CHRYSOTHEMIS Dreaming! How? I saw what I saw!

ELECTRA He is dead, my dear one.
He's not going to save you.
Dead, do you hear me? Dead. Forget him.

CHRYSOTHEMIS OIMOI TALAINA.
                        Who told you that?

ELECTRA Someone who was there when he died.

CHRYSOTHEMIS And where is this someone? It's all so strange.   1230

ELECTRA He's gone in the house. To entertain mother.

CHRYSOTHEMIS I don't want to hear this. I don't understand.
                        Who put those offerings on father's tomb?

ELECTRA I think, most likely, someone who wished
                        to honor Orestes' memory.

CHRYSOTHEMIS What a fool I am—here I come racing for joy
                        to tell you my news, with no idea
                        how things really are.
                        The evils multiply.

ELECTRA Yes they do. But listen to me.   1240
                        You could ease our sorrow.

CHRYSOTHEMIS How? Raise the dead?

ELECTRA That's not what I meant. I am not quite insane.

CHRYSOTHEMIS Then what do you want? Am I capable of it?

ELECTRA All you need is the nerve—to do what I say.

CHRYSOTHEMIS If it benefits us, I will not refuse.

ELECTRA But you know nothing succeeds without work.

CHRYSOTHEMIS I do. I'll give you all the strength I have.

ELECTRA Good then, listen. Here is my plan.
                        You know, I think, our present contingent of allies: 1250

zero. Death took them.
We two are alone.
Up to now, while I heard that my brother was living
I cherished a hope
that he'd arrive one day to avenge his father.
But Orestes
no longer exists. I look to you.
You will not shrink back.
You will stand with your sister
and put to death the man who murdered your father: 1260
Aegisthus.
After all, what are you waiting for?
Let's be blunt, girl, what hope is left?
Your losses are mounting,   ⎤   *grim state*
the property gone and   *of*
marriage   ⎦   *affairs*
seems a fading dream at your age —
or do you still console yourself with thoughts of a
husband?
Forget it. Aegisthus is not so naive   1270
as to see children born from you or from me —
unambiguous grief for himself.
But now if you join in my plans,
you will win, in the first place,
profound and sacred respect from the dead below: ✓
your father, your brother.   ✓
And second, people will call you noble.
That is your lineage, that is your future.   ✓
And besides, you will find a husband,
a good one: men like a woman with character.   1280
Oh don't you see? You'll make us famous!
People will cheer! They'll say
"Look at those two!" they'll say
"Look at the way they saved their father's house!
Against an enemy standing strong!
Risked their lives! Stood up to murder!
Those two deserve to be honored in public,
on every streetcorner and festival in the city —
there should be a prize for heroism like that!"

So they will speak of us.   1290
And whether we live or die doesn't matter;
that fame will stand.
Oh my dear one, listen to me.
Take on your father's work,
take up your brother's task,
make some refuge from evil for me
and for you.
Because you know,
there is a kind of excellence

excellence in me and you—born in us—   1300
and it cannot live in shame.

CHORUS   In times like these, speaking or listening,
forethought is your ally.

CHRYSOTHEMIS Well yes—and if this were a rational woman
she would have stopped to think before she spoke.

mad   She is, unfortunately, mad.
Tell me, what in the world do you have in mind
as you throw on your armor
and call me to your side?
Look at yourself! You are female,   1310
not male—born that way.
And you're no match for them in strength or in luck.
They are flush with fortune;
our luck has trickled away.
Really, Electra,
who would think to topple a man of his stature?
Who could ever get away with it?
Be careful: this sort of blundering
might make things worse for us—
what if someone overhears!   1320
And there is nothing whatever to win or to gain
if we make ourselves famous and die in disgrace.
Death itself is not the worst thing.
Worse is to live
when you want to die.
So I beg you,

270

before you destroy us
and wipe out the family altogether,
control your temper.
As for your words,   1330
I will keep them secret—for your sake.
Oh Electra, get some sense! It is almost too late.
Your strength is nothing,

you cannot beat them: give up.

CHORUS Hear that? Foresight!—
no greater asset a person can have
than foresight combined with good sense.

ELECTRA Predictable.
I knew you'd say no.
Well: 1340
alone then.
One hand will have to be enough.
One hand *is* enough.

Yes.

CHRYSOTHEMIS Too bad you weren't so resolved
on the day father died.
You could have finished the task.

ELECTRA Yes, I had the guts for it then, but no strategy.

CHRYSOTHEMIS Forget strategy—you'll live longer,

ELECTRA I gather you don't intend to help.   1350

CHRYSOTHEMIS Too risky for me.

ELECTRA You have your own strategy, I see.
I admire that.

But your cowardice appalls me.

Terrible to sound so right and be so wrong

CHRYSOTHEMIS One day you will say I was right.

ELECTRA Never.

CHRYSOTHEMIS The future will judge.

ELECTRA Oh go away. You give no help.

CHRYSOTHEMIS You take no advice.

ELECTRA Why not run off and tell all this to mother?   1360

CHRYSOTHEMIS I don't hate you that much.

ELECTRA At least realize you are driving me into dishonor.

CHRYSOTHEMIS Dishonor? No: foresight.

ELECTRA And I should conform to your version of justice?

CHRYSOTHEMIS When you are sane, you can think for us both.

ELECTRA Terrible to sound so right and be so wrong.

CHRYSOTHEMIS Well put! You describe yourself to a fault.

ELECTRA Do you deny that I speak for justice?

CHRYSOTHEMIS Let's just say there are times
when justice is too big a risk.   1370

ELECTRA I will not live by rules like those.

CHRYSOTHEMIS Go ahead then. You'll find out I was right.

ELECTRA I *do* go ahead. You cannot deter me.

CHRYSOTHEMIS So you won't change your plan?

ELECTRA Immorality isn't a plan. It is the enemy.

CHRYSOTHEMIS You don't hear a single word I say.

ELECTRA Oh, it was all decided long ago.

CHRYSOTHEMIS Well, I'll be off.
It's clear you could never bring yourself
to praise my words, nor I your ways.   *words/*   1380
                                              deeds

ELECTRA Yes. You do that. You be off.
But I will not follow you,
no.
Never.
Not even if you beg me.
When
I look in your eyes I see emptiness.

CHRYSOTHEMIS If that is your attitude,
that is your attitude.
When you're in deep trouble,   1390
you'll say I was right.

                              Exit CHRYSOTHEMIS.

CHORUS Why is it—   *strophe* 1
we look at birds in the air,
we see it makes sense
the way they care
for the life of those who sow and sustain them—
why
is it
we don't do the same?
No: 1400
by lightning of Zeus,
by Themis of heaven,
not long

free of pain!
O
sound going down

to the dead in the
ground,
take a voice,
take my voice,   1410
take down
pity
below
to Atreus' dead:
tell them shame.
Tell them there is no dancing.

Because   *antistrophe 1*
here is a house falling sick
falling now
between two children battling,   1420
and there is no more level of love in the days.
Betrayed,
alone
she goes down in the waves:
Electra,
grieving for death,
for her father,
as a nightingale
grieving always.
Nor   1430
does she think
to fear dying,
no!
She is glad
to go dark.
As a
killer
of furies,
as a pureblooded
child   1440
of the father who sowed her.
No one well-born   *strophe 2*
is willing to live

with evil,
with shame,
with a name made nameless.
O child,
child,
you made your life a wall of tears
against dishonor: 1450
you fought and you won.
For they call you
the child of his mind,

child of his excellence.
I pray you raise your hand   *antistrophe 2*
and crush the ones
who now
crush you!
For I see you subsisting
in mean part,   1460
and yet
you are one who kept faith
with the living laws,
kept faith
in the clear reverence
of Zeus.

                    Enter ORESTES *and servant with urn.*

ORESTES Tell me ladies, did we get the right directions?
         Are we on the right road? Is this the place?

CHORUS   What place? What do you want?

ORESTES The place where Aegisthus lives.   1470

CHORUS   Well here you are. Your directions were good.

ORESTES Which one of you, then, will tell those within?
         Our arrival will please them.

275

CHORUS Her—as nearest of kin, she is the right one to
        announce you.

ORESTES Please, my lady, go in and tell them
         that certain Phocians are asking for Aegisthus.

ELECTRA OIMOI TALAIN'.
         Oh no. Don't say that. Don't say you have come with
         evidence of the stories we heard.   1480

ORESTES I don't know what you heard.
         Old Strophius sent me with news of Orestes.

ELECTRA Oh stranger, what news? Fear comes walking into me.

ORESTES We have his remains in a small urn here—
         for he's dead, as you see.

ELECTRA OI 'GO TALAINA.
         Oh no. No. Not this thing in your hands.
         No.

ORESTES If you have tears to shed for Orestes,
         this urn is all that holds his body now.   1490

ELECTRA Oh stranger, allow me, in god's name—
         if this vessel does really contain him,
         to hold it in my hands.
         For myself, for the whole generation of us,
         I have tears to keep,
         I have ashes to weep.

ORESTES (to servant with urn) Bring it here, give it to her, whoever
         she is.
         It is no enemy asking this.
         She is someone who loved him,
         or one of his blood.   1500

ELECTRA If this were all you were, Orestes,
         how could your memory

fill my memory,
how is it your soul fills my soul?
I sent you out, I get you back:
tell me
how could the difference be simply
nothing?
Look!
You are nothing at all,   1510
Just a crack where the light slipped through.
Oh my child,
I thought I could save you.
I thought I could send you beyond.
But there is no beyond.
You might as well have stayed that day
to share your father's tomb.
Instead, somewhere, I don't know where—
suddenly alone you stopped—
where death was.   1520
You stopped.
And I would have waited
and washed you
and lifted you
up from the fire,
like a whitened coal.
Strangers are so careless!
Look how you got smaller, coming back.
OIMOI TALAINA.
All my love   1530
gone for nothing.
Days of my love, years of my love.
Into your child's fingers I put the earth
        and the sky.
No mother did that for you.
No nurse.
No slave.
I. Your sister
without letting go,
day after day, year after year,

transference [handwritten margin note]

and you my own sweet child.   1540
But death was a wind too strong for that.

One day three people vanished.
Father. You. Me. Gone.
Now our enemies rock with laughter.
And she runs mad for joy—
that creature
in the shape of your mother—
how often you said you would come
one secret evening and cut her throat!
But our luck canceled that,   1550
whatever luck is.
And instead my beloved,
luck sent you back to me
colder than ashes,
later than shadow.
OIMOI MOI.
Pity,
PHEU PHEU
oh beloved,
OIMOI MOI   1560
as you vanish down that road.
Oh my love
take me there.
Let me dwell where you are.
I am already nothing.
I am already burning.
Oh my love, I was once part of you—
take me too!
Only void is between us.
And I see that the dead feel no pain.   1570

excessive [handwritten margin note]

CHORUS Electra, be reasonable.
Your father was a mortal human being.
Orestes too—we all pay the same price for that.
Control yourself.

ORESTES PHEU PHEU.

What should I say? This is
impossible! I cannot hold my tongue much longer.

ELECTRA What is the matter? What are you trying to say?

ORESTES Is this the brilliant Electra?

ELECTRA This is Electra. Brilliant no more.   1580

ORESTES OIMOI TALAINES.
It hurts me to look at you.

ELECTRA Surely, stranger, you're not feeling sorry for me?

ORESTES It shocks me, the way you look; do they abuse you?

ELECTRA Yes, in fact. But who are you?

ORESTES PHEU
What an ugly, loveless life for a girl.

ELECTRA Why do you stare at me? Why are you so sympathetic?

ORESTES I had no idea how bad my situation really is.

ELECTRA And what makes you realize that? Something I said?

ORESTES Just to see the outline of your suffering.   1590

ELECTRA Yet this is only a fraction of it you see.

ORESTES What could be worse than this?

ELECTRA To live in the same house with killers.

ORESTES What killers? What evil are you hinting at?

ELECTRA My own father's killers.
And I serve them as a slave. By compulsion.

ORESTES Who compels you?

ELECTRA Mother she is called. Mother she is not.

ORESTES How do you mean? Does she strike you? Insult you?

ELECTRA Yes. And worse.   1600

ORESTES But have you no one to protect you?
         No one to stand in her way?

ELECTRA No. There was someone. Here are his ashes.

ORESTES Oh girl. How I pity the dark life you live.

ELECTRA No one else has ever pitied me, you know.

ORESTES No one else has ever been part of your grief.

ELECTRA Do you mean you are somehow part of my family?

ORESTES I'll explain—if these women are trustworthy.

ELECTRA Oh yes, you can trust them. Speak freely.

ORESTES Give back the urn, then, and you will hear everything.   1610

ELECTRA No! Don't take this from me, for god's sake,
         whoever you are!

ORESTES Come now, do as I say. It is the right thing.

ELECTRA No! In all reverence no please—don't take this away.
         It is all that I love.

ORESTES I forbid you to keep it.

ELECTRA O TALAIN'EGO SETHEN.
         Orestes! What if

they take from me
even the rites of your death!   1620

ORESTES Hush, now. That language is wrong.

ELECTRA Wrong to mourn my own dead brother?

ORESTES Wrong for you to say that word.

ELECTRA How did I lose the right to call him brother?

ORESTES Your rights you have. Your brother you don't.

ELECTRA Do I not stand here with Orestes himself in my hands?

ORESTES No, in fact. That Orestes is a lie.

ELECTRA Then where in the world is the poor boy's grave?

ORESTES Nowhere. The living need no grave.

ELECTRA Child, what are you saying?   1630

ORESTES Nothing but the truth.

ELECTRA The man is alive?

ORESTES As I live and breathe.

ELECTRA You—?

ORESTES Look at this ring—our father's—

ELECTRA Father's!

ORESTES —and see what I mean.

ELECTRA Oh love, you break on me like light!   *light*

ORESTES Yes like light!

ELECTRA Oh voice, have you come out of nowhere?   1640

ORESTES Nowhere but where you are.

ELECTRA Do I hold you now in my hands?

ORESTES Now and forever.

ELECTRA Ladies, my friends, my people, look!
         Here stands Orestes:
         dead by device
         now by device brought back to life!

ORESTES I see, child. And at this reversal,
         my tears are falling for joy.

ELECTRA IO GONAI.   *strophe*   1650
         You exist!
         You came back,
         you found me—

ORESTES Yes, I am here. Now keep silent a while.

ELECTRA Why?

ORESTES Silence is better. Someone inside might overhear.

ELECTRA By Artemis unbroken! I would not
         dignify with fear
         the dull surplus of females
         who huddle in that house!   1660

ORESTES Careful! There is war in women too,
         as you know by experience, I think,

ELECTRA OTOTOTOTOI TOTOI.
         You drive me back down my desperation—
         that unclouded

282

incurable
never forgotten
evil
growing inside my life.

ORESTES I know, but we should talk of those deeds   1670
          when the moment is right.

ELECTRA Every arriving moment of my life   *antistrophe*
          has a right
          to tell those deeds!
          And this chance to speak freely is hard won.

ORESTES Precisely. Safeguard it.

ELECTRA How?

ORESTES When the time is unsuitable, no long speeches.

ELECTRA But how could silence be the right way to greet
          you — simply   1680
          coming
          out of nowhere
          like a miracle?

ORESTES It was a miracle set in motion by the gods.

ELECTRA Ah.

          That is a vast claim
          and much more beautiful,
          to think
          some god
          has brought you here.   1690
          Some god: yes! That must be true.

ORESTES Electra, I do not like to curb your rejoicing
          but I am afraid when you lose control.

[handwritten margin note: needs to limit her]

283

ELECTRA Oh, but my love —
         now that you have traveled back down all those years

         to meet my heart,
         over all this grief of mine,
         do not
         oh love —

ORESTES What are you asking?   1700

ELECTRA Do not turn your face from me.
         Don't take yourself away.

ORESTES Of course not. No one else will take me either.

ELECTRA Do you mean that?

ORESTES Yes, I do.

ELECTRA Oh beloved,
         I heard your voice
         when I had no hope
         and my heart leapt away from me
         calling   1710
         you.
         I was in sorrow.
         But now
         I am holding you,
         now you are visible —
         light of the face I could never forget.

ORESTES Spare me these words.
         You don't need to teach me my mother is evil
         or how Aegisthus drains the family wealth,
         pours it out like water,   1720
         sows it to the wind.
         We've no time for all that — talk is expensive.
         What I need now are the practical details:
         where we should hide, where we can leap out
         and push that enemy laughter

practical

right back down their throats!
But be careful she doesn't read
the fact of our presence
straight from the glow on your face.

emotional

You must keep on lamenting   1730
my fictitious death.
Time enough
for lyres and laughter
when we've won the day.

ELECTRA Your will and my will are one: identical, brother.
For I take all my joy from you,
none is my own.
Nor could I harm you ever so slightly
at any price: it would be a disservice
to the god who stands beside us now.   1740
So. You know what comes next.
Aegisthus has gone out,
mother is home.
And don't worry:
she'll see no glow on my face.
Hatred put out the light in me a long time ago.
Besides, since I saw you
my tears keep running down—
tears, joy, tears all mixed up together.
How could I stop?   1750
I saw you come down that road a dead man,
I looked again and saw you alive.
You have used me strangely.
Why—if father suddenly came back to life
I wouldn't call it fantastic.

Believe what you see.
But
now you have come,
I am yours to command.
Alone,   1760
I would have done one of two things:
deliver myself or else die.

ORESTES Quiet! I hear someone coming out.

ELECTRA Go inside, strangers.
You are bringing a gift
they can neither reject nor rejoice in.

Enter OLD MAN.

OLD MAN Idiots! Have you lost your wits completely,
and your instinct to survive as well—
or were you born brainless?
You're not on the brink of disaster now,   1770
you're right in the eye of it, don't you see that?
Why, except for me standing guard at the door here
this long while, your plans
would have been in the house
before yourselves!
Good thing I took caution.
Now cut short the speechmaking,
stifle your joy
and go in the house. Go!
Delay is disaster in things like this.   1780
Get it over with: that's the point now.

ORESTES How will I find things inside?

OLD MAN Perfect. No one will know you.

ORESTES You reported me dead?

OLD MAN You are deep in hell, so far as they know.

ORESTES Are they happy at this?

OLD MAN I'll tell you that later. For now,
the whole plan is unfolding beautifully.
Even the ugly parts.

ELECTRA Who is this man, brother?   1790

286

father

ORESTES Don't you know him?

ELECTRA Not even remotely.

ORESTES You don't know the man into whose hands you put me,
once long ago?

ELECTRA What man? What are you saying?

ORESTES The man who smuggled me off to Phocia,
thanks to your foresight.

ELECTRA Him? Can it be? That man was
the one trustworthy soul I could find in the house,
the day father died!   1800

ORESTES That's who he is. Do not question me further.

ELECTRA (*to the* OLD MAN) I bless you like the light of day!
I bless you
as the savior of the house of Agamemnon!
How did you come? Is it really you—
who pulled us up from the pit that day?
I bless your hands,
I bless your feet,
I bless the sweet roads you walked!
How strange   1810
you were beside me all that time and gave no sign.
Strange—to destroy me with lies
when you had such sweet truth to tell.
Bless you, father!—Yes, father.
That is who I see when I look at you now.

There is no man on earth I have hated and loved like
        you
on the one same day.

OLD MAN Enough, now. As for all the stories in between—
there will be nights and days

Pylades

to unravel them, Electra.   1820
But for you two, standing here,
I have just one word: act!
Now is the moment!
Now Clytemnestra is alone.
Now there is not one man in the house.
If you wait you will have to fight others,
more skilled and more numerous. Think!

(haha)

ORESTES Well, Pylades, no more speeches.
         As quick as we can
         into the house—after   1830
         we pay our respects
         to the gods of this doorway.

emphasizes
Orestes' conviction
in this play

                    Exit ORESTES *and* PYLADES *followed by the* OLD MAN.

ELECTRA King Apollo! Graciously hear them.
         Hear me too! I have been devout,
         I have come to you often,

         bringing you gifts of whatever I had.
         Now again I come with all that I have:
         Apollo wolfkiller! I beg you!
         I call out—
         I fall to my knees!   1840
         please send your mind over us,
         inform our strategies,
         show
         how the gods reward
         unholy action!

CHORUS   Look where he comes grazing forward,   *strophe*
         blood bubbling over his lips: Ares!
         As a horizontal scream into the house
         go the hunters of evil,
         the raw and deadly dogs.   1850
         Not long now:
         the blazing dream of my head is crawling out.

murder scene

Here he comes like a stealing shadow,   *antistrophe*
like a footprint of death into the rooms,
stalking the past

with freshcut blood in his hands.
It is Hermes who guides him
down a blindfold of shadow—
straight to the finish line: not long now!

ELECTRA My ladies! The men   1860
are about to accomplish the deed—
be silent and wait.

CHORUS How? What are they doing?

ELECTRA She is dressing the urn. They are standing beside her.

CHORUS But why did you come running out here?

ELECTRA To watch that Aegisthus doesn't surprise us.

CLYTEMNESTRA (*within*) AIAI IO.
Rooms
filled with murder!

ELECTRA Someone inside screams—do you hear?   1870

CHORUS Yes, I hear. It makes my skin crawl.

CLYTEMNESTRA OIMOI TALAIN'.
Aegisthus, where are you?

ELECTRA There! Again! Someone calls out.

CLYTEMNESTRA Oh child my child, pity the mother who bore you!

ELECTRA Yet you had little enough pity for him
and none for his father!

hither a 2nd time

CHORUS Alas for the city.
Alas for a whole race thrown and shattered:
the shape that followed you down the days   1880
is dying now, dying away.

CLYTEMNESTRA OMOI.
I am hit!

vengeance talking
always pent up desire

ELECTRA Hit her a second time, if you have the strength! ✗

CLYTEMNESTRA OMOI MAL' AUTHIS.
Again!

ELECTRA If only Aegisthus could share this!

CHORUS The curses are working.
Under the ground
Aeschylus   dead men are alive   1890
with their black lips moving,
black mouths sucking
on the soles of killers' feet.

Here they come,
hands soaked with red: Ares is happy!
Enough said.

restrained
ELECTRA Orestes, how does it go?

ORESTES Good, so far—at least so far as Apollo's oracle was
good.

ELECTRA Is the creature dead?   1900

ORESTES Your good mother will not insult you anymore.

CHORUS Stop! I see Aegisthus coming, yes, it is him.

ELECTRA Children, get back!

290

ORESTES Where do you see him—

ELECTRA There—marching right down on us
full of joy.

CHORUS Go quick to the place just inside the front door
You have won the first round. Now for the second.

ORESTES Don't worry. We will finish this.

ELECTRA Hurry. Go to it.   1910

ORESTES Yes I am gone.

ELECTRA And leave this part to me.   ← *wants to play a role*

CHORUS Why not drop a few friendly words in his ear—
so his moment of justice may come
as a surprise.

Enter AEGISTHUS.

AEGISTHUS Does anyone know where those Phocian strangers are?
People say they have news of Orestes
dead in a chariot crash.
You!
yes you!—you've never been shy   1920
to speak your mind.
And obviously this matter most concerns you.

ELECTRA Yes, of course I know, for I do keep track
of the fortunes of the family.

AEGISTHUS Where are they then,
the strangers?—tell me.

ELECTRA Inside the house, for they've fallen upon
the perfect hostess.

AEGISTHUS And it's true they bring a report of his death?

ELECTRA   No—better: they have evidence,   1930
          not just words.

she would never say this

AEGISTHUS   We can see proof?

he does not perceive it

ELECTRA   You can, indeed, though it's no pretty sight.

AEGISTHUS   Well this is good news. Unusual, coming from you.

Cassandra

ELECTRA   Relish it while you can.

AEGISTHUS   Silence! I say throw open the gates!
          for every Mycenaean and Argive to see—
          in case you had placed empty hopes
          in this man—
          take my bit on your tongue   1940
          or learn the hard way.

ELECTRA   As for me, I am playing my part to the end.
          I've learned to side with the winners.

antithetical

                    A shrouded corpse is disclosed with ORESTES *and*
                                      PYLADES *standing beside it.*

AEGISTHUS   O Zeus! I see here a man fallen by the jealousy of god
                    —but
          if that remark offends,

restraint   I unsay it.

          Uncover the eyes. Uncover it all.
          I should pay my respects.

ORESTES   Uncover it yourself.   1950
          This isn't my corpse—it's yours.
          Yours to look at, yours to eulogize.

AEGISTHUS   Yes, good point. I have to agree.
          You there—Clytemnestra must be about in the house—
          call her for me.

word game

ORESTES She is right here before you. No need to look elsewhere.

AEGISTHUS OIMOI.
          What do I see!

ORESTES You don't know the face?

AEGISTHUS Caught! But *who set the trap?*   1960

ORESTES Don't you realize yet
         that you're talking to dead men alive?

AEGISTHUS OIMOI.
          I do understand. You are Orestes.

ORESTES At last.

AEGISTHUS I'm a dead man. No way out.
          But let me just say—

ELECTRA No!   *stops speech*
         Don't let him speak—
         by the gods! Brother—no speechmaking now!   1970
         When a human being is so steeped in evil as this one   *of Orestes*
         what is gained by delaying his death?
         Kill him at once.   *1828*
         Throw his corpse out
         for scavengers to get. || *excessive*
         Nothing less than this
         can cut the knot of evils
         inside me.

ORESTES Get in with you, quickly.
         This is no word game: *word game*   1980
         your life is at stake.

AEGISTHUS Why take me inside?
          If the deed is honorable, what need of darkness?
          You aren't ready to kill?

                    threat to audience?
                    killing on stage?

293

ORESTES Don't give me instructions, just get yourself in:
You will die on the spot
where you slaughtered my father.

AEGISTHUS Must these rooms see
the whole evil of Pelops' race,
present and future?   1990

ORESTES They will see yours, I can prophesy.

AEGISTHUS That is no skill you got from your father!

ORESTES Your answers are quick, your progress slow.
Go.

AEGISTHUS You lead the way.

ORESTES No, you go first.

AEGISTHUS Afraid I'll escape?

ORESTES You shall not die on your own terms.
I will make it bitter for you.
And let such judgment fall   2000
on any who wish to break the law:
kill them!
The evil were less.

Exit ORESTES *and* AEGISTHUS, *followed by* ELECTRA, *into
the house.*

CHORUS O seed of Atreus:
you suffered and broke free,

you took aim and struck;
you have won your way through
to the finish.

Exit CHORUS.

294

NOTES

A few formal terms: The basic divisions of a Greek tragedy, according to the tradition, is into prologue, parodos, episodes, and stasima. A Greek tragedy contains a variety of levels of speech, in the most general terms the meter of spoken verse (iambic trimeters) and lyric. The prologue and the episodes are usually in iambic trimeter. Characters may speak to each other or to the chorus. A lyric exchange between the chorus and one or more characters is a *kommos*. The *parodos* is the entry song of the chorus (in the *Electra* this takes the form of a *kommos* between Electra and the Chorus). A *stasimon* is a choral song that divides two *episodes*. The *episodes*, which are mostly in iambic trimeter, are what we would call scenes; the final *episode*, which ends the drama, can also be called the *exodos*. These choral songs are typically constructed of strophe, antistrophe, and epode. A strophe is a stanza, while an antistrophe is a stanza whose metrical form closely follows that of a strophe. An epode is a single stanza which follows a paired strophe and antistrophe, but whose metrical form is unique.

The scene: the door to the palace is in the background, and beside it stands a statue of Apollo. ORESTES *and* PYLADES *are distinguished from the* OLD MAN *by their dress, since he is a servant.* ORESTES *and* PYLADES *are dressed as young men of nobility and are wearing travelers' hats.*

1–162 / 1–120 *Prologue* In two parts: a dialogue in iambics spoken by Orestes and the Old Man and a monody by Electra, beginning at 115 / 89. The Old Man is called Paedagogus here (roughly equivalet to "tutor") because he is the servant who raised Orestes

6 / 5 *The grove of Io . . .* This may not be a specific place, but rather it may refer to all of Argos. There are parallels between Orestes' story and that of Io, which are given in the Glossary.

7–9 / 6–7 ...*the marketplace / named for Apollo, / wolfkiller god* This Argive feature is not identified, but "Lykaios" is a regular epithet or cult name of Apollo. It can be derived from *lykos*, the Greek word for wolf. In addition to the mention here of the marketplace named for Apollo wolfkiller, Clytemnestra and Electra both pray to Apollo usuing this title. In Clytemnestra's speech (870 / 655) this phrase is translated "Lycian king," suggesting another possible derivation of the name, from the god's cult in Lycia (an area along the south coast of what is today Turkey).

10 / 8 ...*the famous temple of Hera* The Argive temple to Hera is approximately a mile south of Mycenae.

17 / 12 *From the hands of your sister* Neither Aeschylus nor Euripides say that Electra saved Orestes, and this is probably the invention of Sophocles.

107 / 77 *IO MOI MOI DYSTENOS.* This is a traditional cry of grief. *Dystenos* means wretched. Inarticulate or nearly inarticulate cries of grief, pain, sorrow, surprise, etc., are common in this play. See On the Translation in this volume.

115–62 / 86–120 Monody (sung verse); the meter changes in the Greek text from iambic trimeter to a lyric meter, in this case lyric anapests to give Electra an expressive lament accompanied by the *aulos*, an ancient double reed instrument used to accompany song in the theater.

144 / 107 *nightingale* See Philomela in the Glossary.

163–333 / 121–250 *Parodos* The Chorus engages in a lyric exchange (*kommos*) with Electra.

199 / 148 *the bird who calls Itys!* Philomela again, here linked to Niobe (see Glossary); at **201 / 149**, the nightingale is called "the angel (i.e., messenger) of Zeus," since Zeus is the god in charge of the seasons (Horai), who are his daughters, and the nightingale announces the arrival of spring. The nightingale may be the "messenger of Zeus" for another reason as well, since in mourning the death of a relative, as Electra does (cf. **1422–29** /1074–77, where she is compared to a nightingale), so displays "the clear reverence / of Zeus" (**1465–66 / 1097**).

282 / 210 *pain on pain to pay* This repeats the alliteration of *p* in the Greek line: *poinima pathea pathein poroi.*

334–647 / 251–471 *First episode* Electra begins with a monologue, and the rest of the scene is a dialogue between Electra and Chrysothemis.

338 / 254 *I am ashamed...* In the Greek text, Electra's first word is "I am ashamed." Perhaps there is a hint here that Electra is the opposite of Clytemnestra, who said "I am not ashamed" at the beginning of two major speeches in Aeschylus' *Agamemnon* (856 and 1373).

444 / 328 *Enter* CHRYSOTHEMIS As we will soon hear, Chrysothemis is more richly dressed than Electra, who is herself probably dressed as a servant. There is no embroidery on Electra's "belt," and thus we can assume that such embroidery is visible on Chrysothemis' costume as it is on that of Clytemnestra. As a noble woman, Chrysothemis probably should have an attendant, but she carries at least some of the offerings in her own hands.

466 / 344 *not a word is your own* Kells claims this charge is not fair, but it seems accurate to me. Chrysothemis is not simply in the wrong. By accepting the benefits of a corrupt government, she shares responsibility for its acts to some degree.

468 / 345 *sensible* This term (*phronein*) is prominent here, just as it was in the dialogue of Antigone and Ismene in Sophocles' *Antigone*. It can apply both to "justice" and to "expediency." Electra ironically uses the word in its expediency signification. Chrysothemis later ends her speech with this word ("sensible," 530 / 384).

543 / 396 *we have masters, we must bend* This is the language of "expediency." Electra counters with "lick their boots"—that is, Chrysothemis' position is one of base flattery (*thopeia*). Chrysothemis counters with a charge of stupidity (*aboulia*, 546 / 398). Prometheus uses similar language in a similar situation in Aeschylus' *Prometheus Bound*. He sneeringly urges the Chorus to "flatter" Zeus (*thopte*, 937). Hermes urges him to "think straight" (*eu phronein*, 1000). He accuses Prometheus of preferring audacity to "good thought" (*euboulia*, 1035).

586 / 429 *plain stupidity* Chrysothemis ends her account of the dream and returns to her earlier remarks, repeating the word *stupidity* (*aboulia*) (see preceeding note).

648–91 / 472–515 *First stasimon* The Chorus reflects on Clytemnestra's dream: justice will come.

663–69 / 489–94 *Vengeance...where marriage should never have happened!* The Greek word for vengeance is *Erinys* ("Fury"). Once again, the Chorus uses archaic language. In the very difficult Greek of this passage, the marriage of Clytemnestra and Aegisthus is said to be "without a bed, without a bride" (*alektra, anumpha*). The pun on Electra's name in *alektra* (actually in effect a false etymology of the name) is evidently intentional: the same pun appears in 1266–67 / 961–62 when Electra tells Chrysothemis that she will grow old "unbedded" (*alektra*) if Aegisthus and Clytemnestra remain in power. Thus the actions of Clytemnestra and Aegisthus have made their own marriage dysfunctional (i.e., their children have no inheritance rights, no status) and made marriage impossible for everyone else in the royal line. Electra herself is only one embodiment of that frustration.

As goddesses, the Furies (*Erinyes*) are depicted by Aeschylus in the *Eumenides*, the third play of the *Oresteia*, as horrifying women, with snakes in their hair. They prosecute Orestes before an Athenian court on the charge of matricide and dog-like in their pursuit of their prey. Sophocles provides several hints that Electra and Orestes represent the Furies of the traditional story in some sense. This is particularly clear when Clytemnestra says that Electra "drank / my lifeblood neat" 1064–65 / 785–86). The Chorus describes Orestes and Pylades as "dogs" (1850 / 1388) as it enters the house, and this, too, is close to the concept of the Erinyes in the *Oresteia*.

692–1391 / 516–1057 *Second episode* Clytemnestra enters, and the first part of the episode is her dialogue with Electra. The Old Man then enters and gives his messenger speech, followed by comments by all three actors, after which Clytemnestra and the Old Man exit. Electra remains and sings a *kommos* with the Chorus. Chrysothemis enters; the sisters quarrel; Chrysothemis exits.

745 / 554–55 *...about the dead man and my sister as well* We need only examine the speech that follows to see that this is not spoken in complete candor. Electra is an artful rhetorician as well as a passionate one.

755–67 / 563–73 *Ask Artemis... Hence, the sacrifice* Aeschylus does not give a specific human action as the cause of Artemis' wrath at Aulis. Rather, the seer Calchas infers that wrath from an omen. Euripides more or less follows the version given here. These events are the subject of Euripides' *Iphigenia in Aulis*.

788–90 / 587–89 *You share . . . making children* The Greek has a wonderful run of *p*'s here: "palamnaioi, meth hou / patera ton amon prosthen exapolesas, / kai paidopoieis." Electra is literally spewing. The children of Clytemnestra and Aegisthus were Aletes and Erigone. There are references to plays by Sophocles with each of these names. (See Hyginus, *Fabula* 122 for stories about these children and Electra and Orestes.)

816 / 607 *bitch* This word is not found in the Greek text, and there seems to be no hint here (as there is elsewhere) that Electra is a "dog" and hence a Fury. Rather, this translation refers to the Greek word *shameless*, also a quality associated with dogs.

870 / 655 *Lycian king* Cult name of Apollo; see note on 7–9.

946–56 / 701–8 *Achaea . . . Boeotian* The competitors seem to be diverse in geography and in chronology. One is from Achaea, on the north coast of the Peloponnese; one is a Spartan from the central Peloponnese; two are from Libya (and thus strictly speaking postheroic); one is from Thessaly in north eastern Greece; one is Aetolian, from west of Delphi; one is a Magnesian and one is an Aenian—both tribes in Thessaly mentioned in Homer; one is an Athenian; and one is a Boeotian.

990 / 735 *He had put his faith in the finish* There may be some allegorical point in this detail. In Book 10 of the *Republic*, Plato has Socrates defend just action by saying that the just man finishes the race, while the unjust man is tripped up. Here Orestes does not seem to finish the race, but of course he will in fact do so.

1077 / 792 *Nemesis! Hear her!* Electra appeals to the goddess of retribution to punish Clytemnestra for saying that her son Orestes is "well off" being dead. Clytemnestra's reply probably refers to Orestes' death threats against her, for which Nemesis has punished him.

1092 / 807 *she went off laughing . . .* Here as often in Greek literature and in Sophocles, a person wronged imagines his or her enemies laughing.

1119–65 / 823–70 *Kommos* A second lyric exchange between Electra and the Chorus (cf. 163–333 / 121–250).

1125 / 830 *Don't make that sound* There is a very interesting scholium (an ancient or medieval note preserved in our manuscript tradition) on this line: "It is necessary for the actor to look up to heaven as he makes this cry and to hold out his hands. The chorus restrains him by saying 'Do not say anything excessive.' "

1203 / 903–4 *Beloved Orestes* In a play full of expressions of love, this is the most extreme: "most beloved of all mortals."

1204 / 905 *I said not a word* Literally, "I did not utter a word of ill omen." Jebb assumes she refrained from reproaching Orestes for coming too late. He rejects the view that a cry of joy would be ill-omened at her father's tomb. I believe the remote model here is Odysseus' remark to the old maid after she sees the suitors have been killed in the *Odyssey* (quoted in the introduction, p. 214). What Chrysothemis refrains from doing is letting out a shout of celebration.

1246 / 944 *If it benefits …* Chrysothemis' use of "benefit" (*opheleia*) marks this as an expediency position.

1266–67 / 961–62 *marriage / seems a fading dream at your age* Electra says that *Chrysothemis* will be unbedded (*alektra*)! See note on **663–69**.

1275 / 968 *profound and sacred respect …* Chrysothemis will get the reverence (*eusebeia*) of the dead. One of Electra's key words.

1277 / 970 *noble* The Greek word here is *eleuthera* (free). Chrysothemis claimed earlier (**460 / 339**) that she was free. Electra has at this point stripped away all of Chrysothemis' rationalizations.

1303 / 990 *forethought* (*prometheia*) The Chorus points out the glaring deficiency of this speech. What Electra proposes defies probability, and thus it prepares us for Chrysothemis' speech.

1304–5 / 992–94 *and if this were a rational woman / she would have stopped to think before she spoke* Chrysothemis immediately uses two key words to a person of her character, "rational" (literally "wits" [*phrenon*]) and "stopped to think" (literally "caution" [*eulabeia*]).

1334 / 1014 *you cannot beat them: give up* Electra ended her speech with a heroic slogan: the noble prefer death to shameful life. Chrysothemis answers with one from the world of politics: the weaker must yield to the stronger.

1335 / 1015 *Foresight!* (*pronoia*) The Chorus has the values of any group and thus it places success above all. It cannot help but be alienated by Electra's disregard of good sense. The result, dramatically, is to leave Electra isolated at this point. She persists.

1342 / 1019 *One hand will have to be enough* A more literal translation is "the deed is to be done" (*drasteon*). The use of the verbal adjective is typical of Sophoclean heroes.

1392–1466 / 1058–97 *Second stasimon* The Chorus praises Electra.

1436–8 / 1080 *As a / killer / of furies* . . . The twin furies are Aegisthus and Clytemnestra, so called because of the ruin they have caused.

1439–41 / 1081 *as a pureblooded / child / of the father* . . . "Pureblooded" translates *eupatris* ("of good father"); the plural *eupatrides* was a term used in the Athenian aristocracy. Electra of course is literally "of a good father" for by her behavior she ratifies his virtue.

1467–1845 / 1098–1383 *Third episode* Orestes enters, Electra laments over the urn, and Orestes reveals himself. Electra and Orestes sing a duet. The Old Man enters, and the three characters speak, after which Orestes and the Old Man exit into the palace. Electra gives a short prayer and follows.

1482 / 1110–11 *Old Strophius sent me with news of Orestes* Orestes seems to get the names wrong. Phanoteus is the one who is supposed to be sending the body to Argos. Although it is not mentioned in this play, elsewhere Strophius is said to be Orestes' ally and the father of Pylades. His error passes without being noticed. Perhaps it is a sign of his nervousness.

1614 / 1208 *No! In all reverence* . . . Literally, "not by your chin," a traditional gesture of appeal. It is a stage direction. Electra holds the urn in one hand; she appeals to Orestes with the other.

1650–1716 / 1232–87 A lyric exchange involving only actors. Electra shifts into lyrics at this point to express her overwhelming emotion, but Orestes responds in spoken iambic trimeter. Her joy knows no bounds; he keeps reminding her that there are bounds.

1846–59 / 1384–97 *Third stasimon* This short song uses traditional religious language to describe what has happened. The stage is momentarily empty—an unusual event in Greek tragedy.

1850 / 1388 *the raw and deadly dogs* ... The Furies; see note on **663–69**.

1856 / 1394 *with freshcut blood in his hands* An exact translation of this startling line.

1860–2008 / 1398–1510 *Exodos* In the final scene, Electra enters, and in a short
kommos (**1860–1915** / 1398–1441) three excited actions occur: Electra
and the Chorus respond to Clytemnestra's off-stage cries; Electra queries
Orestes after he leaves the palace; the Chorus sees Aegisthus coming and
Orestes reenters the palace to await him. Aegisthus enters (the meter
reverts to iambics) and speaks to Electra. Electra opens the door, and
Orestes and Pylades exit from the palace with a covered corpse.
Aegisthus, Orestes, and Electra speak. Aegisthus enters the building,
forced inside by Orestes. Choral comment.

PHILOCTETES

Translated by

CARL PHILLIPS

With Introduction
and Notes by

DISKIN CLAY

INTRODUCTION

THE LEGEND AT THE EDGES OF THE ILIAD

The wrath of Achilles, directed first at Agamemnon and then at the Trojan who killed his friend Patroklos in battle, begins with the first line of the *Iliad* and ends with the last. In its stark simplicity, this wrath is the story of the *Iliad*, which opens with Homer's appeal to the Muse, "Sing goddess, of the wrath of Achilles, the son of Peleus" and ends with these words: "And so they carried out the burial of Hektor, breaker of horses." The legend of the archer from Malis who will arrive at Troy only after the deaths of Hektor and Achilles lies on the penumbra of the *Iliad*. Philoctetes' fate in the epic of Ilion is perfectly matched by his ten-year isolation on the island of Lemnos, where he was abandoned as the Achaians crossed the northern Aegean to make their assault on Troy. This legend, which is located at both edges of the *Iliad*, is the subject of Sophocles' *Philoctetes*.

Philoctetes is recalled near the beginning of the *Iliad* in the Catalogue of Ships (*Iliad* 2.716–28). His contingent of seven ships is said to have been manned by archers from Methone, Thaumakia, Meliboia, and rough Olizon—places that are only names to us now. His force of 450 men comes under the command of a subordinate named Medon when Philoctetes is abandoned on the "divine island of Lemnos"—"in the pain and anguish of the brutal bite of the snake that intended his death."

I wish to thank Sir Hugh Lloyd-Jones for the gift and guidance of the three volumes of his edition of Sophocles for the Loeb Classical Texts; Stephen Esposito for providing me a copy of William Arrowsmith's unpublished lecture on "The Sacrament of the Bow"; William Arrowsmith for his inspiration as a translator of dramatic texts; and, finally, Andrea Purvis, who in March 2000 helped me guide my colleague Carl Phillips.

Philoctetes remained on Lemnos as his comrades battled on the plains of Troy, "but soon memory of Lord Philoctetes would return to the minds of the Achaians" (*Iliad* 2.716–20). Homer's description of Philoctetes' state of mind on Lemnos, where he "sat in anger and in grief," echoes what he had just said of Achilles, as he had withdrawn to his ships from the Greek army in anger and resentment (*Iliad* 2.694). Both warriors will be sorely missed by the Achaians (*Iliad* 1.240 of Achilles).

Apparently, what made the Achaian army on the plains of Troy think of a comrade who had been left on Lemnos for ten long years does not need to be explained to Homer's audience. It requires some explanation for the reader of Sophocles' *Philoctetes*. Philoctetes' history is situated on the edges of the Homeric epics. There is a great deal of epic history that Homer excluded from his *Iliad*. He only glances at the antecedents of the Trojan War in the fateful choice offered to Paris by three rival goddesses, Hera, Athena, and Aphrodite, at the end of the epic (*Iliad* 24.25–30). Priam is king of Troy when the forces of Agamemnon reach the Troad, but Homer can take his audience back to the antecedents of Priam's kingship in Dardanos (as recalled by Aeneas in *Iliad* 20.215–41 and 304–5).

The Greek tragedians are more attentive to the events that followed the conclusion of Homer's *Iliad*. When they choose to write of the history of Troy, they concentrate on the events that took place in the interval between the death of Hektor and the capture of Troy; and then on the fate of the Trojans who survived the destruction of their city. The traditions that lay on the periphery of the *Iliad* were known in antiquity as "The Epic Cycle," and Sophocles was said to have been attracted to this fascinating and un-Homeric poetry.[1] Aeschylus wrote a play, much appreciated by ancient readers (including Sophocles), on the award of the arms and armor of Achilles after the "best of the Achaians" was killed by the arrow Paris aimed at his heel. His *The Decision over the Arms* [of Achilles] might be reflected in the episode we find in Sophocles' *Philoctetes*; one of the invented complaints Achilles' son, Neoptolemos, adduces to explain to Philoctetes his disaffection with the Greek army is the decision of the army to award the arms of his father to Odysseus (360–76 / 359–81). Sophocles' *Ajax* is the dramatization of the rage and frustration of Ajax, who, after Achilles, could claim the coveted

---

1. According to the learned Athenaeus of Naucratis in Egypt, "Sophocles was delighted by the Epic Cycle and composed entire plays that closely followed its plots," Deipnosophistai 7.277C. Accessible accounts of the Epic Cycle can be found in G. L. Huxley, *Greek Epic Poetry from Eumelos to Panyassis* (London 1969), 123–61, and Malcolm Davies, *The Greek Epic Cycle*, second edition (London 2001).

title "best of the Achaians" (*Iliad* 2.768–69), but saw the award of the arms go to the guile and eloquence of Odysseus.

After Achilles falls to Paris' arrow, the forces that bring about the destruction of Troy combine in rapid succession. In the anticipations to be found in Sophocles' play the events of this legend unfold in four stages: Odysseus manages to capture the Trojan seer, Helenos, who had unwisely left Troy at night. The seer is brought before the Greek army and forced by Odysseus to reveal that Troy will not fall until Philoctetes brings his bow from Lemnos and Achilles' son comes to Troy from Skyros (603–21 / 614–25 and 1332–42 / 1329–47); persuaded by Herakles, Philoctetes arrives at Troy, with the bow of Herakles, which will spell the doom of Paris. Before he goes into action, his wound is healed by Machaon and Podaleirios, the two physicians who serve the Greek army—or by Asklepios himself; finally, he and Achilles' son join together to take Troy (1490–1511 / 1329–47 and 1614–32 / 1418–40). In Sophocles' version of this part of the Troy tale, Neoptolemos is as necessary to the capture of the city his father could not take as are Philoctetes and the bow of Herakles. This combination of events might be termed "double determination." But, in this case, the determination does not involve the combination of divine and human forces as it often does in the *Iliad*; it involves two warriors whose legends are situated on the edges of the *Iliad*.

There is one crucial condition for the fall of Troy not mentioned in the *Philoctetes*. This is Odysseus' strategem of the wooden horse left for the Trojans by the departing Greeks as an offering to Athena. In the *Odyssey*, Odysseus tells Achilles that Neoptolemos had entered the Trojan horse with him and conducted himself bravely (*Odyssey* 11.523–32). The omission of any mention of the strategem of the Trojan horse seems a deliberate slight to Odysseus.

The actual capture and sack of Troy is the matter of post-Homeric epics; it is not the matter of the tragic poets of Athens in the last three decades of the fifth century.[2] What happened after the capture of Troy was the subject of three of the surviving plays of Euripides. He treats the fate of the women of Troy and the killing of Astyanax, the son of Hektor and Andromache, in his *Trojan Women* (produced in 415), a play that ends with the certainty of the imminent destruction of the city of Troy. The fate of widowed Hecuba (who in the *Trojan Women* is awarded as part of the plunder of Troy to Odysseus) and her son Polydoros is the subject of his *Hecuba*; and his *Andromache* takes Hektor's widow (awarded to Neoptolemos in *Trojan Women*) to Greece as a concubine

---

2. Sophocles wrote a *Philoctetes at Troy*; only reports of it survive.

of the son of the man who murdered her husband. In Euripides' *Andromache*, Pyrrhos (as Neoptolemos is called here) has none of the inherited nobility of the Neoptolemos of Sophocles' *Philoctetes*.[3]

The tragic legend of Philoctetes is, then, situated at the edges of Homer's *Iliad* and in some ways frames it. Philoctetes is the only Greek warrior to take part in the two Greek expeditions against Troy: in the first expedition against the city of Laomedon he is accompanied by Herakles and Telamon, father of Ajax. He takes no part in the action of the *Iliad*, which is intensely concentrated on the plains of Troy during a period of four days of combat and one day of truce in the tenth year of the siege. The legend of Philoctetes, as it connects with the second expedition against Troy, begins with his receiving the bow and arrows that will be fatal to Paris and to Troy from Herakles on Mt. Oita, the mountain that rises to the south of the plain of Malis—a mountain often mentioned in Sophocles' play—both as the rugged symbol of his home and the place of Herakles' immolation (682–89 / 664–70). In Sophocles' play it is Philoctetes who consented to put a torch to Herakles' pyre; he received in gratitude the bow given to him by Herakles. Consumed by the poison daubed on the shirt of the centaur Nessos gave Herakles' wife Deianeira and she gave her husband, Herakles will serve as the model for the sufferings of Philoctetes on Lemnos (1607–13 / 1417–25). In the scenes exhibiting the intense pain of the two heroes, the *Philoctetes* is a pained echo of Herakles in the *Women of Trachis*.

Philoctetes has a close relation to Herakles; he had served him as both stopped to sacrifice at the sanctuary of Chryse on the small island of that name that once lay off the coast to the east of Lemnos.[4] This was at the beginning of the first Greek expedition against Troy and Herakles' assault on the city of Laomedon. It is finally Herakles who persuades the adamantly resentful Philoctetes to sail to Troy with the hated Odysseus and the young warrior who had returned his bow to him (*Philoctetes* 1598–1646 / 1419–51). When he is finally cured by the physicians of the Greek army on the Troad and has helped capture

---

3. Interestingly, the club house (*lesche*) of the Knidians above the temple of Apollo at Delphi contained Polygnotos' version of the sack of Troy on its right wall. Neoptolemos, who was said to be buried nearby, evidently played a major role in this pictorial narrative, as is clear from the description Pausanias gives in his *Description of Greece*, 10.25–26. Polygnotos painted the *lesche* in the fifties of the fifth century; his painting survived until the time of Pausanias in the mid-second century A.D. It is Apollo who is responsible for the murder of Pyrrhos at Delphi (Euripides, *Andromache* 1161–65).

4. A bell crater now in Vienna shows the richly clad statue of the goddess surmounting a column placed behind an altar where Herakles is about to sacrifice, illustrated in Figure 2 of "Chryse I," *Lexicon Iconographicum Mythologiae Classicae* III.2 (Zurich and Berlin 1986).

Troy with the bow of Herakles, Philoctetes is instructed to deposit some of the spoils from Troy in the sanctuary of Herakles on Mt. Oita as a memorial to the divine power of Herakles' bow (1620–24 / 1429–33).

Philoctetes' knowledge of the location of the island and sanctuary of Chryse was essential to the Achaian armada, as the Greeks made a second expedition against Troy. Sacrifice to Chryse was, apparently, necessary for their reaching Troy (as was sacrifice to Artemis at Aulis, as the fleet left the Greek mainland). It was at this sanctuary that Philoctetes was bitten by the snake that guarded the place. The agony and loathsome suppuration from this poisonous wound to Philoctetes' foot caused the Greek army—and Odysseus as their agent—to abandon him on Lemnos. He was to remain on the island Sophocles makes uninhabited and desolate during the siege of Troy, until the frustrated Greek army sends Odysseus and Neoptolemos to persuade him—or force him—to come, with his bow, to Troy. Sophocles' play opens as Odysseus and Neoptolemos have arrived on Lemnos and approach the seaside cave that has been Philoctetes' shelter; it ends as Herakles appears at one of the two mouths of Philoctetes' cave to resolve the human impasse and seal the fate of Priam's Troy (1598 / 1409). The words of Herakles, now a divine resident on Mt. Olympos, persuade Philoctetes to accompany Odysseus and Neoptolemos back to Troy. No strategem of Odysseus or noble appeal of the son of Achilles or the Chorus can bring this about. The irreconcilable conflict between two opposed worlds of value prompts Sophocles to adopt the Euripidean device of introducing a deus ex machina to break the human impasse.

LEMNOS *friend, sufferer, duty*

We begin on Lemnos. Lemnos was populated long before the destruction of Troy (if Schliemann's Troy VI is Priam's city). The coastal site of Polichni belongs to the Late Bronze Age (1500–1000 B.C.). For Homer, Lemnos had close associations with Hephaistos (because of its vulcanism) and was populated. When Zeus hurled Hephaistos down onto Lemnos—Milton's "th' Aegean isle"—he is cared for by a people called the Sinties (*Iliad* 1.590–94). In the *Odyssey* (8.294), the Sinties are described as speaking like animals, and Homer has Hephaistos returning from Olympos to "the strong city of Lemnos" (*Odyssey* 8.284–85). It is remarkable that Sophocles, who wrote his *Philoctetes* after Aeschylus and Euripides had written theirs, should make Lemnos a bleak, uninhabited island and thus leave Philoctetes there in a state of utter isolation. The isolation of Philoctetes on Lemnos is only one of the salient differences between the earlier Philoctetes plays of Aeschylus and Euripides and Sophocles' play. Euripides gives Philoctetes a Lemnian companion by the name of Aktor. In 431 (the date of Euripides' *Philoctetes*) there should have been nothing unusual about Lemnians as companions to the outcast Philoctetes; in 450 the Athenians had sent a group of colonists out to the island to secure control of the seaways to Thrace and up into the Black Sea. Its two principal cities, Myrrhine and Hephaistia, were important Athenian settlements, and Athena of Lemnos was worshipped on the acropolis of Athens. A cult of Chryse seems to have been located near the Pnyx in Athens. There was also an important Athenian cult of Herakles on the island. Lemnos was well populated at the date of Sophocles' *Philoctetes*.

As the play opens, Odysseus and Neoptolemos have landed on Lemnos in search of Philoctetes. They find no trace of humans on the Lemnian shore, only the cave of Philoctetes above them, with its two openings. The foul rags that Philoctetes uses to bandage his wound are the only signs of the island's single human inhabitant; they are visible on the rocky side of the cave. The term that most often describes Philoctetes in Sophocles' play is *eremos*—alone, isolated, companionless. But finally, he will be true to his name (a combination of *philos*, "friend," and the verb *ktasthai*, "to possess") as he finds a true friend in the young Neoptolemos.

As the sailors from Skyros first encounter him, it is clear to them that Philoctetes has become savage (**220–21** / 225–26 and **1479** / 1321). His "bed" is made of leaves (**41** / 33); his "roof" of rock (**1400** / 1262). His food is described as fodder (*phorba*, **49** / 43 and **1221** / 1107)—a word for the food of beasts. He lives by his bow, and the association of bow (*biós*) and life (*biós*) is latent in Sophocles' Greek. The few visitors who are driven to the island refuse to take Philoctetes with them, leaving him once again with no human contact (**503–7** / 494–96). And, when he finally readies to leave the island, Philoctetes invokes the world of nature that has become so familiar to him (**1647–71** / 1452–68), as he had in his long lyric invocation of the life he would lead on Lemnos without his bow (**1648–66** / 1081–1162):

> I . . . call upon this island . . . ,
> chamber that kept watch over me,
>
> water-nymphs,
>
> nymphs of the meadows,
>
> the muscled crashing of sea against headland,
> where often my head, though
> inside the cave, was drenched by the south wind's beating,

and often the mountain of Hermes sent
back to me in answer
my own voice
echoing,
groaning,
as I weathered the storm.

But now,
o streams and Lycian spring,
we take leave of you—I leave you
at last, . . .

Farewell, Lemnos, surrounded by sea . . .

This is the passage that inspired in Matthew Arnold "the eternal note of sadness" as he stood on Dover Beach:

Sophocles long ago
Heard it on the Ægæan, and it brought
Into his mind the turbid ebb and flow
Of human misery.[5]

PHILOCTETES BEFORE *PHILOCTETES*

Of all the tragedies produced in Athens in the competitions of the festivals of Dionysos only seven survive of Aeschylus, seven of Sophocles, and eighteen of Euripides. (Each year three tragic poets competed with three tragedies and a satyr play in the festival of the Greater Dionysia.) By good luck, we can compare the distinctively different talents of the three great Athenian tragedians as they dealt with the theme of Orestes and Electra and their revenge on their mother, Clytemnestra, for the treacherous murder of their father, Agamemnon. In the unique case of Aeschylus' *Choephoroi* (*Libation Bearers*), Sophocles' grim *Electra*, and Euripides' realistic play of the same title, we have a sequence of three extant plays treating the same subject written over nearly half a century (from 458 to approximately 413). In a sense, these plays are "trilogies" in that we can see the three tragic poets whose works have survived in dialogue. In them, we can attend to the silent dialogue of Sophocles with Aeschylus, and of Euripides with both Aeschylus and Sophocles. Euripides' staging of the scene in which Electra recognizes her brother can only be fully appreciated as a sophisticated reenactment of the same scene in Aeschylus' *Choephoroi* (*Electra* 508–52; *Choephoroi* 154–211).

---

5. There is also the striking description of Oedipus as a promontory battered by the sea in Sophocles' last play, *Oedipus at Colonus* 1240–48.

We cannot directly assess the very different dramatic thought and art of the three tragedians in the treatment of any other theme. But Dio of Prusa could. In the late first century or early second century of the imperial period, Dio's library in Prusa contained the Philoctetes plays of Aeschylus, Euripides, and Sophocles. To exercise his mind, he spent a day reading the plays and wrote (and must have delivered in public) a comparison of the three tragedies. These three Philoctetes plays were never entered in competition one against the others, and Dio possessed the refinement not to decide on the superiority of one poet over the others. Yet, as a skilled and erudite public speaker (*sophistes*), he was clearly attracted to Euripides' treatment of the character of Odysseus, who was for the Greeks the archetype of the sophist and demagogue—and, then, of the successful orator of Dio's age (Speech 52). Indeed, Dio gives a prose version of the prologue and first episode of Euripides' *Philoctetes* (Speech 59).

Sophocles' *Philoctetes* won first prize at the competitions of the Greater Dionysia of 409. We know that Euripides entered his *Medea* and *Philoctetes* in the competitions of 431 (and won third prize). As readers of Sophocles' *Philoctetes*, we face the unusual sequence of Aeschylus, Euripides, and then, after an interval of twenty-two years, Sophocles. (We do not know the date of Aeschylus' play.) Dio takes up the discussion of the three Philoctetes plays in this order. As we will see, there are signs in Sophocles of the impact of the dramatic art of Euripides. His *Philoctetes* is his only extant play whose intractable human conflict is resolved by a deus ex machina. The god who appears—not from the machine, but on the upper ledge of the cave above Philoctetes' cave—is Herakles.

Although Sophocles' *Philoctetes* comes last in sequence, Dio places Sophocles between the extremes of Aeschylus' rugged grandeur and Euripides' admirable—and highly imitable—rhetorical agility; he is "intermediate" (*mesos*) (Speech 52 §15). This is Sophocles' position in the dramatic contest between Aeschylus and Euripides in Aristophanes' *Frogs*, a play produced in 405, two years after the death of Euripides and the year after the death of Sophocles. Standing between the two extreme representatives of Attic tragedy, Sophocles is described as "easy-going in Hades and easy-going on earth" (*Frogs* 82; cf. 787).

But in his treatment of the Philoctetes legend, Sophocles stands at an extreme. To assess the distinctive shape of his *Philoctetes*, Sophocles' reader—and ancient audience—must place his play in a context larger than a recognition of the two Philoctetes plays that preceded his in the Theater of Dionysos. When it was first produced, Aeschylus' *Philoctetes* did not enter into dialogue with an earlier play; Euripides' *Philoctetes* is

INTRODUCTION

not merely a dialogue with Aeschylus; and Sophocles' *Philoctetes* is not merely the third play in Dio's trilogy. Although Philoctetes is mentioned only three times in the Homeric epics,[6] and plays no role in the action of the *Iliad*, Sophocles' characterization of Philoctetes' stubborn and archaic heroism is informed by Sophocles' deep understanding of the extremes of heroic character represented by Homer's Achilles and Odysseus. Sophocles also knew and could appreciate infinitely better than can we the post-Homeric epics that dealt with his theme. He had prepared for his *Philoctetes* by producing his *Ajax* and *The Women of Trachis*. He also wrote *The Madness of Odysseus, Phoinix, The Islanders of Skyros*, and *Philoctetes at Troy*—all now vanished with little trace.[7] As important, Sophocles also knew the political culture of Athens during the period of the Peloponnesian War, a period that saw the sudden and dramatic influence of the sophistic movement in the Athenian political assemblies, law courts, and theater. One of the most important of the Athenian sophists was Euripides.

We have already observed how Sophocles also departs from both Aeschylus and Euripides in depopulating the island of Lemnos. The prologue to his play opens with Odysseus' description of the island (1–6 / 1–2):

> This coast—
>
> This shore—
>
> This is Lemnos, the sea
> surrounds it. No man
> lives here—even
> steps here.

It is clear from Dio that the choruses of both Aeschylus' and Euripides' plays were made up of Lemnians (Speech 52 §7). By contrast, Sophocles provides the abandoned warrior with no human companionship: only the sea, the grey rocks, and the birds and animals that provide Philoctetes with his livelihood. None of the occasional visitors who are forced to land on the island are willing to take Philoctetes off it (300–314 / 303–13); Philoctetes is forced to ask some of the departing visitors to take a message to his father (503–7 / 494–96).

The effect of Philoctetes' isolation in Sophocles' play is twofold: it makes the great archer, who possesses the formidable bow of Herakles, as savage and elemental as the island he inhabits, a place of rugged cliffs,

---

6. We have seen him in the Catalogue of Ships, *Iliad* 2.716–28. He is mentioned again in the *Odyssey*, as the greatest archer of the Greek army (8.219) and as having safely reached home, unlike Odysseus (3.190).

7. They can be appreciated in the Loeb edition of Sir Hugh Lloyd-Jones, *Sophocles*, vol. 3, Fragments (London 1996).

raging surf, air pierced with the cry of birds, and the fire of Hephaistos. His isolation also makes Philoctetes a throwback to a vanished heroic past and at the same time the object of pity for Neoptolemos and his Skyrians. The other way in which Sophocles reshapes the tragic myth of Philoctetes is that he adds Neoptolemos to the embassy of Odysseus. The result is that the young son of Achilles is caught in the tension between his loyalty to Odysseus and the Greek army at Troy and his admiration and sympathy for the hero who represents the values and stubbornness of the father he never knew. In this sense, Philoctetes is no longer isolated once Odysseus and Neoptolemos land on Lemnos. He comes to occupy an extreme, and the young Neoptolemos is caught between the powerful forces of Odysseus and Philoctetes.

DRAMATIS PERSONAE

Aristotle spoke epigrammatically of Sophocles' contribution to the development of Attic tragedy: "the third actor and scene painting."[8] In Greek tragedy at the time of Sophocles' *Philoctetes* the speaking parts were divided among three actors: the protagonist (first actor), deuteragonist (second actor), and tritagonist (third actor). In the case of his *Philoctetes*, a single actor plays the parts of Neoptolemos and Philoctetes, but the versatile actor who plays the part of Odysseus also plays the part of the Trader (548–641 / 542–627) and of Herakles at the end of the play (1598–1638 / 1409–68). This actor is—to employ the Homeric epithet that describes Odysseus in the first line of the *Odyssey*—*polytropos*, a man of many turns.

No character in a Greek tragedy stands in isolation; conflict and contrast are essential to drama and characterization. This is true of the Homeric epics. The case of Odysseus is instructive. In the *Iliad*, Menelaos is described as being taller than Odysseus when both stand before the Greek army; but, when both are seated, Odysseus is the more majestic figure. As a speaker, Menelaos' delivery is rapid; he does not use many words and his voice is clear. When Odysseus comes to address the assembly, he leaps to his feet and then stands stock still with his eyes fixed on the ground as rigidly as the scepter he holds motionless in his hand. He seems a dolt. But, when he begins to speak, he speaks with a strong voice and his words fall on the ears of his audience like great flakes of snow. Such is the Trojan Antenor's description of Odysseus (*Iliad* 3.204–24). In the case of Odysseus, unlike any other Homeric hero, appearances are deceiving. Helen confirms Antenor's description as she identifies Odysseus to Priam from the walls of Troy: "This the crafty son

8. *Poetics* 4.1449 18.

of Laertes, Odysseus, who was raised on Ithaca, a rocky place to grow up in. He knows many twists, and turns, and clever strategems" (*Iliad* 3.191–202).

Odysseus is the most fully described character in the Homeric poems, not only because he manages to survive the *Iliad* but he also becomes the hero of the *Odyssey*. His wit, eloquence, and guile combined with his prudent but conspicuous bravery make him unique among Homeric heroes. But, as Antenor's description makes clear, Odysseus' character cannot be understood in isolation; it is revealed in a system of meaningful contrasts.[9] In his *Philoctetes*, Sophocles creates a tension between Odysseus and Philoctetes that, like Philoctetes' bow, is never relaxed. This tension is so intense that Odysseus cannot at first face the suffering warrior he was commanded to abandon on Lemnos. The young[10] Neoptolemos is caught between these two antagonists, who represent not only the conflict between authority and Philoctetes' deeply injured pride, but a conflict between the heroism — if heroism is the word for it — of adaptability and cunning and the fixity of the blunt, archaic heroism of Philoctetes. Odysseus is prudently unwilling to get within range of Philoctetes' bow; Philoctetes is imprudently willing to let himself be caught in the net of lies Odysseus throws over him. The world in which Odysseus lives and moves so deftly is the world of Athens of 409, when eloquence was, in the words of the sophist Gorgias, a "great potentate"[11] in every public arena. This was a world split between words (*logoi*) and reality (*erga*); it was a world in which speech became reality. In contrast to the versatile Odysseus, who moves on and off stage, and whose deeds are words, Philoctetes is virtually immobile because of his injured leg. His language is often reduced to inarticulate cries of agony, and his hatred of the Atreidai and their agent Odysseus is as inveterate and incurable as his wound.

No dramatic detail makes the vanished world of stolid heroism and the contemporary world of agile sophistry more apparent than the interview of Neoptolemos with Philoctetes, who has had no word of the fate of the warriors who had been his companions as far as Lemnos on their way to Troy. Here Sophocles rehearses the dramatic scene from the Underworld in which Odysseus sights the great warriors who died on the Plains of Troy and interviews Agamemnon and Achilles, and attempts to get a response from Ajax (**403–37** / 403–36; cf. *Odyssey*

---

9. As when Priam notes that he is shorter than Agamemnon by a head (*Iliad* 3.193).

10. By sober chronology, Neoptolemos, who is often addressed as "child" (*pais*), would be about ten at the time of the embassy to Lemnos. He is usually presented as about eighteen or an ephebe.

11. So described by Gorgias in his display piece, *In Praise of Helen* § 8 in Hermann Diels and Walther Kranz, *Die Fragmente der Vorsokratiker* (Berlin 1952) 82 B 10. See note on l. 145.

11.387–564). Ajax, Neoptolemos tells Philoctetes, is dead. It is Ajax, who, after Achilles, was recognized as "the best of the Achaians."[12] Nestor lives on, but in grief for the loss of his son Antilochos, who fell at Troy. Patroklos, too, is enlisted in the nation of the glorious dead. But the sons of Atreus, Diomedes, and Odysseus still live on: "War" Neoptolemos says, "will always prefer those who are most noble" (437 / 436–37).

Philoctetes now asks about "one who is hardly noble, but is clever." Neoptolemos is puzzled for a moment and hesitates: "Whom do you mean, if not Odysseus?" (441 / 438–41) The worthless creature Philoctetes had in mind is in fact not Odysseus, but Thersites. It is a measure of Odysseus' rapid decline in the age of Sophocles that the son of Achilles should think of Odysseus and not Thersites, notorious in the *Iliad* for his comic ugliness and abusive and incoherent speeches before the Greek army at Troy. Thersites is hated by both Achilles and Odysseus (*Iliad* 2.211–42). In this episode of the *Iliad*, it is Odysseus, the upholder of authority, who beats the upstart Thersites with the gold scepter that is the emblem of Agamemnon's kingly authority, to the universal approval of the assembly (*Iliad* 2.243–77). Yet Homer admits that this, the worst of the Achaians, is an appealing speaker (*Iliad* 2.246).

Recalling his interview with the soul of Ajax in the Underworld, Odysseus claims that not only the Achaians but Athena awarded him the arms of Achilles (*Odyssey* 11.547). Athena suggests guile; her particular attachment to Odysseus is motivated by the intelligence they both share in common. In his *Ajax*, Sophocles had handled the theme of the consequences of the award of the arms of Achilles (and implicitly his title as "the best of the Achaians") to Odysseus and not to Ajax. Sophocles' *Ajax* resembles his *Philoctetes* in one crucial feature: both plays dramatize the injured pride of a warrior who has been disgraced by Odysseus and the sons of Atreus; and in both the shamed and injured warrior becomes isolated from his society. And, in a sense, Sophocles stages a contest over the divine bow of Herakles in his *Philoctetes*. Character does not carry over from Homer to the tragedians or from one tragedy to another, but it is worth noting that Ajax's contempt for Odysseus and the sons of Atreus is matched by Philoctetes' contempt for Odysseus and his commanders. In the earlier play, when he has regained his sanity, Ajax calls Odysseus "the most fawning, dangerous, and despicable sharper" (*Ajax* 955–60).

In Sophocles' *Philoctetes*, Neoptolemos is a new presence on the stage of the Theater of Dionysos. It appears that Sophocles invented the part of

---

12. Both in the Catalogue of Ships (*Iliad* 2.768) and in the judgment of his mortal enemy Odysseus, who attempts to speak with him in the Underworld (*Odyssey* 11.469–70).

Neoptolemos in the embassy to Philoctetes; in Euripides' *Philoctetes*, Odysseus' companion was Diomedes.[13] The young son of Achilles is caught and vacillates between the extremes of human values represented by Odysseus and Philoctetes. When Odysseus cajoles him to play his part in deceiving Philoctetes and bringing him aboard their ship, he flatters him by addressing him as the son of Achilles and tells him "you'll have to be as noble as your birth is" (57 / 51). Neoptolemos' response to Odysseus' appeal to play this role "for a brief, shameless part of the day" (94 / 83) is predictable: "Son of Laertes, I hate doing things that are painful even to listen to" (97 / 86–87). He is reenacting the part of his father and displaying his inherited genius. His words recall those his father addressed to Odysseus.

Neoptolemos' reply and the embassy of Odysseus to Lemnos subtly recall an earlier embassy from the *Iliad*, that sent by Agamemnon to the tent of Achilles on the shore of Troy. In *Iliad* 9 (122–61), Agamemnon lists for Odysseus, Ajax, and Phoinix the gifts he will give Achilles to persuade him to relent in his anger and return to battle against Troy. He ends by saying that Achilles should give way to him, "in as much as I am more kingly than he and older than he in years" (160–61). When he comes to the tent of Achilles, Odysseus repeats Agamemnon's offer, but diplomatically omits his last injunction. Achilles could not have heard what Agamemnon had said, but his response seems to be directed against Odysseus as well as Agamemnon, whom he mistrusts: "Zeus-born Odysseus, son of Laertes, man of many shifts.... More than I hate the gates of Hades I hate the man who says one thing and conceals another in his heart!" (308–13). He has a similar response to Odysseus' suave flattery as they meet in Hades (*Odyssey* 11.467–91).

In his initial reaction to Odysseus' proposal, Neoptolemos plays the part of his father. But he relents and plays the part Odysseus has assigned to him for just about half the play. What turns him away from his false role in Odysseus' plot to capture Philoctetes is the sight of Philoctetes' bow: "And what is it you're holding now — / is *that* the famed bow?" (669–70 / 654). Now begins what William Arrowsmith has called "the sacrament of the bow."[14] In entrusting this "sacred" bow to the young son of Achilles, Philoctetes has enacted the meaning of his name and acquired a friend. It is precisely at this point of the play that Neoptolemos and the confederate Chorus of his subjects stop acting their roles in Odysseus'

---

13. As is clear from Dio's description of the play, *Speech* 52 §14.
14. In an unpublished lecture given at Hope College in 1976. I am grateful to Stephen Esposito for making a transcript of this lecture (which I heard Arrowsmith deliver on Martha's Vineyard in June 1977) available to me. It is entitled "Heroism and the 'sacrament of the bow' in Sophocles' *Philoctetes*."

cunning plot and come to pity the atrocious suffering of the owner of the bow. Despite Odysseus' threat of violence (1390 / 1254–55), Neoptolemos is determined to return the bow to its rightful owner. He will not make a tool of Philoctetes or separate him from his bow. After three frustrated attempts to leave Philoctetes' cave for their ship and return to Skyros and Malis, Neoptolemos and Philoctetes join forces to face the threat of violence from the Greek army. Philoctetes will protect Neoptolemos and Skyros "with the arrows of Herakles" (1593 / 1406). At these words Herakles appears. In an uncanny way, the seemingly mismatched solidarity of Philoctetes and Neoptolemos recalls the revenge Odysseus takes on the suitors in the *Odyssey*, with the bow given him by Iphitos and his young son by his side.

The conflict of Sophocles' *Philoctetes* has no solution. The words of the Chorus that open Seamus Heaney's *The Cure at Troy* recognize the human impasse.[15]

> Philoctetes.
>   Hercules.
>   Odysseus.
> Heroes. Victims. Gods and human beings.
> All throwing shapes, every one of them
> Convinced he's in the right, all of them glad
> To repeat themselves and their every last mistake,
> No matter what.

DRAMATURGY

The Play within the Play

In the *Philoctetes*, Sophocles' dramatic art is invested in characterization, the plots devised by Odysseus that mimic his own larger construction, his use of a conspiratorial Chorus, the stage property of the talismanic bow, sudden entrances and a long delayed exit, and the final deus ex machina that seems to settle all that is left in suspense and assure the Troy tale of its expected ending. Sophocles' dramatization of the mission of Odysseus and Neoptolemos to bring Philoctetes from Lemnos to Troy is, as we have seen, inspired by the embassy of Odysseus, Ajax, and Phoinix to the tent of Achilles in *Iliad* 9. This embassy can be sighted just behind the stage of Sophocles' play. Within the play, there are three fictive embassies that are an integral part of the plot of the play; they are all part of Odysseus' plot to capture Philoctetes and his bow by guile. They are introduced by Odysseus, who rehearses for Neoptolemos the lying tale he is to tell Philoctetes about the insult of the award of the arms of his father to Odysseus by the

---

15. *The Cure at Troy: A Version of Sophocles' Philoctetes* (New York 1991).

Greek army (**63–76** / 55–69). Even at the end of the play, Neoptolemos cannot reveal to Philoctetes that he was lying about the arms (**1532–39** / 1362–66).

The prelude to Odysseus' lying tale has Neoptolemos arrive at the Troad to discover that the arms of his father had been awarded to Odysseus, who, when reproached, had the audacity to reproach the young Neoptolemos for not being at Troy when he was needed (**380–81** / 379–80). In his own shame and anger Neoptolemos does what Achilles only threatened to do (first in *Iliad* 1.169–71): sail back home. This, in the plot of Odysseus' play, is the insult that brings Neoptolemos to Lemnos on his way home to Skyros. It is a tale designed to elicit the sympathy and confidence of Philoctetes, who had been disgracefully treated by both the Atreidai and Odysseus, "that worst of all evil men" as Neoptolemos describes him on cue (**385** / 384; cf. **73–74** / 64–51).

The first fictive embassy of the *Philoctetes* is the embassy of Odysseus and Phoinix, the tutor of Achilles, to bring Neoptolemos from Skyros to Troy (**341–53** / 343–53); it is the prelude of the mission of Odysseus and Neoptolemos to Lemnos. A part of what Neoptolemos tells Philoctetes about this mission reflects the legend of the fall of Troy, but it includes an Odyssean accent of deception. According to Neoptolemos, Odysseus and Phoinix managed to persuade him to come to Troy by claiming that, with Achilles dead, *only* his son could take Troy. This contradicts the oracle Herakles delivers at the end of the play: Neoptolemos and Philoctetes were *both* needed to finally capture the city (**1625–29** / 1433–37). The oracle of Helenos that the Trader repeats to Neoptolemos and Philoctetes also contradicts the oracle of Herakles: according to the Trader, Philoctetes *alone* was needed for the capture of Troy (**622–25** / 610–13). Neoptolemos and the Trader both play their assigned parts in Odysseus' drama staged on Lemnos with skill.

The second fictive embassy is announced to Neoptolemos and Philoctetes by the Trader. His role is played by the actor, who also plays the role of Odysseus. The Trader arrives on the scene with one of Neoptolemos' sailors just as Neoptolemos had promised to take Philoctetes off the island (**548** / 542). His tale is that he, too, has come from Troy and, finding Neoptolemos on Lemnos, can warn him of a new "plot" of the Argives against the already outraged boy. An embassy made up of "old Phoinix" and the sons of Theseus is on its way to Skyros. Neoptolemos asks the relevant question: "To bring me back by violence, or with words?" (**567** / 563). Philoctetes will ask the same question. What explains the absence of Odysseus on such a mission is the fact that he was sent with Diomedes (his companion in the Doloneia of the *Iliad*) on still another mission to bring Philoctetes to Troy. This is the third false embassy. The Trader feigns that he does not quite know who Philoctetes is as he announces their quarry (578–79 / 573). Him they will bring to Troy either by force or persuasion.

The plot of Odysseus' play on Lemnos in which Neoptolemos, the Chorus, and the "Trader" all play their assigned parts, is well described by Odysseus as a "clever strategem" (*sophisma*, 20 / 14). It is cunningly contrived to accomplish its ends by words and it plays effectively on the pride that Odysseus and the Atreidai had mortally wounded. The last of the lying embassies rehearsed by the Trader casts both Neoptolemos and Philoctetes as the quarry of the Greek who had insulted them: Philoctetes in truth and Neoptolemos in Odysseus' fiction. No force can drive Philoctetes onto Neoptolemos' ship and deliver him to Troy; although Odysseus once offers to use force (1075 / 983), he relies on words and, like Sophocles, produces his own play within a play.

The Complicit Chorus

The Chorus members of the *Philoctetes* are subjects of Neoptolemos from the island of Skyros. (In this it resembles the Chorus of Sophocles' *Ajax*, which is made up of sailors from Salamis.) It has accompanied Neoptolemos from Skyros to Troy and has now come to Lemnos in the mission to bring Philoctetes to Troy. There are two striking features of Sophocles' use of the Chorus in the *Philoctetes*: the lyrical portions of the play are severely reduced when compared to the other plays of Sophocles (including his last play, *Oedipus at Colonus*); the Chorus enters into the action of the play with more involvement in its plot than any other Sophoclean play.

It is not clear from the language of the play when the Chorus of the *Philoctetes* enters the orchestra. It might appear after Odysseus and Neoptolemos have made their entry on stage. Certainly it has assembled before the audience sometime before it speaks. As a participant in the action—and the plot—of the *Philoctetes*, it is closely associated with Neoptolemos and Odysseus from the beginning of the play. The Chorus members are the subjects of their king, as Neoptolemos is for some part of the play subject to Odysseus and the mission on which they were sent by the Greek army. In its first words (148–90 / 135–90), the Chorus asks for instructions from Neoptolemos. The subservience of the Chorus abolishes the distance between the actor on stage and the Chorus members in the orchestra. Its invocation of the scepter of Zeus that its "master," the boy Neoptolemos, possesses introduces the first of the three sacred objects that figure as bearers of power and authority in the play: the other objects are the arms of Achilles, fashioned by the god Hephaistos on Olympos, and the bow and arrows given to Philoctetes by Herakles on the summit of Mt. Oita. Only these appear on stage. The *skeptron* Agamemnon takes up in the assembly of the Greek army at the beginning of the *Iliad* is a hereditary possession fashioned by Hephaistos and passed down from Zeus to Agamemnon (2.100–6). The *skeptron* Achilles takes up in the assembly is seen very differently. Just as it will never sprout leaves again once cut from a tree, Achilles' oath never to return to battle for the Achaians is immutable (*Iliad* 1.234–44). Neoptolemos' men respect the traditional symbol of their king's authority.

The first reflections of the Chorus turn to Philoctetes, who has not yet appeared from the lower opening of the cave. It can hear but it cannot see his agony and desolation (201 / 203). It enters into a dialogue with Neoptolemos and, as he appears, it addresses Philoctetes (313 / 317). In a formal ode, whose strophe is separated from its antistrophe by more than the 100 lines in which Odysseus rehearses his plot, the Chorus invokes the Earth, Mother of the Gods. In the strophe, it represents to Philoctetes the fictive scene on the Troad in which and their injured king witnessed the award of the arms of Achilles to Odysseus. By its complicity in Odysseus' plot, it succeeds in catching Philoctetes in its toils. It enlists Philoctetes in a community of loathing for Odysseus and the Greek army. In the long-delayed antistrophe, it expresses once again its pity for Philoctetes' life on Lemnos.

In the only formal *stasimon*[16] of the play (696–751 / 676–728), the Chorus returns to the theme of Philoctetes' sufferings, once again in his presence. It can discover no parallel in history for his sufferings and finds him innocent of any offense against god or man. The far-fetched example of Ixion, who was punished by Zeus by being bound to an eternally rotating wheel, is no precedent for Philoctetes' sufferings. The Chorus concludes by endorsing Neoptolemos' promise to take him home. The depth of its involvement in Odysseus' plot to trick the object of their professed sympathy is evident as Philoctetes falls asleep, exhausted by the pain of his wound. The Chorus sings a lyric invocation to Sleep (Hypnos), the healer of mortal suffering. It is at this crucial moment that Neoptolemos resists its urging to leave with the bow entrusted to him and abandon Philoctetes on the island.

---

16. That is, a formal song accompanied by dance and divided into *strophe* (turn) and *antistrophe* (counter-turn) when the chorus of fifteen have taken their position in the orchestra (after the *parados*, or entry song). In form, the other choral songs of the play are *kommoi*, or antiphonal lyrics (originally laments). These are 873–913 / 827–64 in which Neoptolemos responds to the Chorus and 1200–1344 / 1081–1217 in which the Chorus responds to Philoctetes.

This moment is the pivot on which the play turns. Philoctetes awakes and Neoptolemos revolts from his long subordination to Odysseus and turns to Philoctetes whom he has now acquired "as a friend" (690 / 671). The Chorus had reminded him of the favorable wind that had sprung up; Neoptolemos resists this wind. This wind has as much power over him now that he has received the bow of Herakles as has Odysseus' persuasive eloquence at the beginning of the play. Odysseus' plot would require him to abandon his inborn character "for a brief, shameless part of the day" (94 / 83). After the "sacrament of the bow," Neoptolemos is incapable of this.

In a striking way, it is Philoctetes and not the Chorus who sustains the choral lyric for the rest of the play. His language is lyrical (in terms of both diction and meter) as he imagines what his life on Lemnos would be without his bow (1200–1344 / 1081–1222). Formally this final song is a dirge of lamentation (*kommos*) in which Philoctetes laments his fate as once again he is abandoned on Lemnos but now without his bow. The Chorus responds in short perfunctory comments about Philoctetes being responsible for the destiny he is lamenting and exonerates itself and Odysseus of any treachery. It is only at the end of the second antistrophe that Philoctetes pays any attention to what the Chorus says and only because it has finally commented on his suffering (1287 / 1170). The worlds of the subordinate Chorus and the wounded Philoctetes stand far apart. The Chorus justifies Odysseus' plot by claiming that he was aiding "friends" (1261 / 1145). The Greeks at Troy are not Philoctetes' "friends." For the Chorus, Philoctetes and his bow are the means to preserving the "community" of the Greek army at Troy; for Philoctetes, his bow is the only means of sustaining his life on Lemnos. The decision of Neoptolemos to return the bow to the man he has acquired as a friend incorporates Philoctetes into another world of friendship.

Philoctetes is not entirely wrapped up in himself and the grim thought of his life on Lemnos without his bow. Unlike the island he says farewell to as he leaves for Troy, the Lemnos of these lyrics is not uninhabited. In the second strophe he imagines Odysseus seated on its shore gloating over the arms of Herakles (1236–53 / 1123–39). (Actually, Odysseus never gains possession of his bow.) In this song, the other inhabitants of Lemnos are the birds and game his bow (which he calls "my means of living" in 1239 / 1126) brings down. In his final farewell to the island and in the presence of Herakles and his bow (1647–71 / 1452–68), Lemnos becomes what Homer called it, a "sacred island" (*Iliad* 21.79). It is haunted by nymphs of the meadows, Hermes, and Apollo of the Lycian spring. The Chorus finally recognizes the divinity of the place; it prays to the sea-nymphs as it sails to Troy. The homecoming it prays for will be delayed by the short episode of savagery that follows the capture of Troy.

The Bow

τῶι οὖν τόξωι ὄνομα Βίος, ἔργον δὲ θάνατος
Life is the name of the bow; its work death.
—*Herakleitos frg. 48,* Diels and Kranz, *Die Fragmente der Vorsokratiker*

The bow of Philoctetes once belonged to Herakles, who gave it to his companion on Oita in thanks for lighting the pyre that consumed his body, freed him from pain, and rendered him immortal. He had employed it in the first Greek expedition against the Troy of Laomedon. Herakles the archer is impressively shown kneeling on one knee with the bow bent on the East pediment of the temple of Aphaia on Aegina (c. 500–480 B.C.). In Sophocles' *Philoctetes* the bow is both a prop to support Philoctetes as he limps on stage from his cave in the middle of the play and an object of awe. We do not see it at first. It is only when Philoctetes brings his bow from his cave as he prepares to leave for Skyros and Malis that it makes its long-delayed epiphany on stage. The young Neoptolemos stands in awe of it and asks if he can touch it and worship it, "as I would a god" (**673** / 657). In first allowing Neoptolemos to hold his bow and then in entrusting it to him, Philoctetes reenacts the scene on Mt. Oita when Herakles entrusted the bow to him. As they enter the cave to gather Philoctetes' few possessions, Neoptolemos both holds Philoctetes' bow and supports Philoctetes himself. Philoctetes gives Neoptolemos his bow as he faints from the recurrent pain of his infection (**790–93** / 762–66), and it remains in Neoptolemos' possession until he finally realizes that he cannot take leave of "his very nature" (**956** / 902–3). After an outraged Odysseus has left the stage in frustration, Neoptolemos returns the bow to its rightful owner (**1437** / 1286–87). Neoptolemos has discovered that the bow and its owner are inseparable.

As the two new comrades prepare to leave the island, the younger man supports the older, who carries his bow. Philoctetes tries to assure Neoptolemos that he will protect him against any reprisals by the Greek army with the arrows of Herakles (**1593** / 1406). As he mentions the name Herakles, Herakles appears on the rock platform at the base of the upper cave.

The prospect of the two comrades facing insuperable odds is strangely reminiscent. In Book 21 of the *Odyssey*, Odysseus and his son Telemachos face the suitors. Odysseus is armed with a bow given to him by Iphitos, who was murdered by Herakles (*Odyssey* 21.11–33). In a test of strength, Odysseus strings this great horn bow, drives an arrow through twelve ax heads, and with the help of Telemachos begins the slaughter of the suitors in his palace (*Odyssey* 21.258–22.125).

The tension between Philoctetes and Odysseus is not something that can be unstrung and relaxed like a bow or lyre. It is only Herakles who can resolve this tension and determine the destruction of the city he had attacked with Philoctetes a generation earlier. He has a divine influence on a man to whom he had given his bow and who has come to resemble him in his suffering. The snake that struck Philoctetes' foot has the same effect on him as the shirt of the centaur Nessos that consumed Herakles' body with its poison. The epiphany of Herakles as a deus ex machina is carefully prepared for. The appearance of his bow brings his divine power to mind. In his agony, Philoctetes had directed the attention of Neoptolemos and the audience upward to the ledge Herakles will stand on at the end of the play (854–58 / 814–16):

> PHILOCTETES There now—over there—
> NEOPTOLEMOS What are you saying? Where?
> PHILOCTETES Up—
> NEOPTOLEMOS What—Are you turning delirious again?
> Why are you looking up at the sky?

The cue that brings Herakles on stage are Philoctetes' words "the arrows of Herakles" (1593 / 1406). There is little to prepare for this Euripidean resolution to human conflict in the tragedies of Sophocles. The striking precedent was Sophocles' *Athamas*, a lost play on the career of Athamas, his divine wife, Nephele, and his human wife, Ino. From indirect evidence we know that the threat to Athamas' life as a sacrificial victim was averted by the appearance of Herakles.[17]

The device of resolving a human impasse by the appearance of a god is familiar from the theater of Euripides. The *Hippolytus* opens with a prologue spoken by Aphrodite, a goddess offended by Hippolytus' exclusive devotion to the virgin Artemis, and ends with the appearance of Artemis on the roof of Theseus' palace in Troizen. As Hippolytus lies maimed and at the point of death below her, she tidies up the human tragedy of Hippolytus, Phaedra, and Theseus by offering the consolation of the cult of the dying Hippolytus will receive in death. Perhaps the closest parallel in Euripides to the last scene of Sophocles' *Philoctetes* is from another lost play of Euripides, the *Antiope*. By our good luck, we

---

17. See Sir Hugh Lloyd-Jones, *Sophocles, Fragments*, vol. 3, for what little is known of Sophocles' two Athamas plays.

know from a papyrus the shape of Euripides' "solution" to the conflict of this play. The two sons of Antiope and Zeus, Zethos and Amphion, are locked in a contest over their two very different ways of life: the political and the musical. The human conflict between the twin brothers has no solution, just as the struggle between Odysseus and Philoctetes over two forms of heroism can have no resolution. In the *Antiope*, it is only the appearance of Hermes at the end of the play that resolves the tension of the sons of Zeus and assures the building of the walls of Thebes.

The appearance of Herakles in Sophocles' *Philoctetes* assures the destruction of the walls of a city built by Apollo and Poseidon. The future seems honorable and prosperous for both Philoctetes and Neoptolemos, who will combine to destroy the city of Priam. But Herakles' words to the two warriors headed for Troy are ominous (**1633–34 / 1440–41**):

> But remember, when you conquer the land,
> to respect what is sacred to the gods.

Anyone present in the Theater of Dionysos in the spring contests of 409 understood how the young Neoptolemos became the bloodthirsty Pyrrhos once he reached Troy. Pyrrhos is slaughtered at Delphi, the shrine of Apollo; Philoctetes finally returns safely to his home to Malis (*Odyssey* 3.190).

Diskin Clay

ON THE TRANSLATION

It's proverbial, of course, that something gets lost in translation. What gets lost is an entire sensibility unique to—and enacted by—the original, and what too often gets compromised is a parallel uniqueness contained by—and enacted by—the language into which the original has been translated.

Rather than try to replicate in English certain strengths of the Greek original, I have tried to replicate the *effect* of those strengths by determining and then employing the particular strengths of English, with attention to how those strengths contribute to free verse especially. I had no interest in trying to force the accentual-syllabic English into the quantitative jacket of Greek, or in seeking to match up the Greek line with, say, the English blank verse line, as if the two were the same or even close.

The most immediately obvious aspect of my translation will be the frequent and radical shifts in line length throughout. In part, I felt this would be a means of conveying the constant shifts in morality, in the notion of trust, and in emotional temper in the course of the play. I want the lines to reflect, as well, the wildness of the landscape in which they occur, and the ruggedness—the harshness and brutality—that characterized the military life in the Homeric age during which this play takes place. The risk here is one of randomness and self-indulgence; to these, I can only counter with an assurance to my readers that, in the course of many years of reading the play in the original and in the many translations that have appeared and continue to appear, I have worked hard to hear the nuances—emotional, psychological, and in terms of language—that resonate through the Philoctetes legend as Sophocles himself wanted it to be told; and I have then gauged my lines accordingly.

I intend for there to be an audible pause at the end of each line, a sharp stress at each line's beginning—the silences are just as important as the spoken parts, and a vocal hesitation is not unrelated to a hesitation of psyche. In a play of so little physical action, relatively speaking, what is clear in the Greek—and crucial to bring to the fore in the English—is that there *is* action, and a great deal of it; but in this play more than any of the other extant tragedies, the action is almost entirely intellectual, psychological, and of the gut. The Greek registers these shifts via metrical shift—there is, if not a metrical equivalent for each state of being human, then a capacity for the Greek to accommodate the nuances of those states with the meter. To read Greek is to know sonically the difference between sudden grief and frenzy, between bliss hoped for and bliss received. My hope is that these shifts might be recognizable, here, in the shifting of line length and in the ways in which the possibilities of line length and line break get deployed on the page.

In addition to line length and line break, syntax and the manipulation of it have been essential tools for me in drawing forth the nuances of (to give but one example) the stalling that is sometimes crisis, sometimes wonder, other times a moment of internal resolve on the part of one character or another. I wish to emphasize that I am in no way seeking to imitate the inflected quality of ancient Greek; rather, the intention here is to take fullest advantage of the capacity for syntax to reflect and enact psychology and emotion, and to make the reader (and listener) an active participant in such psychology or emotion. The result is, necessarily, not entirely demotic, but this has not seemed inappropriate, finally, for a play in which neither the characters nor the moral dilemmas they play out are ever without seriousness and rigor. And again, so much of the action of the play occurs at the level of "ordinary" conversational exchange: no word is without its valence here, and I have worked to calibrate the syntax so as to make these valences most clear.

Given the extraordinarily high number of exclamations of agony and pain in the play, I had to arrive at a means of conveying those moments without seeming redundant and ultimately risking an unwanted comic effect. Too many instances of "alas!" and "ah me," and melodrama, stirring, rears its head. After much debate, it seemed to me inaccurate to merely transliterate the Greek exclamations—they announced right away their being out of place, given that the point was to render an English translation; as well, such expressions are as untranscribable as gesture itself. To attempt that sort of transcription or transliteration seemed to me to have the effect that occurs when we convey pain and assault as "aargh" and "pow," respectively. Fine for the comics, but unsuited finally to the higher seriousness of tragedy. With the exception, therefore, of the occasional "alas" or "ah me"—which, after all, people *do* still say in English—I have chosen to replace such moments with a

Complexity of intimacy

stage direction indicating the need (and freedom) for the actor to express pain as seems most authentic and appropriate—and for the reader, accordingly, to do the same on the level of imagination.

The lyrical moments in tragedy occur in the choruses. Here, though, *Philoctetes* proves to be a sometime exception. Ordinarily, to enter the choral passages is to step from the dramatic, narrative mode and into the more reflective, meditative, and more suspended or static mode we call the lyric. But it is easy to read this particular play in English and miss the lyric quality of many of the choruses, since they often consist of dialogue, conversational exchange between the soldiers and another character in the play, and are therefore indistinguishable, *in terms of content*, from the narrative body of the play. Consider, for example, such passages as 148–214 and 1200–1287, both of them instances in which the Chorus has a dialogue with, respectively, Neoptolemus and Philoctetes—or, more accurate, the choral lyric is variously interrupted or complemented by the recitative dialogue of the other character. In the Greek, the choruses are immediately distingusihable by their lyric meters and their strophic patterning. I have adhered to my choice of flexible line length in the choruses, but have coupled that with a tempered regularity—that is, the stanzas themselves are heterometric, but matched (within a single chorus) in terms of the number of lines per strophic movement—so as to bring forward, visually at least, the patterns of strophe and antistrophe that especially distinguish the choruses from the text around them.

What I have most hoped to bring out in my translation is the complexity of the intimacy with which this play is at every point charged. There is an intimacy born of isolation—consider the intimacy that marks the relationship between Philoctetes and the island (and its animal inhabitants); that to which he was once abandoned has become all he knows and therefore clings to. A parallel intimacy exists between Philoctetes and the all-but-anthropomorphized bow—not to mention the intimacy between arrow and bow: an intimacy so heightened, that each is useless without the other. To this extent, we might call the relationship between bow and arrow a symbiotic one—and quickly see it as a paradigm for one aspect of the relationship between Philoctetes and Neoptolemos.

Another aspect of that relationship is filial-once-removed, as it were: Neoptolemos is a man without a father—has never, in fact, seen his father alive—and quickly adopts a filial relationship to his father's comrade-in-arms, Philoctetes. Part of the recognition and acceptance of this relationship is indicated by how often Philoctetes refers to Neoptolemos as "teknon"—child, or son—a form of address that not only reinforces the father-son relationship, but is resonant as well with the multiplicity of things that Philoctetes is to Neoptolemos: a superior officer as well as a father figure; an elder, and at the same time a man whose chance for heroism depends entirely on the younger man who is his subordinate.

Fraternity is another important component—and form of intimacy—in this play. Philoctetes is the only all-male tragedy that survives; and not only is the cast made up entirely of men, but of soldiers, who are joined together and dependent on one another even more than the average group of men; after all, the success of military action depends on working in concert. In the line of battle, each man becomes as much protector as the object of protection—the difference it could make was that between life and death. Again, bow and arrow. Somewhere in here, it is not only possible to see an erotic aspect of intimacy at work—it is necessary, I believe, to do so. By this, I mean the way in which it is impossible to remove entirely the erotic—the homoerotic—from the fraternal. There is a difference between the sexual and the erotic—it is of the latter that I speak here.

It is my sense that the absolute maleness of the cast has everything to do with the increasing claustrophobia—psychologically—of this play. What is claustrophobia, finally, but intimacy at too intense a pitch—intimacy as much with place as with people, in this case. And an intimacy with ideas or conventions—specifically, trust and duty, on which so many of the intimacies in the play crucially and perilously depend. Again, it is through line length and syntactical inflection that I have hoped to convey the intricacies of intimacy—itself ever shifting—across the play.

This translation is of the Greek in the Oxford Classical text of A. C. Pearson, as reprinted in Webster's edition of the play (*Sophocles: Philoctetes*, T. B. L. Webster, ed., Cambridge University Press, Cambridge, 1997). With regard to method, I translated the play flat out, as it were—leaving no word untranslated, nothing elided in terms of content—in a single week. Then began the process of lineation, which, as in my own poems, got determined after many readings of the text aloud. Several mail exchanges took place between myself and Diskin Clay, whom I thank for pointing out to me the occasional awkwardness or possible misstep, and for his enthusiastic support of and belief in the necessary strangenesses I have brought to the translation of this play, with the hope that *Philoctetes* might be understood as Sophocles himself wanted his audience to understand it.

CARL PHILLIPS

PHILOCTETES

Translated by

CARL PHILLIPS

With Introduction
and Notes by

DISKIN CLAY

CHARACTERS

ODYSSEUS son of Laertes

NEOPTOLEMOS son of Achilles

PHILOCTETES son of Poias of Malis

CHORUS a contingent of sailors, who have arrived on Lemnos with Neoptolemos from the island of Skyros

TRADER actually Odysseus in disguise

HERAKLES

Nonspeaking parts The men of Odysseus who enter at 1061.
One of Neoptolemos' men, who accompanies Neoptolemos and Odysseus from the opening of the play until 147.

Line numbers in the right-hand margin of the text refer to the English translation only, and the Notes on the text beginning at p. 399 are keyed to these lines. The bracketed line numbers in the running heads refer to the Greek text.

*The scene is a cliff, on the coast of the island of Lemnos. Overlooking the sea, there
is a cave with two entrances, one above the other. Some rags draped on the rocks to
dry are the only signs of human presence.*

ODYSSEUS *enters the stage platform, followed by* NEOPTOLEMOS *and the sailor
who does not speak.* ODYSSEUS *gestures to the rock cliff above and addresses*
NEOPTOLEMOS, *who stands nearer to the stage building. The orchestra represents
the shore of Lemnos. The* CHORUS *begins to assemble in the orchestra after*
ODYSSEUS *begins to speak.*

ODYSSEUS This coast—

This shore—

This is Lemnos, the sea
surrounds it. No man
lives here—even   *no man's land*
steps here.

Neoptolemos, son of Achilles—himself, of all the
        Greeks, the noblest father—
it's in this place that, at the command of those in
        charge, I left
the Malian, the son of Poias, his foot
all but consumed by   10
the disease with which it festered—
                            Always,
no sooner would we attend to the usual libations
        or sacrifices,
he'd fill our whole camp with his wild and far-from-
        good-omened
cries—
            Groaning: howling: *un—manned*

Why speak of it now?   *of Aias, Herakles*

333

This is hardly the hour for long speeches—
he may find out I'm here,
I may give away the very plan by which   20
I intend to snare him, soon enough.

Your job: help me with the details—specifically,
look for where these rocks become a double-mouthed
        cave—
forming in winter a sort of twin sun-seat,
while in summer a breeze can send sleep through the
        cave at both ends...
Below it, to the left, you should see
a small spring of drinking water—if it's still there,
        that is.
Go ahead,
quietly,
signal whether he's still in the same place,
        or elsewhere,   30
then I'll tell you the rest of the story,
and you can hear it—our goal's
the same one.

NEOPTOLEMOS Odysseus—Sir—what you speak of, it
             isn't far. At least I think I can see the cave you've
             mentioned.

ODYSSEUS Above? Or below?

NEOPTOLEMOS Above. No sound of footsteps.

ODYSSEUS Make sure he's not camped out asleep.

NEOPTOLEMOS I see a sort of house, but it's empty—nobody there.

ODYSSEUS No sign of anyone living in it?   40

NEOPTOLEMOS Some ground cover, crushed, as if from someone
             lying on it.

trick

ODYSSEUS But the rest is deserted? Nothing beneath the roof?

> NEOPTOLEMOS *enters the cave above the stage platform*
> *and looks about.*

NEOPTOLEMOS A wooden cup—the work of an amateur—along with
some firewood.

ODYSSEUS They must be his—his stores, such as they are.

NEOPTOLEMOS —And these too: some rags drying out, pus-heavy...

ODYSSEUS Well, it's clear that he lives here, and isn't
too far away. How far could he go,
with his foot diseased all this time?
He's gone to look for food, maybe,
he may know of some herb that eases the pain.   50
Send the man you have with you as a scout, so that
    no one catches me—
of all the Argives, there's none he'd rather take than
    me.

> *The silent sailor moves away to stand guard on stage*
> *near the entrance of the cave.*

NEOPTOLEMOS He's going—consider the path guarded.—If you
    need anything,
say so.

ODYSSEUS Son of Achilles,
for the business you're involved in,
you'll have to be as noble as your birth is—
not only in body, but also, should you learn of
    something you haven't
heard of before, you must help me.
You are, after all, my assistant—   60

[handwritten: noble? lies revealed]

[handwritten: wants promise but is tricking him]

NEOPTOLEMOS What is your command?

335

arms of Achilles

ODYSSEUS With your words,
capture the mind—the very soul—of Philoctetes.

When he asks you who you are, where you're from,
say:
"I am the son of Achilles." This needn't be kept
secret.

And—

And you are sailing home, you've abandoned
the Achaian fleet,
full of hate for those who first entreated you with
prayers to leave home,
saying that you were their only hope of sacking Troy—
and then they didn't give you the arms of Achilles
when you came and,   70
quite rightly, asked for them.
No—instead, they gave them to Odysseus.
Say whatever you wish about me—the most
abominable things you can think of,
it won't bother me. If you
don't do this, you bring grief to all the Argives:

not giving anything up

for if this man's bow isn't captured, you'll have no
chance at all of taking Troy.

As to how it is that any dealing with this man can
be trustworthy and safe
for you, and not at all for me—Listen:
You sailed under oath to no one,
nor out of necessity,   80
nor as part of the first expedition—
I can't say the same for myself, however, on any of
these counts.
Therefore, if, while still in possession of his bow, he
should see me,
—I am dead, and you
with me, as my accomplice.

tongue, and not deeds   *trickery*

This is what we must devise,
you to be the one to rob him of his invincible arms.
I know you aren't, by nature, the sort to lie,
or to plot evil, but

—isn't it sweet to gain victory?—   90

dare to. Let us be honest
at another time;
for now,
for a brief, shameless part of the day, give me   *give me*
yourself—   *yourself*
and ever after, be known as the most honorable
       of men.   *not possible*

NEOPTOLEMOS Son of Laertes, I hate doing things that are painful
          even to listen to.
      I wasn't born to act by deception,
      nor, so they say, was my father before me.   *Bk 9 Iliad*
      I'm willing to take the man by force,   100
      not by trickery—he can hardly take *us* by force, on a
          single leg.

      Though sent as your helper, I refuse to be called
          a traitor.
      I'd rather fail while acting nobly, than win dishonestly
      any victory.

ODYSSEUS You're the son of a noble father.
      I myself, when I was younger, had an idle tongue,
      and a working hand.
      But now that it comes to the test,
      I see that it's the tongue, and not deeds,   *tongue not deeds*
      that commands all things for mortals.   110

NEOPTOLEMOS But what do you order me to say, if not lies?

ODYSSEUS I'm telling you to seize Philoctetes by trickery.

trickery v. persuasion

NEOPTOLEMOS But why by trickery? Why not,
        instead, persuasion?

ODYSSEUS He isn't persuadable, and you won't likely take him
        by force.

NEOPTOLEMOS What makes him so sure of his strength?

ODYSSEUS His arrows—as inescapable as is the death they bring
        with them.

NEOPTOLEMOS And it's not safe even to approach him?

ODYSSEUS Not unless you take him by trickery, as I've said.

*Shame
redefined*

NEOPTOLEMOS Don't you think it's shameful to tell lies? 120

ODYSSEUS No—not if lying is a means to safety.

NEOPTOLEMOS How can you look me in the eye and say such
        things aloud?

ODYSSEUS When to act means to gain an advantage, there's no
        need for scruples.

NEOPTOLEMOS What advantage is there for *me* in his coming to Troy?

ODYSSEUS Only this bow of his will take Troy.

NEOPTOLEMOS Then I'm not the one who will take the city,
        as you said?

ODYSSEUS Neither you without the bow, nor the bow
        without you.

NEOPTOLEMOS In that case, it must be captured.

ODYSSEUS Especially since, in doing this, you'll take away
        two prizes.

338

Wise + brave   _shame_

NEOPTOLEMOS What are they? I'd be quicker to act, if I knew.   130

ODYSSEUS To be called wise. To be called brave.

NEOPTOLEMOS Fine then. I'll do it, and
put all shame aside.

ODYSSEUS Then you remember what I told you to do?

NEOPTOLEMOS Yes, I've agreed to it, haven't I?

ODYSSEUS You stay and wait for him here—I'm off,

                              CHORUS _enters._

so he won't catch sight of me.
I'll send the scout back to the ship,
but if you seem to be taking too long,
I'll send the same man back, but disguised,
          as a captain—   140
that way, he won't be recognized.
He's a spinner of tales, that one—
Take only what seems most useful in what he says.
I'm going to the ship now—I leave the rest to you.
May Hermes the cunning leader be   _Hermes_
our leader, along with Victory,
and Athena too—she has always protected me.

                    Exit ODYSSEUS _and sailor._

CHORUS What is it,   _strophe_
what must I hide, my lord—
I, a stranger in this, a strange land—   150
or what say to a man so suspicious?
Tell me.
For his cunning surpasses that of others,
as does the wisdom of kings—those who wield the   _Cunning_
          divine scepter of Zeus.
All this ancient mastery has come to you, young man—
tell me, then: what must I do to help you?

alone

NEOPTOLEMOS For now—since perhaps you'd like to look at
        the place
where he lies—look with confidence.
But when the terrible wanderer comes from his
        quarters,
keep an eye out for my hand-signal,   160
and try to help as seems best.

CHORUS The care you speak of has long been our own,
        my lord—   *antistrophe*
to keep watch over your best interests.
But where does he live, what house?
That much, at least, I need to know,
to be on guard for
—and avoid—being
ambushed by him.
Where is he now—
at home? Outdoors somewhere?   170

NEOPTOLEMOS Well, you can see his house here, with the double
        openings—a rocky resting-place—

CHORUS And the victim himself?

NEOPTOLEMOS It's clear to me that it's out of hunger he makes his
        labored way
somewhere. For this is the sort of life he is said
        to lead—
in pain,
painfully hunting with his winged arrows, no man
approaching him with any respite from
his sufferings.

CHORUS I pity the man. No one cares for him,   *strophe*
he has no one to look to. Wretched. Alone, always.   180
He suffers this terrible disease—with each need as it
        comes, he's
lost again. How does he keep going?
Strategems of the gods—unlucky race of man,
to whom there is no fair measure in this life.

This man may well be no inferior in birth to the
      best-born, *antistrophe*
yet he lies alone, apart from all others,
except the spotted and hairy beasts—pitiable
in his hunger, in his sufferings, his miseries
      without cure.
And babbling Echo, appearing in the distance, merely
throws back to him his pitiable complaints. 190

NEOPTOLEMOS None of this surprises me.
      For, as I understand it, these sufferings are the will of
         the gods,
      and came upon him from savage-minded Chryse,
      and the things that he now endures, companionless,
      these too must be the design of the gods,
      so that he cannot send his invincible weapons
         against Troy
      until the time when it is determined that Troy must
         be destroyed
      by those weapons.

CHORUS Silence!—

NEOPTOLEMOS What is it? 200

CHORUS I heard a sound—as of someone in great
         pain— *strophe*
      here, or—or over there.
      It's coming to me, yes: the voice of one who makes
         his way in agony—
      from afar, a man suffering—heavy groans—
      his lament coming clearly.
      You should take—

NEOPTOLEMOS What? Tell me.

CHORUS A new plan of action, *antistrophe*
      since he isn't far off, but somewhere inside— 210

and he's not playing flute-songs, like some meadowing
    shepherd, but
either stumbling somewhere and in hardship
he lets go a far-reaching howl, or perhaps
he has seen the ship-grudging harbor.

> PHILOCTETES *has barely emerged from the entrance to*
> *his cave closest to the stage; he hesitates as he listens to*
> NEOPTOLEMOS *speak to his men, then limps toward*
> *the group.*

PHILOCTETES Strangers—
    who are you, who have oared your way here,
    a desolation
    no better to drop anchor at than to live in?
    What nationality, what race might I say is yours?
    Your attire is that of Greece, the country most beloved
      by me.
    Let me hear a voice—do not fear me and   220
    panic at my wildness, no; but
    pitying a man so ill-starred and alone and suffering as
      I am, and with
    no friend, no companion—please, speak—if you have
      in fact come as friends—
    Do answer—
    for it isn't right that we should not have at least this
      much from each other.

NEOPTOLEMOS Stranger, since you wish to know it—
    this much first: we are Greeks.

PHILOCTETES O most welcome voice—To be addressed by such a
      man, a Greek,
    after all this time!
    Child, what need brought you here and caused you
      to disembark?   230
    What impulse?
    Which, of all the winds, the most favoring?
    Tell me everything, that I might learn who you are.

NEOPTOLEMOS I am from the island of Skyros.
             I sail for home.
             I am called Neoptolemos, son of Achilles.
             And now you know everything.

PHILOCTETES Son of a dearest father, of a dear country,
             nursling of old Lykomedes,
             on what mission have you come here—and where are
                  you sailing   240
             from?

NEOPTOLEMOS At the moment, I sail from Troy.

PHILOCTETES What do you mean? For you certainly weren't a
                  shipmate of
             ours at the beginning of the expedition *to* Troy—

NEOPTOLEMOS Were you also a part of that effort?

PHILOCTETES Child, don't you know me, even looking at me?

NEOPTOLEMOS How should I know someone I've never seen before?

PHILOCTETES So you don't know my name, or anything of the
                  sufferings with which
             I am utterly destroyed?

NEOPTOLEMOS No—nothing.   250

PHILOCTETES How wretched I am,
             how hated by the gods,
             if no word of my plight has reached home or, for
                  that matter,
             any part of Greece at all.
             Those who abandoned me here, against all that is
                  holy, they
             mock me in silence,
             while my disease continues and only grows worse.

343

Child—son of Achilles—
I am he whom perhaps you've heard of,
the master of the arms of Herakles, the son of Poias—   260
I am Philoctetes,
whom the two generals, along with Odysseus,
disgracefully left behind in this wilderness—

I'd been stricken with a grievous disease,
after being bitten by a venomous serpent.
On top of this,
having put in here with their fleet en route from
          sea-ringed Chryse,
they left me here—me, and my sickness.
Then, as—how gladly!—they saw me,
exhausted from so much tossing at sea,   270
sleeping in a rocky cave along the shore—
then, they abandoned me, leaving some
worn rags, and a small supply of food—the stuff
of beggars. I hope *they* come to as much!
What sort of waking from sleep do you imagine
          it was, child,
when they'd gone?
Of what sort, the evils I lamented, shed tears for,
seeing the very ships that I'd set out on now
gone entirely, no man around, who might help me
          when worn by disease.
Looking at everything, I discovered nothing was here
          except   280
suffering—of this, there was a great abundance.

Time, as it does, passing,
I made do for myself under this makeshift roof.
This bow, felling doves in flight, found what food
          I needed,
and whatever the arrow, drawn back in its string,
          brought down for me
—alone, abject, I crawled up to it,
dragging my miserable foot behind me.

344

If I needed drinking water in winter, when all water
    had turned ice,
still I managed, though suffering, to break up some
    wood.
Even then, no fire forthcoming—but by rubbing stone   290
against stones, I soon made the hidden flame appear,
which always rescued me.
For this roof, along with fire, provides me everything
except some respite from disease.

Come, child—now you need to learn about the island
    itself.
No sailor travels to it willingly.
For there's no harbor, really, nor anywhere that one
    might sail to
for conducting trade or enjoying any hospitality.
This is no destination for men of any sense.
Perhaps someone unwillingly comes here—for
    many things   300
can happen in the course of a man's life—
these people, when they *do* come, feel sorry for me,
at least according to their words,
and they've even given me a bit of food, or some
    clothing,
out of pity.
But this one thing, when I mention it, none is willing
    to do:
namely, to bring me home to safety.
Therefore, I am wasting away—for ten years now,
in hunger and in suffering,
feeding the disease whose hunger is endless.   310
Such things the Atreidai and violent Odysseus did
    to me—
may the Olympian gods give to them in return what I
    have suffered.

CHORUS Like the strangers who have come here before,
    I too pity you, son of Poias.

NEOPTOLEMOS   And I myself am witness to your words, that they
                          are true—
                      I know this, having also found the Atreidai and fierce
                          Odysseus to be evil men.

PHILOCTETES   What complaint do you have with the ruinous
                          Atreidai,
                      what suffering is behind *your* anger?

NEOPTOLEMOS   May I satisfy someday my anger by this hand of mine,
                      so that the Myceneans will know—and Sparta too—   320
                      that Skyros is also the mother of brave men.

PHILOCTETES   You've spoken well. But tell me—what is it, that
                      makes you come accusing them so angrily?

NEOPTOLEMOS   Son of Poias, though it's with difficulty that I tell you,
                          I shall tell you
                      the things I suffered at their hands, on
                          reaching Troy.
                      For when the fated time came for Achilles to die—

PHILOCTETES   Ah, no—Say nothing more, until I learn of this first:
                      the son of Peleus is dead?   330

NEOPTOLEMOS   He is dead—shot by no man, but by a god, they say—
                      struck down by Apollo.

PHILOCTETES   Then both of them—the slain and the one who slew
                          him—are noble indeed.
                      But I don't know whether I should first inquire into
                          your suffering,
                      or should grieve for this man.

NEOPTOLEMOS   I believe your own griefs are enough for you—
                          poor soul—
                      no need to grieve for the sufferings of anyone else.

PHILOCTETES I suppose you are right—

    Tell me, then, of your situation, how they
       insulted you.   340

NEOPTOLEMOS On a garlanded ship,
    they came for me—
    godlike Odysseus, and Phoinix, the man who had
       reared my father.
    They said—the truth,
    or not, who knows?—that it was not the gods' will,
    now that my father had died,
    for anyone but myself to take Troy's citadel. And
       saying this,
    they did not need to spend much time urging me
    to sail soon—especially given my longing for the
       dead man,
    my wanting to see him while still unburied;   350
    for I had not seen him, ever.
    Moreover, there was the good news that if I went
       to Troy,
    I would capture it.
    I had sailed two days, when by oar and the wind's
       favor
    I reached hateful Sigeion.
    And immediately, the entire army, once I'd
       disembarked,
    surrounded me,
    swearing they saw Achilles again, though he was dead.

    —For he did lie dead.

    And I, wretched—when I'd wept for him,   360
    soon approached the Atreidai—my friends, or so
       it seemed—
    and requested my father's weapons and whatever other
       effects there might be.
    Alas—

they told me the worst thing possible:
"Son of Achilles, you can certainly have anything else,
but another man is lord of those arms now—the son
        of Laertes."

I burst into tears, and fell into a heavy rage, and said
        in grief:
"You monsters—you have dared to give to someone
        other than me
the arms that by rights are my own, before informing
        me?"

And Odysseus said—for he happened to be standing
        there—   370
"Yes, they gave them to me,
and rightly so.
I was there,
I am the one who saved the weapons and the corpse
        of Achilles."

not true!
cf Iliad

I was infuriated, and insulted him in every way,
leaving nothing out, since he was going to rob me of
        the arms that were mine.

When it had come to this point,
and even though he wasn't prone to anger,
he was stung by what he'd heard, and answered
        me thus:
"You weren't where we were; no,   380
you were off where you shouldn't have been.
And now that you have spoken so insolently, you will
        never sail to Skyros
in possession of these arms, or anything else."

made up?

Hearing myself reproached with these terrible words,
I sailed for home, deprived of what is mine, by that
        worst of all evil men,
Odysseus.
Not that I blame *him* so much as I do

evil/example of their teachers

those in power; for the entire city, the whole army
is in the hands of those who rule; those men who are
    wanting
in discipline become evil by the example of their
    teachers.   390

That is the whole story.
And he who hates the Atreidai,
may he be a friend both to me and to the gods alike.

CHORUS Mountainous, all-grazing Earth—   *strophe*
        mother of Zeus himself, you
        who dwell in great Paktolos, rich in gold—

        when the arrogance of the Atreidai came against him,
        when they gave to the son of Laertes this man's
            father's arms

        even then, holy mother, I called upon you,
        the blessed rider of bull-devouring lions,   400
        an object of wonder beyond all others.

PHILOCTETES Strangers, you've sailed here, it seems,
        bearing a mark of suffering not unfamiliar to me,
        for it fits what I know myself of the deeds of
            the Atreidai, and of Odysseus.
        For I have known him to put his tongue to any
            speech that is evil,
        any outrage, by which he might bring about an
            injustice.
        But what I *do* wonder is
        how the mighty Ajax can have endured seeing these
            things, if he was present.

NEOPTOLEMOS He was no longer alive—
        had he been, I'd never have been stripped of my arms. 410

PHILOCTETES What do you mean? Even he lives now among
        the dead?

349

NEOPTOLEMOS Put it this way: he no longer lives in the light.

PHILOCTETES Alas—but Diomedes,
and Odysseus, begot by Sisyphos and sold to Laertes—
they aren't dead, when they more rightly *should* be!

NEOPTOLEMOS Indeed—be assured of that—in fact, even now they
are thriving in the Argive army.

PHILOCTETES Alas...
And my old friend, noble Nestor, of Pylos,
is *he* alive?
For he'd have stopped their outrages, by his wise
counsel.   420

NEOPTOLEMOS Just now, he fares badly,
since Antilochos—his son—has died and left him.

PHILOCTETES Ah—you have spoken of two men,
whom I would least wish to have meet with death,
alas—
What is one to look toward, now that these men
are dead,
while Odysseus—whom
it would be more fitting to call dead—
is very much alive?

NEOPTOLEMOS A clever wrestler, that one.   430
But even cleverness gets often enough tripped up,
Philoctetes.

PHILOCTETES By the gods, tell me this:
where was Patroklos in all of this—he who was
everything to your father?

NEOPTOLEMOS Dead also. I shall teach you something in a very
few words:
war never chooses to take the disgraceful man,
but will always prefer those who are most noble.

worse > better

PHILOCTETES   I can attest to that. On this subject,
              let me ask you about one who is hardly noble, but is
                 clever and wise
              where his tongue's concerned—how's *he* faring now?   440

NEOPTOLEMOS   Whom do you mean, if not Odysseus?

PHILOCTETES   Not him, but a certain Thersites, who was never
                 content to speak
              just once, even when no one wished him to speak to
                 begin with.
              Do you know if he's alive?

NEOPTOLEMOS   I've not seen him myself, but I have heard he's
                 living still.

PHILOCTETES   How fitting! Nothing evil has ever died.
              On the contrary, the gods guard it well. Somehow,
              whatever is villainous and thoroughly wicked—this
                 they bless,
              even keeping it from Hades.
              But what's just, what's noble,   450
              this they destroy always.
              How to account for this, how approve it,
              when in looking upon matters divine, I find the gods   Challenge?
              themselves are evil?   age old question

NEOPTOLEMOS   I for one, from now on, shall look upon Troy and
                 the Atreidai from
              a great distance,
              and I shall be on guard against them.
              When the worse man is stronger than the better man,
              and what's good is destroyed and what's wicked
                 is in power,
              I shall not bear such men, not ever.   460

              No,
              from now on let rocky Skyros be enough for me,
              so that I can have some pleasure at home.

—But now I head for the ship. And you, son of Poias,
goodbye,
and farewell,
and may the gods relieve you of your sickness, as
        you wish.

To his companions.

—Let's go, so that whenever the god sees fit for us to
        sail, we may do so.

PHILOCTETES But—
are you going already?   470

NEOPTOLEMOS Yes—we must take advantage of the chance to set sail,
not when it calls from afar, but now,
while it's at hand.

PHILOCTETES By your father—by your mother—
child, if there is anything dear to you at home, by
that too, I beg you:
do not leave me here, alone, suffering such evils—
living among them—as you see, and have heard.
Don't think me a burden.
There's a lot of trouble, yes, to my being brought
        along with you,   480
but undertake it, all the same.
For, among noble men, the disgraceful deed is an
        object of hate, but
the noble one is well spoken of.
In refusing my request, you win for yourself
shame only;
but in doing it—child, if I return to Oita alive,
the greatest honor, that of good reputation, is yours.

Come—
it's an inconvenience of not even an entire day—
        dare it,
take me aboard, and put me in the hold,   490

well spoken of

on the prow, at the stern, wherever
I'll be the least burdensome to your crew.

Promise—
by suppliant Zeus himself,
child, be persuaded—I fall on my knees before you,
even as weak and suffering as I am, and so lame.
Don't leave me here to suffer as an outcast from the
    step of men,
no.
Either take me safe to your home, or to Chalkodon
    on Euboia.
From there, it's not much of a journey for me to the
    swift-flowing river of   500
Spercheios, so that you might show me to my dear
    father
—for a long time now I have feared he is no longer
    with us.
For I sent many messages to him by those who have
    chanced here,
many requests begging him to make the journey here
    himself and
deliver me safely home.—But he is either dead,
or the business of the messengers, likely enough,
outweighed my own, and they voyaged straight home.

But now—for in you I come across both a leader and
    a messenger—
save me,   *leader + messenger*
have mercy on me,   510
since for better or worse, men must
endure what's terrible and
dangerous, both.
When free from distress, we should be on the alert for
    what's terrible,
and when life is going well, look especially
then to our lives,
that they haven't been destroyed while we weren't
    looking.

CHORUS Pity him, my lord.   *antistrophe*
He has made clear the struggles of many all-but-
        unbearable troubles,
such as may no friend of mine come to know.   520
If you hate the wicked Atreidai, lord,
I myself would make from their evil an advantage for
        this man,
and I would take him on our well-fitted, swift ship
to where he is eager to go—namely, home,
escape from the wrath of the gods.

NEOPTOLEMOS See that you don't now seem generous-minded,
and then appear a stranger to your own words, when
        you've had
your fill of contact with his disease.

CHORUS Far from it, you will never be able to accuse me of
        that, or not justly.

NEOPTOLEMOS It is disgraceful, though, for me to appear less
        willing than   530
yourselves to do what is proper. If it seems best,
        let us sail,
let's set out quickly.
For the ship won't refuse to carry him—
may the gods carry *us* from this land safely,
to wherever we wish to sail.

PHILOCTETES Dearest day, sweetest man, beloved sailors—
by what deed might I show you how full of love you
        have made me
toward yourselves?
Child, let us go—having given, though, due
        homage to
the inside of this house, not exactly a house—   540
that you might learn how I survived, how brave I was.
For I believe that, except for myself,
no one would have endured it, having looked inside.

But, by necessity, I learned to bear my hardships.

Begins to enter the cave.

CHORUS Stop—Stand still.
          Two men are coming, a captain from your ship, and a
                foreigner—
          find out about them first; then go in.

*Enter Odysseus, disguised as a trader. He is
accompanied by another member of the crew who
does not speak.*

TRADER Son of Achilles—I asked this fellow, a trader like
                myself, who was standing
          guard with two others over your ship—I asked him to
                tell me where you were—
          seeing as I'd encountered your crew, not planning to,
                but   550
          just happening to drop anchor in the same spot.
          For as a sea captain I sail with a small crew from
                Ilion to
          grape-bearing Peparethos—home—.
          When I heard that all these sailors were yours,
          I decided not to make my journey in silence, without
          speaking to you and finding some recompense.
          For you aren't completely aware of your own affairs—
          what new plots there are concerning you among
                the Argives,
          not just plots—no longer in-progress—
          no: in effect already.   560

NEOPTOLEMOS Stranger, if I am not an evil man,
             the courtesy of your forethought will remain as token
                   of friendship.
             Tell me the deeds of which you've spoken,
             so I may know the latest plans against me among
                   the Argives.

TRADER They have gone in pursuit of you—Phoinix, and the
sons of Theseus—
complete with a ship's crew.

NEOPTOLEMOS To bring me back by violence, or with words?

TRADER I don't know. I stand simply as messenger before you.

NEOPTOLEMOS And Phoinix and his shipmates, are they doing this
willingly,
as a favor to the Atreidai?   570

TRADER Be sure of this: these things are not the future—
they are happening even now.

NEOPTOLEMOS But how is it that Odysseus is not prepared to sail
here as his own messenger?
Does some fear hold him back?

TRADER Odysseus and the son of Tydeus were off in search of
somebody else,
when I myself set out.

NEOPTOLEMOS Who was this man whom Odysseus sailed in
search of?

TRADER He was a certain—
but first, tell me who this man here is.
And when speaking, don't speak too loudly.   580

NEOPTOLEMOS Stranger, this is the renowned Philoctetes, no doubt
known to yourself.

TRADER Then don't ask me anything else.
Sail as quickly as you can.
Get off this island.

PHILOCTETES   *To* NEOPTOLEMOS.
What is he saying, child?

in the open (handwritten)

What business is the sailor conducting with you
    in secret?

NEOPTOLEMOS I don't know quite what he's saying. But he ought to
        say what he has to say
in the open,
to you, me, and these men with us.

TRADER Son of Achilles: do not slander me before the army   590
        for saying what I should not.
For, in doing many favors on their behalf, I enjoy   *looking* (handwritten)
        many benefits in return,   *to* (handwritten)
though a poor man myself.   *benefit* (handwritten)

NEOPTOLEMOS I am hated by them.
    This man is my dearest friend, for he hates
        the Atreidai.
If you have come to me as a friend,
you must hide from us nothing that you have heard.

TRADER Watch what you're doing, young man.

NEOPTOLEMOS I have long been careful, and am careful even now.

TRADER I shall lay all blame on you.   600

NEOPTOLEMOS Do so. Now speak.

TRADER Fine—I shall.
    The two men you heard about—the son of Tydeus,
        and mighty Odysseus—
it is after this man here they're sailing,
bound by oath, either to bring him back by the
        persuasion of words,
or that of sheer force.
And all the Achaians heard Odysseus say this clearly:
he was more confident of getting this done than was
        his accomplice.

NEOPTOLEMOS But, after all this time, by what reasoning do
                   the Atreidai concern themselves
          with a man whom, years ago, they cast out?   610
          What can they be longing for?
          Or is it the violence and anger with which the gods
                   punish wickedness—
          have these brought them to this point?

TRADER I'll explain everything, since obviously you've
                   not heard.
          There was a certain seer of noble birth—son of Priam—
                   called Helenos,
          whom this man—Odysseus, who is called every
          foul and insulting name—he
          captured Helenos by trickery,
          coming upon him alone and at night.
          Taking him prisoner, he showed him off in fetters to
                   the Achaians   620
          —a lovely quarry, indeed.

          Helenos prophesied everything to them,
          how they would never capture the citadel of Troy,
          if they did not persuade this man and bring him
          back from the island where he lives now.

          And as soon as the son of Laertes heard the seer
                   say this,
          he immediately announced to the Achaians that he
                   would bring the man back
          and show him to them;
          that the man would likely come freely,
→   but if not, then he would bring him against his will.   630
          And that, should he fail to accomplish this,
          let any one who wants to
          have his head.

          Now you've heard everything.
          I advise you to make haste, you and anyone whom
                   you care about.

PHILOCTETES That man—he is nothing but damage! He swore
             he'd *persuade* and bring me to the Achaians?
             I shall, I suppose, be persuaded when I'm dead
             to come up from Hades and into the light, like *his*
                  father—

TRADER I don't know about any of that—   640
        I'm going to the ship. And may the gods bring all
             the best.
                         Exit TRADER *and his companion.*

PHILOCTETES Is it not terrible, child,
             that the son of Laertes would hope by softening words
             to lead me to his ship, and then display me in the
                  midst of the Argives?

             No—I'd rather listen to what I hate most,
             the serpent that made of my foot a useless thing.
                                                        —But

             that man is capable of saying and daring anything—
             and now I know he'll come.

             Let us go,   650
             that a great sea may separate us from the ship of
                  Odysseus.
             Let's go—
             timely haste at the hour of need has been known to
                  bring sleep
             and relief, later.

NEOPTOLEMOS Fine—when the wind eases off of the prow, we'll
                  set out.
             But at the moment, it's against us.

PHILOCTETES When fleeing evils, the sailing is always good.

NEOPTOLEMOS I know—but the wind is also against *them*—

PHILOCTETES   The wind is never against pirates,
    when there's a chance to rob and to seize by force.   660

NEOPTOLEMOS   Then if it seems best, let's go—take from within
    whatever you need and want.

PHILOCTETES   There *are* some necessary things, though not in great
    supply.

NEOPTOLEMOS   What can there be, that isn't on my ship?

PHILOCTETES   I have an herb, with which I always dress this wound;
    it eases the pain.

NEOPTOLEMOS   Well, bring it—And what else will you take?

PHILOCTETES   Any of these arrows of mine that may have fallen
    around here,
    and gone unnoticed—
    I won't leave them for anyone else to take.

        Brings from his cave a clump of herbs, arrows,
                and his long bow.

NEOPTOLEMOS   And what is it you're holding now—
    is *that* the famed bow?   670

PHILOCTETES   This is it—there's no other, save this which I bear in
    my hands.

NEOPTOLEMOS   May I look at it more closely—and hold it—
    worship it, even, as I would a god?

PHILOCTETES   For you, not only this bow but
    anything else in my power to give
    will be yours.

NEOPTOLEMOS   Indeed, I desire it, but in this way—if it is the gods'
    will,

yes, I wish it;
but if it isn't, then never mind.

PHILOCTETES Your words are blameless—and yes, it   680
is right, by the gods:
you alone have enabled me to look upon the light of
the sun,
to see Oita again, and my old father, my kin. You
have raised me up when I lay beneath the heel of my
enemies.
Be confident—you may touch it,
then give it back to me,
and boast that to you, of all mortals, because of your
kindness,
it was granted to touch it.
For I myself first acquired it by doing a kindness.

NEOPTOLEMOS I don't regret at all knowing you and having you as
a friend.   690
For whoever, in enjoying a kindness,
knows how to return one as well—he is a friend
more valuable than any possession. Go inside.

PHILOCTETES I shall have you accompany me,
for the disease makes me need you for support.

NEOPTOLEMOS, *holding the bow, supports* PHILOCTETES
as they enter the cave together.

CHORUS I have heard the story,   *strophe*
but have never seen the legendary intruder on the
marriage bed,
he whom the all-powerful son of Kronos made
prisoner upon a revolving wheel in Hades.

But I have known neither by hearsay nor as witness   700
any man, of all mortals,
with a more hateful fate than this man,

who has done no harm to anyone,
has killed no one, but—a just man to
those who are also just—
has long been perishing undeservedly.

What amazes me is this—
how it is, how in the world, when
all alone, hearing
nothing but the waves always   710
crashing, how he managed to endure a life so full
        of tears.

He was all by himself, had   *antistrophe*
no one who might approach him,
for there was no other inhabitant,
no neighbor in his misery
with whom, in mutual agonies, he could
bewail his slow-murdering, flesh-eating disease.

None who might help him, with soothing herbs, to
find sleep, some respite from the hot, oozing
blood of his foot's wounds in their wild   720
festering—

no one who might come to him with food gathered
from the nourishing earth.

But here and there, instead, he made his way,
crawling, like a child without its dear nurse, toward
whatever source of ease might arise,
whenever the wasting disease happened to let up.

Taking no food—   *strophe*
not, at least, by the sowing of the sacred earth—
nor anything else that   730
laboring men enjoy, except when he was able to
bring down with the winged arrows of his quick bow
some food for his belly.

A wretched life,
which for ten years has not known the pleasure
of even a drink of wine—
no,
no sooner might he see a pool of stagnant water,
he'd approach it.

But now,   *antistrophe*   740
he has come upon the son of noble men,
and will attain good fortune, and
greatness, as a result.
For his rescuer intends to bring him
by sea-crossing ship, over many months,
to his ancestral home, home of the Melian nymphs,
along the banks of Spercheios,
where Herakles of the bronze shield
drew near to the gods,
a god himself,   750
radiant in holy fire, beyond the hills of Oita.

NEOPTOLEMOS *and* PHILOCTETES *emerge
from the lower cave.*

NEOPTOLEMOS Come. Why are you silent, not speaking, as if
struck into silence by something?

PHILOCTETES   *Lets out a scream.*

NEOPTOLEMOS What is it?

PHILOCTETES Nothing terrible—come.

NEOPTOLEMOS It isn't the pain of your sickness coming upon you,
is it?

PHILOCTETES Not at all—on the contrary, I feel like I'm rallying,
just now—Oh, gods!—

NEOPTOLEMOS Why do you call upon the gods and groan like that?

PHILOCTETES So that they'll come to us as kind protectors.   760

Suddenly screams again.

NEOPTOLEMOS What are you suffering from?

PHILOCTETES *remains silent in a paroxysm of pain.*

Won't you speak?
You seem to be in trouble.

PHILOCTETES I am all but dying, child; I can't hide my agony from
        you—ah,
it goes through, is piercing straight through me, and
        I am
miserable—half-dead—I am being devoured—

Oh, by the gods themselves, if you have a sword
        handy,
cut my foot off, as quickly as possible,
cut it off,   770
never mind my life—

do it!

NEOPTOLEMOS What is it now? What
causes you to raise such shouts and groans?

PHILOCTETES But—you know already.

NEOPTOLEMOS What?

PHILOCTETES You *know.*

NEOPTOLEMOS What is wrong with you? I *don't* know!

PHILOCTETES How can you *not* know?
                              Shrieking suddenly.

NEOPTOLEMOS The burden of the disease must indeed be fearsome.   780

PHILOCTETES Fearsome—untellable—But—
Have mercy on me.

NEOPTOLEMOS What shall I do?

PHILOCTETES Don't be afraid and—don't betray me—
the disease—its attacks—arrive at various times,
when they've had their fill, I suppose, of wandering
elsewhere.

NEOPTOLEMOS Oh, you are
wretched indeed, clearly wretched in all your
suffering.
Would you like me to hold you—to hold you close?

PHILOCTETES Not at all—no! But take the bow you asked me for
just now—   790
and, until the present pain of the disease eases off,
guard it,
protect it.
For sleep overtakes me, whenever this pain would
leave—it
cannot leave
before then.
So you must let me sleep in peace.
And if *those* people show up in the meantime,
I beg you:
do not give the bow to anyone, willingly or
unwillingly,   800
lest you end up killing yourself
and me, your suppliant.

NEOPTOLEMOS Don't worry. It'll be given to none but you and me.
Give it to me—and here's to luck!

PHILOCTETES Here, take it—but offer a prayer to avert the gods'   protect
envy,   N.
so the bow won't destroy you,
as it did me, and the one who owned it before me.

NEOPTOLEMOS Dear gods, let these things be granted us—
and that our voyage may be swift and favorable,
to wherever the god deems just and   810
as the mission itself dictates.

PHILOCTETES   *Shouts in agony.*

Child—
I fear your prayer goes unfulfilled—
for even now, the bloody wound is dripping,
the blood oozes from somewhere deep,
and I half-predict some new development—ah—
my foot, what agonies you cause me!
The pain, it
creeps forward—   820
it's coming nearer—ah,   ah,   ah—!

You understand.   Don't run away.   *Shrieks.*

Oh, Odysseus,
would that this pain might run you straight through
        your chest!
And—

                                        Again shrieking in agony.

And you two generals, Agamemnon, Menelaos:
if only instead of me
you might nourish this sickness, for as long a time!

Oh   my...   *Sudden cry of pain.*   830

Death—Death—
how is it that, though you are called upon each day,
you can never come?

Son—noble one—take me up
and burn me in the fire called Lemnian—
please—as

cf Aïas

I myself agreed to do for the son of Zeus,
in exchange for these arms, over which you now stand
        guard—

What do you say, my friend?
What do you say? Why silent? Where are you?   840

NEOPTOLEMOS For some time, now, I've been in pain for you,
                grieving over your sufferings.

PHILOCTETES But be assured that the pains come to me suddenly,
                and
             as swiftly depart. Only—
             I beg you—
             don't leave me here alone.

NEOPTOLEMOS Don't worry—I'll stay with you.

PHILOCTETES You'll stay?

NEOPTOLEMOS Yes, of course.

PHILOCTETES I don't think it's fitting for you to swear an oath—but   850

NEOPTOLEMOS It isn't right that I go *without* you.

PHILOCTETES With your hand, make a pledge.

NEOPTOLEMOS I promise to stay with you.

PHILOCTETES   *Looking up to the rock platform and higher*
                                              entrance to the cave.

         There now—over there—

NEOPTOLEMOS What are you saying? Where?

PHILOCTETES Up—

NEOPTOLEMOS   *Grabbing hold of* PHILOCTETES.

What—Are you turning delirious again?
Why are you looking up at the sky?

PHILOCTETES Let me—
Let me go.   860

NEOPTOLEMOS Where to?

PHILOCTETES Anywhere, just let go of me.

NEOPTOLEMOS I won't.

PHILOCTETES You'll destroy me, if you touch me.

NEOPTOLEMOS All right, I'm letting go of you, now that you're
thinking a bit more clearly.

PHILOCTETES Oh Earth, dead as I am, take me—
for this agony no longer even lets me stand up.

Collapses.

NEOPTOLEMOS   *To the* CHORUS.

I think sleep will soon come to him:
his head is stretched back;
and a sweat drips from his entire body;   870
and a dark vein, bleeding violently, has broken from
the bottom of his foot.
Let's allow him some peace, friends, so he can fall
asleep.

CHORUS Sleep, ignorant of agony, of grief   *strophe*
ignorant, Sleep—may you come to us
like a sweet breeze, full of blessing, lord—blessing us.
Hold over his eyes this flashing light
which stands over them now.
Come to me—Oh, healing one, come!

Child, watch where you stand,
where you walk,   880
take thought for what is next—
for already, you can see how . . .
Why are we waiting to take action?
Timely action, which holds sway in all things,
wins great victory when paired with swiftness.

NEOPTOLEMOS But this man hears nothing. And anyway, as I see it,
we capture our quarry—his bow—in vain, if we sail
        without him.
For the victor's garland is not the bow, but Philoctetes—
the gods said we should bring *him.*
To boast, with lies, of deeds that remain undone   890
is disgraceful.

                                                        slipping

CHORUS But the god will see to these things.   *antistrophe*
Answer me, quietly,
give me, however brief, some answer.
For in sickness, sleep is sleepless,
sharpsighted,
sees everything.
But whatever you are most capable of,
that thing,
whatever it is, see to it that you do it secretly.   900
You know whom I'm speaking of.

But if you share his opinion in this matter,
the problems are unresolvable, baffling
even to the wise.

A wind, child; a wind—   *epode*
The man is sightless, helpless,
lies as if shrouded in night—a good sleep is
        without fear—
and he commands no hand or foot or
—or anything else, but lies
like someone on the threshold of Hades.   910
Look, and see whether what you say

is timely; this much I can grasp:
those efforts most succeed, which know no fear.

NEOPTOLEMOS Be silent, and don't lose your heads.
For he moves his eyes now—he's raising his head.

PHILOCTETES Oh light that follows sleep, and—
beyond my hopes—watch kept by these strangers!
For I could never even have prayed for this:
that you would have pity on and endure my agonies
and
stay with me and—help me.   920
The Atreidai certainly didn't manage to do as much,
noble generals that they are!
But yours is a noble nature, born of those in
turn of noble nature—
all my suffering you found manageable,
my shouting, my foul smell.
And now, since there seems to be a moment of
forgetfulness and ease to this sickness,
come and lift me, help me up,
so that when the tiredness leaves me a bit more,
we can   930
set off for the ship and soon be sailing.

NEOPTOLEMOS It's good to see you, beyond what I'd hoped,
free of pain, looking about yourself, breathing still.
For it had seemed that, in your agonies,
you had left us.
But now, get up.
Or, if you'd rather,
these men will carry you. They won't mind the labor,
since you and I have agreed on what's best.

PHILOCTETES I thank you for that.   940
Now—if you'd lift me, as you intended.
Let these men go for now, so they won't grow
oppressed too soon
by my terrible stench—

for there will be effort enough to suffice them, when
    I'm on the ship.

NEOPTOLEMOS Fine, then; stand up, and hold on.

PHILOCTETES Don't worry—long habit will raise me up.

NEOPTOLEMOS Alas—what should I do next?

PHILOCTETES What is it? Where are your words headed?

NEOPTOLEMOS My speech is aimless, I don't know
    where to turn it.   950

PHILOCTETES Why are you at a loss? Don't say this.

NEOPTOLEMOS But that's just where I've come to in this troublesome
    business.

PHILOCTETES Has the burden of my sickness persuaded you
    not to take me aboard, after all?

NEOPTOLEMOS Everything is burdensome,
    when—taking leave of his very nature,
    a man does what he knows hardly befits him.

PHILOCTETES But—in helping a noble man,
    you neither do nor say anything that your own father
    wouldn't have said.

NEOPTOLEMOS I shall be seen as disgraceful—this, for some time, has
    been my agony.   960

PHILOCTETES Certainly not from anything you've done—
    but what you say,
    it frightens me.

NEOPTOLEMOS O Zeus, what shall I do?
    Am I to be found evil on two counts—

371

hiding that which I ought not to,
and saying what is most shameful?

PHILOCTETES This man, if I judge correctly, acts like one who
has already betrayed and abandoned me,
and is about to set sail.   970

NEOPTOLEMOS Not abandoning you—rather,
sending you on what will prove grievous to you—
it's this that has long pained me.

PHILOCTETES What are you saying?—I don't understand.

NEOPTOLEMOS I won't lie to you: you must sail to Troy—
to the Achaians and the mission of the Atreidai.

PHILOCTETES What?! What do you mean?

NEOPTOLEMOS Do not groan, before you've understood everything.

PHILOCTETES What's to be understood?
What do you intend to do to me?   980

NEOPTOLEMOS First, to rescue you from your misfortune;
then—together with you—to go and sack Troy.

PHILOCTETES Is it true—these things—that you intend to do them?

NEOPTOLEMOS A great necessity demands it. Listen, and don't get
angry.

PHILOCTETES I am damned—betrayed!
Stranger, why,
why have you done this?
Give me back my bow immediately!

NEOPTOLEMOS That isn't possible. Both justice and expediency force
me to obey those in command.

how just?

PHILOCTETES You fire—you absolute horror, you most hateful
        strategem of terrible outrage—   990
    what things you've done to me,
    how you've cheated me!
    Are you not ashamed to look at me here at your feet,
        a suppliant to you,
    yourself shameful?

    In seizing my bow, you have snatched, too, my life.
    Give it to me—I beg you—give it back—
    please—

    By the gods of your fathers, do not rob me of my life.

    —But he no longer speaks to me; he looks as if
    he will never return it to me again.   1000

    Oh harbors,
    oh headlands,
    oh mountain beasts in packs, oh rugged rocks—
    for I know none other to speak to except
    you who have always been here with me—
    to you I speak
    of what the son of Achilles has done to me.
    Having sworn to bring me home,
    he instead drives me to Troy;
    having offered his right hand in pledge,   1010
    he has seized and holds onto my bow,
    the sacred bow of Herakles, son of Zeus!

    And he wants to show me off to the Argives
    as if having overpowered a strong man,
    he drives me by force, when in fact he kills a man
    dead already,
    a skein of smoke,
    a mere specter.
    For he wouldn't have taken me, had I been a
        strong man—
    nor even in my present condition, if not by trickery.   1020

But now I have been miserably deceived—
what should I do?—

Give it back!

Even now, come to your senses.
What do you say?

You're silent. And I—I
exist no longer.

Double-mouthed cave,
again—after so long—I return to you,
stripped of all means of living—   1030
I shall wither away, alone, in this dwelling,
bringing down with this bow no winged bird, no
mountain-grazing beast—
but I myself, dying miserably, shall provide the food
for those whom once I fed on;
and those whom I once hunted—
they will now hunt me.
Ah, I shall make slaughter the reprisal for slaughter,
because of one who seemed to know nothing of evil.

                              Turning to NEOPTOLEMOS.

May you die!—but not before I learn   1040
if you've changed your mind again; if not,
 may you die miserably!

CHORUS   What shall we do?
         It is up to you, my lord—
         whether we should set sail already;
         whether, instead, to agree with what this man says.

NEOPTOLEMOS Not now for the first time, no—
         it has long been the case: a terrible pity for this
                  man has
         broken upon me.

PHILOCTETES Have mercy on me, child—by the gods!—   1050
    and do not prove yourself an object of shame
        among men,
    for having deceived me.

NEOPTOLEMOS What shall I do?
    Better never to have left Skyros, I am that
    wrenched by this business.

PHILOCTETES You are not evil. But,
    in having learned from men who *are* evil,
    you seem to have arrived at a disgraceful situation.
    Give to others what is proper:
    sail away,   1060
    but give my weapons back to me.

NEOPTOLEMOS Men, what shall I do?—

                ODYSSEUS *and some sailors suddenly enter from*
                            the side of the stage.

              ODYSSEUS *addresses* NEOPTOLEMOS.

ODYSSEUS You traitor! What are you doing?
    Come back here and give me that bow!

PHILOCTETES Who is that? Not Odysseus—is it?

ODYSSEUS Odysseus indeed—I myself, whom you can see!

PHILOCTETES I've been bought
    —and sold.
    He it was, then, who captured me—
    who stripped me of my weapons!   1070

ODYSSEUS It certainly was—I, and nobody else—I do confess it.

PHILOCTETES   *To* NEOPTOLEMOS.

    Hand the bow back to me—give it back!

ODYSSEUS This—even should he wish to—he shall never do.
But you must come with the bow—
or these men will bring you by force.

PHILOCTETES You worst and most outrageous of evil men—

Pointing to ODYSSEUS's *men.*

these men will drive me by force?

ODYSSEUS Yes—if you don't come willingly.

PHILOCTETES O land of Lemnos, and all-powerful flame forged by
Hephaistos,
must I endure this too?   1080
that this man shall drive me by force from this island?

ODYSSEUS It is Zeus—if you must know—
Zeus, the ruler of this land,
by Zeus himself that these things have been
determined—
I merely serve him.

not serving him

PHILOCTETES Hateful one, what lies you've found to say.
You put the gods before you like a shield, and in
so doing,
you make of the gods liars.

make good men bad

ODYSSEUS No—it is the truth—and this road must be traveled.

PHILOCTETES No!   1090

ODYSSEUS Yes! You've no choice but to obey.

not true

PHILOCTETES Ah, then I am damned indeed.
Clearly, my father sired no free man, but a slave.

ODYSSEUS No—neither of these.
Rather, a man equal to the noblest men,
and you are to sack and utterly demolish Troy.

flattery

PHILOCTETES Never! Not even if it means I must suffer every evil—
so long as I still have my cliff here.

ready to kill himself

ODYSSEUS And what will you do?

PHILOCTETES   *Looking up to the rock platform, then limping*
                                                                toward it.

I shall throw myself from the rocks above,   1100
and dash my head on the rocks below me.

ODYSSEUS   *To his men.*
Seize him! Don't let him do it!

Herakles

PHILOCTETES Oh hands of mine—hunted down by this man—
what things you suffer now, companionless,
no bow.

And you, Odysseus—you who think nothing healthy
        or noble—
how you crept up to me,
how you hunted me,   *Aias*
taking as shield for yourself this boy, a stranger to me
—himself unworthy of you, though worthy of myself—   1110
he who knew nothing but to obey an order.
And now
how he suffers for his mistakes, for what
I've endured.

But your evil soul, looking always out from its
        innermost chambers,
taught him well—
this child with no natural gift for it,   *Odysseus as*
and with no will for it—   *evil teacher*
taught him to be skilled in evil.

377

And now, you wretch, you mean to shackle and   1120
lead me from the very shore where
once you left me alone with no friend,
with no city—
a corpse for the wild animals—
May you die!
How often I've prayed for your death.

But the gods, it seems, have nothing sweet in mind
        for me:
for you have managed to live,
while I suffer all over again the fate of living
wretchedly among so many evils,   1130
to be mocked by the sons of Atreus
and you, their lackey.

And yet,
you sailed with them after being yoked by kidnapping
        and necessity;
whereas I, all the worse for me,
willingly sailed as captain of seven ships—
it is *they* who, according to you, cast me off in
        dishonor,
though they blame *you*.

But why are you taking me now?
Why?   1140
To what advantage?
I, who am nothing now, am long since dead to you.
Most hateful to the gods,
why don't I seem lame and stinking to you, now?
How will you be able to burn sacrifices to the gods,
if I sail with you? How make libation?
For this was exactly why you threw me out, as you
        said then.

May you die miserably!
You *will* die, for having wronged a man like me,
if there is any justice among the gods.   1150

the times have changed

And I know there *is:*
for you would never have sailed on a mission such
    as this
for a man so worthless as myself—not unless
some spur of the gods had driven you to it.

But—oh fatherland and protecting gods—
punish them in due time,
punish all of them,
if you have any pity for me.
For I live pitiably,
but if I could see these men destroyed,   1160
it would be as if I'd escaped my disease itself!

Cf. Aias

CHORUS   Grave is this stranger, Odysseus, and he makes a
        speech as grave,
one that does not give at all in
to his sufferings.

ODYSSEUS   I'd have much to say in response to his words, if
        I could.
But for now, I can say only one thing:
where a man is needed, of whatever kind, I am
        such a man;
if the time called for just and upright men,
you would find no one more noble than myself.
However, I was born desiring absolute victory—   1170

except when it comes to you; now, willingly, I shall
        yield to you.

                    To his men.

Release him, hold him no longer!
Let him stay.
After all, Teucer is with us—he has the skill of
        archery—
as do I: I don't think I'm any worse than you at
mastering this bow, nor any worse a hand at
        taking aim.

mistaken
even if set
upon victory,
he will fail

We have the arms now—who needs you?
Farewell—
and enjoy strolling around Lemnos!

PHILOCTETES *is released by* ODYSSEUS's *men.*

Let's go. Perhaps they'll honor me with your prized
    possession—
you ought to have held onto it.

1180

PHILOCTETES Oh what shall I do in my misery?
Are you to appear before the Argives adorned in
    weapons that are mine?

ODYSSEUS Enough talk—I'm leaving.

PHILOCTETES Son of Achilles—
Have *you* nothing to say to me?
Are *you* leaving, like this?

ODYSSEUS You come here, Neoptolemos!—and don't look
    at him!
Being so noble, you're liable to wreck our good
    fortune.

PHILOCTETES Am I to be left alone by you in this way, strangers?
Will you not pity me?

1190

CHORUS This young man is our captain. What he says,
we say also.

NEOPTOLEMOS Odysseus will say that I am too full of pity—all the
    same, men,
stay—if it is all right with him—
for as much time as is needed for the sailors to
    prepare the ship,
and for us to pray to the gods.
And perhaps this one (*pointing to* PHILOCTETES) will
    think better of us in this matter.
Therefore, let us set off—

380

And you, men, when we call, you set off quickly
    as well.

NEOPTOLEMOS *and* ODYSSEUS *exit.*

PHILOCTETES O hollow cavern—   *strophe* 1200
    hot sometimes; sometimes, like ice—
    so I was never meant to leave you;
    no, you will be with me in my dying.

    O sorry dwelling, filled
    entirely with my suffering,
    what life shall I have again, day to day?
    What hope of finding food,
    where find it?
    You creatures flying above, who once feared me,
    come now through the sharp wind—   1210
    I am powerless, at last, to catch you.

CHORUS Yours is a hard lot,
    but it is you who have damned yourself—
    this fate came from nowhere else, from no greater
        source than you.
    For when it was possible to have sense,
    when a better fate was possible,
    you chose the worse one.

PHILOCTETES I am miserable—   *antistrophe*
    I am wretched—and torn by my hardship: in
    living henceforward with no one else in my misery,   1220
    I shall die finding no food for myself,
    my hands powerless to do so
    without my weapons—their wings, their speed.

    Unseen, hidden,
    the words of a deceitful mind
    have overtaken me. May I live to see
    the man behind those words

[handwritten: bow]

PHILOCTETES *[handwritten: 10 years of wandering]*   [1114–45]

    suffer as I have, and
    for as long.

CHORUS The destiny of the gods has brought this on you—   1230
    no deceit of mine;
    send elsewhere your hate,
    your curse of a prayer.
    I am worried that your friendship
    may leave me.

PHILOCTETES Somewhere, sitting   *strophe*
    on this grey ocean's beach, he makes
    mock of me, brandishing in his hand
    my means of living, which
    none before, ever, had even touched.   1240

    Dear bow,
    wrested from hands as dear,   *[handwritten: personified bow]*
    I'm sure if you have
    any conscious feelings, you look with
    pity on the wretched heir to Herakles, who won't ever
    again use you, no—
                instead, you'll
    be handled by a schemer's hands,
    witness to disgraceful deceits, and to a man
    hateful,   1250
    hated,
    bringing about a thousand deeds of shame—
    he brought as much on me.

CHORUS It is right for a man to say what is just—
    but having said it, for his tongue
    not to put forward hate and pain.
    For this man is one of many who,
    at the command of another,
    has brought about what is best
    overall   1260
    for his friends.

[handwritten: justification sufficient?]

birds as attackers

PHILOCTETES O beasts—winged, bright-eyed,   *antistrophe*
mountain-feeding—
all who dwell here:
no longer will you rush in flight from
your dwelling-places; for I no longer
hold in my hands the former protection
of my arrows—

But come boldly—
You'll find me lame, no longer   1270
a source of fear for you—how
lovely, now, to satisfy your mouths upon
this, my discolored flesh.
For I shall die at once—
where, after all, will my livelihood come from?
Who can live in this way, upon the winds,
when he no longer has possession
of anything that the life-sustaining
earth sends forth?

CHORUS By the gods—if you honor anything at all,   1280
approach the visitor,
who has himself approached you with all good
        intention.
Consider,
and understand clearly:
it is possible for you to escape this fate;   *choice*
for it is pitiable, how it feeds on you,
and he who lives with such suffering has no notion of
        how to bear it.

PHILOCTETES Again, you remind me of my old agony—
you, who are the best of all those who have come
        here before—
Why have you destroyed me? Why are you doing this
        to me?   1290

CHORUS Why do you say this?

383

PHILOCTETES Because you hoped to drive me to the hated land
of Troy.

CHORUS But I think this is best.

PHILOCTETES Leave me—now!

CHORUS What you've commanded is fine with me—
I am pleased to do it.
Let's go—
off to our assigned places on board our ship!

PHILOCTETES   *Shouting.*
Don't go—by the Zeus of prayer and curse—I beg
you.

CHORUS Easy—   1300

PHILOCTETES   *Shouting.*
Strangers,
by the gods—stay here.

CHORUS What are you shouting about?

PHILOCTETES The god, the god,
destiny,
destiny—;
my foot;
how shall I live from now on?

Strangers: come back.

CHORUS And do what?   1310
You seem of a different mind than before.

PHILOCTETES There's no need to hate a man who, torn by suffering,
says something counter to what makes sense.

CHORUS Wretched one—come now, as we've told you to do.

PHILOCTETES   Never—never! Get this clear:
                not even if the fire-bearing wielder of
                lightning should come consuming me in its blaze!
                Let Troy perish,
                and all those beneath it,
                who dared to banish my foot, and me with it!   1320

                But strangers, grant me at least one prayer.

CHORUS   What is it?

PHILOCTETES   Provide me with a sword, if there's one about—
                or an ax,
                even an arrow.

CHORUS   What for?

PHILOCTETES   To cut off my head and all my limbs—
                murder,
                slaughter's my intention!

CHORUS   But why?   1330

PHILOCTETES   That I might see again my father.

CHORUS   Where—in what country?

PHILOCTETES   That of Hades.
                For he is no longer here, in the light.
                O city—
                paternal city,
                if only I might see you, wretched though I am,
                who left your holy stream and
                as an ally
                went with the hateful Greeks, and now   1340
                I am nothing at all.

CHORUS By now I'd be long since en route to my ship,
if I didn't see in the distance
Odysseus and the son of Achilles coming back to us.

> PHILOCTETES *returns to his cave.* ODYSSEUS *arrives on*
> *stage and confronts* NEOPTOLEMOS, *who is carrying the*
> *bow of* PHILOCTETES.

ODYSSEUS Won't you tell me why you're headed back in this
way, and so quickly?

NEOPTOLEMOS To undo the wrong I did earlier.

ODYSSEUS You're speaking strangely—
what wrong did you commit?

NEOPTOLEMOS The wrong of obeying you and all of the Greek army.

ODYSSEUS What have you done that wasn't appropriate to you?   1350

NEOPTOLEMOS I took a man by deceit, by shameful trickery.

ODYSSEUS What man?
You aren't planning something new, are you?

NEOPTOLEMOS Nothing new—but to the son of Poias—

ODYSSEUS What? What will you do?
A strange fear has come over me.

NEOPTOLEMOS He from whom I took this bow,
to him again—

ODYSSEUS Zeus—
what are you saying?   1360
You don't intend to give it back, do you?

NEOPTOLEMOS Yes, for I only have it by having taken it
shamefully and unjustly.

words are slippery   truth is unstable

ODYSSEUS By the gods, are you saying this as a joke?

NEOPTOLEMOS Only if it is a joke to speak the truth.

ODYSSEUS What are you saying, son of Achilles?
What do you mean?   *Can't comprehend clarity*

NEOPTOLEMOS Do you want me to say the same thing twice—
three times?

ODYSSEUS I'd rather have heard nothing from the start!   *rejection*

NEOPTOLEMOS Be clear on this point: you've heard everything.   1370

ODYSSEUS But there is someone—
someone who will prevent you from doing this.

NEOPTOLEMOS What are you saying? Who will stop me?

ODYSSEUS The entire army of the Achaians—and I,
among them.

NEOPTOLEMOS Though you were born clever, you manage to
speak stupidly.

ODYSSEUS Well, in your case,
both words and actions lack intelligence.

NEOPTOLEMOS But if these things are just, they outweigh what is   *justice > clever*
clever.

ODYSSEUS And how is it just for
you to give back what you took thanks to   1380
my planning?   *tricky shit*

NEOPTOLEMOS I shall attempt to undo a wrong that was shameful.

ODYSSEUS Don't you fear the Greek army, in doing this?

387

words as gift

NEOPTOLEMOS   Since I'm in the right,
                    no,
                    I don't fear your army.
                    Nor shall I be persuaded to do anything by force.

ODYSSEUS   Then it's not with the Trojans, but with *you*
                    we'll fight!

NEOPTOLEMOS   Let that be as it will.

ODYSSEUS   Do you see my right hand clasping the hilt of
                    my sword?   1390

NEOPTOLEMOS   Then see *my* hand
                    at *my* sword.

ODYSSEUS   Fine—I'll leave you to yourself.
                    But I plan to go and tell this to the entire army.
                    They will punish you.

creep

NEOPTOLEMOS   You've thought wisely.
                    And should you think this way
                    from now on, perhaps you'll manage to stay out
                    of trouble.

                    ODYSSEUS *exits.* NEOPTOLEMOS *approaches the cave.*

                    But you, son of Poias—Philoctetes,
                    come here, out of your rocky dwelling.   1400

PHILOCTETES   What is all this shouting near the cave?
                    Why are you calling me to come out?
                    What do you need?
                    —Something bad, I am sure.
                    You aren't here—are you?—to
                    bring me some great trouble on top of my other
                    sufferings?

NEOPTOLEMOS   Don't worry. Listen to the words I've brought you.

PHILOCTETES I am frightened.
I was ruined before by lovely words—your words—
when I was persuaded by them.   1410

NEOPTOLEMOS Can't I change my mind again?

PHILOCTETES You were no different in speech
when you stole my bow from me—
trustworthy,
yet secretly ruinous.

NEOPTOLEMOS But not now—
I wish to hear from you what
you've decided:
will you stay here and live out your life,
or sail with us?   1420

not an attempt at persuasion!

PHILOCTETES Stop—don't speak any further!
For whatever you say, it will all be said in vain.

NEOPTOLEMOS Is that your decision?

PHILOCTETES As much, anyway, as words alone can say.

NEOPTOLEMOS I'd like to have persuaded you with my words—
but if what I say is useless in this matter,
well, then I am finished.

he gives up

PHILOCTETES All that you say *is* useless.
For you will never find me generous-minded
toward you,
who stripped me of what kept me alive!   1430
And then you come advising me—
you, the hateful son of a noble father!
May you die, all of you—first the Atreidai,
and then the son of Laertes—
and then you!

action follows words

NEOPTOLEMOS No more cursing—
here, take this weapon of yours from my right hand.

PHILOCTETES What are you saying?
Am I being deceived a second time?

NEOPTOLEMOS No—I swear it,   1440
by holy reverence for highest Zeus.

PHILOCTETES If what you say is the truth, you say what is most
welcome to me.

NEOPTOLEMOS The act itself is clear. Here—
put your right hand out, and take possession of your
weapons.

ODYSSEUS enters.

ODYSSEUS I forbid it!—with the gods as my witnesses,
and on behalf of the Atreidai and the entire army!

PHILOCTETES Whose voice do I hear? Not that of Odysseus, I hope?

ODYSSEUS It *is*, in fact. You see me here—
the one who will drive you by force to Troy,   1450
whether the son of Achilles wishes it or not!

force

PHILOCTETES You won't rejoice in anything, if this arrow finds
its mark!

NEOPTOLEMOS   *Grabbing* PHILOCTETES.
Ah no, by the gods, don't shoot your arrow!

PHILOCTETES By the gods, let go of my hands, dearest child!

NEOPTOLEMOS I won't!

PHILOCTETES Why—why did you prevent me from
killing this man—my hated enemy—with my bow?

NEOPTOLEMOS But killing isn't right for either of us.

PHILOCTETES Well, this much is clear: the leaders of the army,
the false messengers of the Achaians, are no good
        at war   1460
—however bold they may be with their words.

critique

NEOPTOLEMOS That may be so. But you have your bow,
and no reason to be angry with
or blame me.

PHILOCTETES Child, I agree; you have made evident
the stock from which you were born—
not that of Sisyphos as a father, but of Achilles,
who held the greatest nobility when he was among
        the living—
and now too, among the dead.

                              ODYSSEUS *leaves abruptly.*

NEOPTOLEMOS I am pleased to hear you speak well of my father—   1470
of him and of myself.
But now, listen to what I ask of you.

Men must bear the fortune
given them by the gods. But
those who are set upon by
damage that is of their own doing,
such as yourself,
it is just neither to have sympathy for them, nor to
        pity them.
You have become an animal, and refuse
all advice: if someone, thinking on your behalf,   1480
does give advice, you hate him, you
consider him an enemy.

Nevertheless, I shall speak,
calling upon the Zeus of oath-making.
Consider this—and write it deeply into your mind.

*persuasion
of Aias
to
Achilleus*

You are sick with this disease by divine will.
For you came close to Chryse and
the unseen serpent who keeps watch
over that roofless shrine.
There is never to be any respite   1490
from this grave infection—so long as the same
        sun rises
here, and sets there—
until you come willingly to Troy,
and, meeting the sons of Asklepios,
you will be cured of disease,
and will be proven with me and with your bow to be
Troy's destruction.

As to how I know these things are the case,
I shall tell you,
A man from Troy was captured by us—Helenos,   1500
the best of seers—who has said clearly
these things must happen.
And more—
that all Troy must be taken this summer.
He has agreed to be put to death, should he prove to
        be a liar.
Therefore, knowing this, come willingly.
For it is wonderful, to be judged the best of
        the Greeks,
to come into healing hands, and
then, in sacking Troy,
to bring upon yourself the highest fame.   1510

PHILOCTETES   Hateful Life,
            why do you still hold me alive
            and seeing?
            Why won't you let me go to Hades?

            What shall I do? How
            not to believe the words of this man

who has advised me with my best interests in mind?
Am I to yield, then?

But, in doing so, how shall I
in my misfortune come into the light? 1520
Who will speak to me?

Still fears being alone

To the CHORUS.

You, who stand around me and see all of this:
how will you stand for it, my joining the sons of Atreus,
who destroyed me,
my joining the ruinous son of Laertes?

For it isn't the pain of what has happened before
that bites at me; rather, it is what I can see
I will have to suffer in the future.
For those whose mind becomes a mother of evil,
this mind will mother other evils still. 1530

fears future evils

To NEOPTOLEMOS.

You amaze me:
you ought not to go to Troy,
and you should keep me from it, as well.
After all, these men insulted you
by depriving you of your father's prize—
will you now be an ally to them, and force
me to be one also?
Hardly!

Don't go!

But as you swore to me before,
send me home. As for yourself, 1540
stay in Skyros, and let these cruel men be
cruelly destroyed.
Thus will you gain from me and my father, both,
a double favor.
And, in not helping the wicked, you will make it
     clear that
you aren't among the wicked yourself.

separate from the wicked

NEOPTOLEMOS What you say is reasonable; nevertheless,
I want you to trust the gods and my words,
and with me as your friend, sail from this land.

trust

PHILOCTETES To Troy   1550
and to the hateful son of Atreus,
on this foot?

NEOPTOLEMOS To those who will relieve from pain both you and
your foot, dripping with pus,
and will save you at last from your disease.

relief

PHILOCTETES You give strange advice—what are you saying?

NEOPTOLEMOS The things that I see will be the best for us both,
if they're done.

PHILOCTETES And in saying this, you feel no shame before the gods?

NEOPTOLEMOS How feel shame, when helping a friend?   1560

as Philocteles did

PHILOCTETES Do you say this as friend to the Atreidai,
or to me?

NEOPTOLEMOS As *your* friend. Such is my word.

PHILOCTETES How so, if you want to hand me over to my enemies?

NEOPTOLEMOS You should learn, sir, not to be so bold in misfortune.

PHILOCTETES You will destroy me—I know it!—with these words.

NEOPTOLEMOS I won't. You don't understand.

PHILOCTETES Don't I know that the Atreidai exiled me?

NEOPTOLEMOS They exiled you—but now,
see how they would save you.   1570

394

PHILOCTETES Never, if it means I must willingly see Troy again.

NEOPTOLEMOS What am I to do, if I can't persuade you with what
                        I've said?
                    It is time for me to leave this argument,
                    and for you to go back to living as you've been living,
                    without rescue.

PHILOCTETES Let me suffer what I must.
                    And what you swore to me, when you took my right
                        hand—
                    to send me home—
                    do that for me,
                    and don't delay,   1580
                    and don't mention Troy again.
                    There's been enough talk, already.

NEOPTOLEMOS If that is what seems best,   *unlike Agamemnon*
                    let's go.

PHILOCTETES You have spoken nobly!

NEOPTOLEMOS Now steady yourself.

PHILOCTETES As much as I can, I shall.

NEOPTOLEMOS But—how shall I avoid being blamed by   *concern over*
                    the Achaians?   *choice*

PHILOCTETES Don't think about that.

NEOPTOLEMOS But—what if they destroy my country?   *fear*   1590

PHILOCTETES I shall be there—

NEOPTOLEMOS What help will you render?

PHILOCTETES With the arrows of Herakles—

Herakles

> HERAKLES *appears on the rocky ledge at the entry of the*
> *higher cave.*

NEOPTOLEMOS What do you mean?

PHILOCTETES I shall prevent them from approaching!

NEOPTOLEMOS Well, if you will do this, as you say,
then kiss the ground farewell, and come along.

HERAKLES Not yet, son of Poias!
Not until you have heard *my* words.
It is the voice of Herakles you hear,   1600
and his face you see with your eyes.
I have come here from my seat on Olympos,
on your behalf,
and to tell you the plans of Zeus,
persuasion
and to stop you from this road you are now taking.
Listen to me.

First, I'll remind you of my fortunes,
what sufferings and agonies I
suffering → glory endured before winning the immortal
glory which you see before you.   1610
For you, also—know well—it is fated
that from these sufferings of yours your life
will be made famous.
Going with this man to the city of Troy,
end to disease you will find an end to your grievous disease;
of the whole army, you will be declared first in valor,
and with these arrows of mine you will slay
Paris—who was the cause of these troubles—
and you will conquer Troy, and win the best
prizes from the army, and send home the spoils,   1620
to the high plain of your fatherland, Oita,
to your father, Poias.
And whatever spoils you take from this war,
recognize place on my pyre, as tribute to my bow.
Herakles

I advise the same to you, son of Achilles,
for you aren't strong enough to take Troy
without him, nor he without you.
But each of you must guard the other,
even as two lions that feed together.
Meanwhile, I shall send Asklepios to Troy   1630
to heal your disease. For, once again,
the city is to be taken by my bow.
But remember, when you conquer the land,
to respect what is sacred to the gods.
For father Zeus considers all things
second to this alone.
For reverence does not die with mortals—
whether they live or die, it is never destroyed.

PHILOCTETES Uttering what I've longed for,
you appear at last—   1640
I shall not disregard what you have said.

NEOPTOLEMOS Nor shall I.

HERAKLES Then don't waste time now in
preparing for action—the moment to act
is upon you,
and the wind at your stern.

PHILOCTETES Very well, then. In departing,
I shall call upon this island: farewell,   *addresses island*
chamber that kept watch over me,
                                                    room
water-nymphs,   1650 *water-nymphs*

nymphs of the meadows,   *nymphs*

the muscled crashing of sea against headland,   *sea*
where often my head, though
inside the cave, was drenched by the south wind's
        beating,   *wind*
and often the mountain of Hermes sent

back to me in answer
my own voice
echoing,
groaning,
as I weathered the storm.   1660

But now,
o streams and Lycian spring,
we take leave of you—I leave you
at last,

what I never expected.

Farewell, Lemnos, surrounded by sea—
grant me, free of blame, a safe voyage
to where great Destiny itself
carries me,
and the judgment of my friends,   1670
and the god who tames everything—who himself
          has decreed this.

CHORUS Let us leave together, praying
to the sea-nymphs,
that we meet safe voyage home.

                                        Exeunt omnes.

echo
groan

Destiny
judgment of my
*   friends*

Zeus

home

NOTES

1–178 / 1–134 *Prologue*

3 / 2 *Lemnos* An island in the northern Aegean just under Mt. Athos, which looms to
the north. It is a stage on the way from mainland Greece to the Troad. In
Sophocles' time it was an important and inhabited island, and its two
main cities (Myrrhine and Hephaistia) were virtually Attic demes. Remarkably, Sophocles makes it an uninhabited island, despite its description in the *Iliad* as being well populated and the realm of the son of
Jason and Hypsipyle (*Iliad* 7.467 and 21.40).

7 / 4 *Neoptolemos, son of Achilles* The use of patronymics is remarkable in this play
about inherited character. Neoptolemos identifies himself to Philoctetes
in the following words: "I am called Neoptolemos, son of Achilles. / And
now you know everything" (237–38 / 240–41). Philoctetes is described as
the "son of Poias" (9 / 5) and Odysseus himself is called "son of Laertes,"
and even of Sisyphos (97 / 87, and 417 / 414 with note). The description
of Neoptolemos as the son of Achilles initiates one of the major themes
of Sophocles' play, that of nature (*physis*), birth, inherited character, and
nobility.

9 / 4–5 *the Malian, the son of Poias* Malis is a region to the south of Thessaly
occupying the alluvial plain opposite the northern tip of Euboia. In
the Homeric Catalogue of Ships (*Iliad* 2.716–28) Philoctetes' home is
located in Thessaly, but it migrates to Malis because of his associations
with Herakles. Malis is dominated to the south by Mt. Oita, where
Herakles was consumed on a pyre. In Sophocles' time, the summit of
Oita was the site of a cult of Herakles.

55 / 50 *Son of Achilles* This form of address continues the significant repetition of patronymics in the play and suggests that character passes from father to son without the intervention of education or the influence of society. It is clear that Neoptolemos, born on Skyros, has never seen his father. Odysseus calls him the "son of a noble father" (**105** / 96) and Philoctetes says the same as Neoptolemos returns the bow Philoctetes had entrusted to him (**1310–11** / 1467).

79 / 72 *You sailed under oath to no one* This oath was the oath taken by the Achaians to avenge the abduction of Helen by Paris; the necessity was the compulsion put upon both Achilles and Odysseus to join the expedition against Troy. According to a tradition on the periphery of the Homeric poems, to avert his death in Troy, Achilles' mother, Thetis, disguised her young son as a girl and entrusted him to the care of Lykomedes, King of Skyros, where he stayed among Lykomedes' daughters. There Achilles fell in love with Deidamia, revealed himself as a man, and became the father of Neoptolemos, who was born on the island. In the Book of the Dead of the *Odyssey*, Odysseus tells Achilles that he brought his son, Neoptolemos, from Skyros to Troy, where he distinguished himself in battle and entered the Trojan horse with Odysseus (*Odyssey* 11.506–37).

Odysseus' ruse to avoid service in Troy is the counterpart of Thetis' plan to save her son. To evade joining the expedition against Troy, he pretended that he had gone mad and tried to convince the army of this by plowing the sand of the sea shore, apparently, when he was still on Ithaca. Palamedes (whom Odysseus in revenge accused of treason) revealed his deception by throwing the infant Telemachos in the path of his plow. Odysseus stopped in time and revealed himself as both sane and an imposter. This is the subject of Sophocles' lost *The Madness of Odysseus* (*Odysseus Mainomenos*.)

The "first expedition" to Troy was not that of Herakles against the Troy of Laomedon, the father of Priam, but the expedition of ten years past.

100 / 90 *I'm willing to take the man by force* According the prophecy of the Trojan seer, Helenos, to assure the capture of Troy Philoctetes had to be brought to Troy "by persuasion" (*logos*, **624** / 612). But persuasion, if it involves lying, is disgraceful. Odysseus improves the situation by speaking of deceit (*dolos*), not lying.

109 / 99 *it's the tongue, and not deeds* Odysseus evokes the contrast between word (*logos*) and deed (*ergon*) and the supremacy of word over deed that was part of the sophistic culture of Sophocles' Athens.

126 / 114 *as you said* In Sophocles' Greek, the plural "you said" refers to Odysseus and
Phoinix, the tutor of Achilles, who in the later epic tradition were sent to
Skyros to fetch Neoptolemos and bring him to Troy after his father had
been killed there. Neoptolemos refers to their assurance that he alone
would take Troy in **343–47** / 346–47. In his lying tale, the Trader adds the
sons of Theseus to Phoinix in the embassy to Neoptolemos and Skyros
(**565** / 562).

129 / 117 *you'll take away two prizes* The prizes Odysseus holds up to Neoptolemos are
the combination of intelligence (or, in its debased form, "cleverness")
and valor. Among Homer's Achaians, Odysseus is unique in possessing a
combination of guile and bravery. Even the young Neoptolemos is
capable of speaking well in the deliberations of the Achaian army
(*Odyssey* 11.511–12).

145 / 133 *May Hermes the cunning leader be* Hermes Dolios is the much admired
patron of merchants, thieves, and tricksters. He began his career by
stealing the cattle of his half-brother Apollo and was—at the tender
age of one day—brazen enough to deny the theft (Homeric *Hymn to
Hermes* 260–77). Among her other attributes, Athena was the goddess of
intelligence; she was patron to Odysseus at Troy and, then, in Ithaca at
the end of his long voyage home. The elective affinity between the two is
brilliantly displayed in their meeting on Ithaca, as Athena disguises
herself as a young shepherd and Odysseus tries to conceal his own
identity by telling a long lying "Cretan" tale (*Odyssey* 13.222–24 and
254–86).

      Athena is called *Polias* (the Goddess of the City), an epithet she does
not have in the Homeric poems. In Athens, she is associated with Nike,
the Goddess personifying Victory. Athena Polias was one of Athena's
cult titles on the Athenian acropolis. Her elegant Ionic temple (of 421
B.C.) built in commemoration of the Athenian victory over the Persians
rises to the southwestern entrance to the acropolis. It was dedicated to
Apteros Nike (Wingless Victory). Sophocles is clearly forging a connection between Odysseus and Athens.

148–214 / 135–218 *Parodos* (entrance song of the Chorus)

154 / 140 *the divine scepter of Zeus* Sophocles' Chorus evokes the scepter symbolically
involved in the quarrel between Achilles and Agamemnon in the *Iliad*.
The *skeptron* of Agamemnon is described as a hereditary possession
fashioned by Hephaistos and given by Zeus to Pelops and passed down
to Agamemnon by Atreus' brother, Thyestes (*Iliad* 2.100–106).

171 / 159 *you can see his house here, with the double openings* It is dramatically
significant that Philoctetes' cave (which dominates the stage platform)
has two "doors." There might be a revealing parallel to this cave with two
entrances; the cave of the nymphs on the harbor of the sea god Phorkys on
Ithaca also has two entries (*Odyssey* 13.109–12). The entrance facing north
is accessible to men; that to the south is reserved for the gods. As we stage
the *Philoctetes*, Herakles appears at the mouth of the cave not entered by
the human actors of the play. (See stage directions to line 1593 / 1409.)

193 / 194 *savage-minded Chryse* The accident is referred to again in 1487–90 / 1327–28.
Chryse is the name both of a place and a minor divinity (apparently a
nymph) associated with the cult of Apollo. The sanctuary of Apollo at
"sea-girt Chryse" was on a now submerged island off the northeast coast
of Lemnos, where there was also a shrine of Chryse. Pausanias, who
wrote a *Description of Greece* around the middle of the second century
A.D., records the sinking of the island (8.33.4).

197 / 199–200 *the time when it is determined that Troy must be destroyed* The prophecies concerning the crucial role of Philoctetes and his bow in the fall of
Troy are first revealed by Odysseus (125–27 / 113–15) and then the Trader
(622–25 / 603–21). The equally crucial role of Neoptolemos in the taking
of Troy is a part of Neoptolemos' deception of Philoctetes (345–47 / 353),
and then stated clearly by Neoptolemos as Helenos' prophecy at the end
of the play (1490–1510 / 1433–39).

214–675 / 191–695 *First episode*

234 / 239–40 *I am from the island of Skyros* Neoptolemos' father Achilles came from
Phthia in the plains of Thessaly. Skyros, a small island in the Sporades
between the coast of Thessaly and Troy, was the refuge his mother (or
his mortal father, Peleus) found for her young son in her vain attempt to
avert his destiny. As the grandson of Lykomedes, Neoptolemos suc-
ceeded to the kingship of the island.

 The name Neoptolemos means "He who is new to war" (*polemos*). In
the post-Homeric epic, the *Kypria*, this name was given to him by
Achilles' guardian, Phoinix, to signify that, like his father, Neoptolemos
would prove "the young fighter" (Pausanias, *Description of Greece*
10.26.4). When Neoptolemos arrives at Troy, the Achaians greet him as
an Achilles come back to life (358 / 357–58).

247 / 249 *How should I know someone I've never seen before?* Nor does Neoptolemos
know his father whom he had never seen before. Both Achilles and

Philoctetes belong to a vanishing generation of heroes. See note 349 / 350.

260 / 262 *the master of the arms of Herakles* The bow and arrows given to Philoctetes at the pyre of Herakles on top of Mt. Oita. Some of the booty awarded to Philoctetes by the grateful Greek army is to be dedicated on Mt. Oita as "tribute to my bow" (**1623–24 / 1422–23**).

297 / 302 *there's no harbor* There are fine harbors on Lemnos, and in Sophocles' time it was frequently visited by ships from Athens bound for Thrace and the Hellespont. Philoctetes invokes the harbors of the island he is leaving at **1001 / 936–40**.

306 / 307 *But this one thing, when I mention it* The reluctance of the occasional visitors to Lemnos to carry Philoctetes off the island to his home in Malis is simply explained by the fact that he is polluted by his wound. Such pollution (*miasma*) is unlucky for sailors who depend on the winds and the good will of the gods. His cries of agony were ill-omened as the Greeks sacrificed to the gods; Philoctetes explains as much in **1143–64 / 1031–34**.

308 / 311–12 *I am wasting away—for ten years now* The Greek army had been camped before the wall of Troy for ten years after its commanders abandoned Philoctetes on the island on their way there. The period of ten years of warfare before the fall of Troy is recognized in the omen interpreted by Chalkas in *Iliad* 2.311–32 (at line 329) and in Aeschylus, *Agamemnon* 40; cf. Euripides, *Electra* 1154 and *Trojan Women* 20.

316 / 321 *the Atreidai and fierce Odysseus* Odysseus is included with the Atreidai as the object of Philoctetes' fierce anger, but Odysseus alone is associated with the threat of violence (*bia*), as he is in **575 / 592** (where the same word stands for more than the Homeric periphrasis for the "person" of Odysseus). Philoctetes is scrupulously careful to stress this violence. For his part, Neoptolemos recognizes only the Atreidai as being responsible for the abandonment of Philoctetes. He even refers to Odysseus by the most enobling of his Homeric epithets, *dios* ("godlike"); the alternative would have been the formulaic "son of Laertes" or "man of many wiles" (as in *Odyssey* 1.1). According to the prophecy of Helenos, Philoctetes could be *persuaded* but not forced to leave Lemnos for Troy (**624 / 612**). In his only direct encounter with Philoctetes, Odysseus threatens to drive him to Troy "by force" (**1450 / 1297**) and in fact has the men from his ship seize him (**1102 / 1003**).

332 / 333 *struck down by Apollo* According to the later epic tradition, Achilles was killed by an arrow shot by Paris. But it was Apollo who directed his aim to Achilles' vulnerable heel. (The role of Apollo in Achilles' death is alluded to by the dying and prophetic Hektor in *Iliad* 22.359; cf. 19.416–17). This "double determination" of both human and divine agency is illustrated in the case of the death of Patroklos, who was stunned by Apollo, wounded by the Trojan Euphorbos, and dispatched by Hektor, who takes his arms. But Apollo was ultimately responsible for Patroklos' death (*Iliad* 16.777–815).

343 / 344 *Phoinix, the man who had reared my father* Sophocles composed a *Phoinix*, of which we know very little. Phoinix is best known from his role and speech in the embassy to persuade Achilles to return to battle in *Iliad* 9.432–605. He is accompanied in this embassy by Odysseus and Ajax.

349 / 350 *my longing for the dead man* Neoptolemos has no knowledge of his father, living or dead. In this, he resembles Odysseus' son, Telemachos. Both were conceived as the Greek armies gathered for the Trojan war. Neoptolemos' "longing for the dead man" is a longing whose only real object is the reputation (*kleos*) of his father.

355 / 355 *Sigeion* "Hateful Sigeion" is a strategic city on the Dardanelles, which had been an Athenian possession since it was annexed by Miltiades the younger at the beginning of the fifth century. It is hateful because the tomb of Achilles was located there, near the city of Ilion. Here Alexander of Macedon honored Achilles when he crossed into Asia (Plutarch, *Life of Alexander* 15).

362 / 362 *my father's weapons* One set of Achilles' arms were worn by Patroklos as he entered battle as a surrogate of Achilles and stripped from him by Apollo; they were taken by Hektor and recovered from Hektor's body by Achilles (*Iliad* 16.130–39, 792–804, and 17.191). The other set was divine and the work of Hephaistos fashioned to replace these as Achilles returns to battle. They are described in *Iliad* 18.468–614. This divine armor was the object of the contention between Odysseus and Ajax for the arms of Achilles and the arms Sophocles brings to mind.

394–401 / 391–402 AND **518–25 / 507–18** *Choral* interludes Although there is no full "act-dividing" choral ode (*stasimon*) until **696 / 676**, two brief, metrically identical stanzas provide musical and choreographic punctuation. In the first stanza, the Chorus of soldiers from Skyros invokes the Phrygian goddess Cybele, the Anatolian Earth Mother or Mother of the Gods. As the mother of Zeus, she was recognized by the Greeks as Rhea, but she also had a cult as the Mother of the Gods. She had an important cult on Lemnos. The Chorus invokes the Mother, but asks nothing of her. Neoptolemos' sailors are willing participants in the fiction Neoptolemos rehearses to Philoctetes as they recall the fictive prayer they made at Troy to this awesome foreign goddess on the occasion of the award of the arms of Achilles to Odysseus. Her cult stronghold was on Mt. Ida above Troy. Her power extended from Troy to the south to Lydia and Sardis, a city watered by the Paktolos, a river with deposits of gold. Cybele is represented in art and literature as being drawn in her chariot by lions. The second stanza similarly carries forward Neoptolemos' design to win over Philoctetes, although the pity and sympathy expressed need not be entirely feigned.

402–54 / 403–52 Philoctetes, who has been virtually without human contact for ten years, questions Neoptolemos about the warriors who sailed to Troy: Achilles, Patroklos, the "greater" Ajax (the son of Telamon), and the young son of Nestor, Antilochos. All are dead and all were seen by Odysseus in Hades (*Odyssey* 11.465–72). Three were killed in the fighting at Troy; Ajax committed suicide on the shore of the Troad. This interview in the *Philoctetes* is Sophocles' tragic counterpart of the interview of Odysseus with the comrades who fell in Troy in the Book of the Dead of the *Odyssey* (the Nekyia of Book 11). But in this list of Greek warriors, the survivors—Odysseus, his close companion, Diomedes, and the "ugliest" of the Achaians, Thersites—are all base. As Neoptolemos says: "war never chooses to take the disgraceful man, but will always prefer those who are most noble" (**436–37 / 436–37**). Neoptolemos makes no mention of the suicide of Ajax.

414 / 417 *Odysseus, begot by Sisyphos and sold to Laertes* In a form of the legend of Odysseus that surfaces after Homer's *Odyssey*, Odysseus' mother, Antikleia was made pregnant by the wily Sisyphos, King of Corinth. She was bought with a bride price (*edna*) by Odysseus' presumed father, Laertes. Significantly, this genealogy comes from Aeschylus' *Contest over the Arms*, frg. 175 Radt. In the *Odyssey*, by contrast, his lineage is taken back to the trickster Autolykos (*Odyssey* 19.394), who in one tradition matched wits with Sisyphos.

442 / 442 *Not him, but a certain Thersites* This is the sharpest barb cast at Odysseus in the *Philoctetes*. It sticks. In the *Iliad*, Thersites is described as the ugliest of the Greeks who came to Troy. He rises to speak against Agamemnon before the full assembly of the Achaians. For his boldness and effrontery

(his name means brazen), he is beaten by Odysseus to the delight of the army (*Iliad* 2.243–77). Yet Homer admits that Thersites was an appealing speaker (*Iliad* 2.246).

453–54 / 451–52 *in looking upon matters divine, I find the gods / themselves are evil* Philoctetes' dark assessment of the gods who allow men like Odysseus to remain alive changes as he hears Herakles address him at the end of the play. And in the immediate sequel he will invoke "suppliant Zeus" to persuade Neoptolemos to take him off the island (484 / 494).

494 / 484 *suppliant Zeus* Zeus Hikesios, the god who protects suppliants (*hiketai*) who have no other guarantee of protection.

503–7 / 494–99 This passage acknowledges the rare human contact Philoctetes has with sailors who refuse to take him on board. Skyros lies to the south-west of Lemnos; Chalkodon (evidently a city on the island of Euboia) is a reminiscence of a line in the Catalogue of Ships (*Iliad* 2.540), where the leader of the Euboean contingent is said to be the "son of Chalkodon." There is no Chalkodon known on the island, and Chalkodon is probably Sophocles' archaism for the city of Chalkis. The Spercheios is the major river of Malis.

548 / 542 *Son of Achilles* The actor who also plays the part of Odysseus enters the stage. He is disguised as a trader. He presents the second of the lying tales by which Odysseus hopes to convince Philoctetes to sail to Troy. Again the theme of deception (*dolos*) surfaces in the play. In this case, deception is a matter of disguise as well as lies. In disguising a member of the crew of Neoptolemos' ship as a merchant captain—merchants were sacred to Hermes the "trickster" (*dolios*)—Odysseus replicates his own history of disguise as he penetrated Troy dressed in rags with lash marks upon his body (the tale of Helen in *Odyssey* 4.244–50). With Diomedes, he takes a notorious part in the night ambush of Dolon in the episode known as the Doloneia (*Iliad* 10). His feined madness before arriving at Troy, his disguises at Troy, and his strategem of the Trojan horse all prepare for his disguises and anonymity as he returns to Ithaca and remains there in disguise. He even continues to conceal his identity after the killing of the suitors of Penelope as he is reunited with his aged father, Laertes (*Odyssey* 24.303–14).

553 / 549 *Peparethos* Now the island of Skopelos in the Sporades to the south and west of Lemnos.

565 / 562 *They have gone in pursuit of you—Phoinix, and the sons of Theseus* All of
these embassies following on the death of Achilles are reenactments of
the embassy of Odysseus, Ajax, and Phoinix to Achilles in Book 9 of the
Iliad. They figured in the tradition of the Epic Cycle. The embassy of
Diomedes to Lemnos figures in *The Little Iliad*; that of the sons of
Theseus in *The Sack of Troy*.

567 / 563 *To bring me back with violence, or with words?* Neoptolemos' question
reflects what seems to have been an essential condition in Helenos'
prophecy concerning the taking of Troy: Philoctetes would have to be
persuaded to come to Troy. The alternative to persuasion (words, *logoi*)
is *bia* (force). Later in the play Odysseus' men actually seize Philoctetes
by force (1102 / 1003).

611 / 601 *What can they be longing for?* The question and the word *pothos* (a longing
for something absent) recall the language of the *Iliad* and the prediction
that the day will come when the Greek army at Troy comes to *miss*
Achilles and *remember* Philoctetes long out of mind (*Iliad* 1.240 and
2.716–20), just as they recall Neoptolemos' longing for his father (349 /
350).

615 / 606 *Helenos* The Trojan augur, Helenos, figures in the *Iliad* (6.76 and 576).
In the post-Homeric tradition, Helenos was forced by Odysseus to reveal
the fate of Troy. In the *Philoctetes*, his contingent prophecy concerning
the combination of forces necessary to the destruction of Troy must
be pieced together from the deceptive speech of the Trader (613–29 /
603–12) and Neoptolemos' honest words at the end of the play
(1499–1510 / 1336–47). Neoptolemos must be brought from Skyros to
Troy; Philoctetes, from Lemnos, willingly and with his bow. At Troy
Philoctetes' injured foot will be healed either by the brothers Machaon
and Podaleirios, the doctors of the Greek camp, or by Asklepios himself
(1630 / 1437). Philoctetes will then kill Paris, and Neoptolemos will play
his part in sack of the city that had withstood ten years of siege. This
much is not a part of Odysseus' deceit; its truth is authoritatively confirmed by Herakles in 1611–32 / 1421–44. Helenos survives the fall of Troy.
His destiny is to marry Hector's widow, his sister-in-law, Andromache
(Euripides, *Andromache* 1243–47) and greet Aeneas with another prophecy on Aeneas' way to Italy from Buthrotum in northwest Greece
(Vergil, *Aeneid* 3.293–355).

616–17 / 607–8 *Odysseus, who is called every / foul and insulting name* Just as he can
bear the anonymity of disguise, Odysseus can bear the insults he in-

structs his confederates to heap upon him in the presence of Philoctetes. His instructions to Neoptolemos are the same (73–74 / 64–65). In Euripides' *Philoctetes,* he is called "the common plague of all of Greece" (Dio, *Speech* 59 §8).

619 / 606 *coming upon him alone and at night* Odysseus' capture of Helenos at night is meant to recall the night expedition he and Diomedes made against Troy (*Iliad* 10) and their capture of the unwary Dolon and to foreshadow the night in which Troy would be taken.

639 / 639 *like* his *father* Meaning not Laertes but Sisyphos, who persuaded his wife not to give him the proper mourning ritual in death and then persuaded Persephone, the goddess of the Underworld, to release him from Hades to return to life and punish his wife. See note on 414.

669 / 654 *And what is it you're holding now?* It is only at this point of the action that Philoctetes appears with his great bow in hand. Now begins what has been called "the sacrament of the bow."

689 / 670 *a kindness* The kindness of agreeing to put a torch to Herakles' funeral pyre.

690 / 671 *I don't regret . . . having you as a friend* Neoptolemos' words in Greek seem to reflect the meaning of Philoctetes' name as Sophocles understood it: "acquiring a friend." It is a compound of *philos* and the verb *ktasthai,* to gain.

696–751 / 676–729 *Stasimon* This is the only full choral ode of this, the most unlyrical of Sophocles' extant tragedies. It consists of two pairs of *strophe* and *antistrophe* (metrically matched turns and counterturns of the Chorus in its song and dance). The fate of Philoctetes and his abandonment as a cripple on an uninhabited island is something for which the Chorus of islanders can find no parallel in Greek tradition and no example in its own experience. The inappropriateness of the parallel the Chorus seeks in the punishment of Ixion simply stresses Philoctetes' isolation. His life on Lemnos is shared by no human companion; his fate is without precedent in the legends that fill the choral odes of Greek tragedies.

Ixion was a king of Thessaly, who had murdered his father-in-law. Absolved of the stain of homicide by Zeus, the ingrate attempted to seduce Hera. Zeus frustrated this rape by substituting a cloud for his wife and punished Ixion with the torment of being bound to a wheel that turned perpetually. Philoctetes had committed no such offense, but had rather lived a just life (704–5 / 680–85). Yet his fate was to hear the ceaseless roar of the sea without a companion to bring him medicinal herbs or respond to his cries of agony (as the Chorus does now). Only the echoing cliffs respond to him (1655–60 / 1458–60). Without grain or wine, the hunter Philoctetes is reduced to the most primitive form of human life. (Fishing seems out of the question for a Homeric hero.) Even the thought of returning to his father's estate takes his imagination to the mountain nymphs of Malis, the banks of the Spercheios, and the slopes of Oita. The mention of Mt. Oita and Herakles' self-immolation there prepares for the long scene of the crisis of the wound to Philoctetes' foot. This scene both parallels and follows the scene of Herakles' suffering from the shirt poisoned by the blood of the centaur Nessos staged in Sophocles' *The Women of Trachis* (983–1043).

790 / 762–63 *But take the bow* In his paroxym of pain, Philoctetes entrusts his bow to the care of Neoptolemos, first asking him to worship the formidable weapon to avert the divine jealousy (*phthonos*) that had pursued its first possessor, Herakles, and then continued to pursue Philoctetes on Lemnos. Earlier, Neoptolemos had asked to hold and worship Philoctetes' bow "as I would a god" (673 / 657).

823–26 / 791–94 *Odysseus . . . Agamemnon, Menelaos* Even as the bow is transferred to Neoptolemos, Philoctetes would transfer his agony to the Greeks he considers responsible for his abandonment on Lemnos. Elsewhere in the play, Agamemnon and Menelaos are referred to as "the sons of Atreus" (Atreidai) to stress their criminal parentage.

834–85 / 791–94 *Son . . . take me up / and burn me in the fire called Lemnian* There is no active volcano on Lemnos, but the expression Lemnian fire was proverbial and referred to the vulcanism of a mountain known as Moschylos. This is one of the reasons the god Hephaistos was associated with the island, cf. 1079 / 986.

835–39 / 799–803 Philoctetes asks Neoptolemos to perform the same service he had performed for Herakles on Mt. Oita, when he consented to put the torch to his funeral pyre. Neoptolemos' reaction is that of Herakles' son, Hyllos, who refused the request. Philoctetes' request seems to carry the promise that Neoptolemos, too, will receive the bow as a reward for his services.

856 / 814 *Up—* Before Philoctetes falls asleep in a state of exhaustion, he attempts to ask Neoptolemos to help him return to the protection of his cave. Neoptolemos, who fails to understand, thinks he is looking up to the

sky. Sophocles' gesture of drawing the attention of his audience "up" prepares for the epiphany of Herakles at what we argue is the "divine" entrance to Philoctetes' cave (1599 / 1409; see note on 171). As it is, Philoctetes collapses before he can return to his cave.

873–913 / 827–64 *First kommos* Instead of a second and third choral stasimon, Sophocles gives us in this play two specimens of the lyrical dialogue between chorus and actor usually know as the *kommos*, though the term should strictly designate a responsive dirge or lament. The lyrics of this song have two motivations: in the strophe they attempt to lull Philoctetes to sleep and, as they are addressed to Neoptolemos in the antistrophe, to move him to take Philoctetes' bow and sail away with Odysseus to Troy. The favorable breeze, like Philoctetes' helpless sleep, gives Neoptolemos and his crew the occasion to accomplish their mission with Odysseus' sure approval. In the *Iliad*, Hera travels from Olympos to Lemnos where she finds Sleep (Hypnos) and Death (Thanatos) (14.230–31).

995 / 931 *In seizing my bow, you have snatched, too, my life* Sophocles connects the words bow (*toxa*) and life (*bíos*) here and elsewhere in the play. He seems to have in mind a saying of heraclitus that connects the word bow (*biós*) with the word for life: "Life is the name of the bow; its work death," Herakleitos 22 B frg. 48 in Diels-Kranz, *Die Fragmente der Vorsokratiker* (Berlin 1951). The same association recurs in 1239 / 1126, where the bow is called "my means of living."

1012 / 941–42 *the sacred bow of Herakles* Sacred because it once belonged not to a hero, who is the son of Zeus, but a hero who has become one of the immortal gods on Olympos. In the Book of the Dead of the *Odyssey*, Odysseus reports that he saw the terrifying shade (as opposed to the Olympian presence) of Herakles, armed with this strung bow, ready to release his deadly arrows (*Odyssey* 11.601–8).

1135–36 / 1026–27 *I . . . willingly sailed as captain of seven ships* Unlike either Achilles or Odysseus, Philoctetes sailed toward Troy as a willing participant in the expedition. See note on 79 / 72 and Aeschylus, *Agamemnon* 841.

1145 / 1032–33 *How will you be able to burn sacrifices* The excuse given by the leaders of the Greek army for leaving Philoctetes on Lemnos was religious: the offense of his wound and cries of agony would disturb their worship of the gods. This religious pretext is no longer compelling, once the Greeks need Philoctetes and his bow. A passage from Thucydides' *The Peloponnesian War* (6.31.5) makes it clear what the inhibitions of an army setting out to invade a foreign land would have been. In describing the launching of the Athenian armada against Sicily in the summer of 415, Thucydides evokes the trumpet signal enjoining absolute silence on the army before the offering of prayer and libations.

1174 / 1057 *After all, Teucer is with us* Odysseus pretends that he can manage without Philoctetes himself and use his bow without him. Both Teucer, Ajax's brother and the renowned archer of *Iliad* 13.313, and Odysseus himself can manage the bow. In the games on the island of Skeria, Odysseus professes expertise as an archer (*Odyssey* 8.215–20), yet acknowledges Philoctetes' superiority "when we Achaians fought as archers in the land of Troy" (219–20). Odysseus' mastery of the bow is most impressively demonstrated in the revenge he takes on the suitors in *Odyssey* 21 and 22. Teucer has a dubious part to play in the events following the death of Achilles. In Sophocles' *Ajax*, Ajax abuses him as "archer" (1120), and in one tradition (the fiction of the orator Alkidamas' *Against Palamedes*) it was Teucer who shot an arrow into the Trojan camp carrying the forged message with which Odysseus incriminated Palamedes of collaboration with the enemy.

1183 / 1063–64 *adorned in weapons that are mine* The bite of the sarcasm is that Odysseus needs weapons that are all show and disguise his real cowardice, as was the case of the arms of Achilles he won by eloquence and not as a prize for his valor.

1200–1344 / 1081–1217 *Second kommos* This long passage of formal lamentation (*kommos*) is in the form of a lyric exchange between Philoctetes, who is the only actor on the stage, and the Chorus. The *strophe* and *antistrophe* (1200–88 / 1081–1170) have more the character of a lyric monody (solo song) for Philoctetes with responses from the Chorus, than of a true exchange, which only begins with the concluding *epode*, a self-standing, metrically unique stanza (1288–1344 / 1170–1217). The kommos prepares for — yet stands in subtle contrast to — Philoctetes' last words of farewell to the island where he spent ten years in pain and isolation (1647–71 / 1452–68). In his last evocation of the island, the island becomes sacred and the haunt of gods. In this dirge of lamentation, Philoctetes first imagines himself abandoned once again and without his bow (in the first strophe) and then, suddenly, he turns in imagination to the sight of Odysseus, seated on the shore, exulting in the possession of the bow of Herakles (in the antistrophe).

1331 / 1210 *That I might see again my father* Philoctetes' desire to join his father in Hades is more than a symptom of his despair with his life; he wants to return to an earlier and better generation.

1467 / 1312–13 *Achilles, / who held the greatest nobility* Philoctetes' generous praise of Achilles and his nobility both in life and in death deliberately recalls Odysseus' praise of Achilles' power over the dead in Hades. It also recalls Achilles' curt rejection of the notion of there being any consolation of lordship in death: "I would rather serve on the plot of a poor farmer with no land of his own than be king over all the dead who have perished!" (*Odyssey* 11.484–91).

1494 / 1333 *the sons of Asklepios* These are Machaon and Podaleirios, physicians in the army of the Achaians, who cured Philoctetes' wound on his arrival at Troy. At the end of the play, Herakles says that Asklepios himself will heal Philoctetes' wounds (**1630 / 1437**), which amounts to the same thing.

1629 / 1436 *as two lions that feed together* In the *Iliad* the simile describes Odysseus and Diomedes as they set out in their nocturnal mission against Troy (10.297). This episode gives the simile here a sinister connotation.

1631–32 / 1439–40 *once again, / the city is to be taken by my bow* A reference to the first Greek expedition against the Troy of Laomedon a generation before. It included Herakles; Telamon, father of Ajax; and Philoctetes.

1633 / 1440–41 *But remember, when you conquer the land* Herakles' warning to Philoctetes and Neoptolemos casts an ugly shadow over the divinely imposed solution to the fated capture and sack of Troy. It seems to echo the warning of Clytemnestra in Aeschylus' *Agamemnon* against the victorious Greek army's sacrilegious treatment of the altars and temples of the gods of Troy (*Agamemnon* 338–42; cf. 527–28) and the similar warning of King Darius in Aeschylus' *Persians* to respect the shrines of the Greek gods, a warning his son Xerxes did not heed (*Persians* 800–17). The events following the capture of Troy are well known from the poems of the Epic Cycle (*The Fall of Troy* and Lesches of Mytilene's *Little Iliad*) and from two plays of Euripides, especially the *Hecuba* (where they are recalled in 523–68) and *Andromache*. Neoptolemos, the noble son of Achilles in Sophocles' *Philoctetes*, becomes the blood-thirsty Pyrrhos (so well known from Vergil, *Aeneid* 2.526–58), whose savage bloodlust was already commemorated by Polygnotos on the walls of the club house of the Knidians at Delphi. He is held responsible for the murder of Priam at the altar of Zeus in his courtyard and (in the lyric poet Ibycus) of Priam's daughter Polyxena. Ajax, son of Oileus, attempted to rape Cassandra in the temple of Athena, and Odysseus and Diomedes carried off Athena's cult statue, the Palladion. Pindar explained Pyrrhos' murder at Delphi as motivated by the anger of Apollo over his crimes at Troy (*Paean* 6.98–120).

1647–71 / 1452–68 In Philoctetes' final farewell to Lemnos, the island has become "divine," as Homer had described it (*Iliad* 21.79), and he leaves it to the nymphs of its waters and meadows (1650–51 / 1454) who sustained him for so long.

GLOSSARY

ACHAEA: In historical times, Achaea was the name of a region located on the southern coast of the Bay of Corinth.

ACHAEANS (ACHAIANS):   A generic name for the Greek forces who made the expedition against Troy. Homer refers to the Greeks as Achaeans or Dorians or Argives; "Greek" is the name used for them by the Romans.

ACHELÖOS: Monstrous spirit of the major Aetolian river that bears the same name.

ACHERON: A river in the underworld.

ACHILLES: Son of Peleus and Thetis, the greatest of Greek heroes at Troy, father of Neoptolemos. After Agamemnon took away his concubine, Briseis, he refused to fight for the Greeks until the death of his close companion, Patroklos. Returning to battle, he killed Hektor and not long after was himself killed, shot in the heel by the Trojan prince, Paris. After his death, his arms were claimed by Aias but awarded to Odysseus.

AEGEAN: The sea lying between mainland Greece and Asia Minor.

AEGISTHUS: Son of Thyestes, the only of his children who escaped when Atreus, Thyestes brother, took revenge for a wrong by killing Thyestes' children, feeding them to him, and then revealing what he had done. Aegisthus grew up to avenge this crime by killing the son of Atreus' son, Agamemnon.

In Aeschylus' play, *Agamemnon*, Aegisthus tells this story to claim that his cause is just.

AENIAN: The Aenians are a tribe mentioned in the *Iliad* (2.749) as one of the contingents on the Achaean side. Although involved in hostilities against the Spartans in 420 B.C., they are probably mentioned in *Electra* as an epic reminiscence.

AETOLIAN: Adjective from Aetolia. Aetolia lies along the north shore of the Bay of Corinth, to the west of Delphi.

AGAMEMNON: King of Mycenae and Argos, son of Atreus, brother of Menelaos, and commander-in-chief of the Greek forces that sailed against Troy. When he returned to Argos after the fall of Troy, he was murdered by his wife Clytemnestra in conspiracy with her lover, Aegisthus.

AIAKIDAI: Descendants of Aiakos, a son of Zeus; they included Telamon, Peleus, Aias, and Teukros.

AIAS (AJAX): Son of Telamon and prince of Salamis. He was a hero of great courage and enormous size, standing head and shoulders above all others at Troy, but traditionally stolid and slow of speech. Second only to Achilles among the Greek warriors, he went mad with anger and finally killed himself when, after Achilles' death, his armor was awarded to Odysseus.

ALKMENE (ALCMENE): Wife of the Argive exile Amphitryon, the mother of Herakles by Zeus.

AMPHIARAUS: One of the seven who fought and were defeated at Thebes, in support of Polynices' claim on the Theban throne. Polynices bribed Amphiaraus' wife Eriphyle to force her husband to go, and he went knowing that he would die at Thebes. In the battle, the earth opened and he vanished below ground.

ANTILOCHOS: Son of Nestor of Pylos; killed in the Trojan War.

APOLLO: Son of Zeus and Leto, brother of Artemis, god of prophecy, healing, music and lyric poetry. As a light-bringing god, he is

closely connected with, but distinct from, Helios, god of the sun;
as an archer god, he was responsible for the death of Achilles. In
Electra, Orestes is said to have been killed in a chariot race at
Delphi, the site of Apollo's most famous oracle. This tale con-
forms to Apollo's insistence that Orestes kill his father's murderers
with a subterfuge, found in all versions of this story in tragedy.

ARES: Greek god of war. His name often stands for violence of any sort.

ARGIVES: Generic name for the Greeks who made the expedition
against Troy (see also ACHAEANS); it may also refer specifically
to the inhabitants of Argos.

ARGOS: Argos is a city in the Peloponnesos, but in drama more often
refers to the entire region in which Mycenae is located.

ARTEMIS: Virgin goddess and sister of Apollo, associated with animals
and the hunt. Women called on Artemis in childbirth, and she
was in general the protector of the small and helpless.

ASKLEPIOS: The Greek god of healing who is to cure Philoctetes'
wound.

ATHENA (ATHENE): The virgin daughter of Zeus, born of no mother,
but sprung fully armed from her father's head; a patron goddess
of war and the arts and handicrafts in general, and protector of
Athens and Odysseus.

ATHENS: Chief city of Attika.

ATREIDAI: The sons of Atreus: Agamemnon and Menelaos.

ATREUS: King of Mycenae, son of Pelops, and father of Agamemnon
and Menelaos. He served his brother, Thyestes, a dinner con-
taining the flesh of his children after learning that Thyestes had
seduced his wife, Aëropē. After discovering the nature of the
dish, Thyestes placed a curse on Atreus' house.

AULIS: A place on the east coast of mainland Greece and site of a
temple of Artemis. Before sailing to Troy, the Greek fleet
assembled at Aulis.

BARCAEAN: Adjective from Barca, a city in Cyrenaica in Libya.

BOEOTIAN: Adjective from Boeotia, a large plain north of Athens and east of Delphi.

BOSPHORUS: Channel in Thrace connecting the Sea of Marmora (Propontis) with the Black Sea.

CENTAUR: A creature characterized by the fusion of human head and torso with the legs and body of a horse; notorious for its lust (but see also CHEIRON).

CHALKODON: A city on the island of Euboia, perhaps an invention of Sophocles.

CHEIRON: An atypically humane and civilized centaur; immortal son of Kronos and mentor and friend to many Greek heroes, most notably Achilles. He was accidentally wounded and eventually destroyed by one of Herakles' poisoned arrows.

CHRYSE: A now submerged island of the northeast coast of Lemnos; also a minor goddess associated with the sanctuary of Apollo on the island.

CHRYSOTHEMIS: Sister of Electra and named as a daughter of Agamemnon, along with Laodike and Iphianassa, in the *Iliad* (9.144–47).

CLYTEMNESTRA: Sister of Helen and wife of Agamemnon; responsible with her lover Aegisthus for killing her husband upon his return from Troy.

CRETAN: Adjective from Crete, one of the largest islands in the Mediterranean, south of the Cyclades; home of Aëropē, Agamemnon's mother. (See also ATREUS.)

CRISA: A town near Delphi. The hippodrome at Delphi is located below the sanctuary on the more level ground known as the plain of Crisa.

DEIANEIRA: Daughter of Oineus, wife of Herakles, and mother of Hyllos.

DEIDAMIA: Daughter of King Lykomedes of Skyros and mother of Neoptolemos by Achilles.

DELOS: Cycladic island in the Aegean and birthplace of Apollo and Artemis; an important site in the worship of Apollo and seat of one of his important oracles.

DELPHI: The mountain sanctuary of Apollo, where his main temple and oracle are located. The games held here were among the major athletic festivals of Greece.

DIOMEDES: One of the most prominent Greek warriors at Troy; accompanied Odysseus on the night raid against Troy.

DODONA: A town in northwestern Greece; cult-place of Zeus and site of his sacred oak, the oldest of all Greek oracles.

ENYALIOS: Alternate incarnation of Ares.

ERECHTHEUS: A famous king of Athens and a son of Earth reared by Athena, with whom he was often honored.

ERIBOIA: Wife of Telamon and mother of Aias.

ERYMANTHOS: A mountain in southern Greece; haunt of the savage boar destroyed by Herakles during his labors for Eurystheus.

EUBOIA: A large island off the east coast of Boeotia, adjacent at its upper extremity to the territory of Trachis and at its lower to the shores of Attika; site, at the north, of Cape Kenaion, at the south, of Oichalia.

EURYSAKES: Son of Aias and Tekmessa.

EURYSTHEUS: Argive king; notorious as the cruel taskmaster for whom Herakles was compelled, by divine decree, to labor for twelve years.

EURYTOS: King of Oichalia, father of Iphitos and Iole.

FURIES: Female ministers of divine vengeance dedicated to the pursuit and punishment of murderers; born from the blood of Ouranos when he was castrated by his son Kronos.

HADES: Lord of the underworld, brother of Zeus and Poseidon, husband of Persephone; his name is frequently used for the underworld itself.

HEKTOR: Son of Priam and Hecuba, and bravest of all the Trojans who fought against the Greeks. After killing Patroklos, he himself was finally killed by Achilles, who dragged his body behind a chariot to the Greek camp and then around Patroklos' tomb.

HELENOS: Son of Priam and Hecuba; a prophet, he was captured by Odysseus and forced to reveal the secret of Troy's capture.

HELIOS: Greek personification of the sun, conceived of as a charioteer who daily drives from east to west across the sky.

HEPHAISTOS: God associated with metalworking and vulcanism (whence his close connection to the volcanic island of Lemnos).

HERA: Wife of Zeus and queen of the Olympian gods. In the *Iliad*, she is a strong supporter of the Argives, and her sanctuary, not far from Mycenae, was a major shrine in historical times.

HERAKLES: Son of Zeus by the mortal woman Alkmene, and the most renowned of all Greek heroes; worshipped as an Olympian god after his death. He accomplished his famous labors at the command of Eurystheus, and at the end of his mortal existence gave Philoctetes his bow in thanks for putting a torch to his funeral pyre.

HERMES: Son of Zeus and Maia; god of heralds, travelers, and thieves; inventor of the lyre; messenger of the gods. Hermes is a great trickster but also guides the souls of the dead to Hades.

HYDRA: A gigantic, many-headed serpent that plagued the inhabitants of Lerna until destroyed by Herakles as one of the labors imposed by Eurystheus; source of the venom with which the hero tipped his infallible arrows.

HYLLOS: Son of Herakles and Deianeira.

ICARIAN: Adjective from Icaria, a small island in the Aegean.

IDA: Mountain or ridge of mountains near Troy; site of the Judgment of Paris and the source of several rivers, including Simois and Skamander.

IO: Daughter of the river Inachos and the ancestor of the royal line at Argos. Zeus conceived a desire for her, and due to Hera's jealousy she was turned into a cow, guarded by Argus, a creature with a hundred eyes. After Hermes had killed Argus, a gadfly drove Io around the eastern Mediterranean to Egypt, where she regained her human form and bore Zeus a son, Epaphus, whose descendents eventually returned to Argos and produced the line of Argive kings that included Perseus and Herakles. For the story see Aeschylus' *Suppliants* and *Prometheus Bound*.

IPHIANASSA: One of the daughters of Agamemnon in the *Iliad*.

IPHITOS: Son of Eurytos and brother of Iole; treacherously murdered, while a guest at Tiryns, by Herakles.

ITYS: Child of Philomela and Tereus; see also PHILOMELA.

IXION: A king of Thessaly, he was absolved by Zeus for murder of a kinsman, but then attempted to rape Hera. His punishment was being bound to a perpetually rotating wheel.

KADMOS: A Phoencian, the founder and first king of Thebes.

KALCHAS: A celebrated soothsayer, he accompanied the Greeks to Troy as their high priest.

KENAION: A small promontory at the northwest tip of Euboia; site of Herakles' triumphal sacrifice to Zeus.

KNOSIAN: Adjective from Knossos, principal city of Crete famous for its dances.

KRONOS: Son of the primal sky-god Ouranos and father of Zeus, who subsequently overthrew him to become the supreme Greek deity.

KYLLENE: A mountain in the Peloponnessos and site of the birth of Hermes.

GLOSSARY

LAERTES: King of Ithaca, he married Antiklea, who bore him
Odysseus. According to another tradition, Antiklea was
already pregnant with Odysseus by Sisyphos when she married
Laertes.

LAOMEDON: Trojan king, father of Priam and Hesione. With the aid of
Apollo and Poseidon, he built the walls of Troy. When refused
payment, the two gods brought destructive forces against the
city; these forces could only be appeased by the annual offer of
a young Trojan woman to a sea monster. When the annual lot
fell to Laomedon's daughter, Hesione, he made a bargain with
Herakles to destroy the monster. When Herakles completed his
task, Laomedon refused to reward him, whereupon Herakles,
with the aid of Telamon, besieged Troy.

LEMNOS: An important island between mainland Greece and Troy
associated with Hephaistos; scene of *Philoctetes*.

LERNA: Coastal region of southern Greece just south of Argos; home of
the Hydra destroyed by Herakles.

LETO: Goddess of the Titan generation; mother of Apollo and Artemis
by Zeus.

LIBYA: Vaguely defined area on the north shore of Africa, whose main
Greek settlement was Cyrenaica; often used in Greek literature
as a generic name for the part of Africa bordering on the
Mediterranean.

LICHAS: Herakles' herald during his war against Oichalia; delivered
Iole to Deianeira and the fatal robe to Herakles; in some
versions of the story, killed by the hero as punishment for his
unwitting participation in Deianeira's scheme.

LYDIA: A barbarian realm in Asia Minor ruled by Queen Omphale.

LYKOMEDES: King of Skyros, father of Deidamia, and grandfather of
Neoptolemos. Neoptolemos succeeds him as king.

MAGNESIA: Region in Thessaly mentioned in the great catalogue of
forces in the *Iliad*, Book 2.

MALIS: District of Greece just south of Thessaly. Its name means "Sheepland."

MENELAOS (MENELAUS): King of Sparta, son of Atreus and brother of Agamemnon, and husband of Helen; the Trojan War was fought to regain his wife after she went off with the Trojan prince, Paris.

THE MOTHER: An Anatolian goddess, whose cult is associated with Mt. Ida and Troy. Cybele was the Mother of the Gods and in Greek tradition Rhea, the mother of Zeus.

MYCENAE: City on the northern edge of the Argive plain, the traditional location of Agamemnon's palace.

MYRTILUS: Charioteer murdered by Pelops, ancestor of Agamemnon. See also PELOPS.

MYSIAN: Adjective from Mysia, region in Asia Minor, where the Phrygian Great Mother Goddess, Cybele (often identified by Greeks with Zeus' mother, Rhea, and cult-companion of Pan) was widely worshiped.

NEMEA: A valley in southern Greece, approximately midway between Corinth and Mycenae; home of the monstrous lion destroyed by Herakles as his first labor for Eurystheus; later the site of an important sanctuary of Zeus and the festival of the Nemean Games.

NEMESIS: The goddess of retribution for excessive acts.

NEOPTOLEMOS: Son of Achilles, who arrives at Troy after his father's death and participates in the final stages of the Trojan War.

NESSOS: A centaur killed by Herakles in reprisal for an attack upon Deianeira; donor of the charm which finally destroys the hero.

NESTOR: King of Pylos, who took part in the Greek expedition against Troy; accompanied by his son Antilochos, who died there.

NIGHTINGALE: See PHILOMELA.

NIOBE: Mother of many children, she boasted that she was greater than Leto, who had only two. In response Leto's children (Apollo and Artemis) killed all of Niobe's, and she in her grief was then changed into a rock.

ODYSSEUS: Son of Laertes (or Sisyphos) and Antikleia, king of Ithaca, husband of Penelope, and father of Telemachos. A central figure in the *Odyssey*, which narrates his ten years of wandering after the fall of Troy and his eventual return home to his kingdom. Represented by Homer as both brave and wise, he is increasingly portrayed by later authors, especially the tragedians, as a cunning, deceitful, and an extremely articulate demagogue.

OICHALIA: A city on the island of Euboia, off the eastern coast of Attica, and the home of Eurytos, Iphitos, and Iole; attacked and destroyed by Herakles.

OINEUS: Aitolian king and father of Deianeira.

OITA: Mountain in southern Thessaly, famed in antiquity as the site of Herakles' self-immolation and apotheosis; its summit was thus a center of Herakles' cult.

OLYMPOS: Highest mountain on the Greek peninsula, separating Macedonia from Thessaly, and traditional home of the gods.

OMPHALE: Lydian queen to whom Herakles was bound in servitude for a year as atonement for Iphitos' murder.

ORESTES: The son of Agamemnon and Clytemnestra. He took vengeance on the latter for killing the former, and in Aeschylus' *Oresteia*, he went to Athens, stood trial for matricide, and was found innocent. In Euripides' *Iphigenia in Tauris* we are told that these wanderings continued after the trial.

PALLAS: A cult name of the goddess Athena.

PAN: Half goat and half man; the god of shepherds, often portrayed as chief of the satyrs.

PAKTOLOS: A river in Lydia, south of Sardis, flowing with deposits of gold.

PATROKLOS: Close companion of Achilles; killed by Apollo and the Trojan Euphorbus as he took to the field in Achilles' armor.

PELOPS: Son of Tantalos and grandson of Zeus, father of Atreus and Thyestes, among many others. He won Hippodamia as his wife by defeating her father, King Oenomaus, in a chariot race using subterfuge. Pelops won by bribing the king's driver, Myrtilus, to remove the linchpin of the chariot. By then having the driver thrown into the sea instead of rewarding him, Pelops brought down a curse on his house, a curse that descended to his sons, Atreus and Thyestes.

PEPARETHOS: An island in the Sporades to the south and west of Lemnos, now called Skopelos.

PERSEPHONE: Daughter of Demeter, the goddess of agriculture and grain; Persephone was abducted by Hades and made queen of the dead.

PHANOTEUS: Ally of Clytemnestra and Aegisthus in Phocis.

PHILOCTETES: Son of Poias from Malis in Thessaly. As an archer in possession of the bow of Herakles, Philocetes was indispensable to Greek victory in the Trojan War, but was nevertheless marooned on Lemnos by his comrades on their way to Troy because of a suppurating wound that would not heal.

PHILOMELA: Wife of Tereus, king of Thrace, to whom she bore a child, Itys. When Tereus raped Philomela's sister Procne, Philomela avenged her by murdering the child and was turned into a nightingale, the bird whose cries of "Itys" recalls the deed. Sophocles wrote a tragedy (*Tereus*) on this subject.

PHOCIS: The region in which Delphi is located.

PHOINIX: Achiles' old tutor, who accompanied him to Troy.

PHRYGIAN: Adjective from Phrygia, a country in the interior of Asia Minor.

POIAS: Father of Philoctetes; he was a famous archer and is numbered among the Argonauts.

PYLADES: Son of Strophius of Phocis and Orestes' friend and companion.

PYLOS: A city in the southwest Peloponnesos and center of the kingdom of Nestor.

PYTHO: Another name for Delphi, derived from the chthonic serpent-deity from whose control Apollo wrested the site.

SALAMIS: An island in the Saronic gulf separated by a narrow channel from the southwestern coast of Attika. It was the ancient home of Telamon, Aias, and Teukros and the site of the crushing defeat of the Persian fleet by the Greeks in 480 B.C. Athens had taken possession of it early in the sixth century.

SIGEION: A city on the coast of the Troad and the place where Achilles was buried.

SISYPHOS: Son of Aeolus and the most crafty prince of the heroic age. He slept with Antiklea, the daughter of his neighbor Autolykos, a few days before her marriage to Laertes, thereby rendering the paternity of her son Odysseus doubtful. For crimes unknown, Sisyphos in Hades was eternally condemned to roll a giant boulder up a steep hill, only to have it always roll back down again. Odysseus' enemies alleged that Sisyphos was his true father.

SKAMANDER: One of the principal rivers of the Troad, rising in Mt. Ida and flowing into the Hellespont.

SKYROS: A small island in the Sporades and the birthplace of Neoptolemos.

SPARTA: Chief city of Laconia in the Peloponnesos, whose Homeric king was Menelaos, by reason of his marriage to the Spartan

Helen. In the fifth century B.C., Sparta was Athens' greatest enemy.

SPERCHEIOS: The major river of the plain of Malis.

STROPHIUS: Ruler of Crisa in Phocis; father of Pylades; Orestes grew up in his house.

TEKMESSA: Daughter of the Phrygian prince, Teleutas. After Aias killed her father in war, she became his concubine and the mother of his son, Eurysakes.

TELAMON: King of Salamis; father of Aias by Eriboia, his wife, and of Teukros by Hesione, his concubine.

TELEUTAS: Prince of Phrygia and father of Tekmessa; killed in battle by Aias.

TEUKROS (TEUCER): Son of Telamon, ruler of Salamis, by Hesione; half-brother of Aias. He was best archer among the Greeks who came to Troy. Absent at the moment of his brother's suicide, he returned to secure his burial. Banished by his father for failing to save Aias, he went to Cyprus, where he founded the new town of Salamis.

THEBES: Chief city of Boeotia in central Greece and scene of numerous tragedies; birthplace of Herakles.

THEMIS: A goddess of the Titan generation, who is associated with, and even stands for, traditional law and custom.

THERSITES: The ugliest of the Achaean army who spoke out against Agamemnon in assembly.

THESEUS: King of Athens in the generation before the Trojan War. His sons Akamas and Demophon were part of a fictive embassy to Philoctetes on Lemnos.

THESSALIAN: Adjective from Thessaly, a region of northeastern Greece.

TIRYNS: A city in southern Greece; Herakles' home during the period of his servitude to Eurystheus.

TRACHIS: A region of central Greece just north of Thermopylai; site of the palace of Keyx and the scene of Herakles' final homecoming.

TROY: City on the northern-coast of Asia Minor founded by Dardanos. Under its king, Priam, it was besieged and finally, after ten years of struggle, taken by an expedition of Greeks who came to recapture Helen, wife of Menelaos, who had been abducted to Troy by Paris, son of Priam.

TYDEUS: Aetolian hero of the generation before the Trojan War, he fought with the Seven who marched against Thebes. He was the father of Diomedes.

ZEUS: Son of Kronos and Rhea; husband of Hera; the paramount god of the Greek pantheon. "Father of gods and men," he was in fact the sire of several of the Olympian gods, including Aphrodite, Athena, Apollo, and Artemis. He also fathered numerous human offspring, including Herakles, who later became a god.

FOR FURTHER READING

SOPHOCLES

Mary Whitlock Blundell. *Helping Friends and Harming Enemies: A Study in Sophocles and Greek Ethics*. Cambridge: Cambridge University Press, 1989. A lucid exploration of choices and decisions made in the tragedies of Sophocles, with reference to the traditional moral code referred to in the title of this book.

Karl Reinhardt. *Sophocles*. Translated by H. Harvey and D. Harvey. Oxford: Blackwell, 1989. A classic reading of the Sophoclean tragic hero.

Charles Segal. *Sophocles' Tragic World: Divinity, Nature, Society*. Ithaca, NY: Cornell University Press, 1995. Includes important essays on *Aias [Ajax]*, *Philoctetes*, and *Women of Trachis*.

Charles Segal. *Tragedy and Civilization: An Interpretation of Sophocles*. Cambridge, MA: Harvard University Press, 1981. A detailed and insightful structuralist reading of the tragedies.

R. P. Winnington-Ingram. *Sophocles: An Interpretation*. Cambridge: Cambridge University Press, 1980. Humane and thought-provoking studies.

AIAS [AJAX]

Peter Burian. "Supplication and Hero Cult in Sophocles' Ajax." *Greek, Roman and Byzantine Studies* 13 (1972) 151–56. A brief demonstration of the foreshadowing of Aias' heroization in the tableau of suppliants at his body in the final scenes of this play.

Jon Hesk. *Sophocles: Ajax*. Duckworth: London, 2003. This Duckworth Companion contains thoughtful introductions to the play and its context, and it has a detailed bibliography.

ELECTRA

Helene P. Foley. "Sacrificial Virgins: The Ethics of Lamentation in Sophocles' *Electra*." Chapter III.2 of *Female Acts in Greek Tragedy*. Princeton, NJ: Princeton University Press, 2001. A stimulating investigation of the ethics of female lamentation and vendetta in this drama.

Michael Lloyd. *Sophocles: Electra*. Duckworth: London, 2005. This Duckworth Companion contains thoughtful introductions to the play and its context, and it has a detailed bibliography.

PHILOCTETES

P. E. Easterling. "*Philoctetes* and Modern Criticism," in E. Segal, ed., *Oxford Readings in Greek Tragedy*. Oxford: Oxford University Press, 1983, pp. 217–28. A fine overview of the issues.

Hanna Roisman. *Sophocles: Philoctetes*. Duckworth: London, 2005. This Duckworth Companion contains thoughtful introductions to the play and its context, and it has a detailed bibliography.

WOMEN OF TRACHIS

Edith Hall. "Deianeira Deliberates: Precipitate Decision-making and *Trachiniae*." In S. Goldhill and E. Hall, eds., *Sophocles and the Greek Tragic Tradition*. Cambridge: Cambridge University Press, 2009. An interesting study of deliberation and its failure in this play.

Brad Levett. *Sophocles: Women of Trachis*. Duckworth: London, 2007. This Duckworth Companion contains thoughtful introductions to the play and its context, and it has a detailed bibliography.

CPSIA information can be obtained at www.ICGtesting.com
Printed in the USA
BVOW011413251112

306250BV00001B/1/P